HER HUSBAND

ALSO BY DIANE MIDDLEBROOK

BIOGRAPHY

Anne Sexton: A Biography

Suits Me: The Double Life of Billy Tipton

CRITICISM

Walt Whitman and Wallace Stevens

Worlds Into Words: Understanding Modern Poems

Coming to Light: American Women Poets in the 20th Century
(Essays, edited with Marilyn Yalom)

Selected Poems of Anne Sexton
(with Diana Hume George)

POETRY

Gin Considered as a Demon

Ted Hughes, London, July 25, 1960

Diane Middlebrook

HER HUSBAND

HUGHES AND PLATH—A MARRIAGE

LITTLE, BROWN

A *Little, Brown* Book

First published in Great Britain in 2004 by Little, Brown
First published in 2004 by Viking, Penguin Group (USA)

A CIP catalogue record for this book
is available from the British Library

ISBN 0 316 85992 3

Printed in Great Britain by
Clays Ltd, St Ives plc

Little, Brown
An imprint of
Time Warner Book Group UK
Brettenham House
Lancaster Place
London WC2E 7EN

www.twbg.co.uk

To my husband, Carl Djerassi

Contents

Acknowledgments

Grateful acknowledgment is made to the following institutions and individuals holding archival material used in this book, and to their curatorial staffs:

The British Broadcasting Company Written Archives Centre, London; Susan Knowles, Senior Document Assistant

The Department of Manuscripts and the National Archive of Recorded Sound at The British Library, London; Christopher Fletcher, Curator of Literary Manuscripts

Ted Hughes Papers, Special Collections and Archives, Robert W. Woodruff Library, Emory University; Stephen Enniss, Curator of Literary Collections, and Kathy Shoemaker, Associate Reference Archivist, with additional thanks to Vincent Broqua and Victoria Hesford for research assistance

Sylvia Plath Collection, The Lilly Library, Indiana University, Bloomington, Indiana; with additional thanks to Kathleen Connors for research assistance

Sylvia Plath Collection, Mortimer Rare Book Room, Smith College; Karen V. Kukil, Associate Curator of Rare Books

Department of Special Collections, Stanford University Libraries; William McPheron, Curator of English and American Literature, and Roberto G. Trujillo, Head, Department of Special Collections

The Estate of Aurelia S. Plath, for use of an extract from an unpublished letter of Aurelia Plath; and Warren J. Plath, for use of a photograph; with additional thanks to Susan Plath Winston, Permissions agent.

For a range of other contributions to this book, I thank the following:

Al Alvarez, Carole Angier, Lisa Appignanesi, Sam Barondes, Hans Beacham, Eavan Boland, Janet Booth, Joseph Conte, John Cornwell, Karen Croft, Peter Davison, Jean-François Denis, Audrey Droesch, Doris Eyges, Ruth Fainlight, Elaine Feinstein, Donya Feuer, Annie Finch, Mary Ellen Foley, Renee Fox, Nick Gammage, Terry Gifford, Elizabeth Lameyer Gilmore, Lynn Glaser, Langdon Hammer, Michael Hofmann, Ann and George Hogle, Fiona Holdsworthy, Elin Hoyland, Olwyn Hughes, Terry Hurlbutt, Ryan Johnson, Claas Kazzer, Donna Laframboise, Richard Larschan, Joshua Lederberg, Helder and Suzette Macedo, Leah Middlebrook, Nancy Miller, Kate Moses, Joanny Moulin, Jerome Murphy, Eilat Negev, Alicia Ostriker, Marjorie Perloff, Jill Barber Petchesky, David Pye, Nicholas Rankin, Pamela Rosenberg, John Sewell, Linda Gray Sexton, Miranda Seymour, Elaine Showalter, Ben Sonnenberg, Hilary Spurling, Peter Stansky, Marcia Tanner, Kyla Wazana Tompkins, Katharine Viner, Linda Wagner-Martin, Thomas C. Wallace, Judith Wallerstein, Colin Wilcockson, Simon Williams; the members of the Biographers' Seminar at Stanford University; and participants in the Bay Area Seminar in Semi-Baked Ideas convened by psychoanalyst Robert Wallerstein.

Special thanks to my agent, Georges Borchardt; to my editor at Viking, Kathryn Court; and to the manuscript editor at Viking, Beena Kamlani, who made this the book I intended to write, and became a friend.

List of Illustrations

Introduction:
Becoming Her Husband

Ted Hughes met Sylvia Plath at a wild party in February 1956 and married her four months later. He was English, twenty-five years old; she was twenty-three, an American. For six years they worked side by side at becoming artists. Then Hughes initiated an affair with another woman, and the marriage collapsed. Hughes moved out and, exactly four months later, Plath committed suicide, leaving behind their two very young children.

One of the most mutually productive literary marriages of the twentieth century had lasted only about twenty-three hundred days. But until they uncoupled their lives in October 1962, each witnessed the creation of everything the other wrote, and engaged the other's work at the level of its artistic purposes, and recognized the ingenuity of solutions to artistic problems that they both understood very well. This kind of collaboration is quite uncommon between artists, especially if they are married to each other, and after the publication of Hughes's prizewinning first book, *The Hawk in the Rain,* the marriage began attracting the attention of journalists. In January 1961, Hughes and Plath were interviewed for a radio broadcast on the BBC, *Two of a Kind,* that displays them at the apex of their compatibility. The interviewer, Owen Leeming, asked whether theirs was "a marriage of opposites." As if in a movie by Woody Allen, Hughes said they were "very different" at the same moment Plath said they were "quite similar."

Explaining "different," Hughes allowed that he and Plath had similar dispositions, and worked at the same pace—indeed, so deep were
the similarities that he often felt he was drawing on "a single shared
mind" that each accessed by telepathy. But he and Plath drew on this
shared mind for quite different purposes, he said, and each of their
imaginations led a thoroughly "secret life."

Explaining "similar," Plath said that though she and Hughes had
very different backgrounds, she kept discovering unexpected likenesses.
Hughes's fascination with animals, for example, had opened up for
her the subject of beekeeping, which was one of her father's scholarly
pursuits. More of her own history had become available to her poetry
because Hughes was so interested in it, she said: that was how the
similarities were developing in their work—though the work itself
was not at all similar, she insisted. Did she too believe they had a
single shared mind? No, Plath laughed. "Actually, I think I'm a little
more practical."

Just such a dance through the minefield of their differences characterized their partnership at its best. It succeeded because each of
them invested wholeheartedly in whatever the other was working on,
even when the outcome was of dubious merit. In the late 1950s,
Hughes helped Plath develop plots for stories she could publish in
women's magazines, even though he regarded fiction-writing as a
false direction for Plath. At the time, he saw, accurately, that only conventional plots in which people got born, married, or killed released
her distinctive "demons," so he encouraged her to invest in whatever
mode was most productive of tapping these unique sources of energy.
Plath, for her part, loyally defended the incoherent and unmarketable
plays in which Hughes promoted the esoteric ideas he was hooked on,
beginning in the early 1960s—she was as interested in his artistic
strategies as she was in the results. Paradoxically, their intimate
creative relationship enabled each of them to conduct better the
"secret life" expressed in their art.

The rupture in their marriage closed down this literary atelier. But
poetry had brought Hughes and Plath together, and poetry kept them
together until Hughes's death in 1998. Hughes inherited Plath's

unpublished manuscripts, appointed himself her editor and made her famous. In 1965, when he brought out the volume titled *Ariel*, which contained Plath's last work, he said proudly, "This is just like her—but permanent." By that year, the world was ready to agree with him about Plath's importance. Poets rarely become cultural icons, but Plath's suicide had occurred just when women's writing was beginning to stimulate the postwar women's movement. The posthumous publication of Plath's poetry, fiction, letters and journals added her voice to a swelling chorus of resistance to the traditional positions women occupied in social life. The more celebrated Sylvia Plath became, the more people wanted to know what role her marriage to Ted Hughes had played in the catastrophe of her decision to die— especially after it became widely known that the woman Hughes left her for, Assia Wevill, had also committed suicide and had killed the daughter she had borne to Hughes.

Hughes spent the rest of his life quashing public discussion of these painful episodes in his private life. But shortly before his death in 1998, he released two books of poems that explore the subject of what it meant to have been the husband of Sylvia Plath. One was titled *Birthday Letters*. Speaking to Plath as if she were looking back with him from the vantage of their middle age, Hughes reflected on the array of circumstances that drove them together in 1956, and kept them together for six years; and he also proposed an explanation of the psychological issues behind her suicide.

Birthday Letters became a huge commercial success, but most people never even heard about the other book, *Howls and Whispers*, which was published in an expensive limited edition, and was never reviewed in the press. To make *Howls and Whispers* Hughes had reserved eleven poems from the manuscripts that became *Birthday Letters*, as a winemaker sets aside the choicest vintage for special labeling. In its keynote poem, "The Offers," the ghost of Sylvia Plath appears to Ted Hughes three times. On each visit she tests him; on the last visit she warns, "*This time don't fail me.*"

That startling phrase sends a pulse of light back through every page Hughes had published since Plath's death. It points our attention to the theme in Hughes's work of how marriages fail, or how men fail in marriage. Sometimes his work contains a representation of himself as the character who fails, as in *Birthday Letters*. In other writings, such as the translations of the grand works of Western literature with which Hughes occupied himself toward the end of his life—Racine's *Phèdre*, *Tales from Ovid*, the *Alcestis* of Euripides—Hughes brings empathy to the theme of marriage under duress. His versions of these were all produced for the stage, and audiences were quick to intuit that a second passionate story—Hughes's own story—was being explored, inexactly, within the dynamics of a venerable classic.

Though only 110 copies of *Howls and Whispers* were printed, Hughes acquired a large audience for its most important poem, "The Offers," by releasing it in the London *Sunday Times* on October 18, 1998. Ten days later, Hughes died. Whether by accident or design, that sentence spoken by Sylvia Plath through the medium of Ted Hughes would be on record as his last words. *Birthday Letters* offers us a way to see Ted Hughes from inside his partnership with Plath; "The Offers" requires that we see them as inseparable, even in death. "This time, don't fail me" is the voice of poetry itself, which Plath embodied; the persona created in his work is her husband; and that persona is his contribution to the history of poetry.

Hughes began developing this autobiographical persona, her husband, when he was nearly fifty years old. After years of attempting to avoid autobiographical writing, Hughes had come to believe that the voice in poetry had to issue from a human being situated in historical time and place, engaged in attempting to "cure" a wounding blow to his psyche inflicted by an historically significant conflict. The struggle conducted in a poet's art was his way of participating in history. Hughes also saw that no single work of writing stood alone, that a strong writer's work proceeded by accretion over time. Hughes observed that the poetic DNA expressed itself in single, definitive images or a "knot of obsessions" produced early in the poet's career and repeated in variations thereafter. Like the cells of a developing foetus, each work contained the DNA of the whole man, that is, the whole image of the persona.

"The Offers" is the central poem in Hughes's work of self-mythologizing. It marks the turning point in his creative life, showing in a set of images how the poet's powers were summoned back to him following the two successive personal disasters of the suicides of women close to him. What would it mean not to fail the claims that Woman had made on his psyche from childhood on? How could he negotiate the urgency of contradictory needs for separation from her, and for dialogue with her? During the last two decades of his career, these questions informed works of lasting importance by Ted Hughes. These included *Shakespeare and the Goddess of Complete Being*, in which he investigated the conflicted "way of loving" to be found in Shakespeare's writing; and the autobiographical poems wherein Hughes provided himself with a mythical childhood, much in the manner of Wordsworth, setting forth an account of the growth of the poet's mind. But in Hughes's account, marriage was the culmination of that developmental path. And marriage forced a man into the underground of his own darkness. In "The Offers," he is stepping naked back into the world, no longer in the form of a man, but as a persona.

This is the myth that can be pieced together from its scattered manifestations in Hughes's published works and private papers; and Hughes made sure that it could be found. The year before his death, he sold a very large collection of his manuscripts and letters to Emory University in Atlanta. And during the latter years of his career, anxious about his literary reputation, he responded generously to inquiries from scholars and critics interested in his work, and granted interviews about his beliefs and practices, and about his personal life.

In just such ways did Ted Hughes insure that his persona as a poet would survive him and would slowly work its way into the consciousness of posterity. He said as much to Sylvia Plath's mother, Aurelia, back in 1975 while they were editing some of Plath's correspondence for publication. Hughes requested that many references to himself be excised from this book. Aurelia Plath protested that Hughes was asking her to leave out too many informative details. He responded in a long letter, of which he made a carbon copy that he placed in his own archive. "An impartial scholar will eventually—no doubt—put all these notes in quite pitilessly," he assured her. "In time everything will be quite clear, whatever has been hidden will lie in the open."

Hughes was speaking, specifically, about his relationship to Sylvia Plath. He understood that after his death the story of their marriage would belong to the cultural history of the twentieth century. As he knew, the totality of his work contained a unique and poignant account of how they struggled together to become writers: what each gave, what each took; how their marriage floundered and their art did not. *Her Husband* threads together the story Hughes told and the history that surrounds the story. Drawing from his books and papers, it follows a single line of inquiry through the maze of Hughes's life as he enters into the partnership, struggles and prospers in it, loses the partner but not the relationship, and turns the marriage into a resonant myth.

HER HUSBAND

CHAPTER ONE

MEETING
(1956)

Ted Hughes believed that destiny had singled him out to become the husband of Sylvia Plath. "The solar system married us," he claimed, when he re-created their meeting in *Birthday Letters,* locating the astrological coordinates very precisely. The date was Saturday, February 25, 1956, under the sign of Pisces, in the zodiac; the place was Cambridge University, from which Hughes had graduated a year and a half earlier. During the week he was living in a borrowed flat in London, working at a glamorous-sounding day job as a reader of fiction submissions at the film company J. Arthur Rank. But he continued to spend his weekends in Cambridge, hanging out with friends, mainly poets who were still enrolled at the university. They were ambitious, idealistic, apprentice artists, and that winter Hughes joined them in putting together a very small, very literary magazine, *St. Botolph's Review.* One of the contributors, an American named Lucas Myers, lived in a repurposed chicken coop behind the rectory of St. Botolph's Church, off campus. His residence inspired the cheeky title—these poets were ultra-anti-establishment. Friends began peddling copies of *St. Botolph's Review* around the Cambridge colleges on publication day, spreading word that a launch party would be held at rooms in Falcon Yard that night. Sylvia Plath bought a copy from an American cousin of one of the poets, and he invited her to the launch.

Plath accepted immediately; here was an opportunity she had been waiting for. She was studying literature at Cambridge on a two-year Fulbright Fellowship after graduating from Smith, a prestigious women's college in New England. Her writing had won minor literary prizes in the United States and was beginning to appear in such American magazines as *Harper's, Mademoiselle, The Nation,* and *Atlantic Monthly.* Arriving at Cambridge, she had quickly learned that the literary world was tightly networked in Britain; even the limpest student publications were scouted for new talent by London publishers, who were often themselves Cambridge graduates. She immediately began submitting work to college publications. In January, two of her poems had been printed in a little magazine called *Chequer*—and not only published but, to her amazement, scoffed at, in a fierce little low-budget paper called *Broadsheet,* which was produced every two weeks on a mimeograph machine by some of the St. Botolph poets. The men who reviewed Plath's poems disliked on principle the formal verse at which she was very skillful, and on principle they derided what they disliked. "Quaint and eclectic artfulness," the reviewer labeled Plath's style, then added, "My better half tells me 'Fraud, fraud,' but I will not say so; who am I to know how beautiful she may be."

The stapled pages of *Broadsheet* were read avidly by the local poets, and Plath was mortified at being so manhandled. This had been her first exposure to the blokishness of English literary culture. What bothered her most, though, was that little refrain "fraud, fraud." Plath was aware of her shortcomings and didn't like them to be noticed by others. Yet the critic's rhetoric gave her an opening. Did he want to see whether she was beautiful? She would introduce herself. She put on a pair of red party shoes and smoothed back her pageboy with a red hair band, then went to a bar with her date for the evening, where she fortified herself with several whiskeys. But before getting high she had fortified herself another way: she had memorized some of the poems in *St. Botolph's Review.*

The party was well under way by the time Plath arrived in Falcon Yard and climbed in her red shoes up the stairs to the Women's Union, where a jazzy combo hammered music into the babble of raised voices. Plath started working the room, getting noticed. She immediately sought out the reviewer who had called her a fraud; he turned out to be a little chap, "frightfully pale and freckled," quite unimposing in person, after all—Plath too judged poets by their looks. She cut in on men she wanted to dance with, bantering at the top of her lungs. At the end of the long hall, she spotted a good-looking fellow, and learned his name: Ted Hughes, one of the two poets whose work she had memo-rized that afternoon. He caught her watching him and slouched across the room, staring into her eyes. She began yelling over the dance music, and he recognized that she was recit-ing lines from a poem he had writ-ten. He shouted back, "You like?" He steered her into an adjoining room where they could talk, and refilled her glass with brandy, apologizing, lamely, for the bad notice in *Broad-sheet*, though privately he shared the reviewer's opinion. They sparred a bit, Plath nervy and exhilarated. He

Ted Hughes, age nineteen, passport photo, 19 April 1949

suddenly kissed her, hard, and she retaliated—she bit him on the cheek until blood ran. He snatched off her hair band and her silver earrings, and walked out.

Ted Hughes left the party with his current girlfriend. He didn't know, yet, that the solar system had married him. But he was wearing a wedding ring of tooth marks, and for the next several weeks, one of his cheeks would display a scar as did one of hers, a scar just under her right eye, about which he would learn much more during the ensuing months.

Hughes wasn't looking for a wife that night. Quite the contrary—he was in a profound dither about where his life was heading. At the time of his graduation from Cambridge, Hughes had decided somewhat impulsively that he would apply for immigration to Australia, where his older brother, Gerald, had settled. The Australian government pro-vided free passage to British men who agreed to work there; Hughes

envisioned taking up a life of shooting and fishing with Gerald, an avid
sportsman. But Hughes deferred his application for the allotted period
of two years—he was in no hurry. In March 1955—maybe between
jobs—he suddenly wrote to Gerald that he was coming "without
delay," but again he delayed. By February 1956, the deferral period was
almost up, so Hughes reactivated the application, hoping that the long
waiting list would give him as many as nine more months in England.
Nonetheless, he knew he could be assigned a ticket at any time, and the
question came home to him, urgently: What was he actually going to
do, in Australia, anyway? Work as a teacher? or a day laborer? On the
other hand, how much longer could he tolerate the hand-to-mouth
existence he was leading in London and Cambridge? Given these
unmanning worries, Hughes may have been especially receptive to the
kind of flattery Plath lavished on him at the launch party. She had
plucked from *St. Botolph's Review* a poem that glorifies male aggression. It opens with the line, "When two men meet for the first time,"
and goes on to observe that (male) strangers sometimes attack each
other on slight provocation, as animals do, because the animal is still
alive in them:

> their blood before
> They are aware has bristled into their hackles

Plath had thrown herself at Hughes chanting the poem's last words:
" 'I did it, I' "—Hughes's first experience of Sylvia Plath was hearing
her voice pronouncing his words as knowingly as if she had written
them.

She had not written them, but she knew where Hughes was coming from: in the poem's DNA lay works of Sigmund Freud and D. H.
Lawrence that were fundamental to a literary education in those days.
Hughes had read Lawrence avidly in his teens, and Lawrence's notori-
ous celebration of "blood consciousness" appears undisguised in
this poem that Plath picked out to memorize. Plath had read the
same books, and had undergone a similar literary infatuation with
Lawrence—she couldn't miss the allusion. The first, telegraphic

exchange that passed between Plath and Hughes that night was both a party game and a discovery scene in six syllables. " 'I did it, I.' " "You like?" When he kissed her, when she bit him, they were acting out a scene of primitive impulsiveness that would have been at home in one of Lawrence's novels.

Ted Huge

Ted Hughes may not have been looking for a wife that night, but Sylvia Plath was looking for a husband, and Ted Hughes met her specifications exactly. "That big, dark, hunky boy," she called him, in her journal the next day, "the only one huge enough for me." He was a striking man, more than six feet tall, and he normally weighed around 195 pounds. In winter he liked to wear a heavy, brown leather army-issue topcoat that had survived the Great War, which gave his shoulders extra bulk and cloaked his shabby clothes in a bohemian glamour.

An extremely unkempt appearance was unusual at Cambridge in his day. Hughes was acutely aware of the class anxieties expressed in bizarre clothing at Cambridge: grammar school boys like himself attempting to counter the contempt of public school boys through displays of eccentricity. Hughes's contemporary Karl Miller recalled that the most spectacular students "dressed in a weird exacerbation of Edwardian chic—pipe-stem tweed trousers, lapelled and brocaded waistcoats, wilting bow-ties, wafer-thin flat caps." Winter and summer Hughes wore the same shapeless black clothes. He bought his corduroy cheap from a factory owned by one of the prosperous members of his mother's family, up in West Yorkshire, and dyed it black himself. His classmate Glen Fallows thought he looked "as though he'd just climbed out of a fishing smack after a stormy night." A fellow poet, Philip Hobsbaum, was less charitable: "Ted was appalling. He had smelly old corduroys and big flakes of dandruff in his greasy hair."

Hughes was actually quite self-conscious and shy in company, but he hid his unease behind mesmerizing talk. For sociability, he gravitated to the Cambridge pubs where students passed their time singing folk songs. Hughes had a big, distinctive voice, rich and sonorous, the mannerisms of his native Yorkshire detectable under the influence of his elite education. Many anecdotes about this voice appear in the memoirs of people who knew him when he was young. The American writer Ben Sonnenberg tells one of the best stories, about being invited to dinner with Hughes sometime during the early 1960s at the home of the American poet W.S. Merwin. "I felt like Hazlitt meeting Coleridge for the first time: bowled over by his warmth and energy," Sonnenberg writes. While listening to Hughes, "I did indeed fall off my chair. When he helped me up from the floor, I wrote in my notebook, 'He didn't stop talking and I felt the vibration of his voice running down his arm.'" The English writer Emma Tennant tells another good one, about finding Hughes sitting immobile in the middle of a lively London party in 1976, broadcasting a rambling fairy tale to anybody who would listen; she dragged him onto the dance floor, interrupting him long enough to initiate an affair with him. Over the years, a lot of women would want to interrupt Ted Hughes long enough to initiate an affair with him. According to some, Hughes was "the biggest seducer in Cambridge"—it was the chief topic of gossip about Hughes at the time Sylvia Plath met him, and she heard about it the night she met him, from the man who accompanied her to the party.

But even before she laid eyes on the man, Plath thought she had learned something essential about him by reading his work, and she was right. He had published only a few poems and essays, only in the smallest magazines, and usually under pseudonyms. But from the time he was sixteen, Hughes believed he was destined to become a poet on the grand scale. He wanted to be a poet like W. B. Yeats, whose work he studied passionately, beginning in grammar school and right through his years at Cambridge. After discovering D. H. Lawrence, Hughes wanted to be a poet like D. H. Lawrence too; eventually he fulfilled both wishes in a highly original way. In 1956 he was still finding the path into his vocation—it was the sense of *having* a vocation that underlay his friendship with the somewhat fanatical undergraduates whose work appeared in *St. Botolph's Review*.

One of these was the poet Daniel Weissbort, with whom Hughes later founded a journal to publish translations of poetry. At the time they met, Weissbort recalls of himself that he was awkwardly attempting to imitate Dylan Thomas. "I went up to Cambridge the year after Thomas died and I very much remember trying to write like him," Weissbort said. "And of course the idea of the poet as a bohemian wild boy was very attractive, even though I didn't really know what it all meant." For Hughes, the ideal artistic wild man was Beethoven—he often said that the most intellectually useful thing he did at Cambridge was listen to Beethoven. The poet Peter Redgrove recalled his first encounter, as an undergraduate, with Hughes's Beethoven obsession. "A strange yowling was coming out of this doorway of a kind that I had never known before—I was not at that time musical. I knocked and entered. In the brightly lit room a hand-wound gramophone was playing a black disc—this was the yowling. My puzzlement was complete. Hughes's own physical presence was also of a kind I had never encountered before. It was decisive—very few people in my experience had the ability of showing by their physique a kind of knowledge." Hughes told Redgrove that they were hearing Beethoven's last quartet. " 'It is as if the whole of the music is crushed into the first few bars, which are then unraveled,' " Hughes explained. " 'Look! This is the author'—and he unhooked a frowning kindly plaster mask off the wall. 'This is how he walked'—and he waddled this face towards me at chest-level. 'This was his height and how he walked.' " Hughes introduced Sylvia Plath to Beethoven with the same thoroughness as soon as they began spending time together.

Yet on the whole, Cambridge University figures negatively in the myth of himself that Ted Hughes extracted from the facts of his life once he had become an established poet. Cambridge was "almost a deadly institution unless you're aiming to be either a scholar or a gentleman," he said. Hughes was not born a gentleman and did not wish to become a scholar—only some good luck and special pleading got him to Cambridge in the first place. He'd had the good luck as a boy of eleven: after he failed the preliminary exam for admission to the excellent grammar school in Mexborough, the mining town where he grew up in South Yorkshire, his mother had persuaded the

headmaster—a customer at the Hughes family tobacco shop—to permit her boy to sit for the actual exam, which he got through by writing an essay on his desire to be a gamekeeper. Eight years later, he
performed badly on the exam for entrance at Pembroke College, but
his grammar school teacher sent a sheaf of Hughes's poems to the
master of Pembroke, and the poems won Hughes admission as a
"dark horse."

Hughes had arrived at Pembroke in 1951 after serving his compul-
sory term of National Service, as a ground wireless mechanic for the
RAF. He was posted to Fylingdales, a three-man station on the North
York Moors, where he had little to do but read, and he tried to use this
time to widen his taste in literature. He says he tried the poetry of
Walt Whitman, but couldn't make his way into the rhythms, and also
tried without success to read Rilke. He was equally at a loss with the
collections of contemporary verse that he brought along. What he did
read was his mother's Bible, and the works of Shakespeare. At Pembroke he intended to study English literature, to prepare himself for
the profession he envisioned as a poet.

However, the university education he undertook was designed to
make him into a literary critic. The chief literary man at Cambridge
in those days was F. R. Leavis, who achieved a lasting influence on
Hughes's generation through practicing the analysis of literature as an
elegant form of savagery. Hughes had a gift, himself, for the sadistic
side of Leavis's intellectual style, so he understood the attraction. But
Hughes had little taste for the coteries that formed around the scholars whose influence would later be essential to professional promo-
tion. Nor did he join clubs or play team sports. "He was already
fascinated by the Ouija board and the occult," said Brian Cox, who
became a writer and good friend of Hughes. "There were Pembroke
stories about the frightening intensity with which he engaged in these
activities." These included his interest in astrology, which was
advanced enough to be used as the basis of a memorable paper on
"The Scope of Horror," which he presented at Pembroke. Hughes had
learned astrology from his sister, Olwyn, before he entered Cambridge, according to his friend Lucas Myers. "He loved the opulent

lexicon of symbols, the convergences, oppositions, planetary solar and lunar influences, the cusps and houses with which it organized a description of the human character and destiny," Myers says; but was not a literalist about it. "Ted saw astrology not as a science but as an instrument for the vivid expression of intuitive insights."

But he was an indifferent student. His tutorials in English literature felt to Hughes like mere time-serving, and did not feed his hunger for wildness in art, at all. During his second year at Cambridge, he reached a crisis in his studies that culminated in a fabulous and prophetic dream. He had been working late on an essay for a tutorial on eighteenth-century literature, when the door opened and a man in the shape of a fox entered the room. The animal was singed and bloody, as though he had stepped out of a furnace. He strode to the desk and placed his hand, palm down, on the paper Hughes had been writing, and told Hughes he must stop. When the apparition lifted his hand, Hughes saw that the page bore a bloody palm print.

Hughes told versions of that story time and again throughout his life, and eventually wrote it down, for publication. Not surprisingly, the story changed significantly over the years, but the purpose of telling it didn't change: this was Hughes's explanation for dropping English literature for the study of archaeology and anthropology. It was a practical decision, because he had already absorbed much of the required material on his own. From early childhood he had been fascinated by folktales, and at Cambridge had been drawn to the anthropological literature that had influenced the modernist poets Hughes admired, especially T. S. Eliot, Robert Graves, D. H. Lawrence, and W. B. Yeats.

Hughes graduated from Cambridge in July 1954, having achieved a rank of II.1 in his exams. This was a high second-class degree, roughly equivalent to an American B+; Sylvia Plath would achieve the same rank, in 1957—"respectable but not dazzling," as her chilliest biographer put it—when she completed the course in English literature that Hughes had abandoned. But artists didn't need to achieve "firsts," and Hughes wanted to be an artist. He moved to London and continued writing poetry, picking up one job and another while undergoing the typical postgraduate jolt of discovery that his higher education was economically useless.

He resisted moving back to his parents' home in Yorkshire, where his worried mother was waiting to take him in, possibly with the idea of bringing Ted into the family textile business. It was run by his rich uncle Walt, who invited Hughes to be his driver on a trip to the Continent, shortly after Hughes left Cambridge. They visited battlefields; his uncle had been wounded on the Somme, when he was Hughes's age, and the visit impressed Hughes deeply, later surfacing in a number of poems. They also tasted wines on that trip, and discovering the taste of claret became synonymous in Hughes's imagination with the promise of prosperity that might await him. But he didn't want to work for his uncle. Returning to London after this holiday, he took a job as a dishwasher in the cafeteria at the London Zoo. Next, he found work as a security guard; in his off-hours, he entered newspaper competitions, and sometimes won a spot of cash. He wrote to his brother, Gerald, that what he really wanted was to ship with a North Sea trawler for the winter, but he knew their mother would collapse with dismay if her son the Cambridge graduate did such a thing.

But all along Hughes was reading and writing poetry. During his cigarette breaks at the zoo, he studied the big cats, and got one of them rather quickly into a poem titled "The Jaguar" that Sylvia Plath admired in a Cambridge literary magazine before she even met Hughes, and that Hughes always remained proud of. When he became a security guard, he took a late shift so he could write and read while earning eight pounds each night. Whenever he was free, he was a regular at evenings organized by the poet Philip Hobsbaum, whom he had known slightly in Cambridge. Hobsbaum had a bed-sitter off the Edgware Road, where poets gathered to read aloud and discuss the minutiae of poetics. Hobsbaum recalled that on one occasion Hughes spent hours reading passages from the medieval English poem *Sir Gawain and the Green Knight* into Peter Redgrove's tape recorder.

Actually, Hughes greatly coveted a "respectable" job in television or film, the sort of work a swank Cambridge graduate might expect to hold—Philip Hobsbaum held such a job. But Hughes's scruffy bohemianism was a liability in that world, where appearances counted. In a memoir, Hobsbaum recalled the strikingly bad impression Hughes made in the glitzy environment of a TV studio on a day when Hughes met him at the office before going out to "drink lunch" together. "Ted in his hairy overcoat presented a contrast to the tinsel starlets and be-blazered leading men who populated the foyer," Hobsbaum recalled. "His habit of sitting sideways while waiting for me, and squinnying askance at our clients, perturbed our statuesque receptionist, Miss Westbrook. She asked me once, 'Do you think Mr. Hughes is quite right in his head?' " It was Hobsbaum who arranged for Hughes to be employed at J. Arthur Rank, commuting by train to the Pinewood Studios in Slough, to write summaries of novels that had been submitted for possible development into films—then commuting on weekends to Cambridge, to sleep on the floor of Lucas Myers's chicken coop, and put his new-minted poems into *St. Botolph's Review*. Which led him to Sylvia Plath.

Flashy American

Many of these details about Ted Hughes would have been circulating in the pool of Cambridge gossip when Plath began inquiring about him, after the party in Falcon Yard. Plath had acquired a certain notoriety herself, even before the party. The male undergraduates outnumbered the females by ten to one, and all of the women came under close scrutiny. It is recalled in various memoirs that Plath was considered flashy and pushy, even in comparison to the other American women enrolled at Cambridge—it is recalled that even Ted Hughes considered her too "forward," at first. She was opinionated, impatient, sometimes arrogant, and always on the move, even when seated, as one of her housemates at Cambridge remembered. "One foot . . . was always kept swinging impatiently and the fingers of her two hands were always actively interacting—the fingers themselves interweaving, locking and unlocking, the two thumbs rather hostilely opposing each other, stabbing each other with their nails." Riding her bicycle, Plath "would pedal vehemently, head and shoulders straining

Sylvia Plath, dandelion in hand, Wellesley, Massachusetts, summer 1955

forward, as though pure will power rather than her legs propelled her." The vehemence was not dependent on the urgency of trip, no. It was typical. "She rode, say, like a passionate little girl."

Plath was not a little girl, she was a big girl: five foot nine, slim and well-proportioned, with a long waist and broad shoulders. Though she indulged a big appetite for food, her weight normally hovered around 140 pounds. Her most striking characteristic was a physical vitality that, by all accounts, a camera couldn't capture; people who knew her, including Hughes, thought that no photographs of Plath did justice to her looks. She didn't like her nose: "fat," she thought, and squashy, prone to sinus infections that left the internal passages revoltingly clogged with thick mucus, which she perversely reveled in annotating for her journal, more than once—the opening of James Joyce's *Ulysses* had licensed her to write about snot. She had a manner of testing the air with her tongue as she talked, and a habit of gnawing her lips raw, when she was nervous. She often rebuked herself for hanging on to habits she considered childish. But overall she seems to have liked her own looks, didn't obsess about her flaws, and carried herself proudly; her good posture was commented on by at least one of her teachers. One of her boyfriends recalled that she used to gloat a bit about her "hard muscles" and preened over enjoying "athletic sex." Plath referred to herself as "athletic" in her journals and letters, but people who witnessed her in action recall more drive than grace or coordination in her movements. Plath comments about her fictional surrogate Esther Greenwood, in *The Bell Jar,* that she was not a good dancer, for example, and that is what other people remember about Plath too. Perhaps Plath meant by

FASHION NOTE

Bought your May Week outfit yet? Sylvia Plath, American Fulbright Scholar at Newnham, reviews May Week fashions on the centre page.

Sylvia Plath in *Varsity,*
May 1956

"athletic" that she possessed a lot of physical daring. Back in 1952 she had broken a leg her first time out on skis, having launched herself at top speed down a slope reserved for advanced skiers. During her first year at Cambridge she rode a horse for the first time, a purportedly mild-mannered stallion named Sam, who bolted. Plath lost her grip on the reins and stirrups, but she had the physical strength to hang on to his neck as he galloped onto the highway into the path of cars and bicycles, then up onto a sidewalk, scattering pedestrians. She was exhilarated by the fright and danger, and it made a good story, which she embellished in letters to her boyfriends back home.

Nor was Plath averse to showing off this able body. At Cambridge she wrote an article about fashion for the university newspaper, *Varsity,* and posed for several cheesecake shots to be used as illustrations. One of these was published on the front page, another ran with the story: Plath in a halter-neck swimsuit, shot at angles that give maximum column inches to her long shapely legs. They show strong definition in the quads and calves, probably from the vigor of her cycling.

When Plath sent home the clipping, she captioned it for her mother, "With love, from Betty Grable." But here was another of her distinctive traits: Plath was oblivious to the way her self-display jarred the British sensibilities around her and bothered her fellow Americans at Cambridge, who were trying to avoid being noticed for their nationality. To the British, Plath was the caricature of an American girl, loud, overdressed, and gushy. Entering new surroundings, meeting new people, her first response was to exclaim and ooh and aah, to be effervescent. Plath thought she was just being friendly. She had always been alert to the advantage of making a good impression, since she had always been dependent on scholarships such as the Fulbright Fellowship that was supporting her at Cambridge. Indeed, she had taken pains to tone down her appearance before crossing the Atlantic. Plath's hair was naturally a light brown that she referred to euphemistically as "German blond"; during summer holidays from college in the United States she bleached it to a shade she liked to call "platinum." This label was Hollywoodese—Marilyn Monroe's hair was "platinum"—and Plath reveled in the image of herself as a "giddy gilded creature" having fun, fun, fun. But before boarding the ship that would carry her to England, Plath had redyed her hair to light brown; she thought this made her look studious and earnest.

It was the mobility and intensity of her facial gestures and her expressive dark brown eyes that made the greatest impression and eluded the camera. Her skin had an unusual color and sheen that made some people think of translucent wax, others of cellophane. She had thick, juicy lips that she emphasized with brilliant red lipstick. She had an unsettling way of gazing with a scowl as she listened. Plath's Cambridge tutor remembered the first time she caught sight of Plath in the lecture hall. Not knowing anything about Sylvia Plath, the tutor was struck by "the concentrated intensity of her scrutiny, which gave her face an ugly, almost coarse, expression, accentuated by the extreme redness of her heavily painted mouth and its downward turn at the corners." Accustomed to the reserved deportment of English girls, the tutor added, "I distinctly remember wondering whether she was Jewish." One of her Cambridge housemates recalled Plath's face as

"invariably lit by interest in or attention to something or someone. . . . Either she was talking or listening animatedly . . . or she was
silently reading something with eyes very alive and attentive." All in
all, Plath was a decidedly unrelaxing person to be around, though not
everyone found this unpleasant.

The "Diary I"

Plath had left the party in Falcon Yard with the man who was a casual
date for the evening and had accompanied him to his rooms for sex,
returning to her own bed very early Sunday morning. She woke
six hours later with a nasty hangover. She couldn't concentrate on the
essay she was supposed to prepare for a tutorial that coming week, on
Racine's *Phèdre*. Instead, she spent most of the day on a very long,
very literary journal entry.

Ostensibly, the journal-keeper is making notes about daily life. But
the journal of the writer is often more like the barre of the ballerina: she
works out in front of a mirror, watching an ideal version of herself
attempting difficult moves, trying to get them right. Trying to sketch a
character. Compose a scene. Describe her surroundings: food, clothing,
noise, furnishings, weather. Or, turning inward, anatomize a grandiose
fantasy. Grope around in the muddle of her conflicts. Encourage herself.

Plath didn't write poems in this journal. Her most frequent aim
was to compose passages that might someday find their home in a certain kind of novel. Plath's model was J. D. Salinger's *The Catcher in the
Rye*, with a first-person narrator of the sort that Plath called the "diary
I," a character who must be "in her way, limited, but only so she can
grow to the vision I now have of life." Note how Plath separates the "I"
of the written character from the views of the author here. She is speci-
fying that the writer's vision would be deployed through the use of a
female character not identical with the author, though this character
would need to be constructed out of the author's experiences: "that
blond girl. . . . Make her a statement of the generation. Which is you."

In February 1956 two aims occupied the "diary I" of Sylvia Plath.
One was to fall in love; the other was to become a writer. So when

Plath undertook a description of the *St. Botolph's Review* launch party, she was making notes on scenes, characters, and atmosphere—telling the story of the search for an ideal love—and heightening the story by deploying a range of writerly tricks of the trade. "It's hopeless to 'get life' if you don't keep notebooks," she would scold herself.

The drama of her search for a mate was already far advanced in the pages of that journal, where Plath had been keeping notes about her affair with a young American who was currently studying at the Sorbonne, Richard Sassoon. She had met Sassoon during the spring of her senior year at Smith College, when he was a senior at Yale. He was enrolled in a creative writing course when he first began writing to Plath, using his letters as drafts of work he submitted for credit. Sassoon was intellectually vivid and sophisticated—his abundant letters are full of references to painting, poetry, and things best expressed in French. Plath thought of him even then as "Parisian" and enjoyed his

Richard Sassoon at Yale, 1955

outrageousness, his worldliness, his exoticism. His family lived in North Carolina, but his family tree had an attractive British branch as well: he was a distant cousin of the poet Siegfried Sassoon.

As their relationship deepened, Sassoon became passionate, confiding, open in his desire and poetic in its expression ("part of me sleeps at your throat, pressing pleasure at the passage of life," he wrote after one of their weekends together). He treated her to restaurant dinners and theatre tickets, when they began meeting for glamorous weekends in New York. Plath's journal keeps detailed records of what they ate and drank on their *nuits d'amour*.

Sassoon went on from Yale to the Sorbonne in the autumn of
1955, at the same time Plath went to Cambridge. During the Christmas
holidays, she crossed the Channel to see him on her first-ever visit to
Paris, which she remembered later as a romantic reunion with her
"nervous boy & figs and oranges," in a "smoky Paris blue room like
the inside of a delphinium." They spent several days in Paris—Plath
preserved the appearance of respectability by staying in a hotel—
before traveling together to the Côte d'Azur, which they toured by
motor scooter, another romantic episode that Plath wrote up for publication as soon as she returned to Cambridge.

During their holiday in France, some kind of quarrel caused Sassoon to draw back, however, and Plath became apprehensive that he
would jilt her—even though, throughout their affair, Plath had been
strongly ambivalent: allured by Sassoon's mind, but put off by his
body. She disliked feeling that she dwarfed him physically: he was just
her height, which meant that she couldn't wear heels on their glamorous outings. And he was slight of build, while Plath preferred the
looks and manners of a he-man—one of her erotic fantasies was to be
lifted and carried in a man's arms. She tortured herself with a fantasy
of ending up married to some thin, weak man whose intelligence
attracted her but whose lovemaking would make her feel as if she were a
mere outsize female body "being raped by a humming entranced
insect," then giving birth to "thousands of little white eggs." Plath was
acutely conscious of her prospective fertility, and was dismayed by her
attraction to men whose intellects were their principal erotic assets.

When Plath returned to Cambridge after her Christmas holiday
with Sassoon, she resolved to stop writing letters until he signaled
again that he needed her. Beginning in the New Year 1956, Plath
began writing *as if* to Sassoon in her journal, planning to analyze
her conflicts and possibly to cannibalize these letters for her creative
work. Lucky for us, because we get to watch Plath framing her own
life as "a statement of the generation" with regard to choosing a mate.

Partly because Plath fears she has been deserted, the sexual feelings
she records during those weeks are perversely keen. She is also trying
to choose her life's work. At the opening of the winter term, she begins

mulling over what she labels, using capitals, "the dialogue between my Writing and my Life." She cannot justify the choice of writing unless she can prove herself by publishing steadily. Should she give greater priority to Life, then, and relegate Writing to her spare time? As for marriage, she's now worried. Emotionally invested in Richard, she has failed to play the field at Cambridge. In mid-February, she resolves to accept dates from anybody who asks her. Just before getting dressed for the party in Falcon Yard, in fact, she jotted a cost-benefits analysis in her journal, criticizing herself for being too prestige-conscious, and giving herself a pep talk: "The fear that my sensibility is dull, inferior, is probably justified; but I am not stupid. . . . I long so for someone to blast over Richard."

All of these conflicts were waiting in the wings of Plath's journals that Sunday morning after the party, when she settled down with her hangover and her typewriter. Plath took up where she had left off the preceding day, pursuing the theme of her twin quests: mating and writing. This time, not the anxious jilted female but the experienced writer goes to work on the material. Eight men are sketched rapidly, each in the chiaroscuro of a single phrase, the better to highlight the attractive American, Lucas Myers, who gets a paragraph to himself, complete with fashion note: "dark sideburns, rumpled hair, black-and-white baggy checked pants, loose swinging jacket, doing that slow crazy english jive with a green-clad girl." Plath doesn't mention that he was tall, but he was tall. Plath tells how she cut in on the green-clad girl, and how she began declaiming his poem "Fools Encountered" while they danced. They were both awfully drunk, but—she admonishes herself in the journal—Lucas at least had won the right to his tipsy behavior by publishing poems in *St. Botolph's Review*, "sestinas which bam crash through lines and rules." We can see that on February 26, 1956, Lucas Myers has quite evidently (bam, crash) made it onto the short list for the position so recently abandoned by Richard Sassoon.

Dramatically, Ted Hughes now makes his entrance in the journal. Plath spotlights his size and his physicality (big, dark, hunky, etc.), delivering the lines with which she and Hughes enter the history of literature together: "I started yelling again about his poems and quoting . . . he yelled back, colossal." The scene goes on: they stepped into another room, they talked, and then, "He kissed me bang smash on the mouth and ripped my hairband off . . . and my favorite silver earrings: ha, I shall keep, he barked. And when he kissed my neck I bit him long and hard on the cheek, and when we came out of the room, blood was running down his face." She immediately imagines making love with him, "crashing, fighting." He's the only man she's met since coming to Cambridge "who could blast Richard."

In this morning-after session, Plath is not—quite—falling in love, she is looking for a way to typecast the men she met at the party. "Blast"—the word she takes up from the preceding day's entry—gives her the keynote. Plath riffs on the theme that writing is sexy, sexy is violent, writing is violent. In her morning-after notes, "bang," "blast," "crash," "smash," "wind," and "hunger" become interchangeable terms for lust and for writing, and as we see, she applies them in turn to both Lucas and Ted, foils for Richard, who has generated this term in her erotic vocabulary. But "bang" is a new one: Plath may well have picked it up from Hughes's poem "The Jaguar" (he calls its vital energy a "bang of blood in the brain")—she would have seen "The Jaguar" in a recent issue of *Chequer*. Plath confesses that she had been prompted to memorize the poems of Hughes that she found in *St. Botolph's Review* because they were violent in a way she found sexually arousing: "I can see how women lie down for artists." The scale of the poems matches the brawn of the man, "strong and blasting like a high wind in steel girders." Plath strokes in memory the way he pronounced her name: "Sylvia, in a blasting wind." In a daydream about seeing him again, she and he are "banging and crashing in a high wind in London."

Plath had now fixed a set of associations that will roil in her journal entries for the next month whenever she tries to characterize herself as a heroine. Sometimes it is, again, the memory of Richard Sassoon that generates the flow of associations. She envisions "a life of conflict" with him, where writing and food and kids and housekeeping thrive in a tumult of violent energies, "banging banging an affirmation" in every moment, but especially "in bed in bed in bed." Sometimes it is the thought of Hughes—as on the first weekend he was rumored to be in Cambridge after their meeting. "[M]y black marauder," she calls him, "oh hungry, hungry." Sometimes it is her own vocation of writing that calls forth the crash-bang metaphors: "I have powerful physical, intellectual and emotional forces which must have outlets"—promiscuous sex, or writing that reproduces "the flux and smash of the world," even in the small-scale grids of her verse.

In short, that journal entry of Sunday, February 26, the day after Ted Hughes entered her life, shows Plath developing a vocabulary and a point of view for "the diary I of the novel," the activity that is competing with her course of academic study to define the profession she may take up.

But what sort of story might she devise around this "character," her surrogate self? This post-party entry contains an inkling—it contains Plath's very first recorded thoughts about writing the first-person novel that in 1963 would be published as *The Bell Jar*. She will put her protagonist in a situation Plath knew well—"shock treatment"—and compose the scene in a style that no one could dismiss as quaint artfulness: "tight, blasting short descriptions with not one smudge of coy sentimentality."

"Blasting." "Shock treatment." It was bold of Plath to settle on those metaphors and themes. Three years earlier, she had been released from McLean Hospital in Belmont, Massachusetts, where she had been undergoing psychiatric treatment for clinical depression, following a nearly successful suicide attempt. In August 1953, immediately after returning from a stint as guest editor on *Mademoiselle* magazine's annual college issue, Plath had suffered a sudden, debilitating psychological disorganization. She couldn't sleep, eat, or read. It was not merely a reaction to the stress and excitement and letdown of her hectic weeks in New York, but an all-encompassing sense of worthlessness and hopelessness and meaninglessness. Plath was very likely predisposed to this illness; it ran in her family on both sides. On August 24, despairing, terrified by the deterioration of her mind, obsessed with suicidal thoughts, she had crept into a dugout under the family house, where no one might think to look for her, and taken an overdose of pills. Sometime during the two ensuing days of unconsciousness she had vomited them, and had abraded her face against the dirt floor; the scar on her right cheek was the legacy. She was rescued by her brother, Warren, who overheard her faint, semiconscious groans.

During the five-month run of her illness, Plath was put through two courses of electroconvulsive therapy (ECT)—"shock treatment." The first course, administered before her suicide attempt, had, apparently, been botched. The second was overseen by a young female psychiatrist with whom Plath formed a lifelong bond: Dr. Ruth Beuscher. Plath recovered fully, and by early February 1954 was able to return to Smith College, where she had brilliantly completed her degree, written an honor's thesis, and led an active social life.

The remaining challenge of that near death experience, from Plath's point of view, was to make it into a story about her generation, in a first-person novel based on herself. In Plath's journal, "blasting" lays the track along which her associations zoom toward subject matter uniquely her own and—like Hughes's poetry—unsentimental. Shock treatment is the centerpiece of the plot of *The Bell Jar,* and did indeed make Plath's heroine the statement of a generation. Plath presents Esther Greenwood's madness not as an illness but as a response to social pressures that condition the choices and stifle the ambitions of middle-class women in the 1950s—coincidentally, *The Bell Jar* was published in England only weeks before the publication, in America, of Betty Friedan's *The Feminine Mystique,* a nonfiction polemic on some of the same subjects.

And once she has settled on the formula for such a novel, she thinks of testing it on Hughes: "I would like to try just this once, my force against his." By "force" she means, along with the force of her sexuality, the force of her writing. More: she wants to be accepted as a writer by Hughes, by Myers, and by the whole pack of men from whom she has singled him out. "I could never sleep with him anyway, with all his friends here and his close relations to them, laughing, talking, I should be the world's whore as well as Roget's strumpet. . . . Perhaps at dinner they will be laughing at me." Then she asks herself, "Shall I write, and be different? Always, I grab at it, the writing, hold it to me, defend, defend."

She slept on it; and the next day—Monday, February 27—still agitated, she again put off writing the paper on *Phèdre* for her tutorial, skipped her classes, and spent many hours composing and revising a poem based on themes in *Phèdre*. Plath opened with an epigraph from the play: "*Dans le fond des forêts votre image me suit*"—"In the depth of the forests your image pursues me." "Pursuit," she called her poem; she is being stalked by a panther:

> hungry, hungry those taut thighs . . .
> And I run flaring in my skin

Plath later noted that the essay she finally got around to writing on *Phèdre* received low marks for being too focused on the theme of lust. But in the poem, immoderate emotion paid off. A few months later, "Pursuit" was accepted for publication in *Atlantic Monthly,* one of Plath's big breakthroughs as a poet. And as luck would have it, the acceptance letter arrived while she was on her honeymoon—now, that was the sort of thing that *should* happen to the heroine of this story Plath is writing. At the end of his life, when Hughes wrote his own version of Racine's *Phèdre,* he had read those journal entries and watched Plath's imagination seize on Racine's theme of passion as destiny, and apply it to the two of them. He was fastening the end of a personal chain of consequences into its first links.

In Plath the writer, lust is a stimulus to writing, and, as we have seen—as Hughes would see, when he read her journal many years later—the men who could evoke it in February 1956 were easily inter-changeable. Sylvia Plath's journal during the ten weeks between her return from the Christmas holidays in mid-January and her departure for the Easter holidays in late March is one long erotic fidget. She frankly appraises every man she meets for sexual compatibility. Sassoon stayed on the back burner, but the flame could easily be turned up; Lucas Myers greatly intrigued her; and Hughes held the status of a great prize just out of reach. That's the short list, but there's a long list to be found in those pages too.

And though her excitement over Hughes stimulated the desire to write "Pursuit," once she began writing, the poem itself took over—writing poetry "eats up the whole day in a slow lust which I can't resist," she noted. Writing "Pursuit" seems to have been a way of making room for Hughes in the imaginative space previously reserved for the "Parisian" Sassoon alone, for Plath associated Sassoon with the French language and it was partly her study of French that kept him alive in her erotic imagination while their actual relationship withered. "You speak to me through every word of French, through every single word I look up bleeding in the dictionary," she mourned in her journal, shortly after composing "Pursuit," thinking of Sassoon. "My poems are all for you."

Ironically, it was to be those journal entries themselves—not poems, not stories, not novels, not even *The Bell Jar*—that fulfilled the literary aim that Plath the writer brought to her desk on February 26, 1956. Plath was by then such a practiced diarist, her erotic feelings had been so deeply stirred by their meeting, her ambitions were so clear to her that Sunday, that she captured in writing something that needed no further enhancement by generic retouching to achieve its power of communication. Once Hughes released the journals into the public sphere of a library archive, these paragraphs began a slow drip into the public consciousness, to become—along with a few lines from "Daddy," a few lines from "Lady Lazarus"—among the most quoted passages Plath ever wrote.

But that, of course, was much later. After the party in Falcon Yard, Hughes went back to his job in London. In another fortnight he was again in Cambridge for the weekend, and on the Friday night, after drinking late at the Anchor, he went with Lucas Myers around to the house where Sylvia Plath lived with other female students from abroad. Throwing clods at what he thought was her window, he called out her name, but she was out with another man, and anyway he was calling at the wrong window. Saturday night he and Lucas were back, again throwing clods at the wrong window at 2:00 A.M. This time they wakened the tenant, who dutifully went looking for Plath, but Plath was deep asleep and couldn't be roused.

CHAPTER TWO

ROMANCE
(1956)

A month passed before Hughes and Plath met for the second time. It was Friday, March 23; the winter term at Cambridge was over, and students were required to vacate their rooms for a two-week interval. Plath had arranged a three-week trip to the Continent, hoping for a reunion in Paris with Richard Sassoon: she would just drop in on him, as if by chance. Before crossing the Channel, she would stay overnight Friday in London. She reserved a room at a hotel not far from the flat on Rugby Street where Hughes was lodging, as she probably knew. But she made no effort to contact him.

Hughes didn't want to declare his interest, either, so he asked Lucas Myers to play go-between. Myers could meet Plath for a drink somewhere, then just drop in on Hughes at the flat on Rugby Street, as if by chance. Myers admits in his memoir that he had taken a dislike to Plath, and that he agreed to this ploy reluctantly. He duly invited Plath to join him and Michael Boddy, another of Hughes's friends, at a pub called the Lamb, in Conduit Street—a poets' hangout—and shortly afterward suggested a visit to Hughes. It didn't take long to see that Hughes and Plath wanted to be left alone. Myers and Boddy returned to the pub until closing time, then loitered on the curb across from the house for another forty-five minutes before returning upstairs.

They found Hughes and Plath sitting in separate chairs drawn close together, Plath with her legs folded under her, hands framing her face; Hughes with his knees touching her chair, leaning far forward, whispering across the narrow space between them. Michael

Boddy remembered that Hughes and Plath were so absorbed in each other they hardly noticed when he made his way discreetly to the room where he would sleep that night; Myers remembered that Plath was flustered. Hughes offered to walk Plath back to her hotel.

The way Hughes re-creates this episode in *Birthday Letters* indicates that Plath had told him, that night, about the breakdown and suicide attempt she had been through in 1953. But nothing could hold them back from each other. They kissed madly under the stars, slipped past the receptionist, made their way to Plath's room, and

> went in a barrel together
> Over some Niagara

All night they made violent love. When Hughes returned to Rugby Street he was too excited to sleep. He roused Michael Boddy, who helpfully fried up some sausages for breakfast, while Hughes paced and muttered to himself and talked to Boddy into the dawn.

Plath went to Paris, where she looked in vain for Richard Sassoon. But she was also gathering material for the novel she planned to draw from her Fulbright year. She made a brief journal entry about what she called her "sleepless holocaust night with Ted in London." She ate well, taking careful notes about the food and the street life. She attended a ravishing performance of a ballet based on *Phèdre:* "my phèdre," she calls it, thrilling to the prima ballerina's "billowing cloak of scarlet," signifying "blood offered and blood spilt." And she indulged in a couple of harmless brief encounters with prowling men, one of whom lent her a typewriter. Underneath her bravado she was anxious and disappointed, though—she contemplated cutting short her Continental vacation to spend the remaining week of her holiday with Hughes, but reconsidered. Too many other lads had keys to the London flat and were free to turn up unannounced. Also, she reminded herself, there was no bathroom *chez* Hughes. So, before moving on to Rome on April 6, she merely mailed a postcard of Rousseau's *Snake Charmer* to Hughes at Rugby Street, preparing the ground for a meeting when she returned. Meanwhile, Hughes pursued her, smitten, in two brief letters addressed, with little likelihood of reaching her, care of American Express in Paris—but they did reach her, and accomplished their purpose. When she returned from the Continent, on Friday, April 13, she ran directly into his arms.

From then on, they were a couple. Within a week of their second night together she began planning Hughes's future: by the end of April she had included herself in the trip to Spain he intended to make on his way to Australia; on May 4 she confided to her mother that she could think of nothing she'd rather do than marry him when he returned from Australia. Five days later she reports that she has persuaded him not to go to Australia at all. Instead, he plans to take a teaching job in Spain while she finishes her degree at Cambridge. She has a hope—not yet a plan, but a hope—of bringing Hughes to America, to meet her family in Wellesley, Massachusetts, before they set off to be world wanderers. On May 18 she announces that they have decided to marry, and have set the date: June 1957, in Wellesley. Being in love with Hughes made her feel like an earth mother, and she believed that marriage to him would influence her poetry. She wanted to have a lot of babies, eventually. "I shall be one of the few women poets in the world who is fully a rejoicing woman . . . my songs will be of fertility." They will have seven children, but only after they have traveled widely, and published a book apiece—in about four years, she estimated.

The strength of Plath's determination had overtaken Hughes's dawdling resolve. At the time he met Plath, Hughes didn't really have plans, he had soothing notions: there was Australia, but maybe first there should be Spain. . . . Did he dread engulfment by the emptiness and provincialism of Australia the way Plath dreaded returning to the vacuous busy-ness of the Massachusetts suburbs where she had grown up? Hughes disdained the aspiration to ordinariness that he thought he witnessed in English poets of the generation just ahead of him. As he told an interviewer, World War II had set these older poets "dead against negotiation with anything but the coziest arrangements of society." Emigration would put English coziness behind him, in a big way. By May 9 he had taken his name off the waiting list for passage to Australia. Sylvia Plath was going to become his "new world," as he says in *Birthday Letters*. They merged their fantasies of exile and began to envision a vagabond life that would take them to Italy, then Germany, then Russia, learning the languages and paying their way by teaching English.

Then June was upon them, and with it, a promised visit from Plath's mother. Aurelia Plath was a widow, working full-time, and planned to give herself the rare treat of a holiday in Europe, where both of her children happened to be that year: Sylvia on the Fulbright Fellowship, Warren as a Harvard student enrolled in an overseas project in Austria. Plath's letters home during the spring term bubbled with plans to show Aurelia around Cambridge and London, and to show off Hughes. But almost immediately after Aurelia arrived, Plath and Hughes decided to marry—hastily, recklessly, even secretly, on June 16: Bloomsday, the day commemorated in James Joyce's *Ulysses*. They quickly organized the necessary documents, and were wed in London at the Church of St. George the Martyr, "the parish church where Ted belonged and had, by law, to be married," as Plath explained in a letter to her brother. Aurelia Plath was the only family member at the ceremony. When Plath sent the news to her brother two days after the wedding, she didn't explain what prompted the radical change of plans. Plath did explain why she wanted to keep the marriage secret from people in Cambridge: she feared losing her Fulbright Fellowship and place at Newnham College, both of which she believed were reserved for single women. In any case, she was more than ready to take this step. As she had written to her mother a month earlier, "To find such a man, to make him into the best man the world has seen: such a life work! . . . this is my reward for waiting."

Hughes was yin to Plath's yang in this romance, according to his accounts in *Birthday Letters:* knocked down by the panther that sprang through Plath's eyes the night they met; married by the solar system; sent on his way as her companion and guardian more or less in the manner of a big, well-trained dog. But within the deterministic language of the story he tells in *Birthday Letters* can be discerned an explanation of fatedness that Hughes had absorbed from Robert Graves. Hughes's marriage was the doing of the White Goddess, who had laid claim to Ted Hughes through the agency of Sylvia Plath: Hughes had no choice. For behind the improbable momentum of their 112-day dash into wedlock, on both sides, was a big literary education that had taught each of them how to live, and what to do.

Take those first two air letters in which Ted Hughes followed Sylvia Plath to the Continent, and the postcard Plath mailed Ted Hughes from Paris. They were like discrete knocks with knuckles on doors that might be firmly shut. Even more, they were like the echolocation signals that bats transmit, navigating in the dark with exquisite sensitivity to every vibration of the target's presence. Hughes and Plath had been exchanging witty literary badinage from the first moment of their first encounter. But now they were falling in love, and no matter what lovers actually say as they succumb to enchantment, the messages transmitted are simple: *Who are you? Where are you? I am here.* Plath's postcard to Hughes has not survived, so we do not know what words she wrote, but the title *Snake Charmer* itself is a message: *Who are you?* The air letters in which Hughes inaugurated his courtship of Sylvia Plath have survived. In *his* first letter, not knowing her exact emotional whereabouts, Hughes sent an inquisitive signal that exposed his own position: *I am here.* He told her that the memory of exploring her naked body lingered "like brandy"—in his bloodstream, in his brain, warming and enlivening him, as if that brandy he poured into her the night they met at Falcon Yard had saturated her skin, and he had tasted it a whole month later.

Hughes's second message to Plath was more elaborate. He sent her a twelve-line poem, prefaced by a lighthearted note saying he would aim for a 6:1 ratio of poetry to prose, when he wrote to *her*. The poem, though, is frankly anguished. Beginning "Ridiculous to call it love," it says that her departure felled him like a gun blast. He is like a wounded man who, looking up from the ground, sees a bird preparing to sing, and dies reaching toward the song.

Plath surely detected implications in his metaphors that we will never hear, though we can guess that the poem was full of allusions to their first evening alone. In the long foreplay of their whispering session, did Hughes tell her about his childhood forays with a rifle-toting brother on the moors, where they shot birds out of the trees? Did he tell her that, when writing, he felt like a hunter stalking prey? And did the two of them attack each other sexually that night, renewing the excitement of rough play that brought them together at the party? In her journal note on this episode, Plath says that her face was bruised and her neck raw the next day. In *Birthday Letters* Hughes mentions bloody scratches on his back as a later "inscription" of Plath's passion.

In any case, Plath treasured these first love letters from Hughes and passed them on to her mother for safekeeping in the family home in Wellesley, as she habitually passed along other items, such as manuscripts of her poems and clippings of publications. Hughes was shocked to learn, years later, that Mrs. Plath possessed these letters, and that she planned to include them in the collection of Plath's correspondence that she was editing for publication. He protested that the letters were very private, "somewhat sacred" to him.

But every metaphor has a public entrance too. The lover as a hunter hunted is an ancient poetic device, which Hughes has updated in this poem, placing himself with Plath in the long tradition of love poetry in English that dates to Thomas Wyatt's beautiful lyric "Whoso list to hunt, I know where is an hind. . . ." Hughes and Plath had both studied such poetry in books, now they had embarked on living it. The term "lyric" reminds us that poetry was originally voiced to the accompaniment of rhythmic instruments such as a lyre. Thus the importance of Hughes's reference to the song of the bird. The hunted man grasping at the song can be seen as Hughes grasping not only at the woman but at the power of poetry he found in Plath. He has been struck by the gift she embodies, and that gift will be his downfall, says the poem. The Hunt, the Wound, the Bird, the Voice, and the beloved known best after death—through the magical compression of metaphor, this short lyric manages to provide a fairly comprehensive preview of coming attractions in the poetry of Ted Hughes. And any of Ted Hughes's closest friends at

Cambridge would have recognized instantly that it was a poem addressed to the White Goddess.

The White Goddess: "Song"

Ted Hughes's friends watched his courtship of Sylvia Plath with disbelief. Lucas Myers has described his own reaction: "I had expected Ted to preserve his freedom from everything but poetry," Myers writes. "I was afraid Sylvia would pull him into a struggle for income, shoes, tableware, functioning appliances, perhaps into the American English Literature Establishment, a shallow sea hostile to his happiness." If Ted ever were to marry, the suitable choice would be a country girl, in Myers's view, not this flashy American, with her appalling commercial instincts. Ted's other friends, equally baffled by his fascination, adapted a lament to sing down at the Anchor: "I'd rather have my Ted as he used to be / Than Sylvia Plath and her rich mommy." In 1956, all Americans were assumed to be rich, Myers explains.

What the poets seem to have held against her most—or at least, as much as anything else—was Plath's attitude toward poetry. All of the *St. Botolph's Review* poets were devotees of the theories Robert Graves put forward in *The White Goddess*. Graves took the view of an anthropologist, observing that poetry has a religious function in society: it keeps alive the primordial myths and ancient rituals that affirm man's animal instincts. A true poet, therefore, writes from the wild, uncivilized depths of his mind. By the 1950s, *The White Goddess* had become a cult book at Cambridge, and the year before Plath arrived, Graves himself had reinforced its influence by giving at Cambridge an outrageous series of lectures on poetry that got the whole literary world worked up. Graves mocked the poetry that was at the peak of current literary fashion. Gerard Manley Hopkins, Lawrence, Yeats, Ezra Pound, Eliot, W. H. Auden, Thomas—all were ridiculed as "false" poets.

The St. Botolph poets adopted Graves's militant stance in the reviews they wrote for *Broadsheet,* according to Lucas Myers, who was one of this circle, along with Dan Huws, David Ross, and Daniel

Weissbort. They avidly studied Graves's "grammar of the language of poetic myth" and applied it to whatever specimen poems crossed their path. That's why they were so hard on the poetry by Plath that was published in *Chequer,* especially the one titled " 'Three Caryatids Without a Portico' by Hugo Robus: A Study in Cultural Dimensions." Plath's poem referred to a work of modern sculpture—there was no wild nature in it. And the poem was written in "quaint" and "artful" rhymed stanzas—there was no zeal of inspiration in it. The reviewer, Daniel Huws, presumed to speak for the White Goddess in calling such work a "fraud." But his addendum was also inflected by Gravesian theory. Yes, the poem was a fraud, but what if the poet herself was "beautiful"—a representative of the White Goddess, the Muse of "true" poetry?

Well, Ted Hughes believed that she was, and that was the reason he fell in love with her.

Hughes had received a copy of *The White Goddess* as a gift from his favorite grammar school teacher, in 1951 when he matriculated at Cambridge; he later said that this book shaped his poetic conscience throughout his whole career. He was rereading it with his Cambridge mates when he met Plath, according to Lucas Myers.

But his susceptibility to Graves's vision preceded his exposure to Graves's book. The evidence is a beautiful love poem, titled "Song," that Hughes wrote at age nineteen, during that period of solitude on the wild moors of North Yorkshire during his service in the RAF. Hughes said that the poem just "came" to him, "as such things should in your nineteenth year—literally a voice in the air at about 3 a.m. when I was on night duty." In "Song," a young poet recalls how he witnessed the transformation of a woman into a Muse, and how this privilege determined his path in life once and for all.

The transformation described in "Song" occurs in three stages, the usual number in a myth. First, a baptism by the moon turns the lady into cloud and fire, with stars for eyes. Second, an embrace by the sea hardens and silences her. Third, a kiss from the wind makes her yield music—not as a voice making song out of air, but as a shell sounds forth when the wind blows through it.

The poem is not about the lady, though, it is about her effect on the poet. As a result of glimpsing the Muse in the woman, he falls in love; then she abandons him.

> You stood, and your shadow was my place:
> You turned, your shadow turned to ice . . .
>
> You will not die, nor come home . . .
> I follow

His abjection humiliates him in the eyes of other men, but he knows he will wear out his life in trailing after her; only his death will free him from this obsession.

Hughes was proud of the poem. He sent an early version of it to his brother as a birthday present, in 1950. Then he lost the manuscript. In 1957, when he was putting together his first book, *The Hawk in the Rain*, his sister retrieved "Song" for him—out of her memory. "Song" is an old-fashioned lyric, laced into a corset of four stanzas, using only four rhyme sounds. Olwyn Hughes was able to reconstruct the poem almost ten years later by recalling its distinctive metrical form.

Presumably, Hughes had not yet read *The White Goddess* when he composed "Song" in 1949. Yet very Gravesian is the story told in "Song," and very Gravesian these images. A brief summary can illustrate.

The White Goddess affiliates the concept of the poet's Muse with primitive worship of the moon. Graves argues that moon-worship is the oldest form of religion, the White Goddess being the divinity abstracted from the moon's waxing and waning in a cycle that matches the woman's menstrual cycle. The earliest cultures were, logically, matriarchal, Graves argues, because the female body seemed to be directly linked to nature and possessed the power of generating new life. Just as the moon has three phases—waxing, full, waning—so the White Goddess possesses three aspects—Bride, Mother, Crone—which correlate with her powers of sexual allure, maternal care, overseer of death. Thus the Goddess was considered to govern not just fertility but all of the seasonal changes in nature, from gestation and birth through copulation and decay. It is obvious that when he wrote

"Song," Hughes had thoroughly assimilated this iconography. Behind the lady's ongoing transformation we can glimpse attributes of the White Goddess: the new moon lifting above the horizon, reddened by the last sun's rays; the fully risen full moon, imposing, distant, and marmoreal; the waning moon, generating images of wasting and loss.

In Graves's account, the Goddess inspires reverence based on terror. The female is her medium; in ancient days the male was required to propitiate her with adequate ceremonies. Poetry, Graves claims, evolved from masculine rituals of devotion to this Goddess, rituals that expressed the understanding that human beings are ruled by the same forces that bring fruition and death in the animal and vegetable kingdoms, through the female of every species. More radically, Graves argued that all "true poetry" expresses this understanding, and in so doing preserves humanity's connection to nature. And by "nature," Graves meant both the drive to reproduce and the drive to destroy. Muse poetry expresses the "mixed exaltation and horror that her presence excites," Graves asserts. Its truths encompass the most brutal and fearsome aspects of wild nature. In modern life, Graves thought, true poetry could be found mainly in the work of the mad.

Hughes's "Song" hardly fits this definition, in any technical sense: it moves purposefully and knowingly to its melancholy closure. The anecdote Hughes told about fetching it out of the air when he was nineteen years old points to its real importance, which is autobiographical: "Song" gives the origin story of his vocation. There isn't another poem formally like it, on any subject, in all of the rest of Hughes's work; and it is the most forthright love poem he ever wrote. Hughes's sister, Olwyn, identified the woman behind "Song" as a girl with whom Hughes was infatuated back home in Mexborough, but in Graves's theory her historical personhood is irrelevant; it is her sexuality that catalyzes the poet's gift. The moon goddess "demanded that man should pay woman spiritual and sexual homage," Graves said, and "no Muse-poet grows conscious of the Muse except by experience of a woman in whom the Goddess is to some degree resident." In his passionate sexual embrace of the woman who inspired his love, a poet would reach through that female person to the fearsome power she embodied, as a requirement of his art. She would be, for the poet, less a woman than a contact with wild nature. "She is either a Muse, or she is nothing," Graves said. But the Goddess would make an individual woman her instrument only temporarily—"for a month, a year, seven years, or even more." And the poet, having exhausted his attachment, might well turn away from his Muse once and for all—and do so with relief, Graves notes. Or he might seek her again and find her again "through the experience of another woman."

All this lies in the background of Hughes's courtship of Sylvia Plath. "Song" is quite evidently a poem about the impact of Sylvia Plath on Ted Hughes, even if it was inspired by another woman and written more than half a dozen years before Hughes met Plath. It shows us what he was seeking and finding in his bond with her.

"Muse" is not a term Hughes applies to Plath, nor indeed does he use this term freely in either his criticism or his poetry elsewhere. Instead, he signifies the presence of the muse figure in metaphors, most often as the experience of being stricken into helpless awe by a female presence who manifests herself as a voice or a birdlike shape; the presence of the moon is coded as a pulsing blue flame, or aura. Hughes would apply just such a metaphor to his mother after her death, in the poem "Anniversary," published in 1995.

> in her feathers of flame
> . . . matter
> And anti-matter
> Pulses and flares, shudders and fades
> Like the Northern Lights

He used the same metaphor of flaring plumage in *Birthday Letters* to describe Plath's appearance on the night she first came to him, to make love.

> A great bird, you
> Surged in the plumage of your excitement,

> ... A bluish voltage
> Fluorescent cobalt, a flare of aura

The voice that entered him out on the moors at 3:00 A.M. in 1949 showed Hughes a space in his psyche that had been hollowed by his mother's voice, and that Plath would fill exactly. On March 23, 1956, as soon as he made love with her, he knew it.

Plath's Idyll

Plath's education at Smith College resembled the education Hughes had received at Cambridge, in that both had studied, avidly, the works of the great Modernist writers who flourished after the Great War. Plath's letters show how specifically her literary education underwrote the way she accounted, time after time, for falling in love. After Plath returned from her spring break on the Continent in April, she wrote almost nothing in her journal until July, when she and Hughes had settled into their honeymoon flat in Spain. She didn't stop *writing*, though, and of the literary language in which Plath located her experience during their courtship we have a great abundance, because she was testing it on her mother.

Sylvia Plath had a close, almost symbiotic, relationship with Aurelia. Plath's father, Otto, had died of complications from diabetes when Plath was only eight years old and her brother Warren was six. Otto Plath had been a successful man—a professor of entomology at Boston University, author of an authoritative treatise on bumblebees. But he had been an improvident husband and left his widow with no financial legacy whatsoever. She, however, was well educated and ferociously ambitious, and found work as an instructor of stenography at Boston University. Through the rigorous exercise of frugality she had provided her children with elite educations. Both proved to be high achievers academically: Plath held scholarships at Smith every year, Warren was awarded a full scholarship to Harvard. Aurelia was particularly proud of Sylvia's precocious artistic talent, both as a visual artist and as a writer.

From the time Plath was very young, she felt a strong sense of obligation to this self-sacrificing mother. Anytime she was away from home, she wrote frequent, vivid, upbeat letters that emphasized the good use she was making of Aurelia's hard-earned money. So it happened that Plath kept track of her life during the spring term at Cambridge in 1956 in a stream of letters to her mother that depict an idealized episode of happiness.

Plath's idyll opened in March, when crocuses and snowdrops began to blazon the cold lawns and stir her to wistfulness. "I think I am made for a 'great love'. . . ." In mid-April, daffodils rise like early stars over the first paragraphs in which Plath confides that she has fallen, hopelessly, for an unnamed poet she describes as a "large, hulking, healthy Adam." Sixteen days later, the cherry tree under her window has foamed into blossom; Adam is Ted, Eden is Cambridge, and the resident pagans are these idling poets soaking up the sun in meadows bordering the college grounds. "He takes me among cows and coots," Plath exults. She's being silly, she doesn't care! And she loves his lack of refinement. Hughes's unwashed, shabby, disheveled look is, in her eyes, a rustic aplomb, appropriate to a "world-wanderer, a vagabond," "a big, unruly Huckleberry Finn." He is strong, strong, strong, and his talk is as bold as his walk. "No precocious hushed literary circles for us—we write, read, talk plain and straight and produce from the fiber of our hearts and bones."

In preparation for her mother's visit in June, Plath also took pains to describe traits in Hughes that worried Plath herself, though she didn't admit it. In paragraphs suppressed from the published letters, Plath cautions her mother not to be shocked by a certain brutishness that Hughes cultivates. He stalks and bangs about, is a lady-killer, has a streak of cruelty in him—"cruel" is a word she uses several times to characterize him—but Plath assures her mother that these traits are inconsequential. What counts, to Plath, is the brilliance of his mind, the virility of his imagination, his fitness as a father of magnificent sons. Moreover, she intends to reform him with her love.

Plath's descriptions of their idyll teeter with a burden of sexual innuendo; the poems she encloses for Aurelia go all the way. Whether or not the lovers acted out their fantasies—they probably did—Plath's poems show what the fantasies were. They link the lovers to primordial sexual mythologies. When Hughes begins introducing Plath to his animal magic, the lovers become satyr and nymph; by moonlight, the pair of them go owl hunting and he turns into a goat-footed god before her very eyes in the poem "Faun." In "Ode to Ted" she declares herself "adam's woman." By daylight they tramp field and fenland together, and Plath celebrates making love in the open air: "under yellow willows' hazing, / I lay for my love's pleasing," she writes in "Song." This is "wedlock wrought within love's proper chapel," she writes in "Wreath for a Bridal."

And what prodigious other appetites they have. Ted's shabby black corduroy coat has big loose pockets in which he carries up to her college room supplies of fresh trout, shrimp, and herring roe. Plath is jubilant. Ever since enrolling at Cambridge she has been revolted by the stodgy, fatty meals served in the college dining room; she has been squandering Fulbright money on private stores of cheese, fruit, nuts, cakes, wine. Now Ted shows her how to prepare meals in her hearth, using the gas ring meant for heating water. Plath mentions cooking steak, trout, and sweetbreads with mushrooms on that gas ring and describes how she and Ted spent three hours one evening peeling tiny shrimp for a dish of shrimp Newburg. Ted was the first man in her life who really appreciated food, she claimed to her mother, putting out of mind her joyful gourmandizing with Richard Sassoon in some very good New York restaurants the preceding year.

They were a matched pair, as country people used to say of horses. Hughes's towering body put her own in scale, and she bloomed with health under his influence. Each was the other's best critic of their writing, and it delighted Plath to discover that they shared other interests too. One afternoon in May, when Plath proposed to take her sketchbook into the sunny garden, she learned that Ted kept a sketchbook himself, which he filled with drawings of fantastic animals and sprites. On the spot they resolved to make portraits of each other for their first books (they didn't). A game they liked to play was Finish the Quotation: one would say the first words in a line of poetry and toss it to the other. He read his favorite poems aloud to her, from Dylan Thomas, Gerard Manley Hopkins, W. B. Yeats; she ventriloquized them back in poems that she bragged were "drunker than Dylan, harder than Hopkins, younger than Yeats"—the evidence now being in print for all the world to see, in the *Collected Poems of Sylvia Plath,* edited by Ted Hughes.

It was probably during these same months that the lovers developed the private language of pet names that appear in the letters Hughes wrote later that year during the brief period of their only separation, in October, after they had been married for three months. Plath had returned alone to Cambridge from Hughes's family home in Yorkshire, to begin her second year of study. Hughes was broke and stayed holed up in Yorkshire for most of the month, then briefly reoccupied his crash pad on Rugby Street in London while looking for work. They wrote to each other every day, and his long marvelous letters end with pulses of pure echolocation—*lovelovelovelovelovelovelove.* He longs to kiss, suck, lick, and bite her from head to heel, and curses himself for missed opportunities. He punctuates long disquisitions on art and life with litanies of pet names, possibly based on slang for her private parts. He calls her *"puss."* He calls her *"kish"*—which might be a slurry approximation of "kiss," but is also an Irish name for the wattle basket used for lugging turf and potatoes, an earthy Celtic word available for carrying other meanings. He calls her *"ponk,"* and sometimes describes the bed where she lay with him as *"ponky."* In a journal entry written on his birthday, Plath says she gave Hughes *"ponky pooh chocolate for breakfast."* Are they playing with "punk," a word Shakespeare used as a synonym for "strumpet"?

These intimacies, whatever their origins, are directional signals, echolocation, in the stream of prose that Hughes addressed to Plath during that month of separation: page after page, laying out his plans for writing plays, stories, filmscripts, fables for children; crabbing about rejections from publishers; itemizing plots; describing revisions of poems he wants her to type and dispatch; worrying about money, dithering over the prospects for a job in Spain, scheming about work to keep him in London; ranting about the false poets they both knew;

compiling lengthy notes about Cambridge eccentrics for the novel
she's undertaking; joking about his surroundings; and always, acutely
lovesick, yearning and longing, needing her letters, needing her—*kish,
ponk, puss, wife, I am here, where are you?*

But that was in October, when they had known each other for
seven months. During April and May, the months of their courtship,
they spent most of the hours of the day and night together, and wrote
no letters that have survived to show us how they were circling and
advancing and devising codes. The idyll that Plath was writing for her
mother, however, shows us some of the internal processes by which
Plath was orienting herself to receive the messages Hughes was sending. Just as in her journal Plath is often working on a story, in the letters she wrote during the months of their courtship she is writing a
disquisition on love, based on the language of erotic ideology she had
learned in college, from D. H. Lawrence.

By age twenty-three, when she met Ted Hughes, Plath was already
more sexually sophisticated than many a college girl was likely to be in
the 1950s. The summer before entering Smith College, she made
friends with a twenty-one-year-old man named Eddie Cohen, a free
spirit who eventually became her trusted mentor on sexual matters.
Cohen lived in Chicago. He had written her a fan letter after reading
the first story she had ever placed in a "slick" magazine ("And Summer Will Not Come Again," in *Seventeen*). Plath was flattered, and
they embarked on an avid correspondence. When Plath complained
to him about the unfairness of the requirement that women but not
men remain virgins, Cohen took the opportunity of cluing her in. He
recommended a good sex manual written by a doctor, but provided
the basics himself, often drawing his advice from his very satisfactory
sexual relationship with a long-term girlfriend. Reaching orgasm was,
he observed, "mainly a learned process" requiring plenty of practice.
But just as important, he claimed, were a willingness to experiment
and a positive attitude toward the inescapable grossness of sex. He
suggested that she get fitted with a diaphragm.

The intercourse between Plath and Cohen was conducted entirely
by mail. At one point Plath noted in her journal that she hoped she

would never meet him in person; astutely, she saw that writing to him was not an act of communication but of composition, "justifying my life, my keen emotion, my feeling, by turning it into print." In the fifty-plus letters they exchanged Plath practiced a journalistic style in which to capture her experiences as a woman of her time who was forced to undergo the maintenance of technical virginity: "soggy desire, always unfulfilled." It appears that Plath eventually asked Cohen to return her letters, and collaborate to edit them for publication, but they did not follow through with this plan, if it ever was a plan.

During her first two years at Smith, however, Plath did not take Cohen's advice to get fitted with a diaphragm. She achieved what she called "practical satisfactions," in sessions for which the 1950s coined the term "heavy petting." Eddie Cohen had encouraged her to pursue her own orgasm as well as her partner's, and with that aim Plath developed a repertoire of what she called "physical rituals." Her journal kept pace, recording the exquisite pleasure of lying full-length between a man's legs, "leaning into the tender pointed slopes" of their bodies while they kissed and came to climax.

After Plath's hospitalization in the autumn of 1953 following her suicide attempt, her psychiatrist, Dr. Beuscher, apparently proposed that part of her cure might lie in a more straightforward exploration of her sexuality. Plath put the suggestion into practice almost immediately, by losing her virginity in the front seat of a car with a boy she had known a long time. She avoided telling one of her straitlaced college boyfriends that she wasn't a virgin the first time they made love, but Plath's journals indicate that, tact aside, she had unhesitating confidence in gratifying what she regarded as a healthy sexual appetite. At Cambridge she startled her housemate by commenting, out of the blue, "what all these English boys need is a little of our good old sensible American attitude toward sex." Perhaps her sexual confidence was underwritten by access to reliable contraception, at long last. A scene in The Bell Jar includes Esther Greenwood's visit to a doctor to acquire the diaphragm that the psychiatrist based on Dr. Beuscher has prescribed. There is no confirming journal entry: unfortunately, Plath was not keeping a journal during that period of her life.

The journals she did keep during her college years show that Plath drew an understanding of her sexuality from works of Freud and D. H. Lawrence, beginning in her sophomore year, when she claimed that one of her organs of perception was now her vagina. She was dating a Harvard medical student, and considering what marriage to him might entail: a medical student was a prime candidate for this role. In her journal she worries about "the appalling and demanding fire licking always at our loins." The pressure to have sex, in 1952 in Plath's world, was a pressure to marry. Would her hopes of becoming a writer be derailed by these strong sexual urges? Misreading Freud's claim, in *Civilization and Its Discontents,* that women are "little capable" of the sublimation required for making art, Plath had thought Freud was saying that a woman writer should avoid sex in order to channel her libido into her work. Plath's female professors at Smith were, no doubt, points of reference in this misapprehension, since they were all spinsters. When Plath applied Freud to her own ambitions, it made her dubious that she should marry. Sexual satisfaction, she feared, might "lull and soothe" her out of the need to write.

But by the end of her sophomore year, she had found an alternative view in the fiction of D. H. Lawrence. A rapturous literary diction takes over the prose in Plath's journal as she attempts to capture the emotional climate of the embraces she has shared with her boyfriend one May night: not yet intercourse, but close. Sexual union, she tells herself, need not endanger her independence. It could be "a polarization . . . a balance of two integrities . . . with centers of coolness, like stars." She is paraphrasing a passage from the scene in Lawrence's novel *Women in Love* in which Rupert Birkin argues with Ursula Brangwen that the ideal relationship between man and woman is not union but "conjunction . . . like a star balanced with another star." But such a conjunction, Lawrence claims, can occur only between strong, independent individuals. The love he and Ursula share "is only the branches. The root is beyond love, a naked kind of isolation, an isolated me, that does not meet and mingle, and never can."

This passage in Lawrence has given Plath a progressive idea of sexual love. "I plan not to step into a part on marrying—but to go on living as an intelligent mature human being," she affirms. She pens a pair of diagrams: two concentric circles with the woman-circle enclosed by the man? No! Then: overlapping circles of equal size? Yes. "Two stars, polarized: like so." And Lawrence has also given Plath a metaphor that will organize the consciousness of the fictional Esther Greenwood in *The Bell Jar*. Lawrence's Birkin memorably peels a fig in an important scene in *Women in Love;* Plath's Esther will dream she is sitting in the crotch of a fig tree amid branches loaded with ripe fruit. Each is labeled as an opportunity, but she may choose just one. Specifically, if Esther chooses to marry and bear children, she cannot choose to become a famous poet. The dream dissolves with Esther "starving to death" while surrounded with fruit, because—unlike Birkin, we might say—she wants something from life's abundance that her sex disallows.

But before this kind of disillusion set in, D. H. Lawrence was Plath's authority on the subject of finding an enabling partner, because he affirmed the idea that a great love was utterly recognizable. This idea is in the background of the letters Plath wrote during April and May 1956, feeling around in her sense of destiny. What if *Women in Love* could be updated, to replace Lawrence's heroine Ursula Brangwen with someone like Sylvia Plath? Someone who longed to be a writer, and also longed for a great love? Such a heroine would know the Real Thing by instinct: the intensity of a distinctive emotion would be proof. Plath's copy of *Women in Love* is heavily, heavily underlined, marking the trail of her quest for the exact way to understand a true and authentic relationship between the sexes. For example: "she had established a rich new circuit, a new current of passional electric energy, between the two of them, released from the darkest poles of the body and established in perfect circuit . . . from the strange marvelous flanks and thighs, deeper, further in mystery than the phallic source, came the floods of ineffable darkness and ineffable riches. . . ."

It is difficult to make Lawrence the champion of a woman as ambitious as Plath was ambitious. Plath found a way. Her adaptation of Lawrence flows from her belief that while she is immensely strong, too strong for most men to take, Hughes is stronger: "the only man in the world who is my match," she tells her brother, Warren. She will go far, but he will always be out there ahead of her, a primal phallic source. What's more, she's glad. Yet a little flutter in her letter to Warren conveys the feminine anxiety that this issue stirs in Plath, and will always stir in Plath. She *gains* power in connecting to Hughes; he *has* power, no matter what. Or so she believes, or wishes to believe.

Why did Plath switch from writing about these things in her journal to writing about them to her mother, though?

Aurelia Plath was a very literate woman. The daughter of Austrian immigrants with little money, she had put herself through college, gaining both the vocational degree in typing and stenography with which she later supported her family and a master's degree in German and English literature. From Sylvia's babyhood on, Aurelia Plath instigated and fostered Sylvia's acquisition of language; she had given Sylvia her first diaries; she involved herself deeply in Sylvia's emotional life. When Sylvia left home to enter college, daughter and mother transferred their intimacy into a very active correspondence, and this separation was fruitful for Sylvia. She was able to climb off the teeter-totter of daily relationship and address her mother as the perfect reader of the unfolding story of the perfect student and writer that she was becoming, at Smith.

One component of their relationship was a shared view that high-minded literature was a useful guide to life. In April and May, Plath was finding her way through murky emotions by attuning herself to Lawrence's passionate confidence in sexual love. But she was also trying to justify her wish to marry Hughes, and the audience she chose was female: her mother and her benefactress, Olive Higgins Prouty. Mrs. Prouty was a wealthy writer of romantic novels, and author of *Stella Dallas*, a very successful novel, published in 1922, that became the basis of a film and a long-running soap opera on radio. Prouty had endowed the scholarship that supported Plath's education at Smith College, and she also paid Plath's bills at McLean Hospital, ensuring that Plath had the best possible psychiatric attention for her depression. Mrs. Prouty too had suffered a breakdown earlier in her life, and she was deeply touched by the catastrophe that had laid low her brilliant protégée in 1953.

So Plath turned to Olive Prouty as a mentor while working out her rationale for marrying Ted Hughes, writing Mrs. Prouty a lyrical account of this perfect love. Mrs. Prouty paid close attention, but was not persuaded—she thought Ted Hughes sounded too much like Dylan Thomas, a bad husband. She had also seen Plath starry eyed before. She encouraged Plath to enjoy the infatuation, not marry the man.

"To Ariadne, Deserted by Theseus"

Plath, however, was determined to marry the man—he was exactly the partner she had been seeking ever since she had discovered Europe for herself that autumn. During their earliest conversations, Plath and Hughes learned that each of them aspired to a life of exile in the manner of James Joyce, in the manner of Lawrence, in the manner of Hemingway: all writers who had fled the provincialism of their English-speaking origins. Plath was aiming for a year or more of living frugally in southern France and Italy, though she believed she really ought to live in some German-speaking country for a while in order to master her " 'mother and father' tongue"—taking up, and then giving up, the study of German was one of her lifelong foibles. Plath knew all too well what a provincial she was, how deeply she had been conditioned by postwar American suburbia. Once she had crossed the Channel to join Sassoon for the Christmas holidays, and zoomed around the Côte d'Azur on a motor scooter, Plath jettisoned all moderation. Now she aspired to live "on the edge." To Plath that meant living on the Continent, among stimulating people who represented "all the variety of the western world." Even Cambridge—"wet, cold, abstract, formal as it is"—beat Wellesley as a place to read and write, because it was "near the theaters of London and the vital, moving currents of people and art in Europe." She considered her Fulbright Fellowship years as the perfect opportunity to shed her college-girl identity, which she satirized as "gray-clad, basically-dressed, brown-haired, clock-regulated, responsible, salad-eating, water-drinking, bed-going, economical, practical." She might even risk "a certain healthy bohemianism for a while."

But Plath would not dream of traveling in Europe, living in Europe, as a single woman. She viewed her own cultivation as enhancing her opportunity to marry a cultivated man, and she believed that such a marriage would require devoting herself to his success, bearing his children, and demoting her writing to second place. The journal entries and letters she wrote while at Cambridge are utterly consistent on this point: marriage was crucial to a woman's dignity and social status, and if you married, you had a family. You had children; but you had something else too: a man who filled the emotional roles of "husband, lover, father and son, all at once." Therefore her aim was to marry a man richly endowed with family feeling, a man ready to make a home with her, a man whose talent was so great that her own could flourish alongside without disturbing the sexual hierarchy that she never, ever called into question. Hughes was such a man.

Plath's inexorable drive to marry Hughes held a countercurrent, though: she had not recovered emotionally from the shock of being 'abandoned' by Richard Sassoon. Her passion for Sassoon had lasted a long time, fully two years, and she had been devastated in March, when she thought he had stood her up in Paris. But shortly after she returned to Cambridge, shortly after she took up with Hughes, Plath apparently received a letter from Sassoon that explained his absence from Paris, appealed for her understanding, and revived the possibility of resuming their affair.

Sassoon may not have wished to make a home with Plath, but he possessed other assets. He was classy and well-to-do. He was talented—different from Hughes, but talented—and he stimulated Plath's talent. He was a good lover: he too had been Adam to her Eve; he too had made reading D. H. Lawrence "shudderingly relevant." And he was already ensconced in Europe. But she had never regarded him as a good candidate for fatherhood. "Little thin sickly exotic wealthy Richard" was her summary when devising a role for him in her Cambridge novel.

Yet Plath did not terminate her connection to Sassoon. They appear to have corresponded during the spring of 1956; it is certain that Plath wrote to him about her decision to marry Hughes. In June he responded, telling her that he had spent a whole night rereading her letters, reflecting on his own shortcomings, grieving over the ending of their love affair. He commented that though Plath claimed to be very confident about her future, her letter to him had the tang of sour grapes. He told her to count on his devotion if she ever needed it. "Long before I was your *bien-aimé*, I was something else to you, and I think always I was somewhat more than a paramour, always," he assured her. He was now returning to the United States and expected to be drafted into the army, but he encouraged her to write him care of the post office box he retained in his hometown of Tryon, North Carolina.

Fear of being abandoned was a firmly grounded aspect of Plath's emotional makeup, quite probably a psychological legacy of her father's death when she was eight years old. To avert desertion by the men who attracted her, she seems to have developed two, probably unconscious, strategies. One was to date as many men as possible and abandon any one of them before he abandoned her—starting over, so to speak. Regarding her "promiscuity," she notes in her journal, "I was trying to be like a man, able to take or leave sex, with this one and that. I got even." Plath's other strategy was to let slip the controls on a burning core of anger at the perfidy of a man: after her rage flared and subsided, Plath felt refreshed, enabled, more like herself. This energy, Plath's anger, is her most distinctive kind of inspiration, to be found throughout her late poems and in her prose; the masterly "Elm" and "Lady Lazarus" use different artistic methods to explore such anger explicitly.

And it is a theme that shows up very early in Plath's work, in the poem "To Ariadne, Deserted by Theseus," written when she was sixteen. "Ariadne, Deserted" is the first poem in which anguished separation from a strong male figure liberates the creative powers of the female artist.

The mythic Ariadne is a Cretan princess, the sister of Phèdre, the daughter of King Minos and his scandalous queen, Pasiphaë. The queen had copulated with a bull and borne the Minotaur, a monster with the head of a bull and the body of a man; he was kept captive in a labyrinth devised by the architect Daedalus. To feed the Minotaur, the Cretans extracted from the citizens of Athens, their conquered enemy, an outrageous annual tribute of youths and maidens. Theseus, an Athenian prince, resolved to destroy the Minotaur and liberate Athens. When Theseus arrived in Crete, Ariadne fell in love with him, and persuaded Daedalus to provide instructions for navigating the labyrinth. Daedalus gave Ariadne a magic ball of thread that Theseus could fix to the doorpost at the entry to the labyrinth, and follow back to freedom once he had killed the monster. In exchange for Ariadne's collusion, Theseus promised to take her home to Athens and marry her. But he abandoned her on the island of Naxos—Ariadne awoke from sleep to see his sails disappearing over the horizon.

Plath's poem is observing Ariadne immediately after she wakes. Wading into the storm-tossed sea, Ariadne screams and curses for three of the five rhymed stanzas. But in the fourth stanza, her anger subsides, the storm recedes, the sea grows calm, and Ariadne, emotion spent, retreats to the rocks. Here is the ending:

> the small waves break like green glass, frilled with foam
> . . . Why do you stand and listen only to
> The sobbing of the wind along the sand?

Plath isn't speaking *as* Ariadne, she is accosting her. Don't be a sob sister, Ariadne—look around. What are you going to do with yourself now?

For a female artist, the myth of Ariadne has special resonance. Not only does her story include that devious artisanal collaboration with Daedalus; it has a second act that is only hinted at in Plath's poem. Yes, Theseus sailed away; but soon the god Dionysus passed over Naxos in a chariot drawn by sky-borne panthers. He glimpsed Ariadne on the beach, fell instantly in love, and swept her off to Olympus. Zeus bestowed immortality on Ariadne as a marriage gift, and after the ceremony, Dionysus lifted off her wedding crown to set among the stars as the constellation Corona Borealis. Unlike Ariadne's sister, the tragic Phèdre—who also fell in love with Theseus, and married him,

Giorgio de Chirico, "Ariadne," 1913

but died by suicide—Ariadne survived his treachery. More than survived: desertion by Theseus produced the conditions of attaining
immortality. It was a myth that retained its hold on Plath. During a
burst of creativity in 1958, while she was working on a series of poems
about paintings, her attention was arrested by a reproduction of a de
Chirico: an empty cityscape with a sculpture of Ariadne the only figure to be seen in it. Though Plath did not base a poem on this painting, she shaped a journal entry around its important details: "The
trapped train puffing its cloud in a labyrinth of heavy arches . . .
Ariadne, deserted, asleep . . . long shadows . . . unseen figures."

Just as "Song" contains a founding image in the work of Ted Hughes,
"To Ariadne, Deserted by Theseus" can be identified as a founding
image in the work of Sylvia Plath. Both of these poems employ mythic
language to identify the emotional matrix of each poet's creative stance
toward the distinctive subject matter his or her art will seize on. Plath, it
must be noticed, cannot imagine a creativity that is not somehow a
compensation for desertion. "Ariadne" is the first poem in a lineage that

encompasses her most accomplished mature works, from "The Colossus" to "Daddy" and on to the powerful, very last poems, "Words" and "Edge." "Ariadne" is a poem about confronting and surviving desertion; it is set on the shore of the sea, a symbol for Plath of the line that divides the ordinary world from the flow of meanings. Her vision of waves as "green glass"—a metaphor Plath uses very often in her work—makes the sea a translucent medium of representation: something that the self can easily pass through to find and occupy its own reflection. But the most important symbolism in "Ariadne" is its gaze at this female figure who comes down to Plath from classical myth. In this early poem Plath probes the Ariadne myth with anxious questions about how the symbolic heroine will respond to the trauma of abandonment. Is her listening passive, pathologically inert, all too feminine? Or is it creative—will it find in the movement of light and the sound of the waves the stimulus of association, as Plath will do very expertly in, for example, her beautiful autobiographical essay "Ocean 1212-W"? Written shortly after she was deserted by Hughes, Plath's essay conveys a strong and peaceful confidence in her own creative fertility; the paragraphs swell and pile on one another with apparently effortless abundance, one metaphor following another, attuned to "the motherly pulse" of the sea.

And it was against the backdrop of what she considered to be Sassoon's desertion that Plath turned to Ted Hughes in the spring of 1956. Plath's resolve to marry Hughes had some of the pressure of compensation in it, then: she had lost one man but gained another, and she wanted to keep him. Never mind that Hughes had little money, no job, and only a dim sense of where his future might lie, and that his friends didn't like her. It was Plath who proposed. Some inquisitive person once asked Hughes point-blank, why did you do it? And got an answer: "Because she asked me." Why not?

CHAPTER THREE

HIS FAMILY
(1956)

Curiously, Ted Hughes did not invite his family to his wedding. True, the wedding was arranged in haste, but a telephone call home to Yorkshire, or to Paris where his sister, Olwyn, lived, would have been an elementary courtesy. And Hughes continued to preserve his silence on the matter when, the day following the wedding, he made a quick trip to Yorkshire, where he stored some of his gear and gathered necessities for the months abroad.

Plath did not accompany him to Yorkshire; she spent those days from June 17 to 21 giving her mother the long promised tour of London and Cambridge—just the two of them. This was Aurelia's reason for coming to England in the first place. Possibly because the impulsive marriage had required an abrupt and unwelcome change in Aurelia's expectations about having a European holiday, the newlyweds also invited Aurelia to join them for the first week of their honeymoon, in Paris. "She and Ted get along beautifully," Plath told her brother, Warren, who would hear all about it when Aurelia went on from Paris to Vienna, to visit him.

So Hughes shared his wedding and his honeymoon with Aurelia Plath, leaving his own mother entirely in ignorance of this momentous occasion. Was Hughes showing Plath that he kept some valuable part of himself aloof from family relationships (and she was now "family")? Was his obstinacy also, or instead, a leftover scrap of the scorn toward marriage in general that the young bachelors around him shared? Was it maybe also an act of resistance to the pressure Plath had brought to bear with her proposal of marriage? Plath, it appears, didn't understand Hughes's motives, either. After Aurelia returned to Wellesley, Plath worried over his deceitful behavior, in a letter that serves as an early indication of the strife ahead of this newly married couple. The ambiguity weighed on Plath until she persuaded Hughes, in late July, to notify his parents in writing not only that they were married but that they would return to England early enough for a visit to Yorkshire together at the end of the summer. Eventually, Hughes was to transform his family background and his childhood home into a coherent mythology about his development as an artist. At the time he married Plath, it was only a history, asserting itself, often invisibly, in the ways he accommodated himself to becoming her husband.

Leo

Ted Hughes was born at home in the village of Mytholmroyd in the upper Calder Valley in West Yorkshire, on August 17, 1930. No. 1 Aspinall Street was a small workingman's dwelling, one of the terraced houses that lined a canal. He was delivered by a midwife at precisely "solar midnight," according to Hughes. This is a term in astrology, referring to the position of the Sun in an astrological chart. In the Calder Valley that night, the sun reached its lowest point in the zodiac—"solar midnight"—at 12:12 A.M. Greenwich Mean Time. England was on "summer time" (daylight savings time) in August 1930, so in the village of Mytholmroyd the midwife's timepiece would have read 1:12 A.M.

We know the exact hour of Hughes's birth—or at least we know what he said about it—because of a business letter dated 1974, on deposit in the Berg Collection at the New York Public Library. Hughes had just been awarded the Queen's Gold Medal for Poetry and was being asked to lend his hand in good causes. Turning down one such request, he goes on to explain that his natal horoscope foretold he was destined for fame, but ill suited to it—"fated to live more or less in the public eye, but as a fish does in air."

It is useful to know a few details about this natal chart, because Hughes applied astrological portents to some important decision making in his life, and drew on astrological symbols in his poetry. Hughes was born under the fifth sign of the zodiac: Leo, the lion. The Sun is Leo's ruling "planet": the typical Leo is endowed with a strong sense of self, one that wants to shine (Napoleon, for example, was a Leo). But because of Hughes's birth hour, his expression of a strong sense of self would, paradoxically, require seclusion. While the "noon" position of the Sun in the astro-

Ted Hughes's birthplace, 1 Aspinall Street, Mytholmroyd, West Yorkshire

logical diagram is associated with the public realm and outgoingness, the equally powerful "midnight" position is associated with home, and inwardness.

A second relevant aspect of Hughes's natal chart was its "rising sign," or "Ascendant": Cancer. To the astrologer, geography is destiny; the sign that is ascending over the eastern horizon of the geographical locale at the hour of birth is believed to exert strong influence over the social character that the newborn will acquire. Cancer, the crab, is associated with home and family.

The third broadly notable feature in Hughes's chart was the position of the planet Neptune, which is "Conjunct" the position of the Sun in Hughes's natal chart. In the zodiac, Neptune is associated with the making of images, symbols, fantasies, myths. At the hour of Hughes's birth, Neptune was exerting great force on the Sun. As Hughes's talent matured, this muscular influence could be expected to assist his project of shaping an imaginary self within a work of art.

In combination, these astral influences suggested to Hughes the kinds of conflict that made him a "fish in air." The higher he rose into view, the greater would be his disquiet. He would crave a place in the sun alongside the great English poets of his personal pantheon. But he would hate to be dragged out of his proper element, his inwardness. And he would hate being scrutinized.

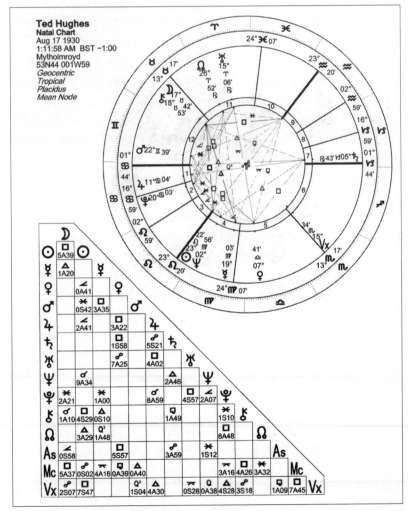

Ted Hughes's natal horoscope

Though Hughes's private papers are full of rough little sketches of astrological charts, for example, he did not divulge his birth hour to the journalists and scholars who interviewed him after he became famous. Nor did he mention it in his autobiographical essays or in his radio broadcasts about becoming a writer, where it would have provided an attractive bit of esoteric lore. Yet he leaked the most valuable detail into a business letter that ended up in a public archive. So, it might be said, the very stereotype of a Leo born at solar midnight wrote that letter in 1974: Hughes accepted the Queen's Medal but wanted to escape the consequences of the fame it shed.

Once you discern that Hughes wished to keep his horoscope a secret, the better to tap its energies for his own uses, you can identify covert traces of it in poems that Hughes regarded as important achievements. Possibly the most significant is its distribution throughout the imagery of "Pike," one of Hughes's best-known poems. Hughes said it was based on a dream he had the night before he married Sylvia Plath. In the dark, in his dream, he cast his line into a black pool,

> For what . . .
> Darkness beneath night's darkness had freed
> That rose slowly towards me, watching

Because of his childhood experiences with fishing, pike, especially, became for him "symbols of really deep, vital life," he said, and he often dreamed of fishing. But "cast" is a term of art in astrology as it is in fishing: to cast a horoscope is to calculate the meaning of the signs in relation to one another. Applying this denotation to "Pike" exposes another dimension of coherence in these lines. The night before Hughes's marriage, a force impersonal and ancient is rising through water to fix its gaze on him—the movement of Neptune into conjunction with the Sun at the midnight hour of his birth is beginning to express its influence in his life. His union with Plath will activate the capacities in him governed by Neptune, his creative powers. The key is given in Hughes's public statements about the poem's relationship to his marriage; the private meaning is unlocked only by knowledge of his horoscope.

Withholding from others something important to himself, by hiding it in plain sight—that is a defensive stance so prominent in Hughes's character, as far back as you can track him, that you might as well say it *is* his character. Hughes's life as an artist was ruled by the need to secrete meanings in his writing that only he would know about. In each important work lies a horde of images imprinted with urgent personal references. It was a brilliant solution to the problem he ascribed to his horoscope. He balanced the warring forces by fashioning a magisterial, a Leonine persona of the Poet, behind which another self could crouch hidden in midnight shadow, peering out.

And this is the self that the solar system married to Sylvia Plath. Pisces—the Fish—is described in handbooks as "the poet of the Zodiac"; Pisceans are thought to be adept at inventing a persona. This sign was Ascendant in Plath's natal horoscope, exerting an influence similar to that of the planet Neptune in Hughes's horoscope. This specific opposition of starry influences meant to Hughes that not just two persons but two artistic personae were jousting that night under the influence of Pisces, the astral sponsor of the poetic imagination. On Saturday, February 25, 1956, the Sun stood in Pisces, as Hughes notes in *Birthday Letters*,

> Conjunct your Ascendant exactly
> Opposite my Neptune and fixed
> In my tenth house of good and evil fame.

Hughes initiated Sylvia Plath into these mysteries while they were falling in love. She wrote to her mother that he always showed up with horoscopes in his pockets, along with fish and new poems. The horoscope wasn't just a courtship ploy, it was one of the charts by which he navigated his career. After Plath had typed up the manuscript of his first book of poems, *The Hawk in the Rain*, to submit it for a prize competition, she noted that Hughes cast a horoscope in order to determine the optimal time for putting it into the mailbox. The book won the prize, and the prize made Ted Hughes famous for the first time; if you believed in astrology, you would see this as evidence for its validity.

"Fixed stars govern a life," Hughes and Plath asserted in their poems, though Plath never did get a proper grasp of astrology—it's one of the faults for which she chastises herself in her journals every now and then, along with her inability to learn German. She had observed, however, that the study of the fixed stars did govern *his* life; and astrology served to make a bridge, for Hughes, between the actual, historical world of day-to-day life, and the occult significance that might be found—if only in retrospect—in the smallest details.

It was only after his marriage to Plath that Hughes began applying his imagination to the place of his birth, the Calder Valley: a deep gorge running through the Pennine Mountains of West Yorkshire, where hillsides rise steeply to plateau on the wild moorland that many readers and tourists know as the setting of Emily Brontë's *Wuthering Heights*. When Ted Hughes was growing up there it was a site of postindustrial wreckage. The Industrial Revolution had made the Calder Valley a prosperous location of the textile trade by 1800: cotton towns in Lancashire, woollen towns in Yorkshire. By the end of the century, business had moved on, leaving a legacy of deteriorating textile mills and clothing factories, and hillsides scattered with abandoned cottages on dilapidated farms. Then the First World War funneled off the able-bodied men. Very few of them returned, and those who did were deeply shocked and disoriented by the war. Hughes would describe living among them as being surrounded by mental patients.

Break off the "Myth" particle in Mytholmroyd and you seem to get an auspicious site for the birth of a future Poet Laureate, but etymologically, the name describes its geographical location on a river mouth. The village lay on a valley floor in a breach of rock, an east-west traffic corridor through which the world traveled on its way elsewhere. But once Ted Hughes began turning his life into stories, he

West Yorkshire Moors: Hughes's "Elmet"

thrust his own myth upon this little town. It became in his telling a cramped passageway, something like a birth canal, out of which he struggled into worldly self-possession.

Hughes's most detailed account of his birthplace is given in a striking voice-essay titled "The Rock" that he wrote for the BBC in 1963. "Everything in West Yorkshire is slightly unpleasant," he begins. This included his hometown. His family home backed onto a polluted canal and stood in the chilly shadow of an enormous cliff that sheered the whole town off from what seemed to be real life, the South of England. Scout Rock was its name, and its influence. It loomed over his childhood like a menacing and inescapable observer—like a policeman, or a bad parent. No town dweller escaped its influence. The valley was "notable for its suicides," he remarked. "It worked on me constantly." After about age forty, Hughes repeatedly ascribed the character traits he most disliked in himself to West Yorkshire parsimony and cautiousness. It often expressed itself in his preoccupation with shrewd and surreptitious or faintly disreputable ways of making money.

There was an escape from Scout Rock: the moors, approachable by a rigorous climb upland, to the north. Once reached, the rolling moors stretched in every direction, surrounding everything in sight. Higher even than Scout Rock, much higher than the valley, they showed themselves only to the sky. A man might seek his fortune in the thriving prosperous cities to the south, but the moors were the home of eternity. Hughes's lifework would attempt to link those worlds, the social and the primordial. From the time he met Sylvia Plath, and under the influence of her practice of submitting everything around her to relentless scrutiny that she transferred immediately into writing, Hughes began absorbing his family history into a coherent autobiography. He centered it on three relationships: to his father, to his mother, and to his brother, Gerald.

William Henry Hughes (1894–1981)

A photograph in the Ted Hughes archive shows Ted's father as a young man posing with his mates in football regalia—soccer, that is. Visible in the distance behind the double row of men on the muddy field is a row of chimneys: "lumbs," in the West Yorkshire parlance, the crumbling remains of the valley's bygone prosperity. The lads are scrappy and stringy, with knobby knees and pale faces. Ted's father stares boldly into the camera, arms crossed, unsmiling, his rough hair bristling. He is taller than most of his teammates and appears more fit. On his youthful face, you can see the distinctive beaky nose and square jaw he passed on to his sons and his daughter. "Billie," he was called by his family members.

According to Ted Hughes, his father played football professionally into his thirties, then gave it up under pressure of his wife's view that she should see more of him on weekends. Billie Hughes was thirty-six when Ted was born, and Ted never watched him in a game. But Hughes knew that football had been his father's passion, and he wrote a tribute to that passion in the poem "Football at Slack," which re-creates the exhilaration of men playing in the deluge of a wild Yorkshire storm:

> The ball jumped up and out and hung on the wind . . .
> Then they all shouted together, and the ball blew back
> . . . While the humped world sank foundering

The father Hughes usually puts into his poems is not an exuberant athlete, he is the silent, psychologically wounded veteran who served in the Great War. Billie Hughes joined the Lancashire Fusiliers in 1915, and was sent to Gallipoli. The assault on Gallipoli was one of the legendary disasters of the war, and the men of the Lancashire Fusiliers were among the hardest hit, mowed down by enemy fire as they came ashore on the Turkish coast. Billie Hughes survived, only to be transported from the beaches at Gallipoli to the trenches of France and Flanders. One of Hughes's poems mentions that his father was awarded a Distinguished Conduct Medal; the citation from the War Office specifies this was "for conspicuous courage and great leadership" in carrying wounded soldiers back from the battlefield to the trenches in Ypres. During his four years of service, Billie Hughes saw the worst horrors that could befall a man. He was spared nothing but death, and was saved by a fluke, when a pay book in his breast pocket, stuffed with mementos of Yorkshire, deflected a piece of shrapnel that would have pierced his heart. At the end of the war, he returned to the Calder Valley, married a local girl named Edith Farrar, and settled down in a world populated by missing persons. All of his former football mates had been killed in the war.

The Beacon, home
of Ted Hughes's
parents after 1950,
Heptonstall Slack,
West Yorkshire

The life he came back to in Yorkshire was pinched and humdrum. In Mytholmroyd, Billie Hughes made a living as a joiner, carpentering sheds and outbuildings. Later, when the family moved to the larger town of Mexborough, near Sheffield, he owned a newsagent and tobacconist's shop, and supplemented the family's income with earnings as a bookie. After Hughes went on to Cambridge, the elder Hugheses moved back to the Calder Valley, eventually into a house called The Beacon in Heptonstall Slack, near Hebden Bridge, another village where Billie Hughes again ran a tobacconist's shop, and played the horses. His children called him "Pa."

The Beacon was the house where Plath met Hughes's parents, when she visited as a bride in 1956. She took copious notes, and immediately wrote them into a story, "All the Dead Dears." It provides a portrait of Billie Hughes in the fictional character of Clifford Meehan, an old man "creaking to his feet" and making his way to a drawer in the china cabinet where he kept his mementos of the Great War: "a cardboard box of souvenirs—medals, ribbons, and the shattered paybook providentially in his breast pocket when the bullet struck (bits of shrapnel still lodged in its faded pages)." He draws from his box a sepia photograph showing wounded veterans in a hospital: five young men. " 'That's me. . . . He's got his leg off. He was killed. He's dead and he's dead.' "

Perhaps it was Plath's example that prompted Hughes to bring his father's war experiences into his own writings. He wrote to his brother, Gerald, that he never knew Pa was a raconteur until witnessing the effect of his stories on Sylvia Plath. A cluster of war poems that were probably instigated by that visit home appears at the end of Hughes's first book, *The Hawk in the Rain*; two of them—"Bayonet Charge" and "Six Young Men"—appear to draw directly on the family's own "first-hand fairy tales" about the Great War; but they have an air of uninvolvement. In 1962, Hughes returned to the subject of Pa's war in "Out," and anchored this theme in his relationship to Billie Hughes's war wounds.

> My father sat in his chair recovering
> . . . While I, small and four,
> Lay on the carpet as his luckless double . . .

The boy intuits that his father is helpless to "outgrow" the grip of the past; the poem ends with the grown-up son refusing, rather brutally, to wear the "whoring" Remembrance Day poppy that is sold in November in honor of the Armistice:

> So goodbye to that bloody-minded flower . . .
> Goodbye to all the remaindered charms of my father's survival

Did Hughes feel that his father, weakened by war, had surrendered too much freedom when he returned to the Calder Valley? That he succumbed to the coziness of bland domestic routine? Hughes once told a friend "how his father, desperate to leave his wife in Yorkshire after meeting a pretty nurse in London, had gone south to find her—only to be discovered almost at once by his pursuing wife, just a few streets away from King's Cross, the station of his arrival and escape." Hughes's letters reinforce the impression that he regarded his father as chronically ineffectual. He grouches to Gerald about how Pa dithers over selling his shop, and how helpless he gets when Edith is ill. He warns Gerald not to tell Pa (or Ma) about the get-rich schemes Ted is hatching—they worry too much. At one point he tells Gerald harshly that he thinks their father had squandered his life; that if Pa ever reflected on himself—which Hughes doubted—he would recognize that he was a failure.

Such attitudes are always in the air when a child is making a foray into independence, even a grown child. In Hughes's poem "Out," the feeling is urgent, though: the father is not "out there" enough, he is "in here." The poem is unusual in being specifically autobiographical. Hughes did not, in his earliest poetry, write auto-biographically very often. He disparaged the realism of such writing, even in poetry—not because it was too frank, but because it lacked the depersonalizing resonance of myth. As he commented in an interview, "Once you've contracted to write only the truth about yourself—as in some respected kinds of modern verse, or as in Shakespeare's sonnets—then you can too easily limit yourself to what you imagine are the truths of the ego that claims your conscious biography."

What did the boy Hughes take from this wounded father that he could use as a poet, then? A clue is provided in "For the Duration," a poem probably written after his father's death. It describes the horrible ordeal for which Billie Hughes was awarded that Distinguished Conduct Medal—after the Victoria Cross, the second highest military honor for gallantry in action that an enlisted man could receive. The poem shows Billie Hughes carrying a wounded man off the battle-field, when a shell burst in front of him and he fell into the trench but did not lose his grip on the man in his arms. "Everybody had his appalling tale." But Billie Hughes does not tell war stories; the boy learns the specifics of his father's heroism from his uncles. His father is more than silent: he *refuses* to tell his son.

> Maybe you didn't want to frighten me . . .
> . . . Why couldn't I have borne
> To hear you telling what you underwent?

"Tell" is rooted in the old English term for counting and reckoning, calculation. A tale is something shaped by art; it can be untrue; it is a near kin to idle talk. "Tell" and "tale" are repeated frequently enough in the poem to trigger recognition that they are being used precisely. The father does not turn the war into anecdotes, and refuses to glorify his own role in it with any kind of rhetoric.

At night, though, the father is not silent; he cries out from bad dreams, and the son hears him struggling, in his nightmare,

> Out of the trench, and wading back into the glare
>
> As if you might still not manage to reach us
> And carry us to safety

The father remembers with his body—this meaning manages to reach his son, several years after the father's death. And those tender closing lines restore the father's dignity to him. *This* father was not traumatized, this father was not fixated; the language of pathology has been replaced by another kind of explanation. The son now sees that behavior so distressing to the four-year-old boy, in "Out," was evidence of his father's absence on a heroic but entirely internal quest. His silence by day and his inner journeying by night through the land of the dead, the ordeal he undergoes in the dark and the aim with which he undertakes it, his bravery and his altruism—even the medal that affirms his superiority in the tribe—all link the father to the other shaman figures idealized in Hughes's work by the time he wrote "For the Duration."

And the son had then matured sufficiently to recognize the ethos of his father's disturbing silence. Billie Hughes was raised to manhood in a cultural milieu that prized silence in men, and in any case offered no language adequate to what he had seen and done in the Great War. The father's trances of agony kept the war dismembered in vital speechlessness and kept it alive for the son to inherit. This is knowledge reserved for men, transmitted only when they are ready to become men—"the soul's food" that awaits a boy "after mother's milk."

Edith Farrar Hughes (1898–1969)

Hughes's mother, Edith, came from an old North Yorkshire family, the Farrars, whose presence in Yorkshire is documented as far back as 1471. The Farrars grew wealthy buying and selling property, and built a great house called Ewood Hall. Their fortune had diminished with the collapse of the textile industry, though when Hughes was a boy the family still owned remnants of land that had once been part of the Ewood estate. The most exalted ancestral Farrars, however, were figures in the far distant past: Robert Ferrar, a sixteenth-century Anglican bishop of the Church of England, burned at the stake by Bloody Mary and commemorated in Foxe's *Book of Martyrs* as a hero of the Reformation. And Nicholas Ferrar, the seventeenth-century Anglican clergyman who founded the religious community at Little Gidding, which T. S. Eliot idealized in *Four Quartets*. And Nicholas's brother John, who immigrated to America as a member of the Virginia Company and was a progenitor of Thomas Jefferson; one of John's later descendants was a founder of the publishing company Farrar Straus. Hughes concealed an ironic allusion to this exalted lineage in the poem "The Martyrdom of Bishop Farrar," with which he ended *The Hawk in the Rain*. "Martyrdom" praises the bishop for his heroic silence; the poem itself is silent about the poet's personal connection to the Farrar line. Hughes's ancestry held psychological importance for him, though. When Plath was pregnant with their first child— who turned out to be a daughter—Nicholas Farrar was the name they chose for a son.

Ted Hughes identified more with Farrar forebears than the Hugheses in his gene pool, and not only because Edith's line was full of literary men. He was attracted to their romantic association with the Celts. The Farrars traced their history back to Elmet, the last independent Celtic kingdom in England. The Celts were the first people who left written records of what they thought was the prehistory of the island, in a "book of invasions" on whose symbolisms of salmon and hawk and eagle Hughes drew lavishly, during the last two decades of his life, when writing his own mythology for the Calder Valley. The Celtic population had gradually disappeared from most of England with the Roman conquest, but it continued to flourish in Yorkshire and regained strength when Roman power diminished. The historical Kingdom of Elmet covered the whole Vale of York until the Anglians seized power in the seventh century, and the name survived in the valley of the upper Calder and the Pennine moorland where the Farrars had their family seat.

Edith Farrar married beneath herself when she wed William Henry Hughes. His parents were Irish and Scots, while one of his grandmothers was reputed to be "half Moorish"—all outsiders, by local standards—and Billie Hughes himself was a workingman. But such local class distinctions appear to have lost force among the younger generation in the aftermath of the First World War; when Edith married, the pool of eligible men had shrunk drastically in the Calder Valley. Edith's youngest sister, Hilda, bore her only child out of wedlock, at age thirty.

Edith, luckier, was twenty-two and William was twenty-six when they wed on May 19, 1920. Her occupation at the time is listed as "Tailoress (Fustian)," and his as "Bench Hand, Woodwork." Their first child, Gerald, arrived a scant sixteen weeks later. It was eight years before daughter Olwyn Marguerite was born; and Edward James—Ted—was the last, the baby of the family.

None of the offspring resembled Edith very much. Her children were tall, lanky, and loose-limbed like their father, whereas photographs show Edith as short and stumpy, with a broad, open face that Hughes described as "leonine." As she aged, arthritis and asthma took their toll. Around the time of Plath's death Edith Hughes began having difficulty walking, and soon thereafter her health collapsed completely. She moved into Ted Hughes's household to be looked after.

Edith Hughes's physical presence asserted a strong influence on Ted Hughes's imagination throughout his life. In letters to Gerald over the years, he monitors her appearance, commenting on her pallors and her sunburns, her weight gains and her weight losses, her symptoms, her moods, her operations, her home remedies, her medical treatments. He speculates freely about psychosomatic features of her indispositions too. A child often feels curiosity and aversion toward a mother's body and learns to conceal his voyeurism. But the adult Hughes's curiosity is direct and intimate and voluble in his letters to Gerald, and also shows up in his work, especially in his stories, where caricatures of aging women appear with surprising frequency. Seen up close and personal, the old ladies of Hughes's fantasy world are almost always physically horrifying: hags, ogresses—powerful, sly characters who trick the hero and subvert his aims. Hughes's extensive reading in psychology and anthropology perhaps licensed this arrestingly uninhibited use of the split-off "bad mother" in his work.

The actual Edith Hughes seems to have been an engaged and ambitious mother during Hughes's early years. In an interview with a Mexborough newspaper in 1985, shortly after becoming Poet Laureate, Hughes credited his mother with giving momentum to his education. He said that when the family moved from Mytholmroyd to Mexborough, his mother took him straight to school, where he was amazed to see, for the first time, a chalkboard filled with "connected-up writing." Cursive script, he means; but this is a kind of origin story. Hughes often claimed that writing by hand was essential to his practice of composition: he needed to feel in his body the pen's resistance as it inked his thoughts into tracks across the empty page. The distinctive italic handwriting that makes his manuscripts recognizable at a distance dates back to the day he entered that schoolroom.

Edith Hughes herself apparently had little book learning. Her most lasting influence on Ted Hughes was the sound of her voice, telling stories in the distinctive West Yorkshire dialect that Hughes's own voice retained throughout his lifetime. "Ours wasn't a house full of books," he remarked. Stories were spoken, not read, and the impulse was always something in the present that reminded his mother of something she had heard or some fancy that crossed her mind. Hughes later commented on the role of the speaking voice in forming his imagination. "Whatever other speech you grow into, presumably your dialect stays alive in a sort of inner freedom, a separate little self. It makes some things more difficult . . . since it's your childhood self there inside the dialect and that is possibly your real self or the core of it. Some things it makes easier. Without it, I doubt if I would ever have written verse. And in the case of the West Yorkshire dialect, of course, it connects you directly and in your most intimate self to Middle English poetry."

Yet Edith Hughes also became the conduit of books into their formerly bookless home. Hughes remembered that it was his mother who provided him with his first truly "literary" experience. When he was about twelve years old, she gave him an encyclopedia of folktales for children. Up to that time, he claims, he read nothing but comic books and boys' magazines. But after his mother had got him a place in a good grammar school, where his teachers began to praise Ted's writing, Edith Farrar bought him, secondhand, a shelf of the classics, including the complete works of Shakespeare. And once Hughes entered grammar school, his sister, Olwyn, was added to the ranks of female influences on his intellectual development. Two years ahead of him in school, Olwyn took Gerald's place as his mentor. "She was the prodigy at school. And I now see that she had marvelously precocious taste in poetry," Hughes said. "Eventually Olwyn got me into the Shakespeare." He thought that the strong interest his mother and his sister took in his development provided the valuable pressure of "perpetual expectations." When his career began to take off in the late 1950s, he wrote repeatedly to his brother about how gratifying it was to fulfill these expectations. His broadcasts for the BBC, in which his voice returned to West Yorkshire over the airwaves, gave Edith special pride. And Hughes's extraordinary voice was to become his most distinctive legacy. During the last years of his life he allocated his precious time to recording poetry: his own, and that of a few other poets whose work he considered urgently important to *hear*. Reading his own work, both in person and for recordings, he sometimes provided a framework of narrative that never appeared in print. Some stories are only for the telling, he had learned at his mother's knee.

It was his mother's Celtic lineage that, Hughes believed, accounted for her skills with language and for his poetic gift. The prehistoric Elmet was a culture that Hughes knew largely through reading archaeology at Cambridge, but he attributed his interest in it to the influence of his mother's prodigious stock of gossip, anecdotes, and local lore. But something more than stories linked Edith Farrar to Elmet, in Hughes's regard: she was psychic. Powers invisible to others streamed over the shoulders of ruined mills and deserted Methodist chapels to endow Edith Farrar with glimpses of another reality still at work in the ancient landscape. She claimed that from time to time she had premonitory visions: that she saw tides of flashing crosses in the sky the night of the Allied landings in Normandy during World War II; that she was overtaken by empathic pain the night her brother died a violent death by suicide. Most unsettling of all, she was visited again and again by an angel, whom she recognized as her dead sister, Miriam. Throughout Edith's life this apparition would visit her bedside when a member of the family was about to die.

Hughes was attracted to hypotheses that occult powers were biologically transmissible, and could run in families. He thought that he too possessed these powers; he accessed them by dreaming. He said, for example, that "Gothic/Celtic" dreaming gave him the elements of a plot that he reworked several times in short stories and radio plays, and that these writings had turned out to predict future events so unerringly that he stopped writing them.

After his mother's death, Hughes began interpreting her as an early influence in the development of his vocation as a poet. A poem titled "Source" looks back to the years before he went to school, and is shaped by the curiosity and worry of a preschooler. It presents the image of a mother naked in her emotions to a child presumed too young to notice. He recalls watching his mother shedding tears, for no apparent reason, as she sits over her needlework. For the child, this emotional situation is thrilling and incomprehensible. His curiosity aroused, he presses toward her. His snuggling has the power to console his mother, relax her, but his pleasure rapidly turns to disquiet. If he draws too close to the songlike rhythms of his mother's weeping, it could

> dissolve yourself, me, everything
> Into this relief of your strange music

In every childhood, the mother's incomprehensible speech provides the first meaning-carrying prosodies, sounds that flood us with the promise of understanding to be shared. But the mother's body that conducts the stream of pleasure is too big a presence, overwhelming. The developmental challenge for a child is to build an island in its flow, a place from which to enliven her attention while escaping engulfment by the force of her emotion. "You escaped," he says of himself at the end of "Source." For Hughes specifically, becoming an artist will require that he separate himself from this influence that he identifies as maternal—both in its power to engulf and its power to nurture—and establish a position from which he can shape to his own ends the mighty fluency that surrounds him. "Source," in effect, updates the concept of the Muse, the explanation of the necessity of a goddess figure as the source of poetic speech. Re-creating the dynamic emotional conditions in which the child's desire emerges—recognizes rebuff, establishes a defense, and acquires a mode of sublimation— Hughes builds into his account of his childhood a principle of continuity with the poet he became.

A mother's weeping carries historical meaning in Hughes's poetry, as well. If all the inhabitants of the Calder Valley were like "mental patients" during Hughes's childhood, the women were the melancholics. For them, the First World War survived as the presence of innumerable ghosts of men cut down in their prime. In the division of labor imposed by war, the men conduct "Senseless huge wars," the women respond with "Huge senseless weeping." But this division exacted a price from the men who returned from the war to the enclosures where women reigned. Made heroic by death, idealized in the memorials of women's stories and picture albums, dead men occupied the top rank in a social hierarchy to which the living returned. And no living man could ever measure up to them; all living males were essentially disappointing. That is one of the subtexts of the autobiographical poems Hughes began writing later in his life, in which the child discerns that the mother's desire is for something that exists only within the closed system of her feelings. That is, her desire is not for the little boy who stands at her knee, watching worriedly; nor is it for the father of that little boy. It is for some ideal form of a man who had disappeared. In the Hughes family, that role was to be played by Ted's older brother, Gerald.

Gerald Hughes (1920–)

As far back as Ted Hughes could remember, his brother Gerald had been a hunter. When Hughes was two years old, playing games with miniature painted lead animals that were sold in shops as toys, Gerald was twelve, and playing another sort of game with animals: hunting and shooting with a rifle on the moors. Shooting was not a pastime among the working people of the mill towns of the Calder Valley, and was not a pastime of their father or the other men in the family. Gerald discovered it for himself, and became "obsessed" with it, according to Hughes. Every morning at four o'clock Gerald left his bed, took his rifle, and made the rigorous climb up a steep hillside out of the valley, onto the surrounding moors. Gerald would pursue the wildlife that foraged on the rough moorland for hours, shooting grouse and snipe, if he was lucky; or rabbits and stoat; but also crows and magpies, even rats. Gerald began taking little Ted on these morning raids as soon as Ted was sturdy and nimble. Ted was six years old when he began going up onto the moors with Gerald—or four, three, or two; as Hughes aged, the boy in the story grew younger. Ted became Gerald's substitute for a hunting dog. "I had to scramble into all kinds of places," he said, fetching the bleeding animals Gerald brought down with his rifle.

This extended period of engrossing play developed Ted's powers of paying attention. Gerald taught Ted at a very early age to observe his surroundings with the patient eye of a naturalist, alert to the smallest movement of any creature in a landscape—Hughes once remarked that he could glance out of a train window at the passing farmland and at once spot the tips of the ears of hares hidden in the corn. Sometimes the big brother took the little brother on camping trips in the Calder Valley. They cooked their food over open fires, slept under a tent, bagged their quarry with one eye out for the gamekeepers.

In his beautiful autobiographical story "The Deadfall," Hughes re-creates two such camping trips that permanently affected his sense of the magical powers that lay coiled in the beauty of the Calder Valley, the feelings that eventually reached artistic expression in his books about Elmet. "The Deadfall" shows how Gerald created a zone of risk in which little Ted—age six, then seven in the story—could establish his own boundaries, advancing just close enough to his brother's daring to experience instructive terror and wonder. Hughes believed that by the time he was seven years old, Gerald's mentorship had created in him another organ of perception, "a subsidiary brain."

One contributor to this strong influence on Ted's development was Gerald's gift for storytelling. Hughes tells how Gerald turned their morning ventures into an elaborate fantasy: "he mythologized his hunting world as North American Indian—paleolithic," Hughes said. Some of the décor seems to have been based on Longfellow's epic *Hiawatha*, which the sons learned from their father—for some reason their father had memorized long passages from this American poem, and liked to recite them. Alone together on the moors, the boys could turn themselves into noble savages; the pursuit and slaughter of little animals became an epic saga. "I lived in his dream," Hughes said.

Ted and Gerald Hughes, Yorkshire, 1947

Gerald also introduced Ted to fishing. Hughes said he was three years old when Gerald first led him down to the canal that ran directly behind their family home on Aspinall Street in Mytholmroyd. The canal had long been polluted by industrial waste, but small, bottom-feeding stone loach were numerous and easy to lure into a fishnet. Years later Hughes could still remember the "long-handled wire-rimmed curtain mesh sort of net" they used—literally made of old kitchen curtains. Hughes says he used to fish there daily, and after he had become a well-established poet, he returned to fishing not only as a retreat from public life but as a return to an emotional home base. "You're not only going fishing," he said, "you're going on some sort of reconnection with the most valuable things in yourself."

This idyllic brotherly companionship ended abruptly in 1938, when the family moved away from Mytholmroyd, with its canal, its looming rock, and its crown of moorland, to Mexborough, the coal-mining town in South Yorkshire, about ten miles from Sheffield, where Ted would eventually go to grammar school. Shortly after the move, Gerald left home. He was now eighteen. Avoiding the trap of the coal pits, where most young men in the town looked for work, Gerald found a job as gamekeeper on a big estate in Devon. A year later he joined the RAF and spent World War II in Africa. He survived the war intact, then immigrated to Australia, and married a blonde party girl (or so went the story Plath heard about this other daughter-in-law). Gerald became an aircraft engineer, but also pursued a number of interests that mightily attracted Ted: painting, poetry, collecting antiques, trading in animal skins. He continued to be an avid hunter and fisherman. On about half a dozen widely separated occasions, Gerald returned to England for relatively brief visits with his family. But he eluded all of Ted's ploys to repatriate him. No temptation and no appeal to conscience could lure Gerald back to Britain, for long. The brothers maintained their closeness by writing letters.

As might be expected, Hughes's relationship to Gerald was not free of sibling rivalry. The positive advantage of having Gerald as a mentor was balanced by the disadvantage of birth order: Ted would never, ever be able to catch up. Moreover, once Ted achieved his full growth, they looked alike, and the similarity provoked comparison; on his visits to the Calder Valley as a grown man, Hughes was sometimes mistaken for Gerald, an experience he appeared to enjoy at the same time he found it unsettling. A studio photograph from the 1940s shows how easily the brothers might be confused with each other, from a distance. They are dressed identically in the photo, and both have the same upcurving, thin-lipped smile. Both are slim and dark-haired, though Gerald's hair is darker: Ted thought Gerald had inherited the "blue-black" hair of their Spanish grandmother. Each bears the imprint of his mother's genes in a hairline with a widow's peak, though Gerald's is the more pronounced.

And indeed, Gerald's status as elder son in the family appears to have been a fairly important pressure on Ted's psychological separation from their mother. No matter how filial Ted strives to be or how famous he becomes, he isn't Gerald, and that is Ted's whole meaning for his mother, he suspects. "You are her best in a way I could never be," Hughes put the case matter-of-factly—by way of chiding Gerald for not writing to Ma more frequently. His insufficiency is the theme of the lovely poem Hughes composed several years after his mother died, "Anniversary." Hughes imagines her as an angel in "feathers of flame," strolling with her sister Miriam,

> Listening to the larks
> Ringing in their orbits . . .
>   . . . telling Miriam
> About her life, which was mine

The poem unrolls like a movie, in which Hughes watches his mother making her own sense of his life; but at the end of the poem he observes that she has been

> using me to tune finer
> Her weeping love for my brother

His insight is based on the memory of a day when his mother caught sight of him from a distance. He watched the joy flare in her eyes, then subside when she recognized she'd got it wrong: it was only Ted.

So Ted stood permanently in Gerald's shadow. But Ted had the advantage of this position as well. In Hughes's account of his development as a poet, Gerald is the sponsor of the "subsidiary brain" formed in young Ted out on the moors, an organ that functioned as a medium of coherent perception long before the little boy had words for what he felt and saw. And this special relationship had an effect of leveling them. Hughes sometimes expressed his bond with Gerald in metaphors of merging or twinning, as in his poem "Two."

> Two stepped down out of the morning star . . .
> Between the dawn's fingers
> With the swinging bodies of hares

The poem brings them down from the hunt into the world where war has broken out. One brother departs, leaving the other disconsolate.

When Hughes was asked about these starry figures, he wrote flatly to his interrogator, " 'Two' is simply about my brother and myself. He was ten years older than me and made my early life a kind of Paradise." Hughes commented, in his letter, that the war intervened, that Gerald had joined the Royal Air Force. But he also added, "the closing of Paradise is a big event." His explanation seems to be one of his foxy stratagems, trotting away from the interesting implications of the poem's mythological language. "Two" presents the brothers as characters out of a Romance. Gerald was the male figure found and idealized by Hughes's emotions very early in his life; Gerald was the guide by whom his soul was instructed in matters of the spirit. The rapturous opening of "Two" is charged with the youthful masculinity of this matched pair; everything exalts them or submits to them, and if the poem is "about" Hughes and his brother, the ten years that separate them in actual life have shrunk to unimportance in this image. The figures are as flawless and predatory as twin gods, hero-comrades in one of the epics Gerald spun for Ted in their wanderings, or primeval hunters out of the song of *Hiawatha* descending through the morning dew, hands weighted with game.

And the image of radiant twins: that too remained an artifact of Hughes's impossible desire to measure up to Gerald, and probably just as much to the point, to differentiate their manhood from that of their father. Ted Hughes's version of masculinity carried the imprint of these two contrasting male figures: Pa, the stricken, passive parent, and Gerald, the adventurous brother. Perhaps because of his position as baby of the family, Hughes is anxious to please both of these senior males, but from Gerald he appears to desire confirmation that he is Gerald's twin rather than their father's son. In his letters ever after Gerald's emigration, Hughes brags to Gerald about his accomplishments—which he sometimes overstates—and about greater glory to come. Always, always, he badgers Gerald to join him in some enterprise that is sure to make them rich. They could buy some big houses in Oxford or Cambridge and let rooms to students. Or buy a mink farm together. They could share the business, take turns living there. Within eight years they would be set for life, and they'd have regained the way of life they lost when Gerald left home: shooting on the moors of Yorkshire or fishing the rivers of Devon, or Ireland, Wales, or Scotland. Hughes proposed one or another such scheme at least once a year from 1958 until late 1974, when Gerald apparently crushed this hope. Hughes took the rejection very hard. It seems he truly believed, during all those years, that Gerald shared his wish to reunite their lives.

Where there is an idea of Paradise, there is an idea of the Fall; so Hughes's poem about Paradise gives us his own version of the Fall as well. "Two" closes with the departure of one of these radiant companions: "The guide flew up from the pathway," leaving the other denuded of feather, drum, and song. This is a pivotal moment in Hughes's myth of the poetic self, defining a parting of the ways. A detail disguised in the poem's ecstatic language is that the actual Ted Hughes cannot have been older than seven years at the time commemorated in the poem: just beginning to acquire book learning, a big event. This is what will eventually separate him from Gerald once and for all. Hughes will transfer the skills of the hunter and fisherman into the enterprise of reading and writing. He will counter the force of Gerald's dominance through mere birth order by acquiring superiority of other kinds.

Two other kinds, to be exact. At the earliest stage of his career, Hughes started writing stories and poems for children. Twinning himself, so to speak, he *became* Gerald, the older brother addressing the eager, susceptible boy that still listened inside his own psyche for Gerald's voice. Hughes's work for children adopts a companionable tone, and this is also the rhetorical stance he adopts in his other literary work, aside from poetry and fiction. When reading Hughes's collected essays in *Winter Pollen,* it is difficult to distinguish pieces that were written for delivery over the BBC's School Service, directed at children, from those written for the general audiences who listened to Hughes over the BBC's Home Service. The voice in these essays is more congenial than authoritative—mulling things over, couching insights in suggestions, hints, and reminiscences. It flushes more game than it hunts. Plenty more where that came from, is the generous idea Hughes conveys: we are all teeming with subjects for poems.

Hughes's second separation strategy was to acquire a set of relations to animals that was entirely different from Gerald's. And this brings us back to the separation theme in the poem "Two": the game dangling from the hands of the glorious brothers. It also brings us back to the question of Gerald's role in Hughes's myth of his persona. The virile, idealized brother in Hughes's writing about his family is a sign of adequacy in the male line: no doubt that is why a brother, not a sister, is necessary to Hughes's myth. However, as strong sons of this wounded father, the brothers inherit the problem of his wound. World War I did not go away: it grew more monstrous and, post-Hiroshima, was continued by other means. Abstracted and enlarged into the threat of total annihilation in a nuclear war, the spectre of destruction fertilized the nightmares of the generation to which Hughes and Gerald belonged. When Gerald left home to become a gamekeeper—and then went off to war—Ted took his place as the family fanatic who spent all his spare time pursuing animals. In Mexborough, Ted befriended John Wholey, the son of a local gamekeeper. The wildlife they pursued in the farm-yards and fields around Mexborough was not even small, it was minia-ture: little songbirds, such as robins and wrens; grass snakes and field mice; "everything that moved." At age eight, Ted was too young to own a rifle, but he had learned from Gerald how to set traps. The boys worked their way up to trapping bigger animals—stoats and water rats, and weasels; they killed the animals and sold their skins. "We lived for it," Hughes said. He began keeping diaries of his kills, diaries that he held on to for the rest of his life (though he didn't place them in his lit-erary archive). It was also in Mexborough that Hughes began fishing for pike, and became obsessed by them, as well.

Wild animals are important subjects in Hughes's poetry from beginning to end. Contact with the vivid energies of animals, especially cats and birds of prey, is often a catalyst in Hughes, a moment when the doubleness of the material world stands revealed, with animals signi-fying the embodied presence of eternity. Eventually, he found it neces-sary to account for the fact that his first intimate knowledge came from killing them. In a long letter written to Moelwyn Merchant, an Angli-can priest and scholar, Hughes took pains to explain the way his earli-est hunting and fishing forays with Gerald, and his boyhood pursuit of ever larger game, were directly connected to the development of his spirituality, specifically to his involvement with shamanism. Hunting on the moors provided his first contact with the divine, he argues. By "divine" he means the undivided consciousness he attributes to ani-mals, which sets them apart from the self-divided human conscious-ness. Hughes derived his understanding of shamanism from reading Mircea Eliade and Carl Jung. Their work explained to Hughes the dis-tinctive mental state of the hunter concealed in foliage, whose unfocused gaze is alert to perceive the faintest movement in the field of vision, as well as the trance of the fisherman, with nerves poised to receive the tremor of a hit on the line. Hughes said it was also the trance of the poet. Through such moments of trance, Hughes believed it was possible to connect with one's lost primeval state of consciousness.

But what justifies the act of killing these messengers? Confronted with political arguments against the sports of shooting and fishing,

Hughes drew his defense from Jung. "Do you know Jung's description of therapy as a way of putting human beings back in contact with the primitive human animal?" he asked his critic. "When I want to kill and eat a salmon I soak myself up to the fontanelle in evolution's mutual predation system within which every animal cell has been fashioned. . . . After sixty years of experience it seems to me that rod and line fishing in fairly wild places is a perfect hold-all substitute for every other aberrant primitive impulse." Hughes uses the term "primitive" in its root sense, meaning "earliest," "belonging to the first stage"—of his own life, and in the culture of *Homo sapiens:* hunting and fishing are the ways that modern men retain a connection to the prehistory of the species. He draws his ideas about the "mutual predation system" from anecdotes written by survivors of attacks by big animals, in which the victims reported experiencing an initial euphoria. Hughes was avidly interested in research on the brain, and seems to have believed that science would soon be catching up with Jung, and with Ted Hughes, in confirming that idea about the way certain emotional states, including the killer instinct, would be traceable to the wiring of ancient portions of the human nervous system.

However, Hughes was not willing to extend this argument to the practice of shooting. In interviews, Hughes told the story of how he came to think of shooting as wrong. It was on a visit to his family in Yorkshire, shortly after he married Sylvia Plath. Walking together on the moor, they found a wounded grouse in the heather. Hughes recognized from its movements that the grouse was mortally hurt, so he killed it. To his amazement, Plath "went berserk." She had a childhood memory of being told a story about "the heather bird," the grouse, but had never before seen one. Now he had destroyed a creature she held precious. "Like an electric shock," Hughes said, he felt "a total kind of transference to me of her feelings. I realized I didn't want to kill anything, any bird or animal, ever again."

What Hughes establishes in this handful of poems that mythologize his family relationships is a suitable childhood for the poet he became. It tells how the child Hughes drew close to the mother's strange music without being usurped: the legacy is his West Yorkshire dialect. It tells how he received his birthright to the knowledge inscribed in his father's nerves: the power to tell. Finally, it shows how he resolved his rivalry with the brother: by becoming not the shooter who pursues animals, but the shaman who is led by them—a clever act of substitution that retains the positive valence of the brother-bond. The legacy of the child's temporary sojourn in paradise with the brother lives on in the shaman's solitary journey inward, during which he does not inflict violence but submits to it, in order to be reassembled in a new form. In Hughes's case, the journey would carry him into the legacy of pain inflicted by the suicides of women close to him, and the violence to which he submitted was psychological.

This was the character that Ted Hughes brought, as a poet, into his marriage to the poet in Sylvia Plath. Hughes's access to poetic inspiration was eventually going to require two specific forms of rebellion against domesticity. Both of these rebellions would be enacted against the women in his life, selfishly and sometimes cruelly. One was escape into solitude—the shaman's act of flight into spiritual ground where an awful transformation awaited him, one from which he could bring back gifts to cure the spirit. The other was displacing the conditions of the hunt into the sphere of the White Goddess, the muse of poetry, where his cold-blooded powers of observation and his predatory skills connected him again and again through his sexuality to the female sources of his inspiration.

This is to look far ahead, however, from the moment at which Hughes and Plath entered into their marriage contract. By the time they arrived at The Beacon, their surprising news had been absorbed, and they received a warm welcome. Plath was very curious about this family she had acquired, and one of her first discoveries was her mother-in-law's passion for gossip. Edith apparently chatted freely to Sylvia Plath about the Farrar family's sorrows: the suicide of Ted's Uncle Albert, and about Ted's mentally retarded cousin—"numb as a tree" was Edith's phrase. Plath carefully recorded their most striking anecdotes and speech patterns in the journals where she was taking notes on all of them. In the story she wrote about them, "All the Dead Dears," Plath fitted Edith Farrar's anecdote about visitation by an angel into a neat little plot with a mildly humorous gothic ending, a vividly realized location, and a memorable representation of the tongue-and-groove fit of the married couple based on Hughes's parents. Their dialogue flows like a well-rehearsed duet that is often performed for visitors: recitations, in which anecdotes about the family's colorful dead are set forth for guests alongside the gooseberry preserves. Through long use, their catastrophes have been softened into anecdotal shapes as homely as carpet slippers.

To Ma, Plath gave the fictional name Nellie Meehan. Plath notes that Nellie Meehan's eyes grow dreamy and her voice rhythmic, as if speaking from a trance; her husband, though never disputing her "undeniable flashes of second sight," herds her gently back onto the path

Sylvia Plath with typewriter in Yorkshire, September 1956

of facts when she wanders. The elders are enjoying their roll call of the dead, though Plath finds an image for what she feels is being held at bay, just beyond the Yorkshire fireside: "Outside, the wind blasted away at the house, which creaked and shuddered to its foundations under those powerful assaults of air." In retrospect this looks like magic thinking on Plath's part: her story sets a ring of wind around these in-laws, to separate their Yorkshire life from her own life with Hughes; and she ends the story by killing off the character based on Edith Hughes.

Plath's incessant note-taking was having a strong effect on Ted Hughes by the time of their visit to the family home in 1956. Her response to Yorkshire seems to have opened his own eyes to the possibility of bringing the Calder Valley into his work. While they were still at his parents' home Plath reported to her own mother that she was spending a couple of hours a day typing stories that Hughes dictated.

In 1956 Hughes did not see his family as *material* in quite the way Plath did. He did not write character sketches and was entirely uninterested in décor and anecdote. It was many years before he himself found imaginative uses for his mother's rhythmic voice and his mother's story about being visited repeatedly by her sister in the form of an angel—the centerpiece of Plath's "All the Dead Dears." The use he found was the definitive poem about his marriage to Sylvia Plath, "The Offers," which he buried in *Howls and Whispers*, where Plath returns in a blue aura to deliver the command to become a poet: "don't fail me."

CHAPTER FOUR

STRUGGLING
(1956–1963)

How mock-heroic is the war between the sexes—the mere, embarrassing grating of his "I" on her "I" behind the little pickets of that pronoun "we" is almost always the active provocation. It's a real war, though, which is why the marriage of Hughes and Plath is of enduring interest. They were so passionately in love, at the outset; they were so attuned to one another, during the years they were struggling to turn themselves into artists. Yet their differences finally became irreconcilable, and their marriage had the most catastrophic ending that could possibly be self-inflicted. When relationships break down, the fault lines can usually be glimpsed by the way the pieces fall. From the elevation of retrospect we can watch the fissures shape in the marriage of Hughes and Plath from the earliest weeks of their life together as Mr and Mrs: a man and a woman with little money and large ambitions living out of the same suitcases, inhabiting the same kitchens, bathrooms, bedrooms; eating at the same table, working at separate desks.

The newly married Mr. and Mrs. Edward James Hughes spent their wedding night in Hughes's borrowed flat in Rugby Street; Plath would later remember, with a shudder, its grease and dust and litter of carrot peels. But six days later they embarked on the honeymoon of their dreams. They planned to spend two weeks in Paris, followed by six weeks in Spain. They would play tourist for a couple of days in Madrid, then seek an inexpensive place to settle on the Mediterranean coast. Their quest led them to Alicante, and on to nearby

Benidorm, a small fishing town perched on a cliff overlooking two large beaches. Though big hotels were already under construction along the coastline, the town was still "primitive," according to Hughes, and suited them very well.

The enforced holiday atmosphere of a honeymoon gives newly-weds plenty of opportunity to discover the ways they are going to make each other unhappy. So it was with Plath and Hughes. An eye-dropper of samples from Plath's journals and Hughes's letters from the summer of 1956 can capture the distinctive conflicts that began to color their marriage from its outset. We can track the stain: it seeped into Plath's writing right up until the time of her death, and into the afterlife with which Hughes endowed their partnership in his own late work. Nothing sensational, the conflicts arose because, to over-simplify, marriage opens a joint account in the language bank, with "we" as the currency, and that pronoun yokes two individual identi-ties with different stakes in marriage.

Take the simple example of how differently Hughes and Plath viewed the question of what it was necessary to pack into their honey-moon luggage. Hughes was already carrying a big psychological bur-den: an anxious need "to earn," as he put it. Plath still had her fellowship money, but he needed a job. Into his rucksack he packed an anthology of Spanish poetry and a Spanish grammar book; he planned to spend the summer months preparing to teach English in Spain that coming year, while Plath finished her degree at Cambridge, though it was a plan he didn't follow up. As a sideline, he planned to translate the poems for an English version of the anthology. He also brought along the red Oxford edition of the works of Shakespeare that he had carried into his service in the RAF and through his years at Cambridge. That summer he would read Shakespeare to Plath while she cooked their suppers.

We know about the books he packed because Plath made a long his-and-hers journal entry describing the way they shared workspace on this honeymoon. Most eye-catching among the items on "his" side of the list is the large bundle of scrap paper that Hughes salvaged from his job at Pinewood Studios and hauled with him all the way to Spain. These were reports he'd written on other people's novels and plays and filmscripts. During the course of the summer, Hughes would use the blank sides of these sheets to draft a whole book of animal fables for children.

The sheets of paper he carried to Spain have apparently not survived, so we cannot guess how much deliberation went into his matching of page with subject, but Hughes normally exercised some selectivity in this practice of writing on scrap paper. Given his superstitious nature he may have been courting movie-magic by bringing these particular scraps on his honeymoon. In a letter to her mother, Plath let it slip that they expected to sell the fables to Walt Disney; Hughes gloated to his brother that he expected his talent for this genre to make him five times as rich as their Yorkshire uncle Walt.

However, when the newlyweds headed for Spain it was on very tight funds. The honeymoon would be a working holiday; one piece of gear in their baggage was Plath's portable Olivetti typewriter. Plath was an inexperienced traveler, and she didn't travel light. In *Birthday*

Ted Hughes and Sylvia Plath in Paris, August 1956

Letters Hughes recalls hauling thirty short-sleeved jerseys to the Continent for her—the round number suggests a guesstimate. Plath, on the other hand, thought Hughes had brought too few clothes: the same baggy sweater and black corduroy jacket he wore summer and winter in England. In Madrid, she spotted a sale of men's clothes and insisted that he buy a summer suit of "cafe-au-lait brownish linen," and "a stylish black tie," a splurge that would put them far over budget by the end of July. Did they bring on their honeymoon Plath's capacious and infamous set of white-and-gold Samsonite luggage, which had prompted many a bloody-minded snicker when she arrived at Cambridge? One of Plath's biographers mentions that the couple carried *a* rucksack. Improbable; but if so, it must have been bursting at the seams by the time Plath added her indispensable copy of Roget's thesaurus, Cassell's thick French dictionary, a paperback edition of *Le Rouge et le Noir*, a *rouge* leather belt and a *noir* linen skirt and a pair of nonsensible open-toe high heeled shoes in which to look wicked, plus who knows how many more pounds of clothes *un*mentioned in her journal; and, most surprising, *The Joy of Cooking*. Plath's big blue-covered Rombauer, like Hughes's big red-covered Shakespeare, stood handily on the worktable where Hughes and Plath spent most of their time every day, getting better acquainted.

Plath's journal also indicates that she carried to Spain a new pair of scissors, and a pair of sunglasses in a white plastic case with a green starfish on it. The sunglasses were a trophy of the summer of 1953, which Plath spent in New York as a guest editor at *Mademoiselle*. In 1961, when Plath settled down to write *The Bell Jar*, she unearthed that plastic sunglass case from the pages of her journal, and, in the novel, cut it up with the scissors, giving the starfish to her baby as a toy.

The baggage they carried to Spain also contributed details to *Birthday Letters*. The scissors appear in "Daffodils," where Plath loses them amid the flowers that flood their Devon garden during the last month of their married happiness. The Shakespeare book plays an even more significant role in the drama. In February 1961, Plath in a fit of jealous fury tore up that copy of Shakespeare—she thought

Hughes was romancing another woman. Hughes *was* romancing another woman in February 1963 when Plath saw on his desk an identical copy of the book she had destroyed, newly inscribed to Hughes by his paramour. In *Birthday Letters* Hughes depicts the discovery of this inscription as the "fatal bullet" that brought Plath down in despair.

The knowledge that Ted Hughes had, and that we have, of February 1963—knowledge of Hughes's infidelity and Plath's suicide—always exerts a strong gravitational pull on efforts to understand them as a married couple. Their story is forever simplifying itself into a tragedy and rushing toward its horrible ending, a process to which Ted Hughes gave a strong push in the fatalistic narrative of *Birthday Letters*, to which we will return. But we, the heirs of their work, can now observe that—aside from their lives—nothing *ended!* Look at that list of items in the baggage they carried on their first journey together. These were not just belongings, as it would turn out, they were raw material. And what the two of them were going through together on their honeymoon was merely one discovery after another about how differently they occupied their mutual habitat in a foreign land, beginning with the gathering and preparation of their food.

Rabbit Stew

In Hughes's narrative about his marriage to Plath, their story begins with his mouth. The first poem in *Birthday Letters*, "Fulbright Scholars," shows Hughes strolling past a newsstand on the Strand near Charing Cross Station. The postwar era of rationing is over: at a nearby stall, he buys a ripe peach, fruit he had never before tasted fresh from the tree—"I could hardly believe how delicious." While eating it, he was looking at the girls in a news photo of the Fulbright Scholars arriving from America: "no doubt I weighed you up, feeling unlikely."

This loose little set of memories provides a deft introduction to some of the big themes of *Birthday Letters*, where each of the realistic details that anchor events in time and place is also literary. The young man Ted Hughes is approaching a crossroads, when he unknowingly encounters an image of Plath hidden in a piece of newsprint: she is already a character in a story. What roles will he be assigned, what character will *he* become, when he reaches the crossroads and joins her?

His act of eating a peach is a clue, associating him with the protagonist of "The Love Song of J. Alfred Prufrock," modern literature's most unlikely suitor. Prufrock's fantasy life seethes with literary allusions; and at the end of his "Love Song," Prufrock too walks on a strand, daydreaming about girls: "I have heard the mermaids singing, each to each." The line refers to a poem by John Donne, a man whose passionate, unwise marriage wrecked a brilliant career, and Donne's poem is about women's treachery. Donne scoffs, you might as well "teach me to hear mermaids singing" as persuade me to trust a woman. But Prufrock knows he is unfit for a grand passion, anyway: "I do not think that they will sing to me."

The Hughes in *Birthday Letters* is a counter-Prufrock: he *is* meant for a grand passion. His mind too seethes with literary allusions, but he *does* dare to eat the peach and, led on by his appetites, he will stumble into sexual complications that Prufrock avoids so comically, so pathetically. And thus does "Fulbright Scholars" thread the strands of *Birthday Letters* into a thick cable of twentieth-century texts that had figured in the literary educations of Hughes and Plath: W. B. Yeats and James Joyce and T. S. Eliot; and, of course, D. H. Lawrence. Each of these great modernists attempted to wrest ordinary marriage into a myth, writing from the perspective of a husband, and their writings lie directly in the background of Hughes's last work. Hughes's postwar marriage will, by the end of the century, have become a major literary event, a catastrophic adventure transfigured by his art. *Birthday Letters* charts its vicissitudes; the Strand in *Birthday Letters* is the site of embarkation, a real place that the book will re-create as a setting in the story of a marriage. This will be Hughes's whole strategy in *Birthday Letters:* cuing the reader's attention to literary classics that prefigure the conjunction of Ted Hughes with Sylvia Plath. Hughes has metabolized these works, which is why *Birthday Letters* opens with a girl and a bite of fruit, the oldest story of all.

Which brings us back to *The Joy of Cooking*. In mid-August 1956 it was sitting open on the newlyweds' dining table/desk along with all the other books they were consulting in Benidorm. Plath made numerous entries in her journal about grappling with the logistics of life on a tight budget in a totally unfamiliar place where she couldn't speak the language; she consulted her "blessed Rombauer" incessantly in the course of finding ways to gain some control over life in this strange environment, a desire she transferred into the labor-intensive project of feeding her husband. Plath acted out—or to be more accurate, felt around in—her new role as a wife by taking charge of the food. She aimed to spend no more than $1 a day. "Good wine is only about 7 cents a bottle!" she wrote her mother, and a kilo of potatoes cost 5 cents. Though Hughes joined her when she went to market—they did almost everything together—Plath writes as though it were her responsibility to satisfy him, rather than to feed the both of them. Shopping was women's work in marriage as she understood it, and the kitchen indisputably an arena of female dominance. So Plath scoured Rombauer for recipes "to keep Ted from roaring protest" at being served the same foodstuffs they ate day after day. The fresh sardines for "one of Ted's favorite suppers" must be purchased early in the morning, then kept fresh in "a homemade water container of several pans covered with a wet-cloth and a plate." Stretching their pesetas, she shopped avidly for bargains, on one occasion bringing home "two shiny purple vegetables" (eggplants, probably) that she didn't recognize but "imagined might be called zucchini"—she trusted that Rombauer would clarify.

On August 17 they celebrated Hughes's birthday with a dinner of rabbit stew. Apparently it was a dish neither of them had ever cooked before. Plath's journal tells how she shopped in the morning for rabbit and "myriad garnishes," and worked her courage up by dosing herself with hot coffee before approaching the stove "like a surgeon before difficult new operation to be performed for the first time." Evidently, Plath was consulting Rombauer's "rules" for dressing rabbit, hare, and squirrel—an illustration on the page facing the recipe for rabbit stew shows two rubber-gloved hands skinning a rabbit. Plath's journal shows how faithfully she followed Rombauer's recipe, until, lacking a supply

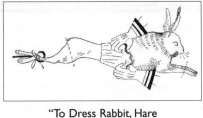

"To Dress Rabbit, Hare
and Squirrel," detail,
The Joy of Cooking, 1953

of vegetable stock, she resourcefully substituted packets of condensed soup mix and a can of peas. Hughes helped out by firing the stove, and by adding the glass and a half of wine that Rombauer regarded as optional—"the French use wine," noted Rombauer, whose home was Missouri.

Sharing housework was a feature of the partnership Hughes and Plath were forming. The resulting stew was "delectable," Plath noted, and Hughes took enough interest in the preparation of the stew that he was able later that year to reproduce it for a Sunday dinner at his family home in Yorkshire. Hughes wrote to Plath—who was back in Cambridge at the time—a detailed account of how he hunted and shot the rabbit, and then how he followed her method in cooking it, except that he put in too many packets of soup mix and got a stiff rather than a succulent result. There was one additional difference in their methods of preparing the stew, of course: Plath shopped for the rabbit at a butcher's stall, and bought it gutted and skinned. Hughes would flush his rabbit out of the brush, then shoot, skin, and dismember, skills he had learned in boyhood in Yorkshire, hunting with his brother on the moors.

And Plath adapted herself to all this strangeness, this foreignness, with zeal; in the privacy of her journal she congratulates herself on proving that she is a good wife. "Never did a new bride queen it over her deep-freeze, washing-machine, pressure cooker, et. al. as I do over my one-ring petrol stove, single frying pan, cold water sink, tangles of straw for cleaning, and iceless storage pantry. . . . If I manage on this narrow leash, I should be in heaven with the most modest of

American kitchens." Nothing illuminates Plath as a figure of her historical moment better than do these entries on her womanly competence, written as if under the aegis of the Good Housekeeping Seal of
Approval.

But Plath also viewed cooking as a practice that advanced her aim
of developing a writing style grounded in womanly experience. After
the honeymoon, when Plath and Hughes had resettled in Cambridge
and Plath was again a student, she spent several hours one day avoiding
the philosophy of John Locke by studying *The Joy of Cooking*, "reading
it like a rare novel." Not as silly as it sounds: Rombauer is a strong narrator in this cookbook, witty and pleasure-loving, and she addresses
the—probably female—reader as an intelligent partner in an interesting kind of expertise. She was also a best-selling author and an
immensely influential cultural figure—*The Joy of Cooking* would
appear on the New York Public Library's list during its centennial celebration in 1995 as one of the 150 most influential books of the century.
Plath's journal entry provides some context for understanding the hidden pathway of association that glides from Locke to Rombauer. She is
groping for a specifically female version of moral philosophy: "I . . . know
& feel & have lived so much: and am so wise, yes, in living for my age:
having blasted through conventional morality, and come to my own
morality." In apportioning value to her own primary commitments,
which she lists as "Books & Babies & Beef Stew," Locke will be no help
to her. The book that will help her, she adds, is the diary of Virginia
Woolf. Plath notes that after a publisher rejected one of Woolf's
manuscripts, Woolf went straight to the kitchen, which she cleaned,
then cooked up a mess of haddock and sausage. In Plath's pursuit of
ethical understanding, her own journal was a pantry, the storage place
for ingredients that the practiced cook knew would be of use.

Hughes didn't seem to recognize the complexity of the issues Plath
brought to the kitchen stove. He viewed her cooking frenzies as sheer
avoidance; "when she's faced by some tedious or unpleasant piece of
work she escapes into cooking," he observed. He also felt its subtle
tyranny, and now and then expressed a subtle rebellion in a low-key
hunger strike. Plath notes in her journal at one point that she is

starving: "When he won't eat I all too easily find it a bother to prepare food for myself." Apparently the tension over food required a bit of negotiation. For one thing, Plath's cooking sent a culture shock through what Hughes called his "West-Yorkshire belly parsimony." She gravitated toward rich main courses such as pork with sour cream, and desserts featuring meringue. Hughes wrote to Gerald that they had arrived at an understanding: if Hughes refused a helping of a "fairy palace" dessert, it wasn't that he lacked admiration for her skills— apparently, Plath was working through Rombauer's rules for cream chiffon pies at the time. "She cooks for relaxation while I eat only by necessity," he said, but he found it hard to resist the temptations she set before him. "During her exams my weight rose from 195 to 205 lbs. Every time I looked up there was a dish that called straight to my lean years in London and hypnotized a stomach made simple-minded by Ma's random recipes."

At the time he wrote this note to his married brother, Hughes was caught in a classic male dilemma, poised between his mother and his wife in a rivalry that Plath expressed via cooking for him. Plath was sharply critical of the "atrocious" food that Edith Hughes served, her "burnt tough meat," her "starchy little pottages and meat pies." Plath was also bothered by what looked to an American eye like dirt and clutter in Edith's Yorkshire kitchen. "It is all I can do not to rearrange her sloppy cupboards." A couple of years later Hughes spoofed this situation in a book for children, *Meet My Folks*. One poem features a mother who can really COOK (caps are in Hughes)—

> Not just kippers in carrot juice
> But Buffalo Puff and Whipped Cream Goose

—and she *never* had to consult a recipe book.

Silent Strangers

After the early morning shopping trip to the public market that supplied the kitchen in Benidorm, Hughes and Plath would settle down to writing. Daily routines were the kind of thing that Plath liked to describe in letters to her mother, so we know that they planned to write for four to six hours a day, 8:30–12:00 in the morning, 4:00–6:00 in the afternoon. In later years, after they had children, they split the day into two parts: Plath took the hours after breakfast, and she aimed to be at work by 9:00; Hughes had the hours between lunch and tea. Despite the evident differences in their dispositions, routines suited both of them, and what they considered good work flowed from Hughes's pen and Plath's keyboard for the whole of their first two months of married life.

But the big dining table that Hughes and Plath converted into a desk was also still a dining table, to which they brought all of their appetites, including their aggressions. In *Birthday Letters*, the poem "Fever" refers to an occasion in Benidorm when Plath came down with food poisoning, and panicked; Hughes came up with a home remedy, his mother's soup. But underneath his sympathy a coldness toward her formed and hardened: she was overreacting, hysterical, infantile.

> I recoiled, just a little . . .
> I said nothing. The stone man made soup.
> The burning woman drank it

Plath's journal records another disturbing episode of conflict. A strange mood of disaffection had fallen between her and Ted; sleepless, she sat alone in their dark dining room, staring at the full moon; restless, she roused him to join her on a sullen walk, "two silent strangers" in a landscape awash with "the blanched light of wrongness."

Hughes's memoir of the occasion in *Birthday Letters* is the poem "Moonwalk." Plath attempted to render this painful event as a scene in a novel, complete with the sounds of donkey bells and the scent of geraniums. A year or so later, she recast it in a startling, lovely poem about the mood itself: "The Other Two." A blissful pair of lovers glimpse, through the gleaming tabletop in their dining room as through the surface of a pond, a second couple enacting an opposite story, a psychodrama of bickering, arguing, estrangement:

> He lifts an arm to bring her close, but she
> Shies from his touch: his is an iron mood.
> Seeing her freeze, he turns his face away

The pair trapped in the table enviously watch the embraces of the ideal pair that come and go freely in the air above them. But the split between their worlds is unstable: at night the other two invade the ideal couple's dreams with their disputes and make them wonder whether they or their opposites are more real.

Plath has perfect emotional pitch in this poem as she explores the uneasiness that can thrive beneath the surface of buoyant, confident happiness. She captures the confidence in the way the poem's opening stanza chimes with its closing line: "We dreamed how we were perfect, and we were . . . the heaven those two dreamed of, in despair." But the poem's form itself expresses the theme of disequilibrium very artfully: Plath uses a seven-line stanza and half-rhymes that leave one line per stanza stranded without a partner, with the rest coupled up.

The poem's furniture is unmistakably the walnut fittings of the honeymoon house in Benidorm, although Plath appears to have written "The Other Two" while they were living in Boston in 1958–1959: the manuscript is typed on paper carrying her Boston address. Did the inspiration to write the poem arise from a return of the burning woman and the stone man, of the iron mood and the icy response? Probably. Plath's journal records similar episodes throughout their marriage. It was the "norm" in their version of normal human misery. But this poem gets closer than the journal ever does to a psychological portrait of the disorienting inner shift that rises in the context of a new and intense intimacy when one or the other partner suddenly turns opaque, unreadable, infantile, ironic. Brilliant, then, was Plath's association of this experience with the dining table where they wrote for money all summer, and ate the food she cooked, and watched each other fumble in their new roles as husband and wife.

The dining table is also associated with the marriage bed in Plath's journal—both, she observes, were built from the same dark-grained wood. In her abundant notes about their domestic life, it is the food that elicits the most sensual entries. About the joy of sex, not a syllable: the newlyweds are up and dressed by the time they appear in the journal, eating a delicious breakfast of bananas and sugar, with brandy milk for Ted and coffee *con leche* for her. One explanation for Plath's silence about their physical intimacy is that she was not keeping the journal for herself, she was using it to make a first draft of articles she hoped to sell in America. Later journals—written after the honeymoon but before they had children—do refer to occasions of lovemaking, and these references are often accompanied by menu notes. "After a supper, or lunch, of mashed potatoes & sausage we fell in bed, made love and slept . . . "; "I rose and made breakfast—coffee, and toast & bacon, and chilled peaches & pineapple. Then making love, hearing the cars come and go . . . "; " . . . Ted's delicious fragrances. . . . We woke in darkness, the sky a memory of orange light, and had tea— toasted tuna salad sandwiches and some excellent canned peaches. . . . " Plath's annotated calendars make the same association: what they had for lunch or dinner, then "love," even "strong love with dear Teddy." During Plath's year of teaching at Smith College, 1957–1958, they seem to have made love every Saturday afternoon after lunch—the end of Plath's workweek. If we want to look for the way Hughes and Plath struggled in their sex life, we might locate some of the issues in those menu notes, which treat sex as routine domestic comfort. They call to mind Plath's comment to her Cambridge roommate about "our good old sensible American attitude toward sex." They also call to mind Plath's aspiration to marry a man who would be a figure of comfort, "husband, lover, father and son, all at once."

Yet the best sex of all, according to Plath's journal, is not associated with food, it's associated with fighting and making up, a practice they proposed to build into their routines, late in 1958. Perhaps it was a New Year's resolution. "We agreed on a Friday afternoon blow-up: all problems and not only that but praise: counting the week's good things. . . . We had a very good f'ing. Enormously good, perhaps the best yet."

Complicated Animals

Before settling down in Benidorm, Hughes and Plath had spent a couple of days in Madrid, where $2.75 a day bought them a room with private plumbing. During their three days in Madrid, Hughes, who had not bathed since their wedding day, reveled in the novelty of the first showers he had ever taken. As Hughes's biographer Elaine Feinstein explains, Ted was raised in the environment of wartime rationing and postwar austerity, when "to use only five inches of bath-water was regarded as patriotic." He hadn't acquired the habit of setting his inner world to rights by cleaning things, including himself.

Plath, on the other hand, was an exemplar of that thoroughly scrubbed, deodorized, gleaming-toothed physicality that Europeans associated strictly with Americans in the 1950s. Her acquaintances in England sometimes observed that she had no *smell*. Her journal shows why not: she mentions bathing, very frequently, and rigorously notes not only the days on which she washes her hair but on the days she should and doesn't. She also records occasions on which she files and lacquers her nails. And on the days that these topics are noted in her journals, she has usually also thrown herself into a frenzy of housecleaning before getting into the bathtub for a long soak, herself. "How cleanliness rests my soul," she muses.

But oh, Sylvia Plath liked the smell of Ted—any of his smells. Plath's nose was an organ of intense erotic connection, celebrated again and again in her journal. "A strong smell of masculinity," she wrote at age seventeen, "creates the ideal medium for me to exist in"; "warm in bed with Ted," she wrote ten years later, "I feel animal solaces." During their year in America, when both were too occupied by teaching to do much writing, Plath transferred quite a lot of her writerly energy into getting Ted's redolence into her prose. On Cape Cod in July 1957 she rejoices at the way their daily dips in the Atlantic left him "smelling lovely as a baby, a hay field, strawberries under leaves." On a winter morning in 1958, "after sweat and fury of the bed," she takes perverse pleasure in the "sticky body of sweats and exudings & odors " that, unwashed, they swaddle into heavy clothes and propel into a day of teaching. On a winter afternoon, "I have run about, a hundred times, to kiss him in his niche or in his bath, to sniff his smell of bread & grapes and kiss his delectable places." On a winter night, chilly, she feels "his warmth & hairy belly & sweet skin smells pull me over to be held & hugged." Spring arrives, and on an afternoon in May, during a nap she dreams that she and Ted are sitting on a lawn near the Smith College Library with other faculty members, who remark that the newly cut grass "smelt of the heat of love, the heart of the love bed." Awake at her desk afterward she analyzes the dream as "an amusing transference of my obsession with Ted's delicious fragrances."

The sense of being bonded to each other through their instincts was one element in their compatibility, not only as lovers but as artists. A striking feature of Hughes's poetics is the way he associates the intensity of poetic inspiration with a strong smell; the image occurs in one of his most famous poems, "The Thought-Fox":

> a sudden sharp hot stink of fox
> . . . enters the dark hole of the head

"Hot stink" is Hughes's metaphor for the way a strong odor delivers a rude reminder that we too are animals. Somewhere in the long passage through evolutionary change, we relinquished the discriminating sense of smell that gives other animals a dedicated broadband access to the world we share with them. Hughes believed that, with discipline and effort and training, we could recover in our human nervous systems the legacy of our animal past. No idea was more important to Ted Hughes than this idea. We human beings had been cut off from animal awareness by the development of a brain capable of ego consciousness, he observed. Yet animal intelligence survives, in men anyway, at the biological level, "founded on the immortal enterprise of the sperm . . . still battling zestfully along after 150 million years. . . . The sperm is looking for the egg—to combine with every human thing that is not itself, and to create a new self, with multiplied genetic potential, in a renewed world. . . . [H]e rattles along on biological glee." The zest of the sperm is not available to consciousness, but intuitions about him, Hughes argues, are embodied in the literary figure of the trickster, which is found in literature across the world and as far back as literature goes.

The individual sperm takes care of itself, but the individual man needs an assist from culture in order to learn to draw upon his animal birthright. Hughes's reading in anthropology led him to the conclusion that the purpose of shamanism—a very early-appearing form of religious practice, found all over the globe—was precisely this: a "technology" developed to restore the connection between animal awareness and human consciousness. Visionary poetry, he said, depicted aims and experiences comparable to shamanist practice; "the shamans seem to undergo . . . with practical results, one of the main regenerating dramas of the human psyche: the fundamental poetic event." The last four plays of Shakespeare seemed to him the greatest example, in English literature, of a shamanist act: a poet working self-consciously to bring about a spiritual effect on the audience, in Shakespeare's case, employing a Neoplatonic philosophy.

These notions and symbolisms were already swarming in Ted Hughes's mind, ready to take up residence in the hive of his writing, when he and Plath began working at either end of the dining table in Benidorm, and he took up his project of writing animal fables. He found in Plath a ready sympathy with his efforts to make animality a medium of exploring human consciousness. Plath kept track of Hughes's progress with the animal fables in her journals and letters, where we learn that by the end of July he had written a whole book of them, to which he gave the title *How the Donkey Became*. As he wrote to Gerald, he could produce one every day before breakfast, then get on with his serious work: "At the end of a year it would be a classic omnibus of animal fables and we should all earn our fortunes on it." He estimated he had in him at least five thousand children's stories, given the "millions" of folktales and fairy tales he had read over the years.

Immediately after they returned to England, Hughes offered these

fables to the BBC for children's programming, and was quite annoyed
to be told that they were too abstract. *Alice in Wonderland* is also
abstract, he groused to Plath. She then sent the manuscript to the
Atlantic Monthly Press in Boston, where she had a good connection
in the poet and magazine editor Peter Davison, who passed them on
to the person in charge of acquiring children's books for Houghton
Mifflin. That editor rejected them as not at all suitable. She said that
some of the fables were "just plain despicable"; that others were disparaging or derisive of the animals; and that still others were
unacceptably ferocious—the fox fable in particular was "too bloody."
Overall, thought the editor, "There is too much viciousness—the animals are portrayed as beasts rather than animals to respect and be
comfortably afraid of."

Hughes bowed to market forces—actually, he enjoyed learning
how to write successfully for children—and eventually published the
book, titled *How the Whale Became*. But he had written the original,
"vicious" stories quite purposefully. As he told his brother, Gerald, the
fables he wrote were filled with "psychic symbols" that were meant to
help children explain their inner lives to themselves. Hughes's writing
for adults had the same purpose, and his most important early work
might well be classified as animal fables: "The Jaguar," "The Thought-
Fox," "The Horses," "The Hawk in the Rain," all included in his first
book of poems, contain significant psychic symbols that few readers
could be comfortably afraid of.

Hughes and Plath were quite complicated animals themselves. Since
Plath is very free with information about what she didn't like as well
as what she did like, we can observe that while Plath didn't object to
the smell of her husband's unwashed body, she did object to his lack
of grooming. She itched to interfere, to improve him. Before their
marriage, Plath had, without questioning herself, briskly applied to
Hughes's appearance a lot of what she regarded as American-style
good sense. Horrified by the general state of the teeth on display
around her at Cambridge, she had insisted on sending Hughes to "an
American-trained dentist who really saved his mouth," incurring

what was for them a big expense (sixty dollars). From the time they met, Plath began mentioning his wardrobe in her letters. She invited Hughes to a reception for the Fulbright Scholars at the American embassy, at which the Duke of Edinburgh was a guest, and wrote to her mother, "I took Ted in his ancient gray 8-year old suit"; a couple of weeks later, when Plath invited him to join some of her American friends at dinner, Hughes had to borrow a shirt from Lucas Myers. In both cases, she assures her mother that she is proud of Ted no matter what he is wearing. Nonetheless, after these public appearances she had insisted that he order some new clothes from a Cambridge tailor: a gray flannel suit and a tweed sports coat. "[M]uch cheaper in England, to have a tailor & a perfect fit, and dear Ted had absolutely nothing to wear. And I mean nothing," Plath wrote to her brother, Warren—she liked to consult him about the ways of men.

Hughes bought new clothes when she insisted, but he remained indifferent about how he looked. After they had been married for a while, Plath's tolerance waned. His appearance annoyed her most when she was irritated with him for other reasons. Ted "sometimes strikes my finicky nerves as coarse—scratching, nose-picking, with unwashed, unkempt hair & dogmatic grumpiness—all unnecessary & unpleasant, about which I am nagging if I say anything." She knew she was in the wrong, and would chastise herself, "Shut eyes to dirty hair, ragged nails. He is a genius. I his wife." And though she continued to feel that they were "amazingly compatible," she sometimes found him "didactic, fanatic." She had a hard time ignoring this strong personality, and often felt relief when he was out of the house. "I can build up my own inner life, my own thoughts, without his continuous 'What are you thinking? What are you going to do now?' "

Did Hughes keep track in his own journal of things he didn't like about Plath? If his journal is ever laid side by side with hers, as he speculated it might be someday, we may learn whether his list of items conformed to her own severe judgments regarding her faults as a companion. To his brother Hughes mentioned, within a year of meeting Plath, that he found her a "superstitious fanciful apprehensive diffident creature." He expanded on this description, harshly, to her mother after Plath's death. He believed that a legacy of Plath's relationship to Aurelia's "tense, watchful anxiety" had been an outsize tendency to panic whenever anything went wrong, "even if it's only missing a train." He thought Plath was constantly in a state of red alert for anything that might disturb the normal course of events in their lives; she needed constant reassurance. The annotations on Plath's weekly diaries reinforce this assessment: she plans everything, including the dates for washing her hair.

Plath herself was aware that she must be hard to live with. She nagged, yes. And she clung to him: Did he dislike it? Did he say so? Possibly, for she notes, "I have never found anybody who could stand to accept the daily demonstrative love I feel in me, and give back as good as I give." She tended to be "sentimental—a gross problem" that she identified in her fiction as well as in her character.

We can also guess at what Hughes considered some of the difficulties of living with Plath, from a note he made about the "oddly combined vehemence and vulnerability in her temperament." It is a neat characterization of an array of behaviors, most exorbitantly displayed in Plath's capacity for sexual jealousy. A journal entry Plath wrote at the end of their year of teaching illustrates the point. Plath had become suspicious that Hughes might be dallying with one of his students in Amherst, the way her male colleagues at Smith seemed to be doing. "I smell it. The house stinks of it." Once she picked up the scent she loped straight through vulnerability into vehemence; an entry she made the following morning shows that she tried to browbeat the truth out of him. On this occasion, Hughes reacted by giving her the silent treatment. She claims that he stonewalled, proposing to make up by having sex. The tension increased for several days, and finally erupted in a spectacular fight. "I had a sprained thumb, Ted bloody claw marks." She lobbed a water glass at him, but, farcically, it bounced back and hit her on the head. "I . . . saw stars—for the first time—blinding red & white stars exploding in the black void of snarls and bitings. Air cleared. We are intact." Plath wrote a slightly different account to her brother: "We have rousing battles every so often in which I come out with sprained thumbs and Ted with missing earlobes but we feel so perfectly at one . . . that we make our own world." Why did this kind of fight work for them? Maybe because their styles of aggression really were compatible? An air of satisfaction is unmistakable in the way Plath accounts for this catharsis, both to herself and to her brother.

But dramas like this one suited Plath's writerly purposes, no doubt about it. Plath made the journal entry almost a month after the occasions. By June 11 she has a new impulse for writing them up. The memory of the fight excites her; she wants to capture the thrill while she is still stoked with the emotions. That paragraph about "blinding red & white stars exploding in the black void of snarls and bitings" forecasts the later imaginative investment Plath will make in resistance to Hughes. It is in finding the boundaries of her neediness, her defensive childishness, that Plath will mature into the poet that we know. It is in warring with Ted that she will locate those boundaries and discover how to use them. The smell and soothe of mammalian rubbing, skin on skin, has its irreplaceable role, but we are rangy predators as well, and seek some of our satisfactions in defending our territory, even if it means drawing blood.

Hughes may have had a use for such fights, himself. When Ted Hughes looks back to those honeymoon days in *Birthday Letters* he sees himself and Plath as struggling with exactly the forces that he was attempting to depict in his animal poems—the terrifying psychic forces that communicate and illuminate our animal nature. *Birthday Letters* is full of just such symbolisms, significant animals that materialize directly out of other writings by Ted Hughes and bring their magic with them. In "Trophies," a big cat leaps at Hughes through Plath's amber eyes: a composite of the jaguar in Hughes's poem of that title and the panther Plath conjured in "Pursuit." Thus the beast that knocks Hughes down in "Trophies" is in effect an animal spirit of his own creation. By far the most common animal in *Birthday Letters* is the dog, with twelve appearances, most of them very significant. Hughes frequently imagines himself as a dog serving as Plath's magical protector, while in

"Afterbirth" he is a dog-headed deity in the service of a goddess figure. Horses appear in three of the eighty-eight poems of *Birthday Letters,* always as allusions to poems by Plath.

And foxes appear in *Birthday Letters,* three times. A centerpiece of the entire volume is the poem "Epiphany," which commemorates a night shortly after the birth of their first child, when Hughes, walking toward the Chalk Farm station of the London Underground, encounters a boy who offers him a fox cub. Hughes is tempted, but pauses to reflect:

> What would you make of its old smell
> And its mannerless energy?

We are surely meant to think of Hughes's signature poem "The Thought-Fox," with its hot stink: his youthful metaphor for poetic creation. But he may also have found a reinforcement of this theme in Plath's journals; *Menagerie with a Red Fox* was one of many titles Plath proposed for the novel she was trying to write about their love affair. Hughes's questions—What would you make of it? What would we do?—point to the struggle at the center of their life together, the tension between the desire for an ordinary family life, and the necessity of protecting that inner wilderness in each other, where each pursued very different artistic aims. In "Epiphany," Hughes claims that his refusal of the fox cub marks the symbolic ending of the marriage.

> If I had grasped that whatever comes with a fox
> Is what tests a marriage and proves it a marriage—
> I would not have failed the test. Would you have failed it?

What comes with a fox? In the privileged retrospect of *Birthday Letters,* Hughes is following a red thread of fox associations in the history of his poet persona: the little ivory fox he found on the site of his separation from Gerald's influence, the dream fox who summoned him to abandon his false pursuit of literary work at Cambridge. What comes with a fox seems to be the capacity for undertaking creative separation. The fox has served each time as the magical agent of release, guiding Hughes back into the authentic solitude of his creativity, his imaginative wildness.

The fox totem has now appeared in his life for the third time at a crucial moment: the birth of his first child. "Epiphany" subtly presses on the question, Who (now) is "we"? For now that we have a baby the answer cannot be "the two of us" anymore, can it? And just as much to the point, Who (now) is "you," given the powerful draw on your attention and mine of this new life that has emerged from our bodies? And, finally, Who (now) am "I"? For as the poem opens, Hughes ascribes to himself a state of psychological disorganization induced by sleeplessness and the "novelty" of fatherhood. About one thing only does "Epiphany" express unambiguous certainty: "I failed. Our marriage had failed." In himself, he means; he doesn't bring home the fox.

The marriage to which he attributes failure is not the actual day-to-day life of the family, but that other marriage, the one enacted by the solar system on February 25, 1956. What Hughes means in his application of the powerful word "fail" is obscure in "Epiphany"—an epiphany is a wholly inward incident, a moment of elucidation to which words are superfluous. But a meaning may be found in a letter Hughes wrote to Plath's biographer Anne Stevenson, after the publication of *Bitter Fame*. Stevenson had described that afternoon in early February 1961 when Plath, in a jealous rage, destroyed Hughes's precious red-bound Shakespeare along with the writing he had underway, as "a turning point" in their marriage. "Ted could neither forget nor forgive this desecration," Stevenson remarks sympathetically. Hughes tells Stevenson that her judgment is mistaken. "Just one instance will show you how far from my world your book is. . . . The truth is that I didn't hold that action against [Sylvia]—then or at any other time." Hughes said he had been dismayed when others attacked Sylvia Plath, thinking he would appreciate hearing them take his side against her; such people "misunderstand utterly the stuff of my relationship to her." He believed that Plath was helplessly in the throes of an instinctual rage during such episodes, and needed him to ride it out with her. "It was like trying to protect a fox from my own hounds while the fox bit me. With a real fox in that situation you would never have any doubt why it was biting you." The *un*real fox in this example is his totem animal, which it is his responsibility to nurture, if he can, within the domestic sphere that is also his workplace. He is defending Plath in her wildness the way he defends the wildness of the fox-totem—as an aspect of his bond with her, misunderstood by others but not by him: the "mannerless energy" that needed protection from interfering outsiders.

Earth Mother

During their honeymoon, Plath made copious entries in her journal about the furnishings in their Spanish flat. These, too, had a projected role to play in the novel of her romance with Hughes. Though she set no scenes in the bedroom, she took stock of features that made it "grand" in her eyes. A full-length mirror amplified the airy spacious-ness that charmed her, while the "sturdy enormous dark wood bed" stood, she noted, "on a floor of stone tiles, giving the effect of living at the cool bottom of a well." Probably an item at hand in this submarine retreat was a plastic clamshell containing a diaphragm. If all went according to Plath's blueprint, they would wait at least four years, or until they had written two books apiece, before having children.

But Plath's unconscious, it turned out, was impervious to the four-year plan. Stronger than her reasonableness was a drive in which sex and reproduction were confounded, and both were implicated in her desire for recognition as a writer. Plath's ambivalence about her own fertility was part of the struggle going on in the marriage, when she lay down with Hughes in the nuptial bed. It surfaced as an issue as soon as she had completed her Cambridge degree in 1957. In June, she and Hughes left England for America, where Plath would be tak-ing up a position as instructor at Smith. Aurelia was providing them, as a long delayed wedding gift, the use of a cottage on Cape Cod from mid-July to the end of August. During this break between completing her exams at Cambridge and preparing to teach courses in literature, Plath became careless about contraception and had a bad scare.

The way Plath managed this crisis can be found on the pages of the journals she was keeping. Hughes and Plath had settled into this "holiday" the way they had settled into their honeymoon, with an intention of writing every day in pleasant surroundings, taking time out for a swim and a beach walk, but never spending a day away from their work as writers. For Plath, workdays started with a warm-up in her journal. She makes her first entry on the opening day of their holiday, celebrating the prospect of a "magic seven weeks" ahead, with no other obligation than to write the fiction she has been planning. Not the novel, not yet. "Slick stories: money-makers: very gay, lively with lots of family." And so she makes a ceremonial beginning: "The virginal page, white. All the dreams, all the promises: wait until I can write again, and then the painful, botched rape of the first page"; and at last the words begin to emerge from her pen, "with great hurt, like giving birth to some endless and primeval baby." Plath's metaphors convey writerly fear of the blank page: *blanc* = white.

But why are these metaphors so physical? Is this a bit of wordplay to prime her pump? Not quite. As we learn two weeks later, Plath has been awaiting her menstrual period. Her journal, however, is not her confidant; it is the place in which she wills herself into writing. For the next two weeks, Plath steels herself against the worry that she is pregnant, by sustaining total silence about her state of mind. Instead, she chastises and exhorts herself not to waste this precious time. Yet all the while, her fear—and her hope—of being pregnant is leaking onto the page in the form of free association. The number of covert references she makes to fertility, childbearing, motherhood is almost ludicrous. The third morning of their magic weeks Plath opens with a note about reading Virginia Woolf's *The Waves* the previous night: "I underlined and underlined." And then Plath makes a vow: "I shall go better than she. *No children until I have done it.*" The same entry records a dream in which Ted's "rosy mother" appears, "holding a lovely droll baby, with two older children at her right side . . . her children or mine?" A short paragraph or two later she churns out ideas for a short story she plans to title "Trouble-making Mother." A few days later she notes a slip of the pen: she has written "mother" for "month."

While this theme is sneaking into her journal, Plath remains oblivious. But on August 9, after her menstrual period begins, she can finally acknowledge that "a growing casualness about contraception" has been putting them through hell. "I have never in my life, except for that deadly summer of 1953, and fall, gone through such a black lethal two weeks." Plath's "overhanging terror" has been that a baby would end their "impregnable togetherness" as writers. The terror was so strong, she claims, "I couldn't write a word about it," though as we can see, her journal is focused on little else. Since she couldn't write about it directly, she was displacing it into stories and metaphors, even in puns such as "impregnable." Four days after the spurt of blood arrived, she could write it up, not only making note of the episode but turning it into a scene: Plath and Hughes, counting the days—thirty-five, forty, sick with worry—then cycling through a torrential rainstorm to the doctor's office for a blood test; this goes into the journal, presumably, for future use in a piece of fiction.

For Plath, establishing that she was a writer had to precede the experience of herself as fully a woman. In 1957, she still had the mind-set of a person being trained, prepared, mentored; she had deferred taking up the life of a writer by accepting the responsibilities of a teacher. When, in 1959, she *decided* to get pregnant and didn't immediately succeed, she sought medical help and was appalled to discover that her heavy, irregular menstrual periods were signs of an irregular ovulatory cycle. She took this to mean that she might be infertile, and her response, at least in her journal, was exorbitant self-pity. "I want to be an Earth Mother," she wailed. If her style is melodramatic, though, the outlook is consistent: infertility was a condition she had ridiculed in other women. Moreover, Plath saw the biological completion of herself in childbearing as a crucial aspect of her development as an artist. If she proved incapable of giving birth, it would mean the end of every aspiration: the end of pleasure, the end of writing—even the end of marriage. "Ted should be a patriarch," Plath told herself. "How can I keep Ted wedded to a barren woman?"

The Luxury of Solitude

Like Doris Lessing's heroine in *The Golden Notebook*, Sylvia Plath compartmentalized the record keeping that supported her life as a writer. She neatly wrote or typed the drafts of poems on loose sheets, leaving plenty of room around the lines for revisions. She pasted the printed documentation of her successes, and those of Ted Hughes, onto the pages of different scrapbooks, his and hers. She used journal entries as a workshop for the making of fiction, or for what we now call "creative nonfiction." During their honeymoon in Benidorm, Plath spent a good deal of time developing in her journal an array of lightly fictionalized events that eventually made their way into the articles she sold to the *Christian Science Monitor*.

One that she didn't use in the published article is a portrait of herself and Hughes at work. The "togetherness" of married couples was a 1950s value; this may have been the pitch she had settled on, composing this charming journal entry. He sits at the head of their dining table in a heavy chair, with books and notebooks and papers helter-skelter around him, and an uncapped bottle of blue ink within easy range of upset. The paper he crumples will lie unheeded where it was tossed. On her side, implements stand in orderly rows, edges of papers and books squared to the table edge. Her French dictionary lies open next to a heavily underlined copy of *Le Rouge et le Noir:* she is translating, not composing; and the bottle of black ink she used for sketching is kept "scrupulously" capped. As Plath pans from his to hers, we get a vivid sense of contrast and a subtle sense of hierarchy: an establishing shot.

And indeed, the scene she sets down is illusory: describing their routines to her mother, Plath mentions that Hughes worked at the dining table, and she wrote at a typing table by the window. My guess is that she kept her back turned to him, and that he sat hunched inside a magic circle of inattention to her presence, focused on the traveling nib of his pen; both of them aiming not to be interrupted. Also, I speculate, aiming not to be observed at whatever little rituals accompanied their spates of composition. Plath and Hughes didn't smoke or drink in conjunction with writing as far as we know, though she often mentions a ritual Nescafé at the day's beginning. However, Plath's annotation of Hughes's fingernail paring and nose picking suggests, to me, that she probably had some embarrassing habits herself—little compulsive gestures acquired in infancy, "playing with yourself," as the phrase has it: fingers, nose, ears, mouth, hair, anything within reach that can be twiddled as you sit there, unblocking pathways of association, feeling your way into the metaphors that perform the role of thinking, in imaginative writing.

During the first three years of the marriage of Hughes and Plath, privacy was hard to come by. After their honeymoon, while Plath was finishing her degree, they rented a small flat in Cambridge where they had to share a bathroom with other tenants; Hughes wrote poems while sitting on the bed. In Northampton, Massachusetts, they squeezed into an attic apartment when Plath took her teaching post at Smith College, and a small dining room again became their study with the dining table their shared desk: it was often piled high with essays submitted weekly by the seventy students whose work Plath supervised. Plath's journal indicates that they had actually bought a desk for the apartment, but it couldn't be made to fit through the narrow doorway. At their next home, a crowded two-room apartment on Beacon Hill in Boston, the kitchen was "crammed up against one wall of the livingroom," which doubled as the writing room, and each had a desk in a window alcove: "a crow's nest," one of their friends observed. Hughes fixed up a makeshift desk with two planks; Plath

 borrowed from her mother's house a little desk, decorated with a tracery of vine leaves, that had belonged to her grandmother. They worked almost elbow to elbow, day after day, and Plath reported that proximity constantly tempted her to whine and worry aloud about her lack of inspiration, which made Hughes "cross and desperate."

Sylvia, detail from original photo shoot in Boston with Ted Hughes, 1959

Plath and Hughes had been married for more than three years—half of their married life, as it happened—before either had a secluded space for work. This was during their residencies at Yaddo, the artist's colony in New York State where they spent September to late November in 1959. Plath occupied the top floor of the house, by herself, since few other artists were in residence at that season; Hughes had a little cabin in the woods. Describing Yaddo to her mother—the grand house, the handsome grounds, the good food, the well-stocked library—Plath reserved her strongest praise for the luxury of solitude.

These privileged months at Yaddo gave significant impetus to work in progress. Both of them were reading and writing seven hours a day, Hughes completing poems that shortly afterward appeared in his second book, *Lupercal*. He also accepted the invitation of a composer in residence at Yaddo to collaborate on an oratorio based on a Tibetan Buddhist text, *Bardo Thödol* (The Tibetan Book of the Dead), a kind of instruction manual for managing the soul's wanderings after death. And he began drafting a play, *The House of Taurus*, based on a theme from Euripides' *Bacchae*, an ancient text that also explores the shaping of the social world by supernatural forces.

As usual, Plath was stimulated by whatever interested Hughes. At Yaddo they continued to practice hypnotizing each other—Hughes taught Plath how, early in their relationship—and also developed a number of meditative exercises derived from Hughes's studies of magic, in order to reach levels of symbolism unavailable to rational consciousness. All the practices were loosely affiliated with his work on *Bardo Thödol*.

But hypnotizing each other may well have been a ritual by which they marked a need for separation for retreat into their own subjectivities, in order to get their work done. According to Hughes, these practices definitely helped Plath, at Yaddo, begin to explore for the first time "the underworld of her worst nightmares." Plath had begun reading the work of Theodore Roethke, whose poetry collection *Words for the Wind* contained a sequence of experimental poems in which he attempted to reproduce the imagery of mental breakdown. Roethke's poetry excited Plath to attempt a similar sequence of "mad" poems. "I have experienced love, sorrow, madness, and if I cannot make these experiences meaningful, no new experience will help me," she mused in her journal. Roethke's example would show her how to use these experiences in her art, and "be true to my own weirdnesses." The result was "Poem for a Birthday," which Ted Hughes admired very much and regarded as Plath's breakthrough into the subject matter of her mature style.

One doesn't have to share Hughes's admiration for this very imitative poem to be interested in why he thought it was a breakthrough. In "Poem for a Birthday" Plath first wrote about the electroconvulsive shock treatment she had undergone in 1953 as treatment for suicidal depression—"the experience that made *Ariel* possible," in his view. That is, Hughes saw analogies among the concepts of the soul's journey after death as codified in Tibetan Buddhism, the shaman's "flight" to the underworld as described by anthropologists, and Plath's 1953 experience of breakdown and recovery. By the time Plath wrote "Poem for a Birthday," Hughes claimed, "an old shattered self, reduced by violence to its essential core, has been repaired and renovated and born again, and—most significant of all—speaks with a new voice."

Plath's own account of this development in her subject matter has a different emphasis—"more practical," as she would characterize her differences from Hughes in an interview later in their marriage. As we have seen, Plath's artistic mission was to find in her unique experience those elements that made her "a statement of the generation" she belonged to. During the months that Hughes and Plath spent in Boston, she had become acquainted with the poets Robert Lowell and Anne Sexton, both of whom had, like Plath, and like Roethke, been hospitalized for treatment of severe mental illnesses—Lowell and Sexton for depressive illnesses, Roethke for schizophrenia. Plath had been excited by the way this new generation of poets wrote about "peculiar, private and taboo subjects," including the experience of breakdown. But it was Roethke's artistic originality that stirred her to emulation. Roethke's poems contained no explanations; they presented an eddying flow of associations from which a reader could fetch themes but not reasons.

Adopting Roethke's techniques, at Yaddo Plath experimented for the first time with finding subjective images for the experience of shock therapy, an experiment that would culminate in *The Bell Jar* and would also produce an extraordinary poem, "The Hanging Man." And in writing "Poem for a Birthday" Plath was apparently able to employ in a practical way the meditative exercises she and Hughes were performing, permitting herself to pursue a rapid associational method of making images—in Hughes's words, "she found herself free to let herself drop, rather than inch over bridges of concepts." Work poured from her during those six weeks: a third of the poems that made it into her first published book, *The Colossus and Other Poems,* were written at Yaddo.

Plath's daring use of her mental breakdown, writing in the experimental mode of "A Poem for a Birthday," was an important achievement. But, to put the matter bluntly, Plath had actually been psychotic. The name "Plath, Sylvia" occurs with striking frequency in the indices to psychiatric literature, as a case history. Diagnostic labels such as "bipolar" and "schizoaffective with predominately depressive features" have been attached with great confidence to Plath herself, because of the personal data that is presumed to be faithfully represented in her novel's heroine, Esther Greenwood; and Plath's journal has furnished significant evidence for the argument that Plath's mood swings were symptoms of a chronic menstrual disorder. As witness of Plath's volatility, and the occasional target of her rage, Hughes might well have thought he was looking at symptoms of mental illness. How did the actual psychotic break in her past affect his attitudes toward her during their marriage?

He answered that question himself in a candid letter written during the last year of his life: "I accepted her temperament & its apparent needs as a given set of facts, to be tended, humoured, cared for, cured if possible." Not that Plath behaved during their marriage as if she were ill. She tended to view the intensity of her emotional states—even the storms of rage that sometimes overtook her—as an artistic resource: "I feel, am mad as any writer must in one way be." But her journals show that she did feel at the mercy of her emotional lability, "as if my life were magically run by two electric currents: joyous positive and despairing negative—which ever is running at the moment dominates my life." Hughes apparently shared the view that writers

were mad in their own way, as a matter of course. Considerable anecdotal evidence indicates that he displayed a high level of tolerance
toward what other people considered inexplicable, antisocial, crazy in
her behavior. Perhaps he didn't consider the extremes of Plath's conduct as signs of pathology at all; in English culture, the useful label
"eccentric" rescues a wide range of behaviors from being regarded
as abnormal. During their years together, he apparently did not fear
another breakdown.

Hughes and Plath left America for England in mid-December 1959,
after completing their residencies at Yaddo and celebrating Thanksgiving with Plath's mother and brother in Wellesley. They spent the
Christmas holiday with Hughes's family in Yorkshire, then set about
house hunting in London. With the help of a friend, they found a very
small flat in Chalcot Square, in North London, near Primrose Hill. It
was a good location, but the rooms were small, the ceilings low, the
stairways narrow—and Plath, in the last trimester of her pregnancy,
felt huge and clumsy in these new surroundings, as she told her
mother more than once. And this time, they had no desks at all. They
did some of their writing in bed, some on the little table where they
ate their meals. Plath joked that they had to shove manuscripts under
the carpet when the cooking pots came out. Hughes decided to set up
a card table in the narrow entry vestibule, where he was never out of
range of Plath's eyes and voice. He reported to his friend Lucas Myers
that on one occasion he counted the interruptions: "She had called out
one hundred and four times in the course of one morning." After the
baby arrived, they turned the small living room into a nursery every
night by setting up a folding cot.

   The strain they were under in these tight quarters was witnessed in
July 1960, by the photographer Hans Beacham, who had been commissioned to make a portfolio of images of British writers. Beacham's
arrival at Chalcot Square "interrupted a serious spat between Hughes
and Plath," he recalled. "They were sullen. Hughes was rude. He
was going to get more attention than she, and she didn't like that
while he *did*. He invited me outside and told me I needed to know

Sylvia and Ted "interrupted in a spat," London, July 25, 1960

that he loathed photographers." Hughes particularly wanted to keep Plath out of the way. "His wish, of course, *forced* me to photograph them together," Beacham said; and later, Hughes acknowledged that he had been "an ogre."

Partly because he exercised impressive powers of concentration, Hughes managed to be very productive during the nineteen months they spent in Chalcot Square. He wrote four plays, many reviews, and most of the poems for his third book, *Wodwo*, and later said that his "tiny cubicle" had suited him very well—he could tell by the quality of the work. When Plath became pregnant again, in 1961, they felt they had no choice but to find larger quarters in which both could work, and by September had scraped together enough money to buy Court Green, a two-story house in Devon, with ten rooms and several outbuildings—Plath meant to have a lot of children. Hughes set up a writing room in the attic; Plath converted one of the upstairs bed-rooms. This placed each of them above the ground-floor bustle of the kitchen, laundry, parlor, and playroom, and it gave each of them com-plete separation from the other.

Plath laid claim to this room of her own by covering the floor with a fine Wilton carpet, brilliant red, a color that stimulated her. She commented to her mother that she realized a solid color was easily soiled but that she planned to wear slippers in her study, and nobody else would be allowed to enter it.

And, ceremonially, immediately after they moved to Devon, Hughes made Plath a writing table, six feet long, out of a thick elm plank of the kind used for coffins, sanded smooth. *Birthday Letters* contains a portrait of Plath the poet at this desk:

> You bent over it, euphoric . . .
> Like an animal, smelling the wild air,
> Listening to its own ailment

That metaphor "ailment" reflects Hughes's belief that all art originated with a wound, a belief that shapes all of his accounts of the way Plath's talent matured: an old shattered self, reduced by violence to its essential core, had been repaired. But what did Plath herself think she was doing when she bent, euphoric, over the first real desk she had owned since her marriage? As it happens, she was about to become the Sylvia Plath that interests us: not a wild animal, but a woman poet conscious of her status as a mother, ambitious to be the voice of her generation. It was at that desk, later, after Ted deserted her and after the cursing and sobbing abated, that she would write the chilly poems of *Ariel,* and most of the other poems for which she is celebrated, in the cold autumn and winter of 1962–1963.

But that is not to say the marriage had failed: far from it.

CHAPTER FIVE

PROSPERING
(1957–1963)

Ted Hughes said that when he met Sylvia Plath at Cambridge in 1956, he recognized at once that "she was a genius of some kind." Plath said the same thing about Hughes, going so far as to forecast in her journal that Hughes would eventually become "the Poet of England," and she "the Poetess of America." When they embarked on marriage, they were still in their midtwenties, still under the influence of university life. They had hardly a clue about the difficulties they would face in the occupation they had chosen to lead as freelance writers, working at home.

A real question posed by their situation, though, is why they chose *that* life. They could have taken up professional work of the kinds that were making other creative young people prosperous during the late 1950s: careers in film, television, or advertising. What motivated the commitment and the deferred gratification required to make a success of poetry, of all possible options open to such clever writers as they already were?

One of the poems of Hughes's *Birthday Letters*—"Flounders"—explores that question, looking back to a moment in their married life when everything might have come out differently. The time is summer 1957; Plath had just completed her Cambridge degree, and Hughes had accompanied her home to Massachusetts. They were indulging in their second honeymoon on Cape Cod—Hughes remarked that learning how much it cost Aurelia (seventy dollars per week) anesthetized him for a whole month. The poem says that they spent a day in a little rented rowboat, fishing in the channel, bouncing in the wake of grand pleasure boats owned by the rich. Suddenly the wind shifted and the tide turned, and they rowed helplessly while their boat was slowly being pulled out to sea. Then their luck turned again: they were rescued by a family in a fast powerboat and towed into a quiet channel, where they ended the day happily making a fabulous catch of flounder.

Hughes unfolds the story as a contemporary fairy tale, in which the bountiful catch of flounder is bestowed on them by a beautiful, nameless goddess. In the opinion of this nameless goddess, they have been "spoiled" by studying literature—it has made them uninterested in American abundance. (We have to infer that this is a goddess of the New World.) She is engaged in a competition with her sister, the goddess of poetry, for the hearts and minds of the young couple. The goddess of poetry, however, demonstrates that Hughes and Plath are under her management. She shuts their ears to the siren song of luxury, so that they heard only the calling of poetry in their life. And from then on,

> we
> Only did what poetry told us to do

The winner, though nameless, is unmistakably the White Goddess, a jealous, marriage-hating deity—Hughes hints at the end of the poem that it was she who denied Hughes and Plath the joy of togetherness envisioned in the ideal marriage of the 1950s. No, the goddess had decreed for them, as artists, the affluence that only she could bestow: fluency. It was through that gift alone that Hughes would become the Poet of England, and Plath the Poetess of America.

Money

In "Flounders," Hughes resists the opportunity to take up an American way of life, yet he apparently felt that he had married up, by marrying an American girl. Eight months after the wedding, Hughes wrote to his brother about the great good fortune his union with Plath had already brought him. Portentous dreams—in which he caught enormous fish—had been telling him that Plath would attract the magic of financial prosperity that seemed to cling to Americans. Hughes had just received confirming evidence, in a telegram announcing that the manuscript of his book of poetry *The Hawk in the Rain* had been selected for publication by the American publishing house Harper Brothers, as winner of first prize in a competition. It had been Plath's initiative to submit the manuscript to this competition. "Sylvia is my luck completely," he said happily, and he predicted that her work would probably make even more money than his.

They never intended to move permanently to America. Plath spelled out their long-range plan in a letter to her mother shortly after completing her exams at Cambridge in May 1957. Plath had accepted an appointment as lecturer at Smith College, her alma mater, beginning in the fall. She and Hughes would arrive in America by the end of June and would stay for two years, teaching and saving money, then apply for grant money to support them in Italy. Plath hoped to have published a novel about her romance with Ted by then. Though Plath hadn't written the book, she was steadily percolating titles for it: *Hill of Leopards. Menagerie with a Red Fox. The Girl in the Mirror. Falcon Yard.* She also intended to have started a second novel, which would put her far enough along in professional life to begin a family. They were waiting until their late twenties, she explained, "because both of us are slow, late maturers and must get our writing personae established well before our personalities are challenged by new arrivals."

College teaching, in America, was a relatively well-paid use of their good educations. The teaching position Plath had been offered at Smith for 1957–1958 paid in the range of $4000 for nine months' duty, leaving them free for writing during the summer. After they arrived at Smith, Hughes was offered a position at the University of Massachusetts in nearby Amherst, for a half year, at nearly the same rate. They were careful managers of their money and were banking a certain amount each month, with their eye on that plan to become itinerant Europeans. Toward the end of the academic year, they were both offered renewals of teaching contracts, which would have provided them a joint income of $8000. It must have been the White Goddess who told them to refuse, since common sense—especially the common sense of Plath's mother—argued for accepting. But they took the plunge, turning down those teaching contracts in order to become writers full-time. Toward the end of his life, looking back on that bold decision, Hughes said simply, "I wanted to keep my energy for myself, as if I had the right." Their income took a plunge too, but in April 1959 Hughes received a $5000 grant from the Guggenheim Foundation, success that justified their gamble.

At first, payment was meager for the kinds of writing they were able to publish; they lived mainly on grants and prize money. Milestones in their economic life, aside from the windfall of the Guggenheim grant, would be the major prizes that Hughes netted: in 1958, £300 for the Guinness Poetry Competition; in 1960, £500 for the Somerset Maugham Award; in 1961, £100 for the Hawthornden Prize. The exchange rate was about 2.8 dollars to the pound in those days, so these were fairly large awards. Plath began pulling her own weight in 1961, with the award of a $2000 Saxton Fellowship grant, plus an enviable "first reading" contract she received from *The New Yorker*, which provided a signing payment, an elevated fee per published line, and a cost-of-living bonus for work accepted—these were unusual benefits in the writer's trade, especially the poet's version of it.

By the time Hughes and Plath separated in October 1962, they had firmly established themselves as writers in a way of life that did not require them to take other jobs; Plath estimated that they made $7000 that year, in grants and fees, of which she earned about a third. When either of them received payment for a publication—book reviews, poems, stories—the money usually went directly into the savings account they retained in Boston. Plath mailed the checks to her mother, for deposit; and often, the stubs went into the big scrapbook of clippings that Plath was assiduously updating as Hughes's star rose. Most of the checks were for fairly small amounts, ranging from $40 to $75, but methodically saving part of their income was a discipline that Plath imposed on them, following the example of her mother.

Ted Hughes felt entitled to prosper. There was money in his mother's family, though not in his childhood home, and an expectation of wealth fueled his fantasy life, as can be observed in numerous letters he wrote to his brother, Gerald, about his schemes, well into his adult life. And he did fulfill his expectations. After Plath died, Hughes became a shrewd manager both of her estate and of the business of poetry, releasing some of Plath's work and significant quantities of his own work in costly special editions, and acquiring a sophisticated agent to negotiate the sale of manuscripts, including the increasingly valuable manuscripts of Sylvia Plath. When Hughes died in 1998, he had achieved the status of "one of the richest British poets this century," according to the *Times* of London; he left over £1.4 million in his will, to his wife.

Hughes didn't marry Sylvia Plath for money, but it seems that at the time they married he regarded Sylvia's family—that is, her mother, Aurelia—as well-to-do. Yankee wealth is hard to gauge by appearances, even for Americans, and Hughes had no index to these appearances, anyway. In *Birthday Letters,* Hughes calls his mother-in-law Prospero, the magician in Shakespeare's *The Tempest.* We remember that Hughes's friends thought she was prosperous, and perhaps that is a pun buried in Hughes's allusion. He seems to have drawn his impression from the quality of the business dress Aurelia wore and the educated precision of her diction. And from her generosity: when the lovers decided impulsively to marry, Aurelia appareled his bride in a new dress that materialized as if by magic out of her luggage. In his poem about the wedding, "A Pink Wool Knitted Dress," he says that his own shabby clothes made him feel like a "postwar utility son-in-law," and he likens himself to the fairy-tale swineherd who steals a pedigreed daughter, a maiden bejeweled by joy.

In fact, Plath's mother was not prosperous. She held a position on the faculty at Boston University teaching shorthand to prospective medical secretaries; the annual salary at the top of her rank in the 1950s would probably have been around $3000. She imposed frugality on herself in order to provide each of her children the benefits of an elite education. One of Aurelia's friends later pointed out that it was generous indeed of Aurelia to send Sylvia away to Smith College, instead of enrolling her at Wellesley College; the Plaths lived in Wellesley, and tuition at Wellesley College, an excellent school, was waived for residents of the town. Hughes witnessed only Aurelia Plath's generosity, not her scrimping.

The two-plus years that Hughes and Plath spent in America— from June 1957 to November 1959—brought Plath a final separation from this mother, and from her alma mater too; and they inaugurated her emergence as an artist. Plath was glowing when she introduced Hughes to the seventy guests who attended the garden party Aurelia held for them in Wellesley at the end of June; and in July, when she and Hughes had settled into their Cape Cod cottage, Plath fully expected to whiz through the ambitious writing agenda she had set for herself. She projected finishing two stories suitable for publication in *Atlantic Monthly,* as well as an article on student life at Cambridge that she would submit to *Harper's.*

Instead, Plath experienced a demoralizing inertia during those weeks. As they were packing up to leave Cape Cod at the end of August, she analyzed the issues precisely: "bridging the gap between a bright published adolescent which died at 20 and a potentially talented & mature adult who begins writing about 25." Plath turned twenty-five that year, on October 27, while she was teaching at Smith. Because teaching anguished and exhausted her, she did not attempt to produce much creative work during that academic year. Instead, she channeled her writerly energy into her journals, and somewhat accidentally produced a work of art.

Portrait of the Artist as a Young Woman

In the journal Plath wrote between the autumn term at Cambridge in 1955 and its abrupt end in November 1959, a woman writes the portrait of a woman becoming a woman writer—the literary equivalent of that image by M. C. Escher in which a hand holding a pen is seen drawing a hand holding a pen. The upper hand dashes forward, rationalizing, judging, commenting, cataloguing; the lower hand eddies, stirring ripples of associations, images, gestures, echoes, repetitions, allusions. A strong intelligence and its unconscious support system show up on the pages as the pages turn. Very slight knowledge of Plath's day-to-day life can be found in the voluminous leaves of writing, because Plath wrote about only what stimulated her into expression, and she heightened the actualities as she went along. Her moods stimulate her; visual effects stimulate her; and so, especially, does any episode that can be dramatized as a scene to be told in the first person. Reading those pages, we watch Plath forming clear, conscious aims as a writer, and then performing in response—sometimes in defiance—as if engaging with semiconscious fluency to her own thinking as it materializes. Her writing itself enacts the process by which writing comes to be.

Plath did not consider herself to be writing a work of literature when writing in her journals. Yet what makes the journal so interesting is its focus on just this one project: becoming a writer. The activity that gave its literary character to the journal crystallized during the fall and winter after her marriage, her second year at Cambridge. Plath had been writing scenes from Cambridge life all along in her journal; now she resolved to pull it into a novel. Hughes offered to help her by writing up a secondary cast of Cambridge "eccentrics." Possibly he was thinking of Kingsley Amis's *Lucky Jim*—he believed Plath could write a wonderful comic novel. The models Plath sometimes mentions are J. D. Salinger's *The Catcher in the Rye,* and Joyce Cary's *The Horse's Mouth;* she too thought she could master a "fresh, brazen, colloquial voice." But Plath also had another kind of book in mind, one that Hughes could not have encouraged. It would probably be titled *Falcon Yard,* and its theme would be "love, a falcon, striking once and for all." She thought she would write it in the first person as "a vivid diary of reminiscence" that would recount "the voyage of a girl through destruction, hatred and despair to seek and to find the meaning of the redemptive power of love."

At the end of their second Cambridge winter, Plath wrote quite a lovely scene for this book into her journal. Then the lower hand froze up. The pressure of aiming for two such clearly defined and mutually exclusive genres—comedy and romance—paralyzed Plath's fluency; no matter how hard she flogged herself, she could not produce a satisfactory effect. Fiction was, to Plath, the supreme test of the writer's skill, and for the next two years she struggled stubbornly to meet the challenge. "I have experienced love, sorrow, madness, and if I cannot make these experiences meaningful, no new experience will help me." But she kept finding out that she couldn't write the novel, she could only write notes about it.

Nonetheless, during her year at Smith, while the upper hand was fidgeting with names for characters, possible literary models, and possible markets for *Falcon Yard*, the lower hand finally set to work. It would have nothing to do with *Falcon Yard*. Instead, it began limning verbal portraits of Plath's colleagues at Smith, deftly capturing their clothes and quirks, their characters, their marriages, their parties, their faculty-lounge hierarchies, their coffee dates with students. Now something genuinely new began to emerge in the journal: an objectifying voice, always witty, sometimes edged with malice. A male colleague is "pale with a mouth like a snail spread for sliding—a man who always keeps the expression on his face for a moment too long." A female art historian has a conversational style like "garish Leger cityscapes where women are turbine engines." Plath is particularly scathing about other writers she meets in Northampton, and they form a subset of characters in her journal. One, a novelist, appeared "ravaged by years of sandblasting." Another, a poet, had a "commercially gilded" look, a head that might have been "struck on a greek coin that since had blurred and thinned from too much public bartering and fingering." She even captures herself in a beaky gaze: "Secret sin: I envy, covet, lust—wander lost, red-heeled, red-gloved, black-flowing-coated, catching my image in shop windows, car windows, a stranger, sharper-visaged stranger than I knew."

This is the pitiless outlook of the satirist, who turns wit on fools and dunces, to reform society by exposing folly to ridicule. And when it wells up in Plath, the effect is mesmerizing. "Grit into art" is her phrase for it. "My voice must change to be heard: brash, concrete," she notes. "Away with blue moony soup-fogs." Plath wrote these little portraits and incidents rapidly, and apparently without a clear plan for their later use. They are simply fulfilling the assignment she's given herself to write in that journal actively until she is free to practice her true calling as a writer. But her lower hand has begun exercising the skill for which, it would turn out, she had a real disposition: satire, caricature, social comedy. Meanwhile, the journal is an incubator: "This be my secret place." And it's an oracle: "Answer me, book."

Plath's teaching job at Smith finally ended in May 1958. As if to make a completely new beginning for the story of her life, Plath wrote new page numbers on the factory-stamped pages of her journal, beginning May 13. For the first time ever she was not officially in school. But she was unofficially in school: she still gladly accepted writing and reading assignments from Hughes, and she immediately imposed on herself a refresher course in German. She also established, in the "new" journal, that completing *Falcon Yard* was going to be most important test of her professional viability. She set herself the project of eliminating the "sentimentality" with which the drafts of the story were accursed, the legacy of the adolescence she was trying to outgrow. "Sentimental" occurs like a litany in these pages, and in a letter to her brother, Warren, about her aims as a writer, Plath designates this as a dislikably "feminine" aspect of her work.

It was in Boston that Plath actually began accomplishing the aim she had identified shortly after returning to America, of transforming herself from a "bright published adolescent" into the "mature adult who begins writing about 25." She and Hughes had found their apartment in Boston at the back of Beacon Hill, and moved in September 1958, planning to spend the next year and a half occupied solely as writers. Again Plath assumed that her new freedom would lead immediately to the rapid completion of her novel; again she was overtaken by panic and immobilized. The difficulties Plath writes about so eloquently in her journal at the time do not seem to represent another episode of depression, however, but a profoundly painful self-confrontation of the kind that many artists undergo when first setting forth on their own. Not able to face the blank page every day, in

Ted and Sylvia, 9 Willow Street, Boston, 1959

October Plath took a secretarial job in the psychiatric clinic of Massachusetts General Hospital. One of her duties was to transcribe the dreams of patients. Plath had temporarily been a patient at this Boston hospital herself during her breakdown in 1954, and the psychiatric records tapped a gusher in her own psyche. She began writing stories that satisfied her, including "Johnny Panic and the Bible of Dreams," in which she achieved the tough, slangy, unsentimental style she would later use in *The Bell Jar*.

And she decided to return to psychotherapy herself, with the psychiatrist who had treated her back in 1953–1954, Ruth Beuscher. She began consulting Beuscher—secretly, at first—shortly after Thanksgiving in 1958. By January 1959 Plath had regained enough self-confidence to try something else: she began attending Robert Lowell's writing seminar at Boston University.

Boston was a city full of poets in the late 1950s. Hughes was welcomed everywhere; Plath was introduced around as Hughes's wife, "who also wrote." His *Hawk in the Rain* had been reviewed in glowing terms by two poets currently living in Boston, Philip Booth and

W.S. Merwin, who wanted to meet him; and a dinner with Bill and Dido Merwin that year inaugurated a friendship that the two couples resumed when the Hugheses moved to London. Plath introduced Hughes to Peter Davison, a poetry editor at the venerable *Atlantic Monthly* and a poet himself. Plath had indulged in a fling with Davison just before she left for Cambridge in 1955; he was now married to Jane Truslow, who had lived in Sylvia's dormitory at Smith. The two couples often saw each other socially, sometimes at the Hugheses' minuscule Boston apartment. Davison recalls in a memoir the tiny table on which they dined. Plath noted in her journal that when she invited Robert Lowell and his wife to dinner along with Steve and Agatha Fassett—he recorded poetry for the Harvard Library's Woodberry Room—she had to figure out how to prepare an entire meal that could be served from one dish per course.

Plath admired Lowell as a poet, and was fascinated by his relationship to his wife, Elizabeth Hardwick. The Lowells' home on Marlborough Street provided Plath with the very model of the sort of literary salon over which she hoped to preside herself someday. But attending Lowell's writing seminar at first disappointed Plath. With a mixture of annoyance and gratitude she observed that she had little to learn from Lowell's teaching—sitting in a classroom "felt like regression." Then Lowell began comparing Plath's manuscripts to those of Anne Sexton, another poet auditing the seminar; Lowell suggested that possibly Sexton's poems could show Plath how to loosen up. Plath took notice, and so did Sexton. They began going out for drinks after class. Sexton tells the story in a memoir she wrote about Plath: "We would pile into the front seat of my old Ford and I would drive quickly through the traffic to the Ritz. I would park illegally in a LOADING ONLY ZONE telling them gaily, 'It's okay, because we are only going to get loaded!'" They were sometime accompanied by the young poet George Starbuck, an editor at Houghton Mifflin with whom Sexton was having an affair.

Sexton says they drank martinis at the Ritz—this would have been very unusual behavior for Plath—and compared notes on their suicide attempts; Plath learned that Sexton too was a "mental hospital

Anne Sexton with her daughters Linda (background) and Joy (foreground), c. 1958

graduate." But Plath found something else to mention in a letter to one of her friends: in Plath's view, Sexton had "the marvelous enviable casualness of the person who . . . never dreamed of herself as a born writer." Sexton, "without ever having gone to college," was writing poems Lowell called "marvelous," on subjects that were "very female," with "no inhibitions." She was also a mother, of two little girls, and she had the looks of a fashion model—writing in her journal about Sexton makes Plath think of getting a better haircut.

So Sexton's name went onto a list Plath was keeping, of women poets who interested her. Plath was trying to figure out how other women solved the problem of becoming a world-class writer without losing any of the benefits of womanhood. At one point, Plath made a ranked list: "Who rivals? In history—Sappho, Elizabeth Barrett Browning, Christina Rossetti, Amy Lowell, Emily Dickinson, Edna St. Vincent Millay—all dead. Now: Edith Sitwell & Marianne Moore, the aging giantesses & poetic godmothers." Plath's *unranked* list of living rivals was very short. In addition to Anne Sexton, whose poems were being accepted for publication at a rapid rate, Plath mentions Isabella Gardner, Adrienne Rich, and May Swenson. It could have included the names of Elizabeth Bishop, Louise Bogan, H.D., Denise Levertov, Muriel Rukeyser, Stevie Smith—but Plath wasn't aiming for coverage: we are learning whose work she envied. Most powerfully, during the months she was auditing Lowell's seminar, she envied the work of Adrienne Rich, Robert Lowell's friend, who had won publication in the Yale Younger Poets Series during her senior year at Radcliffe. Rich was married to a professor at Harvard, and Plath had met her socially after a reading Hughes gave at Harvard in April. Rich was the poet Plath longed to "eclipse" with the brilliance of the poems she was writing that year. Among the female writers of fiction, Plath designates only one rival in her journal, ever, from beginning to end: Virginia Woolf. "What is my voice? Woolfish, alas, but tough. Please, tough." "Her novels make mine possible."

But Plath also kept a list that segregated women writers according to whether or not they had children. Woolf didn't; Rich and Sexton did. For Sylvia Plath—not for all women writers, nor for all women artists, but for Sylvia Plath—one kind of imaginative fulfillment would arrive only through the integration of pregnancy and childbearing into her sense of agency as an artist, and this would be the psychological issue she would resolve as she reached maturity as a woman. That she was beset by anxiety over this we can have no doubt, not only because of the numerous entries in her journal but also because of that succinct passage in *The Bell Jar* where Plath's alter ego, Esther Greenwood, imagines herself sitting in a fig tree, unable to decide which fruit to pluck. "One fig was a husband and a happy home and children, and another fig was a famous poet and another fig was a brilliant professor . . . choosing one meant losing all the rest." By March 1961, when Plath rapidly wrote *The Bell Jar*—it took her only six weeks—she was not green wood. She had arrived at the moment when she could use what she had stored in the pages of her journal, having established herself in motherhood and gained a small foothold in the literary world of London.

Anne Sexton, with *Ariel* behind her typewriter, circa 1966

Plath's extant journal breaks off in November 1959, with the process of maturation still under way. But when a journal succeeds as literature, it succeeds as a genre of unending beginnings and developments. In *The Journals of Sylvia Plath* we are given enough to derive an understanding of the processes by which Plath negotiated the obstacles to fulfilling her deepest ambitions. Her persistence, discipline, and anguish make for sobering and inspiring reading, because we know what she eventually accomplished. The journal shows the unfinished business that lay between her and the finished work on which her reputation rests. She had to find a creative pathway into the negative emotions that stirred her eloquence. And in order to accomplish that task, Plath had to dismantle, within her principal relationships, the structure of parent/child, teacher/student, mentor/apprentice.

Plath had always associated wifedom with the obligation to be second-rate. When she installed Ted Hughes in her life as husband-lover-father-son, Plath was consciously aware of what he could do for her: stay out there ahead of her, like a father, but share his most intimate knowledge with her intellectually and physically, as a husband and lover, and permit her the role of caretaker on which she thrived, like a son. By late 1959, Plath was trying to let go, as a writer, of the need for her attachment to a superior male; and she had rethought the priority list she had written up for her mother at the time she and Hughes left Cambridge, which put getting "our writing personae established" before they had children.

Equally, and at a psychological level quite as primitive, Plath had to dissolve the bond with a mother who had served not only as a nurturer but as a mentor. From Plath's letters home, it can be gathered that throughout her college years in America and England, Plath sent her mother copies of her work in progress—always pointing out to her mother, sometimes in a very condescending manner, the aesthetic effects she was after. When Plath returned to home territory in Massachusetts after completing her degree at Cambridge, strong hostility toward mother figures began showing up in the stories about which Plath sketched notes in her journal. Then, during spring break from Smith in 1958, Plath wrote "The Disquieting Muses," the first poem in which her negative emotions toward her mother are given a symbolic relationship to her writing. Her six months of psychotherapy in 1959 helped Plath bring this hostility into consciousness and to feel around in it.

Hughes never shared Plath's idealization of fertility. As we have seen, at the time of their marriage they both yearned for the romance of a way of life they associated with writer-exiles such as D. H. Lawrence and James Joyce: the freedom to travel and live abroad; as late as the winter of 1958 Plath was putting into her journals detailed fantasies about living in Rome. The advent of Plath's overwhelming desire to become pregnant had startled Hughes, he later told Plath's mother; he thought Plath was sacrificing something deeply valuable to both of them. Plath's journal indicates that they argued over it; she says he called it "nagging." Early in 1959, apparently with Hughes's agreement, she began attempting to conceive a child. She became pregnant in July.

Meanwhile, Hughes and Plath had decided to return to England, where life was less expensive and work for writers was easier to come by. Aurelia Plath recalled seeing them off, after the Thanksgiving holiday. "Sylvia was wearing her hair in a long braid down her back with a little red wool cap on her head, and looked like a high school student." But in fact, Plath had almost grown up.

Literary London

The Hugheses sailed for England on December 9, arriving in time to spend the Christmas holiday with Hughes's family at The Beacon. *Birthday Letters* suggests that Hughes initially proposed to Plath that they themselves settle in Yorkshire; the poem "Stubbing Wharfe" recounts a conversation he and Plath held over Guinness at a pub in Heptonstall Slack. Observing that Plath is sad and homesick, Hughes has an inspiration: what she needs is a house of her own, with a garden. Marvelous bargains could be found, for instance, just across the valley. But Plath wished to keep Ted's family at a distance. She insisted on London.

Hughes and Plath moved into their flat on Chalcot Square on February 1, 1960, and almost immediately they began to feel the great

advantage of their relocation from Boston to London. On the tenth Plath wrote excitedly to Aurelia that the British publisher William Heinemann had accepted *The Colossus and Other Poems* within a week of receiving the manuscript, to her amazement. The editor arranged to meet Plath in a Soho pub to sign the contract. Plath dressed carefully in business clothes, "despite being of an enormous and impressive size"—their baby was due in six weeks. Ted waited in a pub nearby, then took Plath to lunch, and presented her with a gift to celebrate the occasion: the three-volume edition of the poems of D. H. Lawrence.

Blue plaque at 3 Chalcot Square, North London (detail)

In March, when Hughes received news that *The Hawk in the Rain* would receive the Somerset Maugham Award, he learned that the recipient was required to spend the funds on travel abroad, "enlarging his world-view." Suddenly the horizon of foreign travel—abandoned when Plath became pregnant—opened again; gravid Plath wrote to her mother that the award set the Hugheses dreaming of "the Greek islands next winter and all sorts of sun-saturated schemes." *Lupercal* was published that month as well, dedicated "To Sylvia," as *The Colossus* would be "For Ted." To celebrate this occasion, two editors from Faber and Faber—Hughes's publisher—took the couple to lunch at what Plath considered a rather fancy Greek restaurant, and discussed illustrations for *Meet My Folks!* the children's book by Ted that was due out soon after Plath's baby was due out. And indeed, Frieda Rebecca arrived just in time to be named in the dedication.

Reviews of *Lupercal* began appearing at the end of March, and were overwhelmingly favorable. Al Alvarez, an influential arts critic for the London *Observer*, welcomed *Lupercal* as an antidote to the "gentility principle" that was stifling British poetry at the time, "a peculiarly English disease, closely allied to the ideal of muddling through. . . . It didn't seem an adequate response to a century that spawned two world wars, totalitarianism, genocide, concentration camps and nuclear wars." Alvarez arranged to write a piece about Hughes himself as an important new figure in British poetry, to accompany the review in the *Observer*. Alvarez remembered climbing the shabby stairs up to the Hugheses' flat in Chalcot Square—"so small that everything appeared to be sideways," he said. "You inserted yourself into a hallway so narrow and jammed that you could hardly take off your coat." Hughes was as striking in person as on the pages of his books, "a man who seemed to carry his own climate with him, to create his own atmosphere." Plath seemed to Alvarez "briskly American" that day: "bright, clean, competent, like a young woman in a cookery advertisement, friendly and yet rather distant." He didn't recognize her as the author of "Night Shift," a poem he had printed the preceding year in the *Observer* poetry page he edited. This publication had been a great thing, in her eyes, but Alvarez had forgotten the name "Sylvia Plath," until she reminded him. "In those days, Sylvia seemed effaced, the poet taking a back seat to the young mother and housewife." The Hugheses were tickled to see people all around them reading Alvarez's piece when they went to the movies that weekend. Plath noted wistfully for her mother that she was described as Hughes's " 'tall, trim American wife . . . who is a *New Yorker* poet in her own right.' " She was, of course, nine months pregnant at the time.

The articles and reviews about *Lupercal* stimulated a flood of invitations: Hughes was asked to give readings, submit poems, attend literary events. After the baby arrived, Plath was glad to be in circulation again. John Lehmann, editor of *London Magazine*, invited them to a drinks party; *London* had previously published a couple of Hughes's stories and had just accepted Plath's story "Daughters of Blossom Street," plus two new poems; at this party, they were a literary couple. Lehmann delighted Plath by reminiscing about Virginia Woolf. They also met poets and critics that evening they knew only by reputation—Elizabeth Jennings, Roy Fuller, Christine Brooke-Rose. "I must get them all in my diary," Plath vowed.

By far the most gratifying outcome of Ted's fame was the celebratory cocktail party at Faber and Faber in April, where Hughes and Plath met T. S. Eliot and his wife, Valerie. Eliot was the editor at Faber

Ted Hughes with Valerie Eliot and T. S. Eliot, party at Faber and Faber, 1960

who had acquired Hughes's work, and showed encouraging interest in Hughes's desire to write a play in verse. Following the cocktail party, the Hugheses received an invitation to dine at the Eliots' home, where the other guests would be the poet Stephen Spender and his wife, the concert pianist Natasha Litvin. Plath, who was breast-feeding Frieda, immediately began preparing for this occasion by accustoming Frieda to one bottle feeding per day, which a baby-sitter could give her.

Plath wrote her mother a full report of the occasion *chez* Eliot: a warm May evening, a taxi ride though London streets she had never seen before: Little Venice, with its glossy canal, and Palace Gardens, where tall, elegant stucco houses stood on streets lined with blossoming trees. Plath noted the plenitude of "For Sale" signs in these neighborhoods, and proposed that she and Hughes should make "symbolic inquiries" into buying such a house: "Oddly enough, the more we set our sights on, the more good fortune occurs." The Eliots' "drab brick building" itself disappointed Plath, but it concealed a "lavish apartment," and Eliot's kind attentiveness warmed her heart, though it awed her socially into polite reserve. "I felt to be sitting next to a descended god; he has such a nimbus of greatness about him." The arrival of the Spenders enlivened the party, and Plath had a fabulous evening of literary gossip to pass on to Aurelia, along with her awareness that both Spender and Eliot "were instrumental in Ted's getting his Guggenheim and his book printed." This was all they had hoped for in moving to London—what Plath had hoped for, anyway. As Alvarez observed, Hughes kept aloof from shop talk and seemed to dislike literary hobnobbing. He was "self-assured and self-possessed, solidly rooted in a world in which wild animals figured a great deal more prominently than people."

Despite the extraordinary success Hughes was enjoying as a poet, he could not expect to make a living at it. Another avenue had to be found. Surprisingly, he set his sights on the theatre.

During the two years that Hughes and Plath spent in America, Hughes's contemporaries had taken over the English theatre. Young men newly down from Cambridge (notably, Peter Hall) and Oxford (notably, Peter Brook) were making a big splash with bold productions of Shakespeare and of work by young British and Continental playwrights; they were being applauded and promoted by critics as young as themselves (notably, Kenneth Tynan). A wide range of new work was launched by directors taking their cues from ambitious experiments by European theatre companies that were on view all over the Continent. Hall's acclaimed London production of Beckett's *Waiting for Godot* in 1955 demonstrated that English audiences too were ready for the doses of unpleasure on offer in what came to be called the Theatre of the Absurd. Homegrown playwrights such as Harold Pinter, John Osborne, and Arnold Wesker were working different ground, writing social commentary on the failure of the Labour government to reform postwar English society. Osborne's *Look Back in Anger,* which had opened the month before Hughes and Plath got married, furnished the journalists with a convenient label for this whole generation of newcomers who now occupied powerful roles as the principal writers and directors in the British theatre: angry young men. Hughes and Plath took a professional interest in this new arena for writers, and became active theatergoers as soon as they got to London. Hughes's correspondence discusses seeing John Arden's *Serjeant Musgrave's Dance,* W.S. Merwin's *The Golden West,* and John Whiting's *The Devils,* which Peter Hall had commissioned; and Wesker's "kitchen sink" trilogy, *Roots.* Plath mentions Pinter's *The Caretaker,* Osborne's *The Entertainer* (on film), a contemporary production in French of Racine's *Phèdre;* a play called *Chin-Chin,* "translated from the French." When advanced pregnancy made her uncomfortable about going out, she stayed in and translated for her own entertainment a play by Sartre, *Le Diable et le Bon Dieu.*

Hughes thought he might throw his own hat in the ring, since many of the major players were men he had known at Cambridge. He was working on the project he had undertaken at Yaddo, a libretto for *Bardo Thödol* (The Tibetan Book of the Dead) with an oratorio by Chou Wen-Chung, which tracked the soul's forty-nine-day journey from death to rebirth, on which he was collaborating with the composer. Chou planned an ambitious scenario involving a large orchestra and chorus, along with "projected illuminated mandalas," a dancer to mime the action being sung, lighting effects to convey the regions of Hell through which the soul must travel: a grand spectacle. This was right up Hughes's alley—"a sort of Buddhist mass," he called it. Hughes worked on *Bardo Thödol* while they waited for the birth of their own baby, scheduled to arrive under the sign of Aries. Possibly that was the prompt to writing a short verse play that he dashed off and titled *The House of Aries* that spring, and submitted to the BBC's Third Programme, which was scouting material for radio adaptation. He had discarded his *House of Taurus,* written at Yaddo, but apparently liked the astrological-sounding title.

Literary history will not remember Ted Hughes as a playwright, yet it was his principal occupation and the chief supplier of his income during the 1960s. The trendy genre of gritty social realism that dominated the West End stages held no charm for Hughes, but there was plenty of room in the theatre for any new idea in 1960, and Hughes thought he had one. Hughes wanted to see whether he could revive the genre of the verse play.

During those first two years in London, Hughes made several attempts at developing dramatic characters out of psychological elements. *The House of Aries* was only the first. The title referred as well to the Greek god of war, Ares, and the setting was the aftermath of some sort of revolution. Essentially a shaman drama with a quest as its hidden purpose and a spirit leader as the manager of the action, the situation played itself through characters who were "psychic entities" within a single individual. One represented the digestive tract, another the circulatory system; the heroine represented feeling, and the hero represented scientific thought of the kind that had devised the atomic bomb. Or so one gathers from Hughes's comments about the play; the manuscript has apparently not survived. He submitted it to the Poet's Theatre in Boston, and the BBC's Third Programme accepted and produced it, with well-known actors in the main roles. That was a real breakthrough—"early commercial acceptance of his dramatic verse," Plath crowed to her mother. Plath added that T. S. Eliot had expressed an interest in seeing any verse plays that Hughes might be working on.

The House of Aries was broadcast on November 16, 1960, and was given its staged reading at the Poet's Theatre in Boston around the same time. Aurelia Plath loyally attended, and was mighty puzzled by the play. She wrote to Hughes inquiring whether it represented a kind of dream. Plath answered her mother's inquiry rather huffily; she considered the play "marvelously amusing and vivid," and thought it needed no defense. But Hughes, in a long detailed letter, anatomized for Aurelia—probably for himself as well—the faults that had been clarified for him by listening to the BBC radio production. He had been trying to dramatize the fragmentation of the modern self, and got carried away by symbolisms, he admitted. But even a verse play needed character, action and "theatricality," none of which were to be found in *The House of Aries*. It was simply a "verse-piece for voices," and spoken verse is not the same thing as speech, he now saw. The convincing sound of a character's speech, and nothing else, could endow a play with realism. He was "a bit horrified" by what he had permitted to go out over the air with his name on it.

Hughes immediately began drafting another play, *The Wound*, which he considered a great improvement. He commented to his friend Lucas Myers that in his new work the voice of the characters, rather than the voice of the author, was audible—"and what they say is strange to me."

The Wound came to Hughes in a dream, he said, in the course of his ongoing work on *Bardo Thödol*. A soldier with a head wound is being led away from the battlefield by his sergeant; the soldier, Ripley, hallucinates an encounter with a group of women who escort them to a magical château, where they are entertained. The women turn out to be malevolent spirits, and tear the sergeant apart, but one of the young spirit women takes pity on Ripley and leads him away from the scene of destruction. He offers to marry her, but she vanishes as he wakens to find himself being cared for by two other soldiers from his regiment. Hughes said in an interview that *The Wound* was his personal version of the *Bardo Thödol*, "full of all the stock imagery of a journey to the Celtic Underworld." But its anchor in wartime experience and physical pain gave a strong reality-effect to the surreal digression into terror;

the piece had its own coherence quite aside from the allegorical significance it held for Hughes.

Meanwhile, Hughes's work for the BBC had put his name in circulation as a prospective playwright, and notice was taken by the young impresario Peter Hall, artistic director of the newly established Royal Shakespeare Company. Its main theatre was in Stratford, but Hall also developed productions for two London theatres, the Aldwych, in the West End, and the Arts Theatre Club in Soho, a smaller house in which he hoped to showcase new talent. Hall was actively commissioning such work and in April 1961 asked Hughes to submit a play to be considered for the 1962 season. "I couldn't be happier that you want to write for the theatre," Hall told him, "because your poetry has excited me enormously."

This invitation put wind in Hughes's sails. He immediately went back to work on a three-act play he already had under way titled *The Calm*. The setting was a desert island; the characters were eight castaways from a shipwreck who retained only faint and intermittent recollections of their past life—Plath told her mother that Hughes was writing the "dark opposite to Shakespeare's *Tempest*." The manuscript survives only on scattered typescript pages but the action of the play seems to be taking place on the banks of the river Acheron (from classical myth, the river in the underworld where spirits gather after death), with the band of survivors attempting to pool its memories in order for each to recover a sense of self, under the leadership of a superior being called the Helper. A baby is discovered and brought into their midst at some point, supplying the possibility of a new start.

At the time he was writing *The Calm*, Hughes was confident that it would "redeem" his reputation: it had action, humor, a vivid and arresting situation (in his view). He believed that he had reached expression of an authentic level of intensity for the first time, in at least one scene. Another shaman drama, the play contained the ideas to which he was so attached: the quest of the hero and the spirit leader as guide. It too was given a reading at the Poet's Theatre in Boston. Their friend Peter Davison, who was regularly accepting work by Plath and Hughes for publication in *Atlantic Monthly*, wrote that he and his wife had attended the reading and "were fascinated by the strange simplicity of the language, with shapeless forms crouching just beyond earshot." They left the theatre "baffled but reflective," Davison added. Hughes and Plath had high hopes for *The Calm*. "Oh, you wait, we'll be wealthy yet," Plath crowed to her mother.

Apparently, Peter Hall rejected *The Calm*. It was never produced, and the typescript was jettisoned into a common pool of scratch paper in the Hughes household, where it achieved a kind of afterlife, along with other work that was being revised or abandoned. *The Calm* furnished drafting paper for Hughes's *Wodwo*, his libretto for *Bardo Thödol*, initial drafts of a play titled *The Candidate*, and discarded versions of various projects labeled *Difficulties of a Bridegroom*. And Plath too recycled *The Calm* discriminately in drafting some of the poems of *Ariel*. Handling these pages is like overhearing almost inaudible snatches of conversation among the works in progress.

Despite the setbacks, Hughes continued his effort to achieve a dramatically effective expression of his quest plot, by which he was attempting to bring what he viewed as "a technology" of spiritual search into work for the theatre. He was able to sell two of these works to the BBC: *The Wound* and a version of *Difficulties of a Bridegroom*. This odd title was peculiarly talismanic in Hughes's creative life. It referred to *The Chemical Wedding of Christian Rosenkreutz*, the founding text of Rosicrucianism, an allegory based on alchemy that Hughes repeatedly attempted to dramatize for the stage. The "bridegroom" in Hughes's plot was seeking alchemical transformation, and the "bride" was an idea about a so-called female principle, both being wholly allegorical abstractions. In the 1960s, *The Chemical Wedding* was as formative to his thinking about art as *The White Goddess* had been a decade earlier. He worked assiduously on a three-act play he again titled *Difficulties of a Bridegroom* after Plath's death, a succession of scenes based on alchemical concepts, and submitted it to Peter Hall, hoping for production by the Royal Shakespeare Company. Hall apologized for the brutal frankness of his reply: in a nutshell, the play was poetic, but it wasn't *theatre*. The scenes were static, the characters mere vehicles carrying the allegorical freight. The result was "rhetorical and empty," Hall wrote. "Symbolic drama simply has to have a concrete basis, and this I don't believe has. It is a series of fascinating theatrical images which weary by their dexterity."

However, a very much shorter and earlier version of *Difficulties of a Bridegroom* was effectively produced by the BBC as a radio play, and broadcast in January 1963. Radio drama was probably the best medium for the artistic purpose Hughes was pursuing so stubbornly—trying to influence audiences at the unconscious level by dosing them with occult symbolisms—because the drama in his plays is all interior. He wanted somehow to give voice to the array of conflicted "psychic entities" within the divided self of Western man, and to convey the destructive dominance of the "discursive intelligence" in Western civilization, by dramatizing its deadly effect on the fertile emotional life which it seeks to control. Working with the radio producer Douglas Cleverdon, Hughes came close to realizing these artistic aims. Both *The Wound* and *Difficulties of a Bridegroom* were situated in realistic settings, and sound cues were devised to mark the shifts between human and spirit worlds. Cleverdon had the idea of using music to point to the shifts *within* the protagonist's consciousness as well, and the supple voices of the actors—which can still be heard on the BBC's recording of the play—made the emotional richness of the conflicts available to the imagination as no visualization could have done.

Yet it is very hard to fathom why Hughes found this esoteric subject so compelling. Given the financial and emotional pressures in his life during the years he pushed forward with projects based on *The Chemical Wedding,* he surely had some deep imaginative connection to that particular quest story, but the outcome was decidedly unsuccessful, and to a practical mind looks deluded. What was Hughes after? It wouldn't even be an interesting question if Hughes hadn't eventually arrived at an artistic method by which to explore the coexistence of myth and dailiness, but beginning with the poems of *Remains of Elmet,* published in 1979, he did; and the result, eventually, was *Birthday Letters*—poems addressed to the shade of Sylvia Plath, the alchemical Bride of his imagination.

Homemaking

While Hughes set about turning himself into a playwright and establishing himself among the literati, Plath happily played a supporting role: her aim, she told her mother, was to keep Ted writing full-time. They "invested" (Plath's word) in a good bed, a refrigerator, and a stove, all new—to the amazement and disapproval of their English friend Dido Merwin, who later wrote in an unfriendly memoir that she considered these purchases to be a sign of Plath's "besetting insecurity."

But Plath's English mother-in-law thought otherwise. Edith Hughes sent Aurelia Plath a warm letter describing Plath's spotless, well-equipped kitchen, and admiring Plath's skill at homemaking. Being married to a joiner, Edith had an expert eye for woodwork, and noted with special pleasure the polished mahogany plank that the Hugheses laid over a little cupboard to make a dining table and the polished wooden bowl in which Plath arranged fresh fruit. This visit seems to have consolidated Edith's affection for Plath and the feeling was, apparently, mutual; later that summer Plath wrote admiringly to Aurelia about Edith's flower garden in Yorkshire, without adding her usual digs about Edith's housekeeping.

Plath's happiness in nesting was probably intensified by her recognition that after weaning the baby, she would have to get a salaried job to bring in some income. Clearly, they would eventually have to find a bigger place to live, one that gave them both a convenient place to write. Hughes's artistic redirection from poetry to the potentially more lucrative writing for the theatre gave Plath hope that they would actually be able to buy a house. She kept up a running commentary on the subject in letters to her mother. One day Plath spotted a freehold house for sale not far from their flat in Chalcot Square, at 41 Fitzroy Road—the same street on which W. B. Yeats had lived as a boy! But in 1960 the purchase price of such a house, £9250 (about $26,000), was out of reach for them.

Despite the futility of wishing, Plath could not help elaborating, in letters to her mother, the advantages such a house would bestow on their working life. For one thing, it would keep them in London. But since money was a big consideration, Plath was also open to the prospect of buying elsewhere. Cornwall, for example, where an ample house would cost around £5000 (around $14,000; by way of crude comparison, in the United States, where the annual average income in 1960 was $6227, the average price of a house was $18,500). However, because Hughes had no regular job, it would be difficult to get a mortgage: they would probably have to pay cash. Even his rich uncle Walter was chary of acting as a financial reference for the nephew he regarded as unemployed, according to Plath. She noted wistfully that if Hughes were *really* successful—that is, got a play into a West End theatre—they would be able to afford a house in London overlooking Hampstead Heath. And afford a station wagon as well—a *very* American fantasy.

All the while that Plath was daydreaming about real estate, Hughes and Plath were imposing rigorous financial discipline on themselves: still banking money when it came in, still penny-pinching. During their first ten months in England, they didn't even have a radio: when Plath allowed another purchase for their home she chose a vacuum cleaner. They listened to Ted's broadcasts with their upstairs neighbor, who took a liking to them and offered her flat for their use as a study on weekdays while she was away at work. Another writing retreat was made available to them by the Merwins, who traveled a good deal and had a holiday home in France; whenever they left London, they offered the use of their nearby flat.

The focal point of life for Hughes and Plath during the spring of 1960 was their baby daughter, Frieda Rebecca, born April 1. Plath wrote to her family, diplomatically, that she was named for Aunt Frieda, her father's sister, but Hughes told their friend Al Alvarez that she was named after D. H. Lawrence's wife—Alvarez was married to Frieda Lawrence's granddaughter. "We're all besotted with D. H. Lawrence," Hughes told Alvarez. Like everything else that spring, the baby too was a great success.

Plath reveled in her baby daughter, and wrote long, detailed letters to Aurelia about all aspects of mothering. She sent snapshots, but thought they didn't do justice to Frieda's blue eyes and pink cheeks. "Wish I could get her in Technicolor," she mourned. Plath and Hughes found baby Frieda especially enchanting when she began to acquire language. In an interview on the BBC, Hughes commented that she was "like a kind of aerial," bringing a "range of feelings" that weren't in the house before. Or did he mean she was a kind of Ariel, who brought such beautiful unearthly music into Shakespeare's *Tempest*? She was only two months old when Hughes wrote to Aurelia, "At times she seems to be trying to sing. She has a new sound almost every day." By Midsummer Day he reported, "she's found her talking voice and is inventing curious new noises." By Christmas he could offer statistics: she inhaled on every third syllable in the stream of her babble. To one of his male friends he wrote that she was "about the most interesting thing that ever happened in my life, among the three most, say."

A year later Plath was pregnant with their second child, due in January, and the little flat on Chalcot Square had become impossible to tolerate: they had to find another place to live. Hughes wanted to move southwest of London to Exmoor, in Devon, where Gerald had lived in the late 1930s as a gamekeeper, before joining the RAF and leaving England. "The Devon dream must have stayed with me," Hughes remarked the year of his death, reflecting on Gerald's influence in his life. In 1961 he hadn't abandoned his dream of getting Gerald back to England to join a communal living arrangement. For this purpose, Devon was ideal. Part of Exmoor was moorland, like their childhood environment, and it was watered by tributaries of the River Exe that provided abundant fishing. The forests were full of game; Hughes fancied that he might "knock over the occasional deer" to put food on the table. Plath wanted very much to remain in London, but reluctantly concurred that their money would go further if they moved to the countryside, and she had a few plans, herself, about acquiring some household help by relocating her mother to England to care for the children.

The home they eventually bought was near Dartmoor in the village of North Tawton, twenty miles from the city of Exeter. Court Green was a big old thatched rectory, much in need of repair. Parts of the ten-room house had been built in the eleventh century and had walls three feet thick; one edge of the property bordered the churchyard. Hughes wrote gleefully to Gerald that their three acres of ground held a prehistoric mound, possibly a burial mound, along with a large apple orchard. A mile away was a railroad station with good connections to London's Waterloo Station.

It was to the sympathetic mothers-in-law, Aurelia Plath and Edith Hughes, that Ted and Sylvia turned for financial assistance when they finally decided which house to buy. Both mothers reached into personal nest eggs to loan them £500 ($1400) apiece, which, added to the savings Hughes and Plath had accumulated, beginning with their earnings from teaching in 1957–1958, made it possible to buy Court Green outright.

Court Green in early spring, from the churchyard

By September 1961, all arrangements had been made for the move from London to Devon. Plath wrote to her mother that the pest controllers had finished fumigating for woodworm and former owners had left it tidy, but it by no means met her high standards of cleanliness nor her aesthetic expectations. They spent days and days scrubbing, hauling, installing, refurbishing. Plath wanted fresh paint on the floors: a white undercoat, over which the rugs would be laid, with borders of pale gray, to brighten the rooms. Having learned some carpentry from his father, Hughes set about fitting shelves and bookcases in the house, which still seemed empty after they had installed their possessions. After he made Plath's writing table, he made her a sewing table. For Frieda he built a toy box, and devised a gate to keep her off the stairs. The Hugheses joined a discount home furnishing club, and Hughes began scouting the local auctions for useful items. Plath gloated to her mother about the bargains he carried home: a table for twelve cents! A handsome china "biscuit barrel" ("cookie jar" to an American) for sixty cents! A dresser for a dollar! A small slant-top writing desk for the parlor. Several antique mirrors. An upholstered chair for her study, with a good back support.

The move was very tiring, especially to Plath, who was entering the last trimester of her pregnancy. She wrote to her mother tenderly about Ted's caretaking: he insisted that she take a daily rest along with Frieda, and it was he who performed the forty-minute drive to do the laundry and shopping in Exeter, the nearest town with a Laundromat. (Plath's mother promptly gave them the money for a brand-new Bendix washer.) But Plath couldn't sit still. She bought a used sewing machine and supplied herself with many yards of red corduroy for the upholstery, curtains, pillows, Frieda's bedspread. Red, white, and black were her standard decorating colors: vermilion, she said, was her "color tonic." Her most self-indulgent purchase for the house was that fine red Wilton carpet she installed in her own study, but she also ordered equally vivid but less expensive red carpets for the hall runners and stairs, and a good figured carpet for the living room, with red the background color. Hughes liked animal skins on the floor: his splurge was a Chinese goatskin rug with long silky hairs. And in later years, as his affluence increased, so did Hughes's collection: tiger, leopard, python, kangaroo skins, acquired with Gerald's assistance, along with the skins and bones and skulls of foxes, stags, and badgers; and such shamanistic talismans as tigers' teeth, and eagles' claws.

Plath wrote to her mother that she had never seen Ted happier than when they were settling into their new home, "leading, at last, exactly the life he wants." Hughes's poem "The Rag Rug" in *Birthday Letters* offers an image of what domestic happiness felt like to him. As Plath braids the fabric scraps to make a rug, he reads aloud to her from the fiction of Joseph Conrad.

> I could cradle your freed mind in my voice
> . . . I could feel
> Your fingers caressing my reading, hour after hour

Drawing an image from the novel Plath had been working on throughout their marriage, Hughes thinks of such "crimson-shadowed evenings" of reading and listening as if their minds and hands had merged in one gesture,

> reaching to touch a falcon that does not fly off.
> As if I held your hand to stroke a falcon
> With your hand

The huge garden circling the house in Devon was another boon to the Hugheses. These grounds too had been neglected, and exploring them led to further discoveries. Plath plunged into the overgrown flower beds to cut gladioli and zinnias for the house, and found some promising rosebushes among the nettles. Collecting windfall apples, she and Hughes stumbled on an abandoned hill of potatoes ready to be dug. They spotted a cache of raspberry bushes among the brambles, and pulled fruit from the loaded canes. They counted seventy-two apple trees in their orchard, which had been planted to bear fruit from mid-August to mid-October, for eating, for cooking, and for keeping: Devonshire Quarrendon, Early Victoria, Bramley, Pig's Nose. They would be eating apple pie for breakfast during the whole month of September. Elsewhere about the grounds stood an abundance of honeysuckle, lilacs, cherries, and laburnums— flowering trees Plath associated with their Edenic spring romance in Cambridge.

Hughes had appointed himself the head gardener in this new Eden. Immediately after they moved into Court Green, he purchased a set of garden tools at auction and prepared the ground for a vegetable patch and a strawberry bed. By early September, when Plath's brother came to visit, Hughes had mowed the grass and nettles to make a spot of lawn. He planted winter lettuce, for immediate gratification, and sent for seed catalogues, looking forward to spring. After several months Hughes wrote to Gerald that the "digging and dragging and chopping" had made him very physically fit.

But one of the poems of *Birthday Letters* suggests that during those months of hard labor Hughes was suffering, silently, from symptoms of what he thought was heart disease, and dosing himself with Beethoven's music to clear his aorta! Can this be true? Probably. It is one of the endearing things about Hughes that he imposed esoteric experiments on himself. In any case, in the poem Hughes is gesturing to those months of settling into Court Green as the point when he was outgrowing and sloughing off an old self, without any sense of what might emerge from the process. He was not only digging the compacted soil around Court Green and worrying about his heart, during those months; he was digging into compacted questions about what it meant to be a man, to be a father.

Literary Lion

At the time they settled in Devon, Ted Hughes had just celebrated his thirty-first birthday. Court Green would be Ted Hughes's home for most of the rest of his life, and his final resting place as well: before his death, he requested that his ashes be scattered on Dartmoor. His reputation had also taken its definitive shape. During the years of his creative alliance with Plath, he had achieved his maturity as an artist. He was now a literary lion in his prime, who had already made important contributions to English poetry. As the critic Al Alvarez put it, assessing Hughes's whole career, Hughes's characteristic poems gave the effect of issuing from "a permanently open hotline to his unconscious."

As Alvarez points out, most of Hughes's poetry explores the instinctual energies in human beings that reveal our continuity with the animal world. His childhood passion for folktales populated by magical beasts kept a lifelong hold over his imagination, eventually maturing into a set of intellectual pursuits. Yet Hughes's work is not allusive in the manner of earlier Modernist writers who were captivated, as he was, by anthropology's discoveries about the structure of myth—Eliot, Graves, Pound, Joyce. No: Hughes's poetry draws upon that "subsidiary brain" he ascribed to the training in hunting and fishing he had received from his brother, Gerald. His reading explained to him the peculiarly gripping satisfaction of predation—that it was a survival in the human brain of its evolution from its most primitive origins. His writing was intended to give readers a glimpse of instincts underlying their inner lives, including the predatory instincts.

Thinking very like that accounts for the distinctive quality of his poems about animals, although Hughes didn't start writing animal poems to illustrate ideas about evolution. An animal poem was what happened in Hughes's imagination when the sight or thought of an animal connected him to that hotline to his unconscious that Al Alvarez was later to describe as his great strength as a poet. It was always the animal poems in his books that attracted the most curiosity, the most controversy, the most admiration. So central to his achievement are poems about animals that a graph of the artistic development Hughes underwent in the course of writing the three books he produced during his marriage to Sylvia Plath could be drawn through just three points set in place by the changing techniques evident in three animal poems: "The Thought-Fox" (written in 1956), "Thrushes" (1958), and "Wodwo" (1961).

Hughes wrote "The Thought-Fox" before getting to know Sylvia Plath, but it was she who gave the impetus to its publication, and its publication marked Hughes's debut as a promising young poet. "The Thought-Fox" came out in *The New Yorker* in August 1957, just before appearing in Hughes's first book, *The Hawk in the Rain,* and was immediately acquired for reprint in anthologies. That's an important kind of success, because anthologies are often where readers first get acquainted with a poet's work. On the other hand, poems appear in anthologies for predictable reasons: either the poet is indispensably famous—in 1957, Hughes wasn't, yet—or the poem is possible to "appreciate" without assistance from the poet's fame. "The Thought-Fox" is just that latter sort of poem. It unfolds the meaning of the metaphor expressed in the title.

To launch Hughes's *career,* however, required publication of a book and its recognition in the *press.* Because *The Hawk in the Rain* was a prizewinning book selected by a distinguished panel of American and English poets—W. H. Auden, Marianne Moore, and Stephen Spender—it received a good deal more attention than is common for poetry, especially for first books by unknown writers. Al Alvarez, reviewing *The Hawk in the Rain* for the London *Observer,* commented astutely that Hughes "hardly *thinks* at all" in "The Thought-Fox"; Hughes "apprehends the unwritten poem not as an idea or a feeling or a form, but as an ominous physical shock." This summarized what would prove to be the essential originality of Hughes's work throughout his career.

But "The Thought-Fox" is only Hughes's most famous, not his most Hughesian, lyric poem of the sort described—predicted—by Alvarez. In its last lines, "The Thought Fox" deliberately swerves away from its shock image, and limps to an ending:

> The window is starless still; the clock ticks,
> The page is printed

You can hear the poet dusting off his hands: that's all, folks.

The real Ted Hughes (in the sense pinpointed by Alvarez) stepped forth in his second book, *Lupercal,* with the poem "Thrushes." A blaring adjective ushers us into the poem:

> Terrifying are the attent sleek thrushes on the lawn,
> More coiled steel than living

The poet recoils not at the naked appetite the birds display—"attent" at their feeding—but at the smooth, skillful—military—manner in which they accomplish their purpose. Civilization robs men of this animal vitality, the poem suggests. When men are "attent," they are occupied in obsessive sublimation that places them above such naked appetites, in activity such as

> Carving at a tiny ivory ornament
> For years

It "terrifies" this man, on this occasion, to be gripped by this truth, to be suddenly desublimated, in broad daylight, crossing a lawn— some unspecified personal trauma has been released in him, to find expression in the poem's precisely worded imagery: *attent, sleek, coiled.*

Looking back over his own work late in his life, Hughes singled out "Thrushes" as a milestone in the process of developing his poetic method: suppressing a traumatic source and yet "mining it to the limit," in an image that displaces and transforms the personal. If the poem works for a reader, "terrifying" will not seem a ridiculously overstated emotional response. Hughes said he wrote the poem during the first year of his marriage to Sylvia Plath, sitting on the bed in their tiny apartment on Eltisley Avenue in Cambridge. He remembered the occasion because the technique of composition seemed to arise from a part of his brain he hadn't used before, and that he had used again in only a few poems; and that those poems were "special" to him.

He listed them: "Thrushes" was followed by "A Dream of Horses," which he wrote on Cape Cod in the summer of 1957; then "Pig," "Pike," "Pibroch," "The Howling of Wolves," "Gnat Psalm," and "Skylarks." They all have to do with animals; and they all can be seen, indeed, as illustrations of what Hughes meant by pointing to the trauma that underlay his most characteristic art—but avoiding a direct autobiographical method. They are poems that emerge from the solar midnight of his imagination, so to speak. What they keep dark are the ways they express Hughes's legacy of family dynamics: his mother's emotional absences and absorption in the unseen, his brother's mastery in hunting, his father's traumatized silence about the war. In an interview about his radio plays for the BBC, Hughes was asked about the use of violence in his work, "particularly the violence of war." "Well, you write about what you find in your head, don't you?" answered Hughes. "Thrushes" comes from that same part of his head: the part that thinks in images, about war.

The poem "Wodwo" forms the third point in the graph. It was published in *New Statesman* in September 1961, which suggests that it emerged from the matrix of Hughes's efforts to write for the theatre. The "wodwo" is a creature out of folk tradition, a beast in *Sir Gawain and the Green Knight,* with which the hero battles—that is, an imaginary animal available for redefinition by Ted Hughes. Hughes's poem finds a way to dramatize an animal mind and give the animal expressive speech. Hughes's wodwo is a questing, busy, subhuman amphibious creature that has been dropped, it knows not how, into a world where it must find out what it is by discovering what it wants. The sentences of the poem run on without much punctuation, producing the effect of a mind hurrying here and there, sniffing and testing.

> What am I? . . .
> Following a faint stain on the air to the river's edge . . .
> me and doing that have coincided very queerly

As he commented to an interviewer, animals are "continually in a state of energy which men only have when they've gone mad." The observing poet can feel his way into this behavior only by withholding the attempt to analyze it. Hughes's work for the theatre apparently freed him to relinquish the position of drawing a "lesson" from his observations, as he had done in "The Thought-Fox." The poem "Wodwo" is a trophy of that development in his art.

The volumes *Lupercal* and *Wodwo*, the work of his earliest maturity as a poet, contain many of the poems that he himself continued to value, as can be seen in the way he used them repeatedly—especially "The Thought-Fox" and "Pike"—in his radio broadcasts for schoolchildren: a good example is the essay "Capturing Animals," published in *Winter Pollen*. Hughes summarized the artistic goal of this procedure in a letter to the critic Keith Sagar. He was trying to tap a state of "alertness" toward something in nature that lies beyond our usual ways of identifying with other beings, yet is accessible to human consciousness, and can be signaled in the poem.

Uniting these works is Hughes's conviction that art arises from a specific kind of wound or trauma in the individual that is shared by a culture. Hughes believed that human beings in pain are manifesting through their speech their specific experience of suffering, the pain shared by the cultural milieu in which they have been formed. The cultural trauma dealt with in Hughes's poetry is our development, as a species, of the rationalizing consciousness that splits us off from the felt life of the instincts and makes us express them unconsciously, through sublimation, denial. The personal trauma behind Hughes's animal poems was the loss of his brother. Instead of getting over it, Hughes went into it, and discovered that Gerald had disclosed to him a primal connection to the predatory natural world from which all civilization is an expensive escape. Hughes's poems are meant to contact in the reader's imagination whatever survives of the reader's capacity to experience the primal emotions, our biological inheritance as animals. That is to say, all of Hughes's poems about animals emerge from his unconscious questioning of what it means to be a man—a male animal. Resistance to his father, resistance to his brother, what he can use and what he can't use in his legacy from them, press into his animal poems and give them a peculiarly powerful anxiety.

Fertility

If Sylvia Plath had been hit by a bus during the time they lived in London, from February 1960 to September 1961, we would never have heard of her. During those nineteen months in their London flat, while Hughes was prodigiously productive, she wrote only four of the poems that she eventually selected for publication in *Ariel*. She was almost wholly occupied with making a home and becoming a mother. True, by May 1961 she had completed her now famous novel *The Bell Jar*, but Hughes surely would not have wanted to publish it after her death—he disapproved of the satiric portraits of living people in *The Bell Jar*.

So Plath was not very productive as a writer while they lived in London. Yet one or another of the four poems that she had written in their little flat on Chalcot Square—"In Plaster," "Tulips," "Morning Song," and "Zoo Keeper's Wife"—can be found in most anthologies of twentieth-century poetry through which students are now introduced to the great works of Western literature. These poems marked Plath's turning point: Plath was finding her way into the imaginative core of *her* art, at the same moment that Hughes was making successful raids on his own distinctive subject matter. By the spring of 1961, after five years of marriage and the birth of a daughter, Plath had begun to outgrow her excellent education, and to investigate her most intense experiences as a female animal. These four poems contribute an expression of something that is new in contemporary poetry, which has come to be called, incorrectly, a "feminist" consciousness—the suffix "-ist" promoting the impression that a political position is being stated. But Plath's poems are not manifestos. They only do what poetry can do: track a significant emotion along pathways of associations, capturing the spoor in images.

In Plath's case, this was the emotion of being in a "wrong" body. Her "In Plaster" and "Tulips" express the theme of being physically inhabited by a powerful energy that, during an illness, splits off from a female body and declines to be coaxed back. Her "Morning Song" and

"Zoo Keeper's Wife" probe a related theme: the disquieting release of
energies that accompany the maturing of that body in wifehood and
childbearing.

Motherhood produced a momentous, surprising effect in Plath's
art. It extricated her imagination from the overwhelming influence of
Ted Hughes, investing it in the instinctual processes of being female.
Both Hughes and Plath wrote poems about their infant daughter.
Hughes's long, three-part "Lines to a Newborn Baby / For F.R. at Six
Months" was published in February 1961; he believed it had stimulated Plath to write the poem "Morning Song" (which he considered
"much superior"). "Morning Song" is one of Plath's most original and
accomplished poems, and very interesting to read alongside Hughes's
"Lines to a Newborn": you can watch Plath seizing important images
from Hughes and refashioning them to say something entirely different. A swab of imagery from each poem can reveal the symbiosis.
Hughes, warning the newborn about the kind of world she has
entered, illustrates with a metaphor:

> Here the hand of the moment, casual
> As some cloud touching a pond with reflection,
>
> Grips the head of man as Judith
> Gripped that one
>
> > ("Lines to a Newborn Baby")

And here is Plath:

> I'm no more your mother
> Than the cloud that distills a mirror to reflect its own slow
> Effacement at the wind's hand.
>
> > ("Morning Song")

In an interview, Hughes observed, usefully, that he and Plath deployed entirely different methods of composition. "My method was to

find a thread end and draw the rest out of a hidden tangle," whereas "hers was to collect a heap of vivid objects and good words and make a pattern." The contrasting approaches are evident in their poems about the newborn Frieda. Working from Hughes's images of the reflected cloud and the hand gripping the head, Plath produces the startling condensation "effacement at the wind's hand." "Efface-ment," a dreaded outcome of contact, is brilliantly deployed to suggest troubling self-discovery: the cloud produces its own mirror—the reflecting surface of pooled rainwater—as a woman has produced a simulacrum of herself in a child, and fears the loss of her former iden-tity. In Hughes the image is shockingly violent: a beheading. The dif-ference in the poems is Hughes's impersonality—he keeps the emotional charge of his metaphor out there in history, ancient history at that.

"Morning Song" works in the opposite direction: from emotional distance to joyful empathy. At the opening of the poem it is both par-ents that hear the first loud cry of the infant and gaze on it with stunned apprehension. Then the poem's female "I" steps forward to acknowledge that she cannot comprehend emotionally the transfor-mation into "mother" that the child's birth has brought about.

Plath focuses the poem on the woman's sense of alienation from the product of the concealed processes of her own reproductive organs—Plath's acute responses to her chronic menstrual problems underlie the atmosphere of dread in the poem. She probes this unfa-miliar new object with images that convey acute estrangement: a watch set ticking by some processes outside the parent's will; a statue in a museum; a rain cloud. We are ten lines into the poem before the baby evokes associations with an animal: first to a moth, and then to a cat (a mammal, at least!). The eventual attribution of warm blood to the baby reflects a warming and quickening of the woman's feeling. At the exact middle of the eighteen-line poem, the woman wakens to the sound of the baby's breathing; and at the sound of the baby's cry feels herself grow "cow-heavy." Plath's metaphor refers to the involuntary response of the female endocrine system to a baby's cry, releasing milk into the breast. As the baby nurses, the first light of dawn "whitens" the window, preparing the way for the feeling that swells in the poem's last lines:

> And now you try
> Your handful of notes;
> The clear vowels rise like balloons

The postpartum female body "knows" the infant's need and responds; but as the feeding ends, the biological connection becomes a social bond—joyful recognition of the meaning of the baby's actions.

Flattened into such a paraphrase, the poem loses subtlety along with emotional richness, and the gradual onset of maternal emotion *is* the poem. But there is a radical intelligence at work in the poem too, expressed in Plath's use of the baby's mouth as the active agent in their bonding. The woman has been dragged by instinct into the role of nurturing not only the baby's body but its human gift for speech. Human infants are wired for syntax, and start speaking in phonemes at a very early stage of development. And the parents' ears are attuned to this development: the mother cannot resist distinguishing in the infant's experimental babble a prototype of speech, any more than her breast can resist the animal cry of the baby's hunger. In this moment the two of them together have undertaken the baby's initiation into the mother tongue: where cry was, there vowels shall be; where vowels are, there words will form and metaphors arise.

Within the processes of the poem's secret life, Plath is doing a good deal of psychological work as well. In the psychotherapy Plath undertook in Boston, she had been given permission to hate her mother, permission she had recorded with glee in her journal. At that particularly dark moment in Plath's acquisition of maturity, "mother" meant not only Aurelia Plath (though it certainly meant Aurelia Plath), it was an ideal of femininity that created a lot of anxiety in Plath. In "Morning Song" Plath finds a way to reinstate the figure of the mother in her own lineage as a poet. For no infant can do for itself what the mother in Plath's poem is doing for her child: guaranteeing its well-being as it begins to make its way into words. For all her faults, Plath's mother had been a fierce defender and protector of Plath's talent. "Morning Song" undoes some of that "effacement" of the mother that a daughter needs to accomplish; it reinstates her in a position of exchange.

In "Morning Song," Plath's imagination solves the problem of being a woman poet, for within this configuration of infant and mother can be glimpsed an alternative understanding of the myth of the Muse. The poets who invoke her have traditionally been "he." She is always bigger than the needy poet whose existence depends on winning her favor; and her voice prompting him to words builds in his psyche a foundational confidence in his gifts of expression. His connection to her abundance enables his tongue to speak—not her language, but his own. Every human being, regardless of sex, arrives at the possession of language in the same way. So in Plath's poem, the suppression of the baby's sex opens the way for Plath's own identification with the evolution of linguistic mastery: female and male alike are connected to the Muse's power by the hungry tongue. Plath recognized the importance of this skillfully made poem; almost two years later she chose "Morning Song" to open the volume *Ariel*—the work that she forecast would "make her name" as an artist.

Right up until the very end of their marriage in the summer of 1962, Plath and Hughes continued to work in very close proximity to each other's very different writing projects. Hughes communicated something of the flavor of this partnership in a note he wrote about collecting his stories for publication. He recalled that "Snow" was prompted by a question Plath put to him, abruptly, back in 1956 when they were living in Cambridge. She asked him to think, quick, of an idea for a short story. Without hesitation, he replied, "'I'm a castaway, in world of constant snow, with only a chair . . .'" Hughes said he even visualized the chair, and later learned it was a Windsor chair. (He went on to furnish Court Green with Windsor chairs.) Hughes was convinced that this instantaneous creative response that flashed between them was proof that he and Plath shared a mind—that "one single mind" that each accessed by telepathy, and on which each drew for different purposes. This was an idea he held throughout his life, one he spoke about often, including in an interview he gave regarding the publication of *Ariel* in 1965. After Plath became a well-known writer, Hughes became twice shy, as the saying goes, and stopped remarking on it, though he clearly never stopped believing it.

Their working procedure—based on total confidence in each other—was immensely helpful to both of them, and sometimes it paid off. Those poems that each wrote about their baby daughter in 1960–1961 are a good example. It was the paradox of this creative relationship that, as Hughes observed shrewdly in that radio interview *Two of a Kind,* each was also conducting a secret life of the imagination. "Lines to a Newborn Baby" and "Morning Song" were quite evidently the product of the "one brain" shared by Hughes and Plath at the level of the dialogue between images; but Plath's poem is conducting a secret life as well, in which Plath is responding with resistance to her most influential mentor's published work.

By the time Ted Hughes and Sylvia Plath packed up their London life for the move to Devon, they had both accomplished much of what poetry wanted them to do. Plath was pregnant with their second child; and she was also carrying a fine nest egg to Devon, in the literary sense. *The Colossus and Other Poems* had been published the preceding October in London and was due out in the United States; she had received a major literary grant to support the writing of a novel that, unbeknownst to the foundation that awarded the grant, she had already written and packaged for incremental mailing as a progress report to the funding agency. The word "multitasking" hadn't yet been devised to describe this kind of juggling, but it was the way Plath satisfied her mutually exclusive aims of motherhood and productivity as a writer. She was capable of the most rigorous discipline, the most productive concentration in making use of the time she allocated for writing, and in both of these goals she had the unstinting support of Ted Hughes.

However, the publicity and celebrity attendant on his own success was making Hughes interestingly uneasy. Once ensconced at Court Green, he wrote to Gerald that it was a relief to get away from, among other things, "the nervous strain of being suddenly quite famous." That is, Hughes enjoyed being successful, but he did not wish to be on display. From now on, he would base his life in a secluded place and choose his own moments for making forays into the literary world. Somewhere along the way, Hughes had lost his taste for the nomadic life he and Plath had once envisioned. Or so he wrote to his friend Lucas Myers: Europe was too full of tourists, he grumbled. No, what Hughes aimed for in 1961, in buying Court Green, was to reconstitute some version of the family compound he had dreamed of for years. He floated the idea with Lucas Myers—who now had a family of his own to add to the mix and pressed it urgently on Gerald, again.

And he was already far along in the manuscript of his next book, *Wodwo.* It was to be a collection of poetry and prose—stories that Hughes considered worth salvaging, along with poems written after March 1960. The only part of the book that was unwritten when they moved to Devon was the section of concluding poems in *Wodwo:* "Song of a Rat," "Heptonstall," "Ballad from a Fairy Tale," "Mountains," "Pibroch," "The Howling of Wolves." All of these would be funerary poems for Sylvia Plath.

CHAPTER SIX

SEPARATING
(1962–)

During the six weeks between early April and mid-May 1962, Court Green became the earthly paradise that Hughes and Plath had only imagined when they moved from London in September. They had never seen Devon in Maytime, and now, in an abundance that engulfed the house and flowed to the very boundaries of the garden, great drifts of daffodils bloomed and were harvested by the dozens, bloomed and were harvested by the hundreds. Then the trees exploded into blossom: first the cherries, then the young peach tree Hughes had set where Plath could see it from her study window, then the six grand laburnum trees that endowed the grounds with golden rain. Hughes gloated to Plath's mother that Court Green was "soaked with hot sun from morning to night, like a great aviary." He reported that Plath was back at work in her study again—he and Plath had revived their routine of sharing child care and housework, freeing each for a half day of uninterrupted work on literary projects. In March, she had rapidly written a thirty-minute radio play about three women in a maternity ward, which she sold immediately to the BBC; in April, her poem "Tulips" had been published in *The New Yorker;* the American edition of her poetry book *The Colossus* was due out on May 14. After every morning's work she showed Hughes what she had written. An expert craftsman, he recognized the skill of Plath's powers of compression. He wrote to Aurelia in early May, "Sylvia is beginning to produce some really permanent poetry."

Hughes himself was traveling several times a month to London for work at the BBC. His life was agreeably punctuated by these trips, during which he could visit friends and art galleries and bookshops. Plath had for intellectual stimulation only the books she was sent to review for the London papers, and the radio broadcasts that she took care to enter on her household calendar when she spotted one she didn't want to miss. But she was hungry for real contact, real conversation, especially with other couples involved in the same kind of work. Just before leaving London she and Hughes had begun to form some genuine friendships among the literary people they mingled with as a side effect of Hughes's growing fame.

Among the most interesting to Plath were the delightful Suzette and Helder Macedo. The two couples had first met in June 1961, around the time that *Lupercal* was creating a big stir in the papers, mainly thanks to Alvarez's championship of Hughes as the antidote to gentility. The Hugheses had met Sylvester Stein at the cocktail party for Faber authors; his sociable wife, Jenny, organized an informal supper to introduce them to the Macedos. Poets should meet poets, she thought, and Helder was especially interesting, a Portuguese poet who had immigrated to London with his wife to escape the Salazar regime. Suzette, raised in Mozambique, was a skillful translator of works of Portuguese literature and history. She worked as a free-lancer, and in broadcasting, as a contributor on the BBC World Service. Suzette remembered that Plath was overdressed for the party, in a green satin dress cut like a cheongsam; Plath was often just slightly off-kilter in social gatherings, Suzette found. But she was vivacious, an eager conversationalist.

Getting acquainted, Plath found that Suzette shared the outsider's view of British food and British plumbing; they gossiped about clothes and cooking. Plath downplayed her own literary aspirations, telling Suzette that she wasn't in the same league with Ted, as a poet—which was true, at the time; but Suzette was surprised to learn later that Plath had a contract with *The New Yorker* and a book coming out that year. Helder thought Plath was expressing "old-fashioned female uxoriousness" that night, playing the role of "poet's wife." They saw each other as couples several times before the Hugheses moved to Court Green. "Ted was bored by the literary-social milieu and could find a way in five minutes to get from the margins of small talk into the center of a discussion of poetry," Helder said. "And he was *genuinely* curious. There I was, twenty-four years old, and could not go back to the country of my language. I was obsessed with trying to talk to the London natives about my tradition, my world, my coordinates, and this interested him." The Macedos had been one of the early guests to visit at Court Green, in September; they had stopped by for the afternoon on their way back from a holiday in Cornwall, and were led around the house and grounds by precocious little Frieda. It had been a welcome visit, all too short, but it gave Plath the hope that they could lure the Macedos and other sociable Londoners to Court Green, now that the weather was fine.

The first friends to accept an invitation were the writers Alan Sillitoe and Ruth Fainlight. They had all met the preceding spring at the award to Ted Hughes of the Hawthornden Prize for *Lupercal*—Sillitoe was on hand as a previous winner, for his short novel *The Loneliness of the Long Distance Runner*. Plath was especially fond of Ruth Fainlight: she too was an American, she too was a poet with a baby at the breast and an English husband with a brilliant career. During the visit, Fainlight recalled, she and Plath commiserated, over the heads of their nursing infants, about being "nobodies." After Fainlight returned to London, Plath sent her a copy of "Elm," a poem she was very proud of, and which she later dedicated to Ruth.

"Elm" is a disturbing poem, spoken in a savage female voice that emanates from the tree, an ancient fertility symbol. She occupies a place in Plath's imagery similar to that of the moon, always imaged as a crone, who has seen it all, is without empathy, and is strident about illusions such as those that underlay Plath's expectations of marriage.

> Love is a shadow.
> How you lie and cry after it
> Listen: these are its hooves: it has gone off, like a horse

The poem suggests that, somewhere below the threshold of rationality, Plath was detecting a shift in the emotional dynamics between herself and her husband, and that her uneasiness was finding outlets in her poetry. During early April, the second month back at her desk after the birth of her son, Nicholas, Plath wrote several poems in which she appears to be slowly waking up, as if from a lingering sleep, and feeling around in the disturbances, grasping them in imagery. In the five days between April 2 and 7, she rapidly produced a run of extraordinarily accomplished poems: "Little Fugue," "An Appearance," "Crossing the Water," "Among the Narcissi," "Pheasant."

Life at Court Green, even in its glory, was perhaps becoming just too hard on them. They were each spending many hours of each day minding the children while slogging in the house and garden and, during the other hours, scrambling to get the writing done that paid their bills. When work took Hughes to London—a four-hour journey by express train—he returned the same day. When he went out shooting rabbits or fishing in the nearby River Taw, it was to bring home food for the table. Rabbit stew and jugged hare appear in Plath's meal-planning notes for February and March; by early May, Hughes's letters to Gerald report that he is out at five in the morning twice a week, angling, for their breakfasts of trout. Hughes later characterized their life at that time as flawed by "the strangling quality of our closeness." The trips to London and the hunting forays gave him a change of scene, but Plath correctly recognized that there were deeper currents in his restlessness. Helder Macedo thought that Hughes had, by disposition, a deep hunger for privacy and "was always looking for a hiding place."

Plath was not prepared to deal with any changes in him just then. She was still dwelling mainly in the animal pen of the nursery, complaining about "the loving slovenliness of motherhood," but enjoying it too. In letters to women friends she called it "cowlike bliss." She had not yet fully reclaimed the independence of her body, nor did she wish to: she was engrossed in her infant son. Plath was breast-feeding him, and he was a big baby, nine pounds, eleven ounces at birth. Her writing conveys the deep animal satisfaction she took in prolonged physical intimacy with a nursing infant—she had breast-fed her daughter for ten months. Some of her most charming journal notes in 1962 show her soothing her irritable feelings by "nosing" and "sniffing" Nicholas, her "little sweet-smelling peach." To Gerald she described Nicholas as "well-behaved and full of smiles," whereas Frieda was "beautiful but of a rapid, hysterical temperament"; it was "a relief" to be greeted by the baby's "calm little face after one of Frieda's passions." Plath added that Hughes's relatives had observed a resemblance between Gerald and Nicholas, "dark, handsome, Farrar-looking."

Many of the comments that Plath and Hughes made about family life after the birth of their second child are phrased in just such oppositional terms as Plath applies in that letter, suggesting that the foursome at Court Green had subtly fissured into pairs, mother with son and father with daughter. Whereas Frieda's arrival had drawn Hughes and Plath together in passionate fascination, the birth of their second child required a redistribution of resources. Frieda was old enough to feel bewildered by sharing the spotlight. She needed consolation, which she got mainly from her father. He became her playmate as well as her caretaker.

Moreover, it seems that Hughes held rather ambivalent feelings toward his son. During Plath's pregnancy, he had acknowledged that he would greatly prefer the newcomer to be another girl. "I could do with ten daughters," he wrote to Lucas Myers, now a father of daughters himself. "Sons are just momentary hypodermic needles." And he too makes comparisons that convey favoritism. Hughes wrote to Aurelia about Nicholas, "He has a most complicated smile—Frieda's is just a 1,000 kilowatt radiance. He gives the impression of being safe. Whereas Frieda's a bit of a tempest."

These were some of the kinds of instability that already prevailed in the household when Assia Wevill arrived with her husband David to spend the weekend at Court Green in mid-May. The Wevills had taken over the lease on the Hugheses' flat in Chalcot Square back in September. Both David and Assia held day jobs as copywriters in advertising agencies, but David was pursuing a literary career.

They were a good-looking couple. David Wevill is remembered in those years by one colleague as "perhaps the handsomest man I have ever known"; by another as "a Fitzgerald character" with the "look of the young Gary Cooper." Assia had the kind of exotic beauty that turned heads—delicate features, dark eyes and hair, a voluptuous figure: "Babylonian," said a poet who recalled his astonishment the first time he met her. Assia pampered herself with good haircuts, frequent manicures, and stylish clothes selected to conceal her short waist and wide hips; she walked in clouds of Chanel. She was the daughter of a German Protestant mother and a Russian Jewish father; the family had immigrated to Tel Aviv during the war to escape the Nazis. To escape her parents, she had run off to London at age sixteen with a sergeant in the RAF, and married him. She divorced him to marry an intellectual who became a professor at the London School of Economics. Assia and David had met and fallen in love in 1956, while he was still a student at Cambridge and Assia was still the professor's wife: David was twenty-one, Assia was twenty-nine. They married in 1960, after Assia's second divorce. They had no children. Assia too had artistic talents; she was proud enough of her watercolors and sketches to display them in her home. She only dabbled in poetry, but her love of gossip made her a welcome addition to the literary circles

Assia Wevill in a boat on the Serpentine, 1960, here and on facing page.

where David was admired. Among the Wevills' London friends were the Macedos and Al Alvarez, and a loose band of other poets who called themselves the Group and met regularly to share their work: Edward Lucie-Smith, George MacBeth, Peter Porter, Peter Redgrove, Nathaniel Tarn.

Hughes had very purposefully put a good deal of distance between himself and London groups of this sort in moving to Devon, but both he and Plath were intrigued by the glamorous Wevills. Plath's household calendar shows that she planned to serve beef stew and gingerbread for dinner on the evening of the Wevills'

Assia Wevill

visit, dishes that could be prepared in advance, permitting her to join the conversation without keeping an eye on the kitchen. David Wevill recalled for biographers that Plath was an animated participant that night, "intelligent, witty, interested, good company." The four of them sat late at the big round dining table, talking poetry.

This dining table actually belonged to the Wevills. They had asked the Hugheses to keep it for them at Court Green, since it didn't fit into the tiny flat on Chalcot Square. Plath was the first to push back her chair and excuse herself from the conversation that night: she would be awakened early by a hungry baby. Before going to bed she called down asking Ted to join her. But he lingered with the guests. A rough, unpublished poem dated 1962 that lies among the papers in Hughes's archive appears to re-create that visit, and suggests that by nightfall Assia already had him under a spell. Titled "You are like the sunlight," the poem is a handful of images: a woman standing in a flood of noon sunlight watches goldfish gliding in and out of the shadows in a pool; the poet watches her. At evening, the poem says, her dark hair "wed" the darkness of the yew tree; the imprint of her warm body lingered in the grass, and her scent infused the night-blooming flowers; all night, he ached with desire for her.

By the time the two couples gathered at the table the next morning, Hughes was in love. Or so says a poem in *Birthday Letters*, where Hughes describes a dream Assia told at breakfast, about an enormous pike that rose out of a pool, bearing a fetus in the iris of its eye— golden, like the fish in the unpublished love poem in Hughes's archive.

If these events actually occurred in the manner Hughes describes them in *Birthday Letters*, they indicate a calculated act of seduction on Assia's part that was very like the one Plath had conducted years earlier at the St. Botolph's party, quoting "I did it, I" to him. Assia's dream refers to "Pike," a poem that was frequently mentioned in reviews of Hughes's work as an example of his originality. Assia was enough involved in the London poetry scene to have known this. Moreover, according to one of Assia's confidants, Assia had joked about setting out for Devon that weekend in "war paint," to seduce Ted Hughes.

"The Rabbit Catcher"

On Saturday afternoon, May 19, the Wevills returned to London on the train, as planned. The following Tuesday Assia sent Plath a warm letter accompanying the gift of a tapestry kit: Assia had gone to some trouble to find the pattern of roses and ribbons that Plath mentioned liking. Plath immediately began working on the tapestry—"gros point of gross roses," she called it—and according to her daily calendar, she kept at this needlework for the next five weeks, sometimes while listening to French and German refresher courses on the BBC. Those calendar notes strongly suggest that Plath had not yet become overtly jealous of Assia. Plath too had been stimulated by that visit.

Hughes was stimulated enough to hunt her down. Assia Wevill has been described as "rapacious," and that was precisely one of the attractions Hughes later ascribed to her in poems: she was like one of the big cats that hunters prize. His fascination with Assia began to surface guardedly in the frequent letters he wrote to Gerald, to which Plath often added notes. In one, Hughes mentions that divorce seems to be brewing among his acquaintances—he's come to expect it as a matter of course. In another, Hughes comments enigmatically that he thinks it is advisable to dynamite one's life at least once in a decade, just to find out what one can do without. He's ready for something new himself, he indicates. He mentions that he has begun to study German.

In late June, during one of his regular trips to London, Hughes made his move. He dropped by Assia's office, unannounced. Not finding her in, he left a handwritten note: "I have come to see you, despite all marriages." Assia showed this note to Suzette Macedo, who recognized the handwriting. Assia told Suzette that she had replied to this message by folding a rose between blank sheets of paper and mailing it to him.

Meanwhile, during the weeks following the Wevills' visit, Plath was writing poems that give off stark signals of distress: "The Rabbit Catcher," "Event," "Apprehensions," and "The Other." These were not poems about Hughes's infidelity, which Plath had apparently not yet detected; they were poems about feeling the tightly meshed gears of their relationship begin to disengage. In retrospect, that deterioration appears subtle and psychologically complex, and potentially terminal. For example: Plath borrowed from Hughes's abandoned play, *The Calm*, one of the mysterious metaphors in her poem "Event," likening the soul to a maggot. Hughes wrote, in a passage he eventually cannibalized for a poem titled "The Rescue,"

> a shipful of
>
> strangers
>   . . . all the sailors
>   white
> As maggots waving at the rail

Plath wrote, in "Event"

> Love cannot come here.
> . . . On the opposite lip
>
> A small white soul is waving, a small white maggot.

The internal resonances between these two poems is invisible to most readers. But *Birthday Letters* highlights this kind of exchange between them, which was such a distinctive outcome of their creative partnership, by including a poem to which Hughes gave exactly the same title as one by Plath, "The Rabbit Catcher."

Plath's poem is like a short story. A woman is walking on a hot day in the countryside when she spots a line of snares set by a rabbit catcher. She imagines the man who set them as waiting in his own kitchen in a state akin to sexual arousal, and envisions her husband as this man, and herself as his prey.

> hands round a tea mug, dull, blunt, . . .
> How they awaited him, those little deaths! . . .
>
> And we, too, had a relationship—

Plath's "The Rabbit Catcher" is unmistakably a response to "Rabbit Snared in the Night," a poem by D. H. Lawrence from which Plath draws a number of specific images, as well as the theme of sexual arousal. Lawrence wrote,

> Yes, bunch yourself between
> my knees and lie still . . . .
> What are you waiting for? . . .
> You have a hot, unthinkable desire of me, bunny . . .
> It must be you who desire
> this intermingling of the black and monstrous fingers of Moloch
> in the blood-jets of your throat
>
> Come, you shall have your desire
> since already I am implicated with you
> in your strange lust

During 1958–1959, the first year that Plath and Hughes allocated to becoming professional writers, while Plath was attempting to write their romance into *Falcon Yard,* she had turned repeatedly to Lawrence for inspiration—to be "itched and kindled," as she put it. She spent a whole day reading *Lady Chatterley's Lover,* "with the joy of a woman living with her own game-keeper," she wrote in her journal. "Why do I feel I would have known and loved Lawrence—how many women would feel this & be wrong!" In "The Rabbit Catcher," Plath seizes on Lawrence's first-person, present-tense use of sexual metaphors in "Rabbit Snared in the Night," and cleverly imagines a back-story. In Plath's "Rabbit," an ordinary man is sitting at a kitchen table, his hands circling a warm mug of tea as if it were a throat, before venturing into the night to inspect his snares. Plath's poem sits down across that table as a point of view—call it a wife's point of view, with Plath's whole memory behind it, in which D. H. Lawrence merges with Ted Hughes.

It was Ted Hughes who put "Rabbit Snared in the Night," into Plath's hands by presenting her with a set of Lawrence's poetry to celebrate the signing of the contract for her own first book. By 1962, Plath had also read and admired Hughes's story "The Harvesting," a surreal, violent fantasy refracted through the mind of a farmer watching a reaping machine reduce to stubble a field where a large hare will soon be flushed into the path of his gun—a brilliant insider's account of the killer instinct.

Her own gamekeeper. Had a relationship. As far back as they go, Plath had been drawn to the potential for cruelty in Hughes. The "snare" in her poem is, among other things, her own mind, capturing in this reference to Lawrence's rabbit catcher an insight into the predatory content of her husband's hidden fantasy life. If her husband shares traits with Lawrence's rabbit catcher, she shares the erotic position of the creature he has snared. These are psychological structures—"pegs too deep to uproot," as she writes in "The Rabbit Catcher."

By May 1962, when Plath wrote this poem, her art had begun moving out from under Hughes's influence, and out from under

Lawrence's influence too. April and May 1962 are the dates in Plath's *Complete Poems* in which arises the sudden, unaccountable concision of her late style. In the handful of poems she wrote that spring, Plath's talent has been transformed into what I think we can agree to call Plath's genius: the extreme, clenched assertion of metaphorical thought traveling in short stanza-bursts, each line a snare closing on emotional quarry. *Had* a relationship: she had begun the process of stripping D. H. Lawrence's sexual ideology from her imagination's core. "The Rabbit Catcher" is an elegy for everything that had to be outgrown in her femininity to acquire such clarity, such mastery within the medium of the distinctive poetic method and subject matter that would make her name. Defiantly, Plath sent "The Rabbit Catcher" and "Event" to Al Alvarez, hoping he would publish them on the Sunday *Observer* poetry page. He printed "Event" in December, after Plath had moved to London.

Hughes's poem "The Rabbit Catcher"—which was probably written much later—is in dialogue with this very aspect of Plath's poem: its resistance to him, and where it was coming from. He recalls watching Plath rip the snares from the ground.

> In those snares
> . . . Had you caught something in me,
> Nocturnal and unknown to me?

In most of the poems of *Birthday Letters,* Hughes has a ready explanation for Plath's behavior. "The Rabbit Catcher" is an exception. In this poem, he has questions; in this poem, he experiences his own strangeness, through empathy with her fear and despair. The odd adjustments he makes to details he draws from Plath's poem—adding bloody cuticles, replacing the white china with blue—suggest he knows he was being looked at when she made that image.

What had she seen? There is no evidence that Hughes had been sexually unfaithful to Plath before this time; but falling in love with Assia Wevill inaugurated a practice that he pursued for the rest of his life: the creation, alongside his marriage, of a kind of inner game preserve. Hughes's "Rabbit Catcher" suggests that he thought Plath had been clairvoyant about this turn his life was going to take. Not just that he would enter into an adulterous affair with Assia Wevill, but that his life as an artist henceforth would require his wife's acceptance of the sexual practices to which his deepest inspiration was attached. True North in Hughes's libido was the position of predator, imprinted in those early morning escapes from the claustrophobic family home in Mytholmroyd, dominated by his mother, out and up onto the moors with his brother. Escaping from the domain of actual women, the brothers wrote themselves into a complicated fantasy life of voyeurism and violent capture. That era of Hughes's upbringing retained its force in his imagination. And Hughes himself was a shrewd analyst of the role predation played in his creativity. In a letter to a scholar who was preparing an essay on ethical questions raised by Hughes's way of writing about fishing for sport, he was completely straightforward about the kind of allure that fishing held for him: it was a holding place for primitive impulses. He pointed to Jung's observation that psychotherapy served as just such a holding place. "Think of the many extreme ways in which 'civilized' individuals do keep something of that contact," he said; for example, in "hectic bouts of adultery."

In 1962, Hughes was about to make one of those developmental growth-spurts that go on occurring in adulthood, and reveal aspects of the character that have long been in formation but haven't yet asserted themselves. He was about to evolve the adult version of the secretive dual existence that had been a feature of his boyhood and adolescence, when he slipped away from his friends in town to go fishing and shooting. "Up to the age of seventeen or eighteen, shooting and fishing and my preoccupation with animals were pretty well my life," he said in an interview. "I also played with my town friends every evening, . . . kicking around the neighborhood. But weekends I was off on my own. I had a double life."

About a month after Plath wrote "The Rabbit Catcher," Hughes had his first assignation with Assia Wevill. And it was some time that summer or fall that Hughes began working on the version of *Difficulties of*

a Bridegroom for the BBC. In this radio play, he secreted allusions to
their affair: a man driving to a sexual liaison sees a rabbit in the road
and accelerates in order to kill it; on arrival in the city he sells the dead
animal for two shillings and buys two roses for his mistress. *Difficulties
of a Bridegroom* was broadcast on January 21, 1963, and Plath had ears
to hear. She snipped those roses and planted them in a poem satirically
titled "Kindness," again echoing D. H. Lawrence's "Rabbit Snared in the
Night."

> The blood jet is poetry,
> There is no stopping it.
> You hand me two children, two roses

In Plath's private retort to the private message she found in Hughes's
play, the rabbit/hare has acquired exchange value: they were playing
an obsessive game of tag with each other's images.

This brings us back to Hughes's dialogue with Plath's "Rabbit
Catcher." Back in May 1962, his imagination had abandoned Plath,
just as her imagination was deserting Hughes. Hughes's "Rabbit
Catcher" is not an acknowledgment of guilt or a plea to be forgiven.
Instead, it registers his retrospective recognition that he and Plath
had reached, simultaneously, the end of their apprenticeships as
poets. In actual life their romance had ended; the presence of their
children had reorganized the emotional dynamics of their household; and the tight hot intimacy of their sexual bond had been replaced by uncomfortable awareness of irreconcilable differences. In
their creative partnership, Plath had finally outgrown the usefulness
of the D. H. Lawrence figure in her education, and Hughes had
finally grown into the legacy of his early training as a hunter. The
consequence for each of them, as a married couple and as artists,
would be a separation. And though Plath's intuitiveness at their "bad
moments" cannot help but disturb him, he cannot help but admire
the work of art she made of it, either. The expressive power that rises
up in this pivotal poem in Plath's work, and in her as its author,
expresses an imagination alone with its own wildness, in the inner

geography where poetry is made. The volume *Birthday Letters* would be his tribute to that power in Plath.

Yet as the spring of 1962 deepened into summer, Court Green still seemed an earthly paradise to each of them, or so their letters indicate, and they liked showing it off. Hughes's parents visited, in late May, to inspect their son's new home "at its loveliest," as Edith Hughes exclaimed. Aurelia Plath would arrive in late June, to spend six weeks looking after the children, so that Plath and Hughes could work and travel unencumbered. In preparation for Aurelia's arrival, Plath festooned the house with hearts and flowers. She painted hearts on the sewing machine, on the mirror frame, on the cradle for Frieda's doll, and hearts-and-flowers garlands on the baby's cradle and on the threshold to Aurelia's room. She painted hearts and flowers and bluebirds on the children's furniture, and on the beehive in the back garden, where her latest project, keeping bees, was under way.

This efflorescence of sweetness expressed the genuinely optimistic side of Plath's outlook that spring, the outlook supported by satisfaction with her new writing. Ever since she returned to her desk in March, the bipolar currents of Plath's imagination had been running on both its circuits, positive along with negative. While the lower hand worked in the cold black ink of poems such as "Rabbit Catcher," the upper hand had been typing a warm and breezy romance that she meant to give Hughes as a birthday present. Apparently, Plath was resuscitating *Falcon Yard*, the project that had defeated all her efforts to write a novel during their year in Boston. Having finished *The Bell Jar* so expeditiously, perhaps she thought she could now tackle a sequel. A second title appears on some of the surviving manuscript pages from that project: *Venus in the Seventh*, an allusion to the position of the planet Venus in her natal horoscope. One evening when Aurelia and Plath were alone in the house, and Hughes safely out of earshot in London, Plath brought out the manuscript of this novel, and read sections of it aloud to Aurelia. Aurelia's notes do not mention a title, but she does mention that Plath described it as "upbeat" and said she was dedicating the novel to "Ponter," one of her lighthearted

nicknames for Hughes. While living in the United States, Plath and
Hughes had tried to supplement their income by entering slogan contests; he submitted entries under the name Ponter Hughes.

It had always been important to Plath that her mother receive only
the positive signals from Plath's complicated emotional circuitry—
especially regarding the choices Plath had made about her marriage
and her decision to live in England. Despite those painted sema-
phores of gaiety and the cozy occasions of sharing, Aurelia's visit was
giving Plath a good deal of difficulty. Aurelia later remembered "oppressive silences" between the couple. But Plath did not confide any of
her worries to Aurelia; on a drive home to Court Green from a shopping trip, Aurelia recalls, Plath told her, "I have everything in life I've
ever wanted: a wonderful husband, two adorable children, a lovely
home, and my writing." Plath had parked the car and begun to unload
the shopping, when she heard the *blat-blat* of the telephone. She
walked through the door and lifted the receiver, just as Hughes was
rushing down the stairs. The caller asked for Hughes. Plath silently
passed him the phone: she had recognized the voice of a woman pre-
tending to be a man, and knew who it was. When he ended the call,
she ripped the wires out of the wall and fled upstairs.

Hughes followed Plath up to their room, leaving Aurelia to tend
the children. Several hours passed. The baby, needing to be breast-fed,
grew fussy, then frantic with hunger. Aurelia finally took him upstairs,
knocked on the door, and found Plath and Hughes in bed ("though
not in any embarrassing position"); she passed him to Sylvia, then
went to dinner with one of the neighbors, Winifred Davies, the midwife who had delivered Nicholas.

The following day, Plath appeared at breakfast pale and shaky,
unable to lift a mug of coffee to her lips; after wordlessly meeting her
mother's gaze she rose and left the table. Later, Aurelia saw Plath and
Hughes talking earnestly in the back garden; Frieda rushed over to tell
her Grandma that Daddy and Mummy were both crying. Apparently,
Hughes was making a full account of himself to Plath. Shortly afterward, Hughes packed a bag, and they all drove to the station, where he
caught a train to London. Aurelia—who had thought the disturbing

phone call concerned some difficulty about their work—was taken aback when Ted said good-bye "with a strange little laugh" and told her he didn't know when he would see her again. Alone with her mother, Plath explained: Hughes had been unfaithful. She wanted him out of the house.

Immediately upon returning home to Court Green, Plath undertook a dramatic act of revenge. From Hughes's attic study she scooped up manuscripts and letters—"every scrap of paper she found lying loose," Hughes said later. "A clean-out." From her own writing table Plath took the pages of her novel. She dumped the papers in the stone courtyard and set them alight. Aurelia Plath witnessed the scene, and later wrote a letter about it:

> Sylvia had built a huge, blazing bonfire at the end of the cobbled courtyard. (Ted was in London.) I was caring for the children in the kitchen when I became aware of what was happening outdoors. As I stood helplessly in the doorway, with Baby Nick in my arms, struggling to keep Frieda from joining her mother, I saw Sylvia furiously ripping apart the thick Ms., the sequel to the BELL JAR. Distraught, I later brought up the subject of the destruction. All Sylvia would say was that the manuscript had symbolized a period of joy that now proved to have been built on false trust—the character of the hero was dead to her—this had been his funeral pyre.

Another source, who got the story from Plath herself, adds that along with the papers she took, Plath had scraped from Hughes's desk a scum of skin flakes, nail parings, and fallen hair, which she cast onto the bonfire while intoning magic spells; and that one paper fluttered into the air and fell to the ground, singed but readable, displaying the name of her rival, "Assia."

Escaping her mother's worried surveillance, Plath packed baby Nick into the car, leaving Frieda with Aurelia, and went to spend the night with her friend Elizabeth Compton. Aurelia sympathized; she understood that Plath could not face the empty marriage bed that night. A memoir by Compton recalls that Plath was deeply agitated when she arrived and needed to talk. "She told me that Ted was in love with another woman, that she knew Assia and was terrified of her. She wept and wept and held onto my hands, saying, 'Help me!'"

He Said, She Said

This was the way Ted Hughes detonated his marriage, or that Fate detonated the marriage of Ted Hughes. Had he set the timer to go off while Aurelia was visiting, so that she could look after Sylvia and take his place as baby-minder? No, Hughes would later claim, he left because he just couldn't bear to be in the house with Aurelia—Mrs. Plath's gushy sentimentality could be unbearable in large doses. His getaway on July 10 ignited a wildfire that raged out of control, though this was not his intention.

The night of his arrival in London, Hughes dropped in on the Wevills, bringing champagne: he told them it was his birthday. When David Wevill left the flat to buy cigarettes, Hughes told Assia that he was leaving Plath. Or so says a running account of Hughes's pursuit of Assia Wevill in the diary of the poet Nathaniel Tarn, who often got together with Assia for a gossip that Tarn annotated in his journal. He began taking notes in July and continued until a year after Plath's suicide, keeping track of the unfolding drama. (Hughes probably didn't know how freely Assia discussed him with others.) Assia expressed her pleasure that Hughes's manner was so resolute, so "virile"; she was impatient with David, because he had become indecisive, adrift. To get a reaction out of David, she had shown him the note Hughes left at her office, declaring his intentions. David hadn't reacted, which confirmed her judgment about his weakness and hardened her against him.

According to Tarn's diary notes, Assia spent the day with Hughes on July 11, returning home at her usual time, then dressing for a party at the Tarns. The Wevills had arranged to gather beforehand with some friends at a pub: Suzette and Helder Macedo, Al Alvarez—and Ted Hughes. He was staying with Alvarez, who had recently been divorced. By this time, Hughes had told Alvarez that he was leaving Plath, that he was in love with another woman; Alvarez thought he knew who it was.

On Friday afternoon the thirteenth, Assia met Hughes at a hotel, where they spent a long afternoon and evening making love. Assia was shocked at the way he treated her. She said that Hughes's passion was "violent and animal"; it had made her go "quite cold" on him. To Suzette Macedo, Assia added that she had expected something quite different, a romantic interlude. Assia had made all the arrangements for their meeting: she purchased a beautiful, expensive silk negligee for the occasion and ordered champagne and peaches. Hughes had not lived up to the role. He terrified her by tearing off the negligee, sweating profusely—it was not the consummation she envisioned, and she never wanted to see him again. Macedo, who knew Assia loved to dramatize herself and did not mind improving on mere facts, thought that Assia had been as thrilled as she was alarmed by Hughes. Later—much later—Hughes commemorated that day of their first lovemaking in a poem that he published twice, under two different titles, as memorials to the two women that he had first bedded on Friday the thirteenth and who later committed suicide. "Remembering it will make your palms sweat," says the poem, which is titled "Capriccios" in Assia's book, and "Superstitions" in Sylvia's. But in fact, Hughes misremembered the date he first bedded Sylvia Plath: it was not Friday the thirteenth.

When Assia returned home, late on Friday night, she found that her husband, David, had gone wild with jealousy. Assia, chastened by these misadventures, was now remorsefully looking after him. (Tarn commented to himself that David was Assia's "child-husband," and speculated that she hadn't outgrown the need for him yet.) Hughes went back to Devon after this eventful episode. He managed to stay in touch with Assia by telephone, somehow—the telephone at Court Green would not be back in working order until November—and "groaned" when he heard about David's misery. He promised to work behind the scenes to get some of David's work published in *The New Yorker*. He told Assia that in his absence Plath and little Frieda had been "having hysterics." Plath had crashed the car, possibly on purpose, and had ordered Hughes to return the Wevills' dining table.

By July 28, Assia was telling Tarn that she didn't want to conduct a "slinking affair" with Hughes in London, anyway. She said that Hughes would probably stay with his wife.

But what had been set in motion had its own momentum, in Hughes. His return to Court Green was no reunion. Plath's mother moved in with one of the neighbors on July 17, in order to give the marriage some privacy, though she continued to spend most of the day minding the children until her departure on August 4. Plath really had crashed the car—or at least run it off the road, and nothing was harmed—during Hughes's absence. Like burning his letters, it was an act of sabotage and an escalation of the war. Hughes continued to show up at Court Green, but spent more and more of his time in London. Though one of Plath's biographers claims that during these weeks Hughes and Plath were moving in a "civilized" fashion toward a trial separation, completing obligations before they parted company, Plath's letters and the recollections of friends suggest nothing of the kind. In letters, Plath referred to Assia, spitefully, as "this woman he is living with," who'd "had so many abortions she can't have children." For some reason, Hughes assured Plath that he didn't enjoy sex with Assia, she was inert as a "fish on a slab," a jab that Plath passed along to one of Assia's friends. However, Hughes and Plath did maintain an appearance of normalcy in public; they traveled together to Wales on poetry business, and one evening they joined Plath's patron Olive Prouty for a touristy visit in London, staying overnight as her guest at Claridge's and attending a performance of *The Mouse Trap*. In mid-August Plath signed up for riding lessons at a nearby stable.

The peculiarity of the situation prompted Plath to make self-canceling plans at both extremes of possibility. At the end of August she wrote to her mother that she wanted "a clean break" and was "going to try to get a legal separation from Ted." She also wrote to various members of Hughes's family informing them about Hughes's "desertion," and about "his utter faithlessness & irresponsibility." At around the same time she was inquiring into the logistics of spending a winter in Spain with the whole family—and planning a recuperative holiday for herself and Hughes in Ireland in September. Plath had arranged for them to go to Yeats country on the Irish seacoast, and stay in the guest quarters of Richard Murphy, a poet they had met on several occasions in London. She told some of her friends that she hoped to achieve a reconciliation with Hughes.

But Hughes had already made up his mind to separate from Plath. He later said that this decision to live apart—for a limited period of time, he assumed—had been "mutual," and that it was understood that he would be back in a month. As a concession, Hughes agreed to accompany Plath to Ireland, and to help her find a cottage to winter there with the children—she wanted some time away from Court Green. During their visit with Richard Murphy each of them spoke openly to him about their problems. Plath said she had resolved on a legal separation; Hughes said only that the marriage had been "marvelously creative" for him for six or seven years, but had now become destructive. "He thought the best thing to do was give it a rest." Several days into their visit, without bidding Richard Murphy farewell, Hughes set off on his own—Plath and Murphy thought that he had gone fishing or grouse shooting with an American friend— and didn't return, leaving Plath to make her way back to Court Green alone a couple of days later. A telegram from Ted in London was waiting for her, saying he might be back in about two weeks.

Actually, Hughes was in Spain with Assia. The two of them had been planning their surreptitious getaway for some time, Assia making elaborate excuses to Wevill about needing to visit family in Canada, Hughes arranging for the telegram to be dispatched to Plath from London, providing no return address. Plath didn't see or hear from Hughes for the rest of the month, and had no idea of his whereabouts; if the plan to separate had in fact been mutually understood, Plath's letters and conversations with other people during those weeks show no indication of it. When she wrote to her mother about Hughes's baffling absence and silence, she formulated a mournful phrase that would appear in her letters again and again as the distance between them widened: "Ted has deserted us."

Why did he bolt in this brutal manner? Shortly after Plath's death, Hughes wrote a remorseful explanation to Aurelia, in which he pleaded temporary insanity. A whole list of other reasons can be found in his letters to Gerald, where he speaks man to man. In early July Hughes merely hinted that he was being stifled by domesticity itself: "We can't invest body & soul for the safe future of a lot of chairs and window-curtains." After his meeting in London with Assia, he claimed to Gerald outright, without mentioning Assia, that the pressure of coexistence with Plath's extreme possessiveness had driven him away.

This "reason" is the sort of thing one says to justify a big decision after reaching a tipping point, of course, but Plath definitely was the jealous type, never more so than after Nicholas's birth, as is evident in notes she made about their Devon neighbors in 1962. When a pretty sixteen-year-old neighbor began dropping by, Plath started acting like a proctor. Plath writes with just a shred of irony about an afternoon when, hearing the sound of voices below stairs, she "flew down with the baby & materialized at the front door," to find Hughes and the schoolgirl standing "like kids back from the date, she posed & coy." The girl was returning some phonograph records, a mere pretext to see Hughes, Plath opined. Plath dispatched the girl but not the mood of outrage: "For some time I seriously considered smashing our old & ridiculous box victrola with an axe. Then this need passed, & I grew a little wiser." This was not a unique incident of jealous fury, as Plath's earlier journals show. "The one factor that nobody but close friends can comprehend is Sylvia's particular death-ray quality," Hughes wrote to Gerald. "In many of the most important ways she's the most gifted and capable and admirable woman I've ever met—but, finally, impossible for me to live married to."

Hughes's explanations to Plath, or at least Plath's reports of his explanations, pointed to another of her character traits, and brought his disaffection home in a single, wounding word: "sentimentality." "He says all the kindness and sweetness I loved & married him for was mere sentimentality," Plath wrote to her patron Olive Prouty. To her mother, she wrote, "he now thinks all feeling is sentimental & womanish." Hughes may have been alarmed at the way Plath had thrown herself into nesting and motherhood, from the time they left America; and even with a baby at the breast she was writing home about wanting *more* babies. Thus, he may have feared what was portended by those little hearts and flowers Plath was painting so zealously on the cradles, the lintels, the thresholds to the rooms they shared—that she was turning into another Aurelia. The insistent gooey hype in Plath's way of talking and writing to Aurelia about their life may be an example of what he meant by "sentimentality" (wonderful husband, adorable children, lovely home, etc.). It was not just that he disliked the language; he disliked the way it boiled the wildness out of life and bottled it for consumption in irreproachable adjectives. (His own mother's letters use similar phrases: this may be why he chose "womanish.") A few months after they had separated, once Plath resettled in London, Hughes was ready to see the breakup as all for the best, no matter what it had cost. "Now the storm-centre of it recedes into the distance, I can only be relieved that I've done it." And much later, he said that their separation had given Plath necessary room to develop; by the time of her move to London, he said, "she was quite a changed person—greatly matured and a big personality."

Distancing himself from Plath wasn't just the release of a stranglehold, then; it had a positive aim. In one of his letters to Gerald that summer, Hughes said he thought that his puritanical upbringing in Yorkshire had made him too tolerant of deprivation. Now physically fit again, he longed to replenish in himself a "natural supply of joy," and to reinstate some of the old "irregularities—by which I exist." Hughes's biographer quotes a friend's comment that there wasn't much sex in the Hugheses' marriage in 1962. To the extent that Hughes had a well-defined purpose in leaving Plath, it may have been to reorganize their lives to accommodate changes they had undergone since the days when they found themselves perfectly matched. Their physical intimacy may have dwindled, but they apparently still showed each other almost every piece of work they were undertaking—though apparently Plath hadn't shown him the novel she was planning to give him for his birthday, since he later claimed emphatically that it didn't exist. Yet even if this tight working relationship was still functional, even if it loosed the wildness in each of their imaginations,

Hughes had developed other kinds of desires that were never going to be satisfied inside a marriage. He wanted to be out from under her watchfulness; he wanted the hunter's freedom to roam.

It may well be that Hughes's role in raising his spirited little daughter figured in this development. Hughes spent several hours each day in charge of a two-year-old human reservoir of joy, and loved her deeply. His attunement to her was showing up in his work for the BBC, where he had begun presenting programs on writing for broadcast to schools. While these broadcasts were intended for older children, the voice in them has a distinctive ease and lack of condescension: he appears to think it worthwhile to be understood by children. Separation from Frieda caused him great distress, as he wrote to Gerald: "The main grief for me is that a life that had all the circumstances for perfection, should have been so intolerable, and that little Frieda loses a father. . . . She's been my playmate for two years and become absolutely a necessary piece of my life." How could he desert her, then? Did he see himself as correcting the mistakes of the older generation? Was he giving his children the example of another kind of parent than his own had been? Perhaps so, because in Hughes's moral code, preserving the life of the instincts was an *ethical* action. Embracing Assia, Hughes was rescuing his instinctual life from suffocation.

And perhaps he even thought Sylvia Plath might come to understand these aims, with the passing of time.

CHAPTER SEVEN

PARTING
(1962–1963)

Ted Hughes returned to Court Green during the second week of October to pack his clothes and books and papers, and move out. He had hastily arranged temporary lodgings in a London flat that Dido Merwin had recently inherited from her mother and was dismantling for sale. Perched in a room furnished only with a bed and a few boxes of possessions, he would be taking up the way of life he had abandoned to marry Plath—bachelor occupant of a borrowed flat, driving a borrowed car.

Plath unwisely insisted on getting information out of Hughes while he was gathering his belongings to leave Court Green. Where had he been? Why had he tricked her? Did he mean to abandon his children? How much money had he spent? How good was the sex with Assia? Unfortunately, he answered her questions—"fed me the truth, with leer after leer," she told her mother. These awful days revived the dread Plath had felt when she was first getting to know Hughes back in April 1956 and had confided in her brother, Warren, that she worried about Hughes's character, especially his reputation for loving and leaving. She assured Warren, then, that she would be the exception to the rule. Now, she wrote to Warren, Ted was, horribly, "reverting to type."

Bewildered by Hughes's behavior toward her during his last days and hours at Court Green, Plath threw herself on her motherly friend Winifred Davies, the midwife who had taken Aurelia Plath under her roof that summer when trouble erupted. Mrs. Davies did her best to comfort Plath and help her to cope with the panic, but to Aurelia she wrote frankly. Davies believed that Hughes was rebelling against Plath's take-charge personality: "no man really likes that." She also thought she detected in Hughes a good deal of hostility toward baby Nicholas, which she diagnosed as "jealousy of the male." Merely immature, and selfish, he was acting on impulse but doing irreparable damage, she feared, and he was going to regret losing his family once he'd come to his senses.

Hughes himself wrote, much later, a poem about that turning point in his life, "The Mythographers," which finds an explanation for his behavior in the myth of Lilith, the name assigned in the Apocrypha to the Other Woman that God himself created. What Davies classified as immature, Hughes experienced as absolutely instinctual. In Hughes's account, Lilith is the biological female attractant that accounts for the polygamy of the hapless male.

> Her saliva: instant amnesia.
> The cries of his children: pangs
> . . . as he falls, euphoric

Plath observed bitterly that Hughes was humming as he packed to go.

Plath Turns Thirty: *Ariel*

Plath's letters about Hughes's disappearance and final leave-taking are wild with pain. The worst things that *could* happen to her *were* happening to her: she was being deserted; her man was in love with another woman; he was moving to a literary life in London; he was leaving her stranded in the country with the two children—a situation all too similar to the one that had sidelined her own mother. She stopped eating and started smoking; she stopped sleeping and started taking pills to knock her out.

Naturally, and she wanted revenge. As her sense of outrage intensified, Plath began pulling around her a network of other women she could count on to take her side. She found a nanny, Susan O'Neill-Roe, who treated her like a sister. She wrote furious inflammatory letters across the Atlantic to older women with sympathetic eyes—her psychotherapist, Ruth Beuscher; her patron, Olive Prouty; her mother—and received worried letters advising her to pursue legal action against Hughes. Plath followed this advice, and consulted a solicitor in London. She resolved to seize the initiative, and get the upper hand. "If I am divorced," she said, "he can never be unfaithful to me again." Possibly, she even hoped for a dramatic showdown; Assia told Nathaniel Tarn that Plath was naming her in a divorce suit and had engaged a detective to gather evidence. Did she? Intriguing, entirely inconclusive evidence is on offer in Plath's poem "The Detective," written while Hughes was still mysteriously absent.

Plath had eerily forecast a fate like this in "To Ariadne, Deserted by Theseus," the poem she had written as a teenager. Once the hero's ship had disappeared over the horizon, her imagination took charge. Shortly after Hughes's departure she settled into the routine of rising very early and working in her study until the children awoke. Plath was lonely, but her work profited from the lack of distraction, and she rejoiced in the sole possession of her personal island. Hers was the hearth and the children's playroom, hers the orchard and garden, with its hive of honeybees; and she brought to bear on these surroundings not only the whole weight of her grief but the whole weight of her knowledge. Confined by circumstances to Court Green, she retreated to circuitries installed throughout years of education—booklearning, writing, mothering, and housewife's lore. She wrote to Olive Prouty, "I have never been so happy anywhere as writing at my huge desk in the blue dawns, all to myself, secret and quiet."

As the poems flowed out of her, their real project began to clarify. The problem Plath was working on actually had little to do with the grievances against Hughes that she wrote into her disparaging letters. The poems focused almost exclusively on the hidden dynamics of family relationships. The emotional problem-solving Plath conducted in them addressed one large, specific task: divesting herself of an idealization of a fatherly male. Plath was well aware she had required Hughes to play a paternal role in her life, and had benefited from his mentorship, his protective encouragement of her prodigious talent. Her sense of security—false, as it turned out—rested on a belief in his superiority to her. By the time he left for good, the month of her thirtieth birthday, she had a conscious, humiliating, and enraging grasp of her own self-deceit.

During those weeks of solitude, while Plath was islanded in Devon, the lesson began to seep into the workshop of her psyche, where her metaphors were made. This was the turning point in Plath's maturation as a poet: for the first time, she permitted rage to fuel her art. Rage is not a common source of inspiration in the work of any artist, and it is small wonder that Plath resisted its force in her own imagination. Now she let it fly. Before Hughes emptied his study in the attic at Court Green, Plath had been there ahead of him and had helped herself to typescripts of his recent work. After his departure, when she sat down in the early morning dark with her mug of coffee, these pages were her goads to action, and she treated them as opponents in hand-to-hand combat—literally, what with his typing on one side of the paper, her handwriting on the other.

Writing from 4:00 A.M., when her sleeping pills lost efficacy, until eight, when the children needed her attention, Sylvia Plath was more productive than ever before in her life, the negative circuit of her creative energy fine-tuned and running at maximum efficiency. During those months of absorbing the blow of desertion, Plath's imagination was gripping hard on the useful insight that hers was specifically a woman's experience. The positive emotions liberated by this discovery were sometimes maternal: Plath took poetry into previously mute territory in writing about a woman's relations with the infant that had emerged from her body. But sometimes they were brutal.

"Daddy"

If we had to choose only one poem by Sylvia Plath on which to stake a claim to her importance, it would have to be "Daddy," Plath's brilliantly, playfully savage nursery-eye view of the domestic life of a few of Western culture's male authority figures: the father, the professor, and the military officer. The poem is poised between a daughter's tender nostalgia for a father loved, feared, and lost early in life, and that daughter's enraged recognition, at thirty, of the cost of her emotional collaboration with domination by a strong man. A first encounter with this angry poem—it endorses parricide—often knocks readers to the floor, and once they get up and dust off, such readers often turn their backs on Plath for good.

But Plath wasn't addressing these urgent words to her actual father, Otto Plath, though the poem is charged with feelings about him. And though she wrote the poem the day after Ted Hughes moved out of Court Green, apparently abandoning his own role as father, she wasn't writing about him, or only about him, either. No, she was saying good riddance to the attitude behind all those poems she had written in which fathers appear larger than life: as a sea god in "Full Fathom Five," as the hero Agamemnon in "Electra on Azalea Path," as the broken monumental sculpture of "The Colossus." In all of these, a daughter devotes herself abjectly to the service of memorializing an idealized father.

This, exactly, was the psychological program that had shaped not only Plath's poems about fathers, but her search for a husband, as she well knew. In fact, at Cambridge, after Richard Sassoon disappointed her marriage plans, Plath wrote in her journal about her "lust" for a father substitute, her longing "to live with the rich, chastened, wise mind of an older man. . . . I must beware, beware, of marrying for that." As if on cue, Ted Hughes had entered her life: a man she considered older and wiser, whose violent language and rough behavior had really turned her on, and with whom she could act infantile—it was love at first sight. In "Daddy," Plath rebukes herself for not following the good advice she had given herself in her journal: "beware, beware." No, she had fallen for a father figure:

> I made a model of you,
> A man in black with a Meinkampf look
>
> . . . And I said I do, I do

Plath expected her audience to recognize the Freudian principle behind these lines, that the woman's choice of marriage partner was scripted by the girl's emotional bond with her dad; and fathers were supposed to be disciplinarians. Her poem assumes that other women were going to find in the nursery rhymes of "Daddy" an explanation of their own love-hate relationships with strong men. The "I" in the poem gives the reader a place to stand to get a good angle on the mirror. Plath's powerful fantasies about her father provide some high-octane fuel in the poem, but "Daddy" is about more than that. It's about a girl's collusion with a man's sense of entitlement to be in charge of her; and it's a ferocious work of art that—riffing on a single vowel sound and offending left and right—has a lot in common with rap lyrics. How many things can you find to end in "ooo"? Plath starts out slow, with "do," "shoe," "blue." But the higher the ground of the trespass, the better the poem—that's the principle of satire. So: how about "*du*," the pronoun reserved for intimacy, for children, and for animals in the German language? Come to think of it, how about "Jew"? Rhyming has its own wicked logic, and once it gets going—well, here's where it leads:

> [Since] I thought every German was you . . .
> I think I may well be a Jew

"Daddy" is a virtuoso *performance.* When Plath read it to her friend Clarissa Roche during her visit to Court Green in November, Plath got the two of them rolling about the floor hooting with laughter.

Another battlefront in Plath's artistic maturation during those months was separation from her mother. At some point before leaving Court Green to move to London that December, Plath got rid of *all* of Aurelia's letters, hundreds and hundreds of them. And shortly after writing "Daddy"—possibly as a consequence of writing it—Plath wrote an ugly, muddled poem titled "Medusa," that puns on her mother's name. "Medusa" is the name for the immature stage of the *Aurelia* genus of jellyfish, and Plath draws symbolisms out of the resemblance of the body of a jellyfish to a placenta, its tentacles to the umbilical cord. Plath was attempting to divest herself of traits in Aurelia that had earned Hughes's derisive label "sentimental." How could she be motherly without extruding hearts and flowers? Most of Plath's women friends at that time were mothers, and she was actively seeking common ground with them. Notably, on the night Plath discovered Hughes's adultery, she had fled from Aurelia and had sought help from another mother, Elizabeth Compton, a woman her own age. Once Aurelia had returned to Wellesley, Plath again turned to her for moral support. But writing "Medusa," splitting off and silencing this aspect of Aurelia, seems to have cleared some psychological space for the positive images of mothering that infuse other poems of *Ariel*.

Indeed, it seems to have been childbearing that triggered Plath's imaginative metamorphosis during 1962, anchoring her imagination in her womanhood. Plath had always drawn her notions of how to live from literature. Virginia Woolf's published diaries had been a uniquely important resource to Plath in this regard, unique because Woolf was the only female writer whose name appeared along with that of Eliot, Joyce, Lawrence, and Proust on the reading lists from which college students drew their understanding of literary Modernism. But during the months of autumn and winter 1962–1963, while Plath was absorbing the truth that her separation from Hughes was irremediable, inescapable, and opportune, she began reading the work of other women writers. In August, Plath received from her American friend Anne Sexton a copy of *All My Pretty Ones*, the book of poems on which Sexton had been working while they both attended Robert Lowell's writing seminar at Boston University in 1959. Plath thanked Sexton in a warm letter of appreciation. "I was absolutely stunned and delighted" with the book, she wrote. "It is womanly in the greatest sense." A couple of months later in an interview recorded for the BBC, Plath elaborated: Plath admired Sexton's "wonderfully craftsmanlike poems" because they explored "private and taboo subjects" such as being "a mother," and "a mother who has had a nervous breakdown," at that.

    In her own poetry about her children, Plath picked up where Sexton left off. Plath's poems on the taboo subject of motherhood take various forms, but all of them are a variety of custody battle. An aggressive example can be found in one of the poems Plath read on the occasion of that interview in London, "Nick and the Candlestick." It explores what was happening inside the family circle minus Hughes, as Plath sat alone with her baby son at the breast, in a chilly room lit by a candle. In the version Plath read for the BBC, the candlestick is described as a kneeling brass Atlas wearing a panther hide, and "Under the gold bowl of his navel where his phallus and balls should be, a panther claw . . ." The phallic animal Plath associated with Hughes in "Pursuit" has shrunk to the scale of a table ornament, while the infant's presence swells to fill the firmament emptied by Hughes's departure.

> You are the one
> Solid the spaces lean on, envious.
> You are the baby in the barn

Plath's importation of a Christ-child icon in the very last line changes the poem's gears. Unto us a child is born, unto us a son is given: the empty space around the shabby little brass god has been enlivened by the warmth and weight of the living male child in her arms.

The poems in which Plath grappled with Hughes over their daughter are emotionally more complex. They focus on taking Frieda back from Ted, by usurping images from his poem "Full Moon and Little Frieda." Hughes's poem, written during early spring 1962, dramatizes the spontaneous artistry of a young child who is just learning words. It is a quiet evening in the poem, the moment of moonrise, and the child is depicted as taut all over with her attentiveness, like

> A spider's web, tense for the dew's touch.
> A pail lifted, still and brimming—mirror
> To tempt a first star to a tremor

The water in the lifted pail mirrors the sky, and is thus a metaphor for the child's uplifted face; the precision of "brimming" conveys that the rapt passivity of the child's watchfulness is a moment charged with creative possibility. When the child connects thing with word, she does so in an explosive, joyous repetition of a syllable: Moon! Moon! Moon! Moreover, "Full Moon and Little Frieda" is one of those works that reflect Hughes's artistic collusion with Plath. It advances from the point in Frieda's development where Plath's "Morning Song" left off: in Plath's poem, the infant's reach into language is configured in the image of rising balloons ("now you try / Your handful of notes; / The clear vowels rise . . ."); in Hughes, the round moon rising elicits the enclosure of vowels within consonants, notes morphing into words.

Plath, of course, was aware of this genealogy. In the call-and-response manner of their productive collusion, they had established this core vocabulary during 1960 in the poems they addressed to Frieda shortly after her birth. In poems written after their separation, Plath returned obsessively to two of Hughes's images in "Full Moon"—the mirror-pool and the star trembling on the water's surface. These mutate in Plath's poems to convey profound, aching abandonment.

> Intolerable vowels enter my heart.
>
> The child in the white crib revolves and sighs, . . .
> Then there are the stars—ineradicable, hard.
> > ("Event")
>
> The dew makes a star
> > ("Death & Co.")
>
>   this dark
> Ceiling without a star
> > ("Child")
>
> From the bottom of the pool, fixed stars
> Govern a life
> > ("Words")
>
> The mirrors are sheeted
> > ("Contusion")

Submerged in these images is Plath's recognition that all her own separation issues had been revived by Hughes's desertion. According to Hughes, a typescript of "Full Moon and Little Frieda" was lying on Plath's desk at the time of her suicide. Little Frieda herself was inconsolably sad, as Plath's stricken letters show; and Plath identified with that infantile, daughterly grief—these were the poems in which Plath mourned for Hughes.

But Plath had also found a poetic voice for everything that was positive in her single state, in "Ariel," the celebratory work she made on the day she turned thirty, October 27, 1962. Ariel was the name of the horse Plath was learning to ride that fall. Riding lessons were a very agreeable distraction from the difficulties of managing Court Green, "having to take on all a man's responsibilities as well as a woman's," she wrote to her aunt. Plath's morning hours out on Dartmoor also gave her welcome relief from child care, and deepened her friendship with another woman in the protective network she was weaving, the riding mistress. Though Plath's English friends later expressed condescending amusement toward Plath's grandiose references to this workaday horse, Ariel, it is evident from Plath's letters that her developing confidence in riding was a source of genuine pride, and that she felt a powerful bond with the animal.

This raw material underwent miraculous condensation, refinement, and elevation to produce the poem. "Ariel" is the monument in Plath's poetry to the adrenaline rapture of the militant emotions seeking expression in her art. In "Ariel" Plath reclaims freedom for the female artist's body, detached from the child; and she alludes to herself in archaic language: "God's lioness," "the arrow." The female warrior on horseback. As the horse's pace accelerates, the wail of the child she has left behind fades to inaudibility. Someone else will mother the baby this morning. Stripped of all distractions, rapturous in the flow of thought and movement, she loses herself in the momentum of her purpose, reaching the instant of sunrise in the mind:

> at one with the drive
> Into the red
>
> Eye, the cauldron of morning.

Riding, writing. She had written twenty poems that month alone, a dozen of them since Hughes's departure—"Terrific stuff," she reported to her mother, "as if domesticity had choked me." But this was the poem from which Plath finally selected the title for the book she assembled in November 1962 out of the work that burst from her motherhood and her desertion by illusions about Hughes. The volume *Ariel* is the sublime scrapbook of Plath's integration of the duties of her domestic life with the requirements of her art. For about six weeks, Sylvia Plath's actual world was a realization of the aim she had set herself in a journal entry a year after she married Ted Hughes. She had been reading Virginia Woolf's *The Waves*, admiring Woolf's skill at putting commonplace experience into unforgettable images. "I shall go better than she," Plath vowed. "I will be stronger: I will write until I begin to speak my deep self, and then have children, and speak still deeper." Writing the poems of *Ariel* was the way Plath kept that promise.

London on Her Own

Plath had finished all the poems for her new book by December 2. These productive months in her study at Court Green were merely a period of transition in Plath's living arrangements, however. Plath did not intend to spend the winter there. During early September she had entertained a fantasy of living in a little cottage in the West of Ireland, mainly to avoid curiosity and escape painful associations, but in October, her mood elevated by the quality of her new work, Plath decided to advance rather than retreat: she would move to London.

She prepared herself by getting a new look. Her hair had grown very long; it swung to her waist when she let it fall; she usually braided and coiled into a crown atop her head, like a German *hausfrau*. Now she had the front restyled to feather around her face, softening the lines. She had lost a lot of weight and regained the trim figure of her youth; she bought new clothes and shortened old ones. Feeling quite chic, she made several trips to the city, where she confronted the literary world—which was full of Hughes's cronies—with an air of confidence she didn't feel, and made it known that she was glad to be on her own—the point being, she told her mother, "so they won't picture me as a poor, deceived country wife." Plath startled a whole roomful of London writers at the end of October, at a party sponsored by PEN, when she went around the room systematically informing acquaintances that Hughes was having an affair with Assia Wevill, and that she was divorcing him.

In November, Plath's spirits soared when she found a large flat on two floors at 23 Fitzroy Road, in the same neighborhood where Frieda was born. It was the very building that Plath had spotted back in 1960, when she and Hughes were entertaining fantasies about buying a house in London—the building where Yeats had lived as a boy. A round blue plaque bearing Yeats's name stood above the entrance where she would come and go with her own children: to Plath, this felt like destiny. The local tradesmen remembered her too—only fourteen months had passed since Plath's move to Devon. "It was like coming home to a small loving village," Plath told her mother. And since Assia and David Wevill had recently moved out of the Hugheses' old flat at nearby Chalcot Square into a larger one in Highbury Fields, chance encounters with the Wevills were unlikely.

However, Plath kept a jealous eye on her elegant rival by staying in contact with their mutual acquaintances, most of whom had addresses in or near the same area of London. On her business trips that fall, Plath usually stayed overnight with Suzette and Helder Macedo, in Hampstead. Suzette was warmly sympathetic, and lavished welcome on Plath. But Plath knew that Suzette was also friendly with Assia; they often met for lunch and gossip. When Plath spent time with the Macedos, she was determinedly upbeat, self-confident, full of plans; Suzette felt sure that this behavior was meant to be communicated to Assia. One night, Suzette was awakened by the sound of weeping; she went to the door of the guest room, and saw Plath deeply asleep, sobbing, her face bathed in tears. The next morning, Plath left the house before the Macedos awakened, but under the jar of Nescafé on the kitchen table they found the typescript of "Poppies in October," a poem Plath had written on her birthday and dedicated to them. (The dedication was not included when the poem was published in *Ariel*.)

Sylvia Plath with Frieda, December 1962

Sylvia with Nicholas, December 1962

Sylvia Plath showing her restyled hair, with Frieda and Nicholas, December 1962

Plath moved out of Court Green on December 12. Living on her own in London was, at first, a source of relief. "I am out of Ted's shadow," she wrote to Olive Prouty. She lost no time redecorating the London flat, giving it a look deliberately different from the décor of the home she had made with Hughes. She painted the walls white and the floors deep blue—she thought Hughes didn't like blue—and she laid rush matting as an inexpensive substitute for carpets; for seating she bought straw-and-iron "Hong Kong" chairs. Her bedroom walls were papered yellow and white, the floor had a straw mat laid over a black border: "bee colors," she told her mother. This bright room, facing the rising sun, would be her study as well as her sleeping room.

Plath occasionally punctuated this hectic activity to luxuriate in her new surroundings. The weather was mild; she could picnic with the children on Primrose Hill and walk them to the zoo. During those weeks, Plath often wrote to her mother and others of the joy and comfort her children gave her. Baby Nicholas was cheerful and no trouble on these excursions. Frieda, now two and a half years old and very outgoing, was positively a companion, on a good day. Plath was proud of Frieda's lively mind and began imagining ways to share with her children the literary salon she expected to conduct in her London flat when they were older.

The only missing element in Plath's well-planned life was a live-in nanny to occupy the room she had prepared. Without a baby-sitter she could not earn a living to supplement the support Hughes would be paying for the children. Hughes had turned over their joint bank account to her when they separated and had borrowed money to live on himself for the duration, but their ongoing financial arrangements were as yet unsettled.

Doubletake

Writing for money meant writing prose. *The Bell Jar* would be published early in the new year; Plath considered it comparable to *The Snake Pit,* a novel about incarceration in a mental hospital, which had been made into a movie starring Olivia de Havilland. Plath had

high hopes that her own
novel about madness
would establish her cre-
dentials as a writer of
popular fiction. She had
decided to publish *The
Bell Jar* under the pseudonym Victoria Lucas,
partly because it was so
autobiographical. But
possibly Plath also had in
mind establishing another
authorial identity, with a
different name, who
would write for money.
She had toyed with the
idea in 1958: "Sylvan
Hughes" was a pseudo-
nym she had considered
back then.

In any case, before
leaving Court Green,
Plath had started another

Yeats's house, 23 Fitzroy Road, North London

novel. She had written to Olive Prouty that its plot was "semi-
autobiographical about a wife whose husband turns out to be a deserter and philanderer"; she planned to title it *Doubletake*. At the time,
Plath was reading quite a lot of fiction by women, something Ted
Hughes noticed during his brief stay at Court Green in October, and
later commented on to Aurelia Plath. Hughes said that during most of
their time at Court Green earlier, Plath rarely sat down with a book—
she rarely sat still, in any case, without busywork in her hands: the rag
rug, the tapestry kit. Hours that Plath might have devoted to reading,
she devoted to writing. But after she and Hughes separated, this
changed. Hughes listed the books he noticed: the Bible, D. H. Lawrence
(mainly rereading), novels by Patrick White, some biographies and

other general nonfiction, and "several contemporary English novels—mostly by women and quite a few American ones."

Hughes didn't specify the women authors that interested Plath, but Suzette Macedo observed that one of them was the Macedos' good friend Doris Lessing. Plath spoke enthusiastically about Lessing's autobiographical novels, which dramatized the evolution of Lessing's own political and literary involvements through a heroine whom Lessing called Martha Quest. Doris Lessing was hauling daily life right over the border into fiction, where the calamitous events of her own life—including the motherhood Lessing had abandoned—might be seen to resonate with historically significant meanings. When Lessing's new novel, *The Golden Notebook,* came out in 1962, Plath eagerly pounced on the book, and asked Suzette to introduce her to the author.

Suzette arranged a meeting in January, shortly before Plath's *Bell Jar* was published. When they went together to Doris Lessing's flat, Plath, trying to make a good impression, gushed about Lessing's books and made a bad impression instead. Lessing told Macedo privately that she couldn't bear Plath's neediness—"incandescent desperation," as she described it to one of Plath's biographers. Plath didn't seem to notice the brush-off; she was always awkward in situations where she meant to impress people, Suzette noticed, and at that moment, Plath was very high on her own work. Plath was also pressuring Suzette to introduce her to the Macedos' friend Emily Hahn, a staff writer for *The New Yorker.* Hahn was a journalist, a world traveler, now married to an Englishman she hardly ever saw, since her work kept her on the move. Plath listened avidly to the Macedos' stories about Hahn, who presented in the flesh Plath's boldest fantasy of living an unconventional life. The poem Plath dedicated to the Macedos refers to poppies; Plath may have read Hahn's coolly mind-boggling account of acquiring and recovering from an addiction to opium while on assignment in China.

Biographies and autobiographical novels were potential blueprints, not only for Plath's new life but for her success as a writer representative of her generation—Plath's oldest aspiration. Plath's intense interest in fiction and poetry by contemporary women was very much in the foreground of her thoughts during an interview she recorded for the BBC at the end of October, shortly after her thirtieth birthday, when she was flush with the success of all those new poems. The interview was conducted by Peter Orr as a project sponsored by the British Council jointly with the Poetry Room of the Lamont Library at Harvard; forty-five contemporary poets were asked to read new work and comment on their craft.

Peter Orr's interview with Plath captures a valuable moment in her development, when she was quite obviously reorienting herself to become a writer of fiction. Plath told Peter Orr that "taboo" subject matter and "emotional and psychological depth" were the artistic aims she designated for all of her writing, not just her poetry. Referring to Alvarez's influential essay "Beyond the Gentility Principle," Plath said of herself, "I am not very genteel and I feel that gentility has a stranglehold" on English life. She intended to write works that were "relevant to the larger things, the bigger things such as Hiroshima and Dachau." Her latest poems, she said, had been written for the voice rather than for the page: "I speak them to myself" while writing them, she explained, "and whatever lucidity they may have comes from the fact that I say them to myself." They had to sound like a person meaning to be understood. Introducing these poems before she read them— she included "Daddy," "Medusa," "Lady Lazarus," "Nick and the Candlestick," and "Ariel"—Plath made a few comments indicating they should be understood as emerging from the voice of an invented character, not as poems about herself.

But poetry, she added "is a tyrannical discipline, you've got to go so far, so fast, in such a small space" that dailiness is impossible to convey. So at this point she wanted to devote herself to writing novels. "Now that I have attained, shall I say, a respectable age, and have had experiences, I feel much more interested in prose," she said rather primly. No doubt she expected that some people in range of this broadcast might understand what she meant by "experiences."

And writing this new novel was Plath's top priority once she got to London. A card on which Plath made an outline and working notes for it was seen in the mid-1970s by the critic Judith Kroll while she was working on a book about Plath's poetry, *Chapters in a Mythology*.

According to Kroll, Plath's notes refer to the main characters as "'heroine,' 'rival,' 'husband' and 'rival's husband'"; and Plath had described one of the novel's central actions: "rival says to heroine, 'I shall drive you mad.'" Plath also jotted on the card the titles of two French films she had seen in London that apparently influenced her conception of this novel: *Last Year at Marienbad* and *Jules and Jim*. This information suggests either that Plath had taken the novel a stride away from "potboiler" status after moving to London, or that she had started another novel making different use of her material. She reported to Alvarez that she had high hopes for the new novel. "Much better than *The Bell Jar*. I've really got something this time."

It could be done. There was Suzette's neighbor in Hampstead, Doris Lessing, to prove it; there was Suzette's friend, Emily Hahn, off on her world travels, to prove it. There was Suzette herself, extending a hand while Plath was raising her foot to take the next step.

Once the holidays were past, Hughes also settled into a flat of his own, in Soho, and began coming once a week or more, throughout January and early February, mainly to see Frieda. A glimpse of Hughes's way of life by the end of the year can be gleaned from the memoirs of the American Ben Sonnenberg, who was whiling away his time among English theatre people during the early 1960s and writing plays. Sonnenberg was a dandy, an amorist with lots of girlfriends and a fast car, talented, absurdly well read for a man in his twenties. He liked experimental work, and liked to spend money on artists—at one point, running into Ted Hughes on a London street, Sonnenberg learned that Hughes was on an errand to sell some manuscripts. How much do you get for them? he asked, and when he heard five pounds apiece, Sonnenberg bought the lot for ten pounds apiece, on the spot—"I enjoyed transactions like that," Sonnenberg wrote in a memoir of Hughes. "I was quite the debonair young patron of the arts at that time."

One of the artists to whom Sonnenberg gave a commission, the composer Elisabeth Lutyens, decided to throw a bohemian birthday party for him at the end of December 1962 at her garden apartment in Hampstead. Sonnenberg asked her to invite Ted Hughes. Sonnenberg, still a bachelor, turned twenty-six that night, and his principal memory is of annoyance at having no one to take home—he had alienated his current girlfriend, Sally Belfrage, by the insultingly casual way he offered to marry her (insulting in her view). That night, the absence of a partner confirmed his sense of being a young nobody. "You're not as important to anyone here as they are to you," he told himself. "They will remember you hardly at all. . . . So Ted Hughes was the one I went home with."

Sonnenberg was very fond of Hughes, who treated him like "an ideal older brother," encouraging Sonnenberg's work, and helpfully overpraising it, Sonnenberg said. Hughes's birthday gift at the party was a poem by G. K. Chesterton, "The Rolling English Road," which he recited from memory in the baritone voice Sonnenberg liked so much—"energetic, hypnotic, unstoppable."

> Before the Roman came to Rye or out to Severn strode,
> The rolling English drunkard made the rolling English road.
> A reeling road, a rolling road, that rambles round the shire . . .

Hughes had also gone to the party without a companion, and accepted Sonnenberg's invitation to ramble home from Belsize Park Gardens over Primrose Hill, past Regent's Park to Sonnenberg's rooms on Half Moon Street, off Piccadilly. It was now the early morning of the last day of the year. Maybe it was the companionship of another free spirit alongside him in the dark that sent Hughes's mind back to the days before he met Plath, when he had worked briefly at the zoo in Regent's Park, washing dishes in the café. On his breaks from that odious job, Hughes had loitered near the animal cages, and that's when he drafted "The Jaguar." To Sonnenberg Hughes told a story that night, about the way he came up with the poem's ending. Hughes said he'd watched a fly buzz up the jaguar's nostril, and that gave him the poem's last line: "Over the cage floor the horizons come." Maybe he also told Sonnenberg something about his separation from Plath, for at that point her name washes into Sonnenberg's memoir, on a cresting surge of male solidarity. "I can't have liked Sylvia Plath very much," he remarks, "I remember so little about her." One meeting did stay with him. "Sally [Belfrage] and I went to dinner at the Hugheses' when they lived in Chalcot Square. I remember thinking that Sylvia expected too much applause for the dinner she'd cooked and too much approval for the economy of her and Ted's arrangements." Sonnenberg also recalls another walk in Regent's Park, with Ted pushing Frieda's pram, explaining that Plath avoided leaving the house, relying on Ted for news of the outside world. "When I come home she *wrings me out*," Ted had told him.

Sonnenberg himself went on to marry, for the first time, in 1964, a much younger woman, just seventeen, "a lovable child," he said, with "very white skin like paper for me to write upon." The marriage was more or less a side effect of having moved to a larger house, but he planned to take it seriously. "Salvation, protection, reform: these are what marriage would bring." Also adultery. "I in fact believed that adultery was essential to marriage"—a view he had absorbed from books such as Lawrence's *Women in Love* and Joyce's play, *Exiles*. "These works summed up all there was to say on the subject of the infidelity essential to marriage, with its vital homosexual component."

Sonnenberg's style of worldliness was not uncommon in the London bohemia where Plath's friends circulated and gossiped. Plath made tentative excursions into its precincts herself, smoking and talking casually about her divorce. One of the acquaintances she most liked to visit was Al Alvarez. On each of her trips to London that fall, Plath made time to drink whiskey by his fireside and show him her new poems.

Under Alvarez the *Observer* was a conduit of poetry to very large audiences, and he had taken a liking to Plath's work. The *Observer* had published "Morning Song," "Sleep in the Mojave Desert," "Finisterre," "Crossing the Water," "Event," and "Winter Trees." When Plath started showing up to read Alvarez the new poems that were arriving thick and fast in the wake of Hughes's departure, Alvarez was startled and impressed by her cool mastery, her willingness to divulge exactly where she was coming from. "As the months went by and her poetry became progressively more extreme, [her] gift for transforming every detail grew steadily until, in the last weeks, each trivial event became the occasion for poetry: a cut finger, a fever, a bruise. Her drab domestic life fused with her imagination richly and without hesitation."

At some point Plath told him about the suicide attempts in her past—she called the recent car crash a suicide attempt—but with an air of detachment. Alvarez too had been through a deep depression during which he attempted suicide: "We were both members of the club," he said later, and they talked frankly and often about the subject. But it seemed to him at the time that Plath had the attitude of a survivor. And, more significantly, her survival "seemed to entitle her to speak of suicide as a subject, not as an obsession." This was also the quality he found in her art: an attitude "hard, factual, and despite the intensity, understated." Alvarez recalled those occasions by his fireside in his book about suicide, *The Savage God*, published in 1970. He did not think that she was contemplating suicide in the autumn of 1962, and he was almost certainly correct. The occasions Plath spent in Alvarez's company, few as they were, put a strong foundation of confident hopefulness into the move she was making: into London, into independence, into life as a writer. It was to Alvarez, in early November, that Plath brought the poem "Ariel," which she had written on her birthday. He told her it was the best thing she had ever done, and a short time later received a copy written out by hand, and dedicated to him.

Plath appears to have formed a romantic attachment to Alvarez. Their friendship did not become an affair, and Alvarez later felt guilty about letting her down when he knew she was looking to him for comfort. Plath had indicated so in a poem, "Letter in November," which she sent to Alvarez through the post, enclosing a rose petal—the gesture by which Assia had declared herself to Hughes at the outset of their affair. Was this a tease, and if so, did Plath mean Alvarez to recognize it as a tease? He has written about his awareness that Plath was sniffing around him that fall for traces of Ted and Assia. The poem, however, is very accomplished in ways Alvarez was bound to appreciate, and it is utterly direct:

> Love, the world
> Suddenly turns, turns color

"Letter in November" shows us that at least one gift their friendship gave Plath was an uplift of desire, which is its own reward.

Plath's immediate goal, once she was settled, had little to do with romance. She needed to establish a calm domestic routine in which to get her work going again. Her mood grew somewhat more optimistic when she finally hired an au pair near the end of January; she immediately began writing poems: twelve in all, between January 28 and February 5. It appears that she also went back to her novel, *Doubletake*—perhaps in response to Hughes's comings and goings. Hughes was still deeply involved with Assia, who did not want to leave her marriage, though David Wevill knew that she was seeing Hughes. The affair was very public, the source of curiosity and gossip—even Plath knew that Assia was still "dangling" her husband while appearing publicly in the literary world with Hughes. As he would later write, in a poem about Assia,

> The brimming power of your gaze
> Was mainly the accumulated protein
> Of trophies digested

Plath responded to the situation by simulating indifference. She wrote to Olive Prouty that she was keeping up a front with Hughes, attempting to be cheerful, refraining from accusations. But the tone of Plath's letter was wistful: she saw her own loneliness for him reflected in Frieda's undisguised sorrow. She wrote to her mother that Hughes "sometimes is nice & sometimes awful" on these visits. According to Hughes's later memories, the front she kept up was entirely successful. She brooked no dialogue on the subject of divorce: her mind was made up, and her position hard. Unsentimental.

But she was feeling more and more insecure: about money, about the aggravation of trying to train a nanny sufficiently to free her mind for writing. At the end of the first week in February, Plath fired her au pair in a fit of rage after discovering her in bed with a boyfriend, ignoring the children. This meant Plath no longer had the precious morning hours for writing, a severe threat to her financial security. Moreover, for the past month she had been suffering, along with the rest of London, through a long period of extremely cold, harsh weather—the coldest in half a century, it was said—during which a huge snowfall literally brought the city to a halt. Traffic could not navigate the unplowed streets, so food and services of every kind were scarce. Plath's letters describe trying to shop and run errands with the children, navigating the baby's pram along slippery, narrow tracks through the unplowed city streets where the dirty high-piled drifts stood hard as iron. Power outages became routine; pipes froze and burst, leaving the houses without running water—disastrous in a household with two children still in diapers. Worst of all, Plath had no telephone: her service had not yet been installed, despite her insistent requests. She had to queue, in the cold, with the children, at a corner phone box. The relentless hardship of her daily life was compounded by a lingering physical weakness and lassitude from the high fevers and flu that both Plath and the children had suffered immediately after Christmas.

Then, on January 14, *The Bell Jar* was published. The appearance of her first novel should have been the cause of celebration and optimism, but in her current state of mind Plath was exquisitely sensitive to criticism, and she found the few brief, mildly positive reviews mortifying. One she found devastating: the review in the *Observer*, by Anthony Burgess, where *The Bell Jar* was discussed along with two other first novels by unknown writers. Burgess's comments were approving, though not a rave. But what Plath found crushing was to see Hughes's poem "Full Moon and Little Frieda" showcased handsomely in the same issue of the *Observer* where her own work, huddled under a pseudonym, was given hardly a mention. Plath took this personally, as a snub, one that carried implications for her professional future. Keenly perturbed, she dashed weeping down the stairs to the flat of her neighbor for sympathy, though they were hardly acquainted.

Plath's friends, of course, were as occupied as she was by the difficulties imposed on Londoners by the catastrophic weather; and having no telephone, she had little recourse to helpful conversations. Did browsing the printed pages of her own book—usually an exultant moment for any writer—confront her with some of the very symptoms that were now taking hold in her body? *The Bell Jar* told the story of her first, nearly-fatal breakdown. Hundreds of thousands of readers would respond gratefully to the clarity and pathos of its representation of the onset and experience of mental illness. In future years it would be regarded as a reference work on clinical depression. Did it frighten Plath? And did she fear that she could lose custody of her children? Or be incarcerated permanently in a mental institution?

For she was indeed succumbing to the illness. When she finally wrote to her mother about her worry, on February 4, she hinted only that she was "feeling a bit grim . . . seeing the finality of it all and being catapulted from the cowlike happiness of maternity into loneliness." But on the same day, she wrote to Marcia Brown Plumer, a friend from college, a quite clinical description of a psychotic state: "Everything has blown & bubbled & warped & split." We do not have whatever journal notes she made, because Hughes burned this journal. But she had written to her psychiatrist in Boston the terrible words, "I can feel my mind disintegrating again."

The "again" suggests that Plath had diagnosed herself as very sick indeed. During her episode of mental illness, at eighteen, Plath had been treated by a couple of psychiatrists whom she believed had done her harm; now she had ventured to ask whether Dr. Beuscher might be able to come to London. When this proved impossible, Plath confided her psychiatric history to John Horder, the general practitioner who had been treating her. While Plath and the children had been down with flu, he found a live-in nurse who spent a week and saw them through the worst. Now, recognizing that Plath was severely depressed, he prescribed the antidepressant Parnate, possibly chosen because it normally produced improvement comparatively faster than other options—within ten days, rather than three to four weeks. Plath began taking the medication during the week of February 4, and Dr. Horder saw her every day. Her condition was so serious that Dr. Horder attempted to arrange hospitalization where the children could stay with her, but space was not immediately available. He advised her to stay with friends over the weekend; and he scheduled nursing care for her that would begin on Monday morning, February 11.

Complicating Plath's difficulties that week was a change in her relationship with Hughes. Beginning sometime in January, the two of them had begun exploring the possibility of a reconciliation. He told one of his friends, later, that during her first month in London she had "almost completely repaired her relationship to me." He said much the same to Plath's mother, a month after Plath's suicide—though Plath apparently did not mention this prospect of reuniting in any of her letters home. Hughes told Aurelia that during January the two of them had become "closer than we'd been for two years or so," partly because Plath was so evidently thriving in her new surroundings. "[W]e were beginning to get on again and bought a bottle of champagne to celebrate," he said. But her mood had changed abruptly by the end of January, after the publication of *The Bell Jar,* he said. On one of his regular visits she became desperately upset; she felt that his presence in London was disrupting her efforts to establish herself and asked him to leave England for a while. But she had agreed to stop the proceedings for a divorce, and that gave him hope that they might get together again. "The whole crazy divorce business was a bluff," she had admitted. After this meeting, he had canceled his appointments for the coming weeks, thinking he could persuade her to take a trip with him, out of London, and discuss how they might resume their life together.

Hughes didn't specify for Aurelia Plath the dates on which these conversations occurred, but in a letter he drafted some years later he added several significant details, apparently consulting a personal diary, and these greatly change our picture of the ending between them. On Tuesday, during the last week of her life, he wrote, Plath came to his flat in Soho at lunchtime. It was the first time she had been there. Plath told him about the "panics" that were overwhelming her. And she finally let him glimpse what was going on behind the scenes: the gossip she'd been hearing, and the advice she had been getting from friends—presumably including Olive Prouty and Ruth Beuscher, both of whom urged her to seek a legal settlement, as did Aurelia. Hughes was enraged by what Plath revealed. He was especially angered by her reports of the tattle of women friends, which he told her was all "lies." He brought up his idea about arranging a trip out of town together. But when he saw her three days later, on Friday afternoon the eighth, she was again "hard and mysterious." She was leaving for the weekend, and refused to tell him about her plans. It was the last time he saw her alive. "We ran out of time—by days, I think," he said.

Plath's whereabouts that weekend are known. She and the children were staying with her friends Jillian and Gerry Becker, who understood from Dr. Horder that Plath could not be left alone at that time. She came and went on various errands—presumably, her brief meeting with Hughes on Friday was one of them—but mainly she rested during the day and ate well. Plath only hinted that some changes were afoot between her and Hughes, and the hints suggested that she was optimistic. Her nights, though, were horrible, according to Jillian Becker, and the themes of her rambling conveyed a very strong hostility to Hughes.

On Sunday evening, February 10, Plath insisted on returning to her own flat with the children, claiming that she felt much better. Dr. Horder probably called on her that evening. Quite late, she knocked on her downstairs neighbor's door, asking for a postage stamp; she seemed drugged, dreamy—very ill, he thought. Later he heard her pacing the wooden floor over his head for most of the night.

But why did Plath actually do it? Everything knowable has been ransacked for evidence, over many years now, to support an answer simple and concrete. Some people blamed Hughes's infidelity. Others inferred from the timing of her actions that Plath expected to be rescued, and miscalculated the danger. Plath was expecting two visitors that day, but neither of them were able to rescue her: a nurse was dispatched by Dr. Horder and just before lunch Katherine Frankfort, an aquaintance who had agreed to mind the children while Plath went out to lunch with a literary editor. Dr. Horder believed that her death was intentional, but irrational: that she was in the grips of a compulsion attributable to brain chemistry, the biological

Giorgio de Chirico, "The Silent Statue," detail, "Ariadne" series, 1913

condition that her psychoactive medication was addressing with gradual efficacy. Unfortunately, the medication had so far given her only
the strength to act on her hopelessness. Hughes, in a private letter written much later, concurred in this view, though he added that Plath's
doctors in America had established that she was "allergic" to that
particular antidepressant; Hughes believed that it induced the suicidal
thoughts it was supposed to alleviate—that the medication prompted
the suicide, in effect. The whole catastrophe had been brought on by
the publication of that "accursed book" *The Bell Jar,* he said, "that
required the tranquillizers" her doctor prescribed, and that led directly
to her death. Plath's mother held a similar opinion. "She should not
have been alone," Aurelia Plath said in an interview. "It was not a
premeditated and desired end, it was really a chemical thing."

Plath was certainly deliberate that morning, but a compulsion
does not feel irrational to the person acting on it. In the kitchen, she
poured cups of milk and arranged helpings of bread, then carried the

food up a flight of stairs to her children's room. She set it within reach of their beds, and pulled their window wide open. Then she closed the door to their room and sealed it all around with masking tape. On a torn piece of shelf paper, she printed a note giving the telephone number of their doctor—using two different pens: it seems she had to hunt for the telephone number. Then she taped the note to the pram standing in the room next to where the children lay asleep. Her last written words concerned her children's safety.

Then she returned downstairs to the kitchen and blocked the windowsills and entry door with towels and clothing, before pulling down the oven door and kneeling deep into the gas. Her last action on her own behalf was to fold a little cloth and place it under her cheek, for comfort while she drew her last breaths. Depression killed Sylvia Plath.

CHAPTER EIGHT

HUSBANDRY
(1963–1998)

Plath's body was taken to a hospital for autopsy, and then to an undertaker in Camden Town to be embalmed and dressed, and laid in a casket. This is where Ted Hughes would see Sylvia Plath for the last time. He could not face his duties alone: he called on the friendship of Al Alvarez for moral support. Alvarez accompanied Hughes to the undertaker, and also attended the coroner's inquest on February 15. Afterward, Hughes gave Alvarez a little white-framed woodcut by Leonard Baskin, from Plath's flat, as a keepsake, an image of a man with a wolf's head. The funeral was delayed until Monday, February 18, so that Plath's brother and his wife could fly in from Massachusetts. Plath's mother, who was ill and had not yet been informed that Plath's death was a suicide, did not attend, nor did Hughes's mother, who was deeply disturbed by all that had occurred.

Hughes now moved into Plath's rooms on Fitzroy Road to replace her as the children's parent. Frieda was going on three years old; Nicholas was only thirteen months. Hughes decided on a policy of proceeding with the children "as if we had started anew," as if Plath's death had been inevitable and was not to be understood, only endured. He often told his friends, in those early days, "It was either her or me." His friends forebore to ask what he could possibly mean.

But Plath's suicide had sunk into his imagination. He was now thirty-two years old; his adult character was fully formed; and, as time would tell, the main subject of his art had now been consolidated by Plath's angry departure for the underworld.

During the weeks following Plath's burial, Hughes began fumbling toward a literary medium that could capture the complexity of his emotions. Lying in Plath's bed at night, Hughes could hear the wolves howling from their cages in the zoo nearby in Regent's Park. Being a superstitious man, he considered their voices as messages; and during those early weeks he wrote two incoherent elegies for Sylvia Plath that he later published in *Wodwo*, "Ballad from a Fairy Tale" and "The Howling of Wolves."

Hughes once commented that "a man's deeper sufferings and experiences are almost impossible for him to express by deliberate means." In those elegies the "deliberate means" at Hughes's disposal are defeated by the counterforce of his grief. In "Ballad from a Fairy Tale," Hughes recalls a prophetic dream in which he saw an angel who wore on her head a square of satin—its fringed edges "rippling . . . like a flounder." Hughes later acknowledged to a scholar that this satin square was a piece of "funerary furnishing"; presumably he had seen it under Plath's head as she lay in her casket. "Ballad" seems to issue from Hughes's conviction that he and Plath were both clairvoyant, like his mother. The poem tells us that his mother had interpreted this dream for him, but does not tell us what she said: a reader has to know a lot about Hughes's early life to recognize that the dream foretold Plath's burial in Heptonstall cemetery. And a reader has to have read *Birthday Letters* to know that flounders functioned in Hughes's memory as a private symbol for his and Plath's joint commitment to their calling, "what poetry told us to do."

The second poem Hughes wrote during those early days of losing Plath, "The Howling of Wolves," gestures covertly toward the eerie coincidence of the coroner's inquest, February 15, with the date of the ancient Roman fertility festival, Lupercalia, named for the Lupercal, the cave or grotto at the foot of the Palatine hill in which a she-wolf suckled Romulus and Remus. The mother of these legendary children was Rhea Silvia. Hughes had dedicated his book titled *Lupercal* "To Sylvia." During February 1963, Hughes was dwelling in the nightmare of his own metaphors: the wolves appeared to be accosting him personally in the dark. And they were not to be tamed by ceremonies and festivals and magic thinking, such as is found in legends. The poet asks, horrified,

> What are they dragging up and out on their long leashes of sound
> That dissolve in the mid-air silence?

"The Howling of Wolves" and "Ballad for a Fairy Tale" were themselves howls and whispers, numb placeholders for feelings that had not found their way fully into artistic expression. They are worth mentioning because they mark the origin of Hughes's response to the challenge Plath's death posed to his creativity. Only after many years, when he had found his way as an artist through the unfinished business of his marriage, did he return to those first miserable hours with Plath's corpse, and those first nights in the flat on Fitzroy Road, to draw expressive images from the devastation. A poem in *Howls and Whispers* recalls the pallor of the corpse's face. A poem in *Birthday Letters* says, or imagines, that Hughes parted the eyelids of her corpse, and found the eyes as "brown-bright" as he remembered them in his happiest moments with Plath, but now eerily "unmoving and dead." These "brown-bright eyes" recur as an unsettling detail in Hughes's autobiographical story "The Deadfall," in which the boy Hughes inspects a dead vixen while his older brother digs a hole in which to bury it. "I had never examined a fox. It was so astonishing to see it there, so real, so near," he recalls. "When I lifted its eyelid, the eye looked at me, very bright and alive." The echo that links the corpses of woman and fox in Hughes's writing may have been unconscious, but the psychological motivation was consistent: Hughes sought to know the animal as fully as possible, including its condition in death.

And the wolf-howls eventually gave Hughes the closing image of an affecting poem in *Birthday Letters*, "Life After Death." "My body sank into the folk-tale," Hughes writes,

> Where the wolves are singing in the forest
> For two . . .

> ... orphans
> Beside the corpse of their mother

Hughes's image beautifully integrates the ancient Roman legend about Romulus and Remus with the iconography of Plath's last poem, "Edge." In "Edge," the children lie dead next to the mother's body alongside her breasts, described as "pitchers of milk, now empty." In Hughes's poem the singing wolves forecast the children's rescue by a lupine caretaker—Hughes himself. And the phrase "My body sank into the folk-tale" vividly, literally, identifies the remarkable creative leap Hughes had taken, after Plath's suicide, into the first-person voice of a literary character who is telling the story of his life. The process of inventing that literary character can be witnessed in the years between 1974 and 1982, when Hughes oversaw the release of Sylvia Plath's whole literary oeuvre into the public domain and began incorporating his family into a mythic autobiography that accounted for his marriage. The raw material awaited him in the home Plath had abandoned, in the troves of paper that required Ted Hughes's husbandry once he took up his duties as Plath's legal heir.

Since Plath had made no will, Hughes became by default the owner of everything she possessed. He was obliged to open doors into her private nooks and crannies, both in London and at Court Green, taking the blows that fell from all she had concealed from him during their separation. One very unpleasant surprise awaited him in *Doubletake,* the piece of fiction Plath had been working on just before her death, in which she cast Ted as a "deserter" and "philanderer." Hughes also found the letters that Plath's accusations about him had elicited from her female friends—from Olive Prouty, Ruth Beuscher, and Aurelia, all commiserating with Plath over Hughes's failings, and counseling her to assert herself in a divorce suit. Hughes never got over his anger at what he regarded as their meddling; he believed they had goaded Plath into impulsive and misguided actions that painted her into a corner. She'd had to maintain her angry stance out of pride. A couple of fierce poems in *Howls and Whispers* commemorate Hughes's outrage over these letters, as does "Night-Ride on Ariel" in *Birthday Letters*.

The journal Plath had been keeping in 1963 was another awful legacy. "What I didn't find out in my nearly daily visits to her I found out in her diary—complete details," he told Alvarez. These pages were "bitterly sad." When he could finally bring himself to write to Aurelia, a month after Plath's death, Hughes told her that he had discovered, behind Plath's haughty and punitive façade, that "all she wanted to say simply was that if I didn't go back to her she could not live."

It is impossible not to wonder what Hughes was really planning and wishing with regard to his marriage at the time Plath killed herself. The statements to be found among his papers are wildly contradictory: that she was a wonderful woman but impossible for him to live with—that "it was either her or me"; and, to the contrary, that he and Plath were on the verge of a reconciliation, that they had even shared a bottle of champagne to celebrate the end of hostilities.

Of all Hughes's comments about his last meetings with Plath, the claim that they were on the verge of a reconciliation seems most dubious. A cost-benefits analysis would have to put a lot of weight into the emotional cost of reunion, for each of them. If they had taken that trip together, would they have been capable of talking reasonably? Both of them were still the walking wounded, in January 1963, and the wounds were raw. And they were now up against what was immovably, unacceptably characterological in each of them. Looking to the future of their relationship, it seems unlikely that Plath could have accepted Hughes's need for ongoing *ad libidum* predatory separation from his home life, or that Hughes could have tolerated the violent rage this behavior roused in Plath. Moreover, they had probably outgrown what had been uniquely important in their bond—their fascination with each other as their art developed. It seems that divorce would have been the most likely outcome of their separation.

Suppose, then, that Plath had survived, and she and Hughes had divorced. What would have been the consequences for Plath's status as a writer? Anne Sexton had a response to that question: she identified Plath's suicide as an enviable career move. During the brief but intense collegiality of the months Plath and Sexton spent together in Robert Lowell's writing workshop in 1959, they had discussed their case histories as depressives with suicidal compulsions, and agreed on the term "addiction" to describe this symptom. Sexton had used suicide attempts to halt the downward spiral of her own moods at the onset of depression, and considered suicide as a reasonable alternative to another cycle of illness. It was from the perspective of a woman who had been there herself that Sexton wrote the poem, "Wanting to Die," after Plath's death:

> suicides have a special language.
> Like carpenters they want to know *which tools*.
> They never ask *why build*

And Sexton publicly mourned Plath's death in an affectionate memoir, "The Bar-Fly Ought to Sing." But in the privacy of her therapy sessions, Sexton was frank about her anger with Plath for having "stolen" the finale Sexton planned for her own career. "*That* death was mine!" Sexton told her doctor. Suicide was a *glamorous* death, for an artist; the world would now pay more serious attention to Plath's poetry than was otherwise conceivable. Ernest Hemingway's death and Arthur Miller's play *After the Fall*—based on the suicide of Marilyn Monroe—were Sexton's points of reference. More, Sexton knew that her own suicide, whenever it occurred, would seem like a copycat act. This seemed unfair to Sexton, since she was older than Plath.

Ted Hughes apparently found no evidence among Plath's effects to suggest that Plath had planned her death, and most of the papers he sorted through in the flat on Fitzroy Road seem to have been entirely unconsoling. There was an exception: the manuscript of forty-one poems that Plath had assembled before leaving Court Green, which she left in a black spring-loaded binder on her desk. The front pages showed that Plath had deliberated awhile before settling decisively on the title *Ariel,* and suggested that she was designing *Ariel* to begin with a birth and end with a rebirth. She had not arranged the poems

chronologically in the order of their composition, and she had
selected, out of a larger amount of finished work, only certain poems
for inclusion in *Ariel*. Plath pointed out, in a note to herself, the relationship between the first words of the poem she had positioned first,
"Morning Song"—"Love set you going"—and the last words of the
poem she placed last, "Wintering," in which honeybees take flight
from the hive and "taste the spring." The poem "Ariel" was itself a
morning song. Plath had considered titling her book *Daddy*, she had
considered *The Rabbit Catcher*, she had considered *The Rival*, she had
considered *A Birthday Present*. In settling on *Ariel*, she grandly identified the ecstatic, racing energy of "Ariel" as the keynote of the book, a
voice "at one with the drive" of poetry itself.

Did Plath hear in the title *Ariel* a subtle rhyme with *Lupercal*?
Almost certainly. Though *Ariel* was dedicated to her children, it was
aimed at Hughes. *Ariel* was Sylvia Plath's second book of poems, as
Lupercal was Ted Hughes's second book, and both contained forty-
one poems—as Plath knew very well, since she had typed the manuscript and helped him decide on the sequencing of the poems.
Lupercal had established Hughes's position as an important poet.
Plath anticipated the same recognition for her own, and knew that the
book would be read by insiders as a brilliant declaration of independence from the man who had humiliated her.

Hughes apparently did not resent the militant rivalry he found in
Ariel. He was astonished by the artistic mastery in these and the handful of other poems he found among her papers, written since she
moved to London, most of which he had never seen before. Poets who
visited him recall that he kept the typescripts lying on a table, and
would read them aloud to guests. He spoke passionately about his conviction that Plath's poetry had achieved true greatness: "no other
woman poet except Emily Dickinson can begin to be compared with
her." His admiration never abated. When critics later took the line that
Ariel was the work of a psychotic or otherwise deranged mind, Hughes
countered with the view that they didn't know how to read Plath's
work. *Ariel* wasn't a book about going mad, he said; quite the contrary.
The poems revealed the "successful 'integration' " of the rage that had

previously been suppressed in her disposition, a "violent inheriting of a violent temperament." Moreover, he found her anger entirely appropriate to the situation she was in—having learned about his affair with Assia, he means, though he doesn't specify. And a critic should not fail to pay attention to the sense of humor in those poems, he added.

To Hughes, the poems in the *Ariel* binder and the numerous other sheets on her worktable gave vivid evidence of her continuing attachment to the creative partnership that had flourished during their marriage. He found painful evidence in that handful of typescripts Plath had taken secretly, angrily, from his desk at Court Green during his mysterious absence in September, and with which she had been conducting a vigorous dialogue in her own poetry ever since. Among them was that typescript of "Full Moon and Little Frieda," the poem that had caused Plath so much grief and envy in January when it was printed in the *Observer* alongside a negligible review of her *Bell Jar*. Hughes also found copies of "Out" and "The Road to Easington," the poems he had recorded for the BBC in August, the last month they lived together. "I think she got certain things from them," he said. His "Out," with its symbolism of the red poppies worn on Armistice Day, was echoed in two anguished poems by Plath: "Poppies in July," written after she first learned of Hughes's adultery, and "Poppies in October," after he had moved out—the poem she dedicated to the Macedos. Readers who know Plath's work will recognize what she borrowed from Hughes's lines "The poppy is a wound, the poppy is the mouth / Today whoring everywhere."

And Hughes was certain that his "Road to Easington" lay behind Plath's "The Bee Meeting." He saw that she was "mocking the rhythms with a different meaning." He was surely right. His poem begins,

Is there anything along this road, are there answers at the road's end?

Her poem ends:

Whose is that long white box in the grove, what have they accomplished,
    why am I cold

Hughes never afterward included "The Road to Easington" in a collection of his own poems, and only in a private letter did he acknowledge the dreadful message he had read into the "The Bee Meeting." He believed Plath's poem was telling him that her burial ground lay at the end of the road he had taken.

While Hughes was pursuing this investigation of Plath's papers, Assia was at his side. She had moved into the Fitzroy Road flat with Hughes shortly after Plath's funeral and stayed for several months while her husband, David, was away in Canada, attending his dying mother. To Nathaniel Tarn, Assia described Hughes as utterly "crushed" by Plath's death. Assia assigned herself the task of normalizing life in the disturbed household. Hughes's aunt Hilda and his sister, Olwyn, had been helping out as baby-sitters; Assia hired a nanny. She tried to lighten Hughes's grief by encouraging him to visit their friends with her, and she organized informal gatherings in the flat, attempting to restore a semblance of social life.

Assia too investigated the pages of writing Plath had left behind; Tarn thought Assia was "hypnotized" by them. Assia told him that she was very annoyed to find herself and David caricatured as a "detestable and contemptible" couple called "The Goos-Hoppers" in Plath's new novel, which she hoped Hughes would destroy. Assia also told Tarn that she had secretly read Plath's journals, and that these caused her even greater distress than the novel—she was shocked and hurt by Plath's savagery toward her. And nothing Hughes had told her about the marriage had prepared her for the depth of feeling and the passion for Hughes that she found in Plath's journals. "Maybe I'll end up writing the biography of Plath," she told Tarn.

Assia was aware that Hughes's friends blamed her for Plath's death, and she thought that Hughes's own friendships had been damaged as well. During the first months after Plath's suicide, both she and Hughes avoided their old acquaintances, out of shame, she told Tarn. Yet the status of their relationship to each other was far from clear, even to Assia. Though Assia had moved in with Hughes, she had not made up her mind to leave her marriage to David Wevill. Hughes was superstitious about marrying her, she thought. In March, she confided to Tarn that she was pregnant and intended to have an abortion. Tarn speculated that Assia was ambivalent toward both Wevill and Hughes; terminating the pregnancy delayed having to make a decision about what to do about her marriage.

So after David Wevill returned from Canada, Assia rejoined him, and, for the next two years, resumed the life she had been conducting before Plath's suicide. She seemed to have found her equilibrium in these unusual circumstances, poised between two men, holding a good job in advertising that put her in daily contact with the worlds of art and fashion she enjoyed. Lucas Myers, who met her through Hughes in 1964 and spent a month as Assia and David Wevill's guest in London, describes Assia admiringly as a woman "born to conduct a literary and artistic salon." But in Myers's view, Assia had now found herself in a dangerous situation. "She was a touch too elegant for her own well-being, fundamentally very vulnerable, needed a lot of affection, and could remember SS boots outside the railway carriage compartment as her family, half-Jewish, approached the Swiss border."

Hughes's Tribe

Hughes meanwhile was struggling to organize his life to accommodate the needs of his children. From February to July he had an increasingly unsatisfactory nanny looking after them on Fitzroy Road. Then Aurelia Plath announced that she meant to pay a visit to the children in mid-July, shaking Hughes out of a torpor. He had no home in which he could receive Aurelia. He had rented Court Green to Elizabeth and David Compton, who had been such good friends of Sylvia, she had dedicated *The Bell Jar* to them. Hughes thought he would eventually sell Court Green and rid himself of its painful associations. He could not invite Aurelia to The Beacon, his parents' home; his mother was unwell, and she was also deeply disturbed by his alliance with Assia. As a stop-gap, he arranged for the children to stay with his aunt Hilda in Mytholmroyd, and he found lodgings for Aurelia in Halifax, an hour's bus ride from Hilda's cottage.

Before Aurelia arrived, however, Hughes wrote her a cautionary letter, appealing with apparent confidence in Aurelia's emotional intelligence, that she beware of projecting her mourning for Sylvia onto the children. He told her that he feared in himself what he feared in her: now that their feelings "no longer have any worldly object," they will be tempted to make the children into substitutes for Plath. To be loved as a substitute for someone absent had been a horrible legacy in his own life, he said ambiguously; but he was specific about his expectations: Aurelia must recognize the danger to the children that lay in her own terrible grief at this time. On that understanding, he gave his consent for a visit.

Aurelia's trip to England was in part a strategically timed diplomatic errand. She wanted to persuade Hughes to send the children to her in America, and to let her raise them in the prosperous Boston suburb where their mother had grown up. Plath's brother, Warren, had introduced this proposal to Hughes very tactfully at the time of Plath's funeral and had reported back to Aurelia that Hughes at first seemed somewhat receptive, though by the end of Warren's brief visit Hughes had made up his mind to keep the children with him and give "a good try" to handling the job on his own. Aurelia now wanted to assess the situation for herself. Ahead of her arrival, she made an appointment with John Horder, the doctor who had treated Plath and the children while they lived in London, and arranged to meet, discreetly, several of Plath's London friends.

Aurelia spent a grim week traveling back and forth to smoky Mytholmroyd, visiting the children in the "wee" rooms of Hilda's cottage, where there was no room inside or outside for them to play. Once she was back at home at Wellesley, Aurelia wrote Dr. Horder, attempting, unsuccessfully, to enlist him in the argument she meant to have with Hughes about the children's need for a stable home. What she had witnessed in Yorkshire bothered her very much, she told Horder. She considered Hughes's attention to the children to be perfunctory at best, and his arrangements not conducive to their adjustment. She did not intend to give up the effort to change Hughes's mind.

Annoyed by her nosiness, Hughes continued to resist her argument that the children would be better off in America. Nonetheless, he remained on surprisingly good terms with Aurelia Plath. During his marriage to Plath he had built a strong foundation of communication with Aurelia. His letters to her were not merely dutiful—he would describe his literary projects to her, sometimes in overwhelming detail, and seemed to expect that no nuance would be lost on her. Those letters form the most specific and interesting available records of his artistic aims during the early 1960s. He had even written Aurelia into one of his poems, "A Woman Unconscious," which was published in *Lupercal;* it recalled visiting Aurelia in the hospital during the year the Hugheses lived in Boston. The trust he felt is evident in the letter Hughes wrote immediately after Plath's death, in which he poured out his passionate grief, his remorse, his explanation of how everything between him and Plath went wrong during the last month, so irreparably. Aurelia was the one other person who had been familiar with the extremes of Plath's emotional intensity and could appreciate the force of Plath's rage and the pathos of her helplessness.

Aurelia's visits, over the years, required all his forbearance, but he rose to the challenge. Almost every summer until the children were in their teens, Aurelia visited them in England, sometimes staying at Court Green, though Hughes usually organized lodging for Aurelia that would protect his own privacy and give her time alone with the children. Occasionally, the children visited her, and Warren's growing family, in Massachusetts. And though Hughes told other people—and Aurelia herself—that he mistrusted the influence of the "tense, watchful anxiety" that he had seen her exercise over Plath, Hughes retained his respect for her intelligence and generosity. Four years after Plath's death, he remarked that he thought he was now able to see Aurelia through his own eyes rather than through the scrim of Plath's conflicts with her. "An extraordinary woman," he said. "Every time I meet her I'm more impressed."

And it seems that Aurelia's visit in July 1963 produced a significant outcome, motivating Hughes to settle the children in a stable home life. He decided that he wanted them to grow up in the countryside, rather than in London. He was very short of money—his main

Ted Hughes and Olwyn Hughes, executors of the Plath estate, 1978

income at the time was from writing book reviews and children's plays. Despite his aversion to Court Green, it was only sensible to return there. But he needed a nanny. By September, his sister, Olwyn, had agreed to take over this role; she gave up her life in Paris and moved to Court Green, where she stayed for the next two years. Hughes's biographer observes that it was "gallant and generous" of Olwyn, who had lived in Paris since 1952, supporting herself with secretarial work at embassies and at NATO, "and had never been drawn toward motherhood herself."

Olwyn Hughes was apparently sympathetic to Hughes's plight. The rest of Hughes's family was not; and his mother, thoroughly scandalized by Plath's death and by Hughes's continuing association with a married woman, began making trouble for him. She had long been asthmatic and arthritic; now her health deteriorated in a way that Hughes could not help but take personally—she "steals in a mysterious way from illness to illness" was the way he put it. She monitored

Hughes's every effort to organize his life, reacting with alarm even to his plans to take a vacation, as if there were "some strange drastic secret motive" behind it. He was torn between resentment at the shrewdness of her passive interference in his life, and worry about leaving her on her own, to be tended by his father, whom he regarded as useless in the circumstances. By midsummer 1965, Hughes reluctantly began to think he ought to have his parents live with him. Early the next year, they moved to Court Green.

Meanwhile, Assia—still living in London with her husband—had given birth to a daughter, Alexandra Tatiana Elise, who arrived on March 13, 1965. Assia wrote to Lucas Myers, who had become her close friend, that she was ecstatic over the beautiful baby, "sea blue eyes—skin fair as sweetbriar." Assia nicknamed her Shura, and David Wevill provided her with a family name on her birth certificate. But she was Hughes's child, and sometime later that year, Assia left Wevill and took the baby to live at Court Green.

By early 1966, Hughes had given his life something resembling a tribal organization, with himself as chief, surrounded as he was by little children, increasingly dependent parents, a lively-minded sister, a glamorous consort, and a mother-in-law now and then. He'd even had some luck in luring his cagey brother across the seas for a long-delayed homecoming. At the end of 1964, concerns about their mother's bad health had finally persuaded Gerald to break his moratorium. Gerald spent a month in Yorkshire that included the holidays, to his mother's immense delight. Edith Hughes wrote to Aurelia that she had "almost forgotten that so much warmth & love, vitality & joy in life could be embodied in one person."

Hughes's *Ariel*

Hughes's life was almost entirely occupied with these complicated logistical issues in his family life from the time of Plath's death until well into 1965. His own writing languished in this environment—the pressure he was feeling from his parents paralyzed him, he often said. When he was working at all, he concentrated his energies on getting Plath's last poetry into print. He had planned, initially, to produce a complete edition of Plath's poems that would include both *The Colossus* and everything she had written afterward. Having met with considerable frustration, he managed to persuade his own publisher, Faber and Faber, to bring out a smaller book. It appeared under the title *Ariel* in 1965. In conjunction with this publication, Hughes gave a long interview to the *Guardian* in which he spoke in glowing terms about his life with Plath. "We were like two feet, each one using everything the other did. It was a working partnership and it was all absorbing," he said. "There was an unspoken unanimity in every criticism or judgment we made." Even more personal was the note Hughes published when *Ariel* became a Spring Choice of the Poetry Book Society. Hughes's description of the book was a eulogy for the poet, and for their marriage. "She was most afraid that she might come to live outside her genius for love, which she also equated with courage, or 'guts,' to use her word." The poetry of *Ariel,* he added, "is just like her—but permanent."

The *Ariel* Hughes published was not identical with the manuscript titled *Ariel* that Plath had organized in the black spring binder he found on her desk after her death. As editor, Hughes reshuffled the poems, destroying the narrative arc that Plath had described in her notes on the manuscript. He omitted some of the poems Plath had intended to include—he cut "The Rabbit Catcher," for example. And he added poems that Plath had not included, poems written after she finished the *Ariel* manuscript, poems that Plath intended for another book. His most significant intervention was to replace the hopeful poem "Wintering"—the ending Plath had designed for *Ariel*—with "Edge":

> The woman is perfected.
> Her dead
>
> Body wears the smile of accomplishment

Moreover, Hughes provided no editorial notes acknowledging that he had reshaped a book that had been arranged otherwise by its author; he might have avoided censure had he given the book another title. He was later severely criticized for omissions that, defending himself, he said were based on "concern for certain people" at whom certain poems were "aimed too nakedly." Most of these poems had to do with their marriage and were aimed at him, so unsympathetic commentators tended to regard the omissions as a cover-up. The poems that he added he considered self-evidently important artistic achievements, he explained. He did not explain the rationale for giving *Ariel* a different ending, but a good argument can be made in defense of his editorial decision. "Edge" is not only a very beautiful and accomplished work of art, it appears to have been the last poem Plath ever wrote; and in it she forecasts existing only in her work, "perfected": literally, thoroughly made, an artifact. Permanent.

Hughes's *Ariel* was an immediate critical success, and more. Within two decades *Ariel* was standing alongside *The Waste Land* as one of the masterpieces of twentieth-century poetry in English, in having found a poetic mode that is the perfect medium of its culturally significant content, and that conveys an instantly recognizable subjectivity, one that matters to readers. Commercially too, *Ariel* succeeded beyond all expectation. The first U.K. edition of 3100 copies of *Ariel* was published in March 1965, and sold out quickly enough that Faber ordered a reprint of 3200 ten months later, in January 1966. Those were impressive sales for a book of poems by a relatively unknown poet. In the United States, Harper and Row published a slightly different edition, augmented by three poems, in June 1966, and Sylvia Plath became a public figure overnight. American reviewers focused on her suicide, and sought its causes in the ferocity of her poems—*Time* magazine devoted an entire page to "Daddy." Suddenly, Plath was marketable on both sides of the Atlantic. As a consequence of this flurry, Plath's British publisher, Faber, brought out a new edition of *The Bell Jar* in September 1966, identifying the author as Sylvia Plath for the first time; between 1966 and 1977, Faber sold over 140,000 copies of *The Bell Jar* in hardback and paper editions.

And Hughes too was earning money, finally. Out of the blue, early in 1966, he received word that he had been granted a five-year fellowship from the University of Vienna, which, as he confided to Aurelia, would pay him "two thirds a working professor's salary." The award, administered by the university on behalf of the Woursell Foundation, was strictly to support his work as an artist—the contract specified that he was to do nothing other than "exercise my poetic talent," he told Aurelia. This recognition seems to have jump-started Hughes, after long dormancy. He and Assia bundled up the children and took off for a long delayed sojourn in Ireland, where Hughes wrote feverishly for the whole month of March. They then took a tour down the Rhine in Germany, funded by Hughes's Woursell Fellowship. During the course of those months away from Court Green, Hughes at long last completed *Wodwo,* the book he had set aside when he first took up with Assia.

The Wodwo and the Crow

Wodwo had to be a good book; Hughes had established a reputation that he needed to protect, and it had been a long time since he brought out any serious new work. The book he eventually compiled for publication in 1967, out of all the manuscripts he had produced, has three parts: two groups of poems, and a set of stories that included Hughes's radio drama *The Wound,* which is a shamanic tale. A note at the opening of the book informs the reader that "the verse and prose are intended to be read together, as parts of a single work." Elsewhere, to scholars, Hughes noted that the tripartite structure of the book was repeated in several important individual poems, purposely designed, Hughes said, to set forth powerful images, then restrain them with "ritual magic," one part releasing the energy, two parts controlling it.

Hughes confided to his friend Ben Sonnenberg that there was a "story" to be found in *Wodwo:* it told about the death of one life, an invitation to and refusal of another life, and the suffering inflicted when new life was refused. Hughes said he had worked on sequencing the poems in *Wodwo* so that the book would provide to readers a "perpetual mental cure." In his own case, the magic had worked: the book gave him the "mental cure" that permitted him to advance into the poems of *Crow.*

Wodwo is a good book, an ambitious book. Hughes thought that literature should be a force for *uncivilizing* the reader or, better, the auditor. In *Wodwo,* he attempts to write poems that do not impose a historically specific personality on the audience—an identifiable human first-person speaker—because he believed that literature works by penetrating consciousness at a level not reached by the speech of everyday transactions. Hughes's study of alchemy, astrology, and magic and his interest in shamanist practices were expressions of this belief about the workings of language. During this phase of his career, he drew upon these bodies of occult learning in his poetry, without identifying them, for symbolisms through which to express the personal crises in his life, without alluding to them as lived experiences.

Meanwhile, Hughes had not lost his interest in writing for the theatre and, from the late 1960s on, would experience his greatest financial successes in this mode of writing. One milestone was the commission to prepare a new translation of Seneca's *Oedipus* from the director Peter Brook and the actors John Gielgud and Irene Worth, to be produced at the National Theatre. The classical text, Seneca's *Oedipus,* was only a point of departure; Hughes was working directly with the vocalized word, not the written word. Hughes stripped down and speeded up the play, aiming to create "a hurtling momentum . . . an utterance of gasps and howling cries." The goal was to assault the audience's sensibility with violent words and the barest minimum of action—not changing the play, Hughes claimed, but, yes, "changing the audience."

And out of just such a matrix of radical simplifications and black inspirations emerged one of Hughes's most important books: *Crow,* a sequence of brief "songs." They were in fact intended as anti-songs, Hughes explained, "songs with no music whatsoever, in a super-simple and super-ugly language."

> Who owns these scrawny little feet? *Death.*
> Who owns this bristly scorched-looking face? *Death . . .*
> But who is stronger than death?
>   *Me, evidently.*

An invitation from the artist Leonard Baskin precipitated the development of *Crow*. Baskin asked Hughes for some poems to accompany a set of drawings he had made, and the drawings opened a vein. "The Crow is another word of course for the entrails, lungs, heart, etc— everything extracted from a beast when it is gutted," Hughes explained. "The Crow of a man, in other words, is the essential man—only minus his human looking vehicle, his bones and muscles." Hughes's Crow is an irrepressible and sinister trickster figure, whose character appears to owe a good deal to the comic books and folktales Hughes read avidly during his childhood—and also out of his self-confessed obsession with killing and eviscerating small animals during his youth and adolescence. Crow is not a figure of fun. He is a scavenger poking his beak into a destroyed civilization. Wherever he finds a sign of life, Crow pounces on it with unselective appetite.

> When . . . the only face left in the world
> Lay broken . . .
> Crow had to start searching for something to eat

Very late in his life, writing to the critic Keith Sagar, Hughes made explicit the connection between *Crow* and the otherwise unapproachable subject of Plath's suicide. Hughes acknowledged that from 1963 to 1965 he had been floundering in creative lassitude. Then, on the sojourn in Ireland with Assia and the children, Hughes found his way into the style of *Crow,* which was, however improbably, the way he was finally able to write about his own experience of personal devastation. To do so, he had to let a symbolism arise out of his unconscious mind, "obliquely," "inadvertently." According to Hughes's many commentaries on the subject, these short pieces were meant to be incorporated in an epic folktale in which Crow finds a mate after wandering in the ruins of a devastated world. Hughes would always describe the plot of his planned *Crow* saga when he read the poems to audiences; toward the end of his life a recording of *Crow* was released in which he told the story. But he never wrote it up for publication— some stories were meant to be told, not printed.

Crow was the project Hughes undertook while he was living with Assia at their happiest. They never married, but there is good reason to believe that Hughes loved Assia deeply, even after his first infatuation ended. They were more or less a couple for almost exactly the same amount of time that Hughes and Plath were a couple, a little over six years. What Assia brought into Hughes's life when they were most content can perhaps be glimpsed in bits and pieces of poetry to be found in the archive at Emory University. One poem, titled "Auschwitz," was probably written during their trip to Germany; addressed to "my love," it probes for a way to celebrate a life that has escaped the Holocaust. At some point Hughes designated it for publication in *Wodwo*, but changed his mind. Another poem, possibly stimulated by a translation project that he and Assia undertook, is about a man and a woman reading together silently, he feeling her excitement "brightening on the words" while they "double" in him. Hughes and Assia did indeed begin working together professionally in 1966, after Hughes had embarked with his friend Daniel Weissbort on a scheme to bring European poets to English audiences by translating and publishing their work in a newspaper format called *Modern Poets in Translation*. With Hughes's encouragement, Assia produced a much admired English version of poems by the German-born Israeli poet Yehuda Amichai. In 1968, she and Hughes appeared together on a program broadcast by the BBC, with Assia introducing Amichai's poems to English audiences, and Hughes reading them. The year before, as Hughes's biographer reports, Hughes and Assia "made a glamorous couple" at the first International Poetry Festival in London, which Hughes had organized.

Still, Assia couldn't hope to compete with Plath for Hughes's esteem. During those same years that Assia was proving herself as a literary translator, Hughes was actively promoting Plath's reputation. His edition of *Ariel* had arrived in the world like a trump card the week after Assia delivered Shura. It cannot have been easy for Assia to witness Hughes's endless mourning during those years, or to read Hughes's warm, eager praise of Plath's work in the literary press, or to avoid considering herself ill rewarded in her partnership with Hughes.

To compensate, Assia pilfered some of Plath's manuscripts and sent them to her sister, intending to create a nest egg for Shura's support. Assia knew that the manuscripts had increasing monetary value, quite aside from the artistic value Hughes claimed for them, and she felt deeply insecure in her relationship with Hughes. Assia took "quite a lot," according to her sister, who later returned them to Hughes.

Assia and Shura lived with Hughes and his parents at Court Green until late autumn 1967. Hughes reported to Lucas Myers that Frieda and Nicholas had "greatly taken to" baby Shura, "fortunately"; and Hughes found Shura, at age two, "a beautiful precocious little girl." But the senior Hugheses had never defrosted; Billie Hughes refused even to speak to Assia for weeks on end. When Assia could no longer tolerate their disapproval and dislike, she moved back to London, with Shura. She did not reunite with David Wevill, though they remained on good terms until Wevill accepted a faculty position at the University of Texas in Austin in 1968 and left England permanently. Assia found a flat in Clapham, and took up work again in the advertising business. She also continued working on translations of contemporary Hebrew writing. Hughes visited her and Shura in London, where his sister, Olwyn, also now lived; all of them spent the Christmas holidays together in 1967.

Hughes expressed immense relief when Assia left Court Green, along with a bit of shame. "By Napoleonic moves," he wrote to his friend Lucas Myers, "I've got myself some qualified peace. . . . I've withdrawn all investments of distress and agitation, and become a monster of suiting myself." Yet he claimed that he was still attempting to find a home in which he could settle comfortably with Assia—out of range of his parents—and as late as March 1969, he and Assia did some house-hunting in the North of England. It is not clear that Assia favored such a move. Assia was currently taking pills to treat a "serious" depression, according to a writer for whom Assia was translating a play. Assia's friends remembered that she was despondent about losing her looks as she aged and gained weight, and that she talked frankly about suicide when she was in her lowest moods; at one point she asked her sister to accept guardianship of Shura. "I have been literally suicidal," she wrote. She was also aware that after she left Court Green, Hughes had become involved with another married woman, a neighbor in Devon named Brenda Hedden. Hughes said that Assia habitually "tested" him by saying that he and she ought to part for good.

On March 25, lonely and depressed, Assia called Hughes and, according to him, they went over the same old ground: "it was nothing new, nothing we hadn't got over dozens of times before," he said later. "I know if I had only moved—if I had only given her hope in slightly more emphatic words, in that last phone conversation, she would have been OK." After this phone call, Assia arranged to be alone. She dissolved sleeping pills in a drink that she gave her daughter, and took sleeping pills with whiskey herself. She drew a mattress close to the gas stove, turned on the gas, and lay down with her daughter in her arms. She was forty-one and Shura had just turned four when both of them died.

Assia's appalling death, and that of their little girl, plunged Hughes into the deepest misery. Immediately after their funeral, he fled to Ireland, thinking he would look for a house to buy in order to start a new life there with Frieda and Nicholas. Sitting at the bar in his hotel after a solitary dinner one night, he began writing in a notebook he had at hand. He reflected on the satiric poem "Gulliver" that Plath had written about him in November 1962, after he left Court Green. Plath had depicted him as a fallen man, immobilized by "petty fetters," hated by everyone, staring vacantly at the sky. That's how he saw himself, at that moment: immobilized by guilt, "tied & married" to trivialities, incapable of work, sunk in "the slow, steady, nearly numb tearing" of pain. He had been prey to horrible nightmares, in which Assia's face, and Shura's, rose before him, tempting him to believe that the "bitter misunderstanding" could have been avoided.

Hughes had been undergoing terrible "black moods" ever since Plath's death—depressive periods stronger than anything he had ever experienced before, he told his brother—and he thought they were at least partially responsible for Assia's suicide. "People who live with me contract the gloom from me," he speculated, "but they don't have the supports that I have to defend themselves from it." To Aurelia he wrote that he thought Sylvia's death "threw my whole nature negative," creating disaster for others. He thought the remedy was to get away from Court Green, "which has gradually become a hell for me." He urgently wanted to remove the children from what he described, in dire terms, as the "psychological inferno" of the life he had imposed on them ever since Plath's death. Frieda was by now nine, Nicholas seven.

In May 1969 another blow sent Hughes reeling again—his mother, who seemed to be convalescing, died suddenly after learning what had become of Assia and Shura, information that Hughes had tried to keep from her. Hughes believed that the shock had killed her, adding yet another woman's death to a lengthening list of fatalities caused by his blunders. In the depths of his despair he thought that intimacy with him had been deadly to all of them, and that he himself was damned.

This time Hughes fled haunted Devon for Yorkshire, where with a windfall of prize money he impulsively bought Lumb Bank, an enormous house not far from his parents' home—it was like trying to bury his head in his mother's lap, he acknowledged. Shortly afterward, he invited Brenda Hedden—the woman he began seeing after Assia left Court Green—to leave her husband and join him and his children, bringing her children. Aunt Hilda wrote to Aurelia Plath that Mrs. Hedden was serving as Hughes's "housekeeper," though her letter hinted there was more to this arrangement than she wanted to mention. Poems Hughes drafted that autumn indicate that he too felt he had done wrong, in making such a selfish "retreat from a dilemma of pain": it was of a piece with his other false moves involving women and children, letting "my lovelies drift & die."

This new arrangement did not last long. The following year, Hughes married Carol Orchard, a beautiful young woman from Devon who had trained as a nurse. They wed very privately in a London registry office on August 19, 1970, two days after Hughes's fortieth birthday. Hughes wrote to his friend the poet Peter Redgrove that Carol was "not very interested in literature," which he apparently regarded as a good thing, but that she had "perfect taste and judgment" in what interested her, and, very much to the point, she was "exceedingly good for me." She provided his children with a mother, and for the next several years endowed his home life with peace and orderliness greater than he had ever known. "Carol has pulled us all out of the fire," was the way he put it to Aurelia Plath.

Stewardship

No matter what new involvements were shaping the trajectory of the actual life and work of Ted Hughes, after 1965 the ongoing consequences of his marriage to Sylvia Plath stalled him in a public role he was helpless to defy. Hughes once remarked that the clamor surrounding every publication of Plath's writing made him feel as though he and his family dwelt in a "mausoleum," with himself on display as a "second-hand relic husband." His metaphor of living in a tomb points to the double bind that Plath's literary legacy imposed on him. He could neither avoid his responsibilities to her writing, nor—because he had to act on her behalf, and speak on her behalf—fulfill them in a way that satisfied anybody, least of all himself. That was because he found it difficult to draw a bright line between his rights as owner of her manuscripts, and his responsibilities as their custodian.

After Olwyn Hughes moved back to London in 1966, Hughes assigned her the role of literary agent, handling the business transactions of the Plath estate. His scheme would keep the money in the family, and keep the noses of strangers out. But the appointment of his sister as gatekeeper of the public dissemination of Plath's work proved immensely compromising to Hughes's own reputation. Olwyn adopted a stance of militant defensiveness on behalf of the family's interests; permission to quote Plath's work in scholarly manuscripts was refused if the estate disagreed with the point of view. It appeared to outsiders that Hughes was using his sister to protect himself from questions, and had appointed Olwyn to censor rather than broker the discussion of Plath's work.

The husbandry of Plath's papers burdened Ted Hughes's life even with his sister in charge of tedious business details. He refused to relinquish the burden for many years, however, out of mere "sentimentality," he told his brother. Yet he appears to have been downright careless in looking after these papers. How, for example, was it possible for Assia to read Plath's journals "secretly," as she said she did in 1963, and steal a substantial number of Plath's valuable manuscripts after Shura's birth in 1965? It appears to have been possible because Hughes did not secure them. In September 1963, when he moved with his children back to Devon, he apparently continued to leave the papers handily out in the open. His friend Lucas Myers recalls in a memoir that Hughes invited him to stay at Court Green for a spell of visiting and writing. Myers was there for four months, from December 1963 into March 1964. "Sylvia's unpublished literary legacy was standing on a table in the living room at Court Green when I was there," he observed; "in the succeeding years, Ted let it out bit by bit."

During those years, manuscripts disappeared, and so did other items. A letter Hughes wrote to his sister-in-law complains that visitors have walked off with "everything that had her or my signature, her manuscripts, towels, sheets, tools—whenever I wasn't actually on watch, something was pinched." A poem in *Birthday Letters* mentions the theft of Sylvia's fountain pen; a letter to Aurelia Plath complains that memorabilia hunters had plundered his collection of family snapshots. On one occasion some visitor had even removed the exposed film from cameras belonging to his wife and his son, and reset the counters to disguise the theft. In 1967, sending Gerald a limited edition of a book of poems, Hughes cautioned him to keep it in a safe place, a lesson he says he has learned the hard way by watching personal copies of his first editions disappear on "centipede legs." To the critic Keith Sagar he ascribed the disappearance of valuables from his home to a character trait, "my easygoing general readiness to let anything pass."

The greatest losses to posterity, under Hughes's stewardship, were undoubtedly the last prose manuscripts Plath left in the flat on Fitzroy Road: the two journals she kept between 1960 and 1963, and the novel she was working on—the one Assia told Tarn she hoped Hughes would destroy. Hughes did not destroy it, at least not right away. The novel was still in the estate's possession in 1968, when Olwyn Hughes mentioned it in a letter to Plath's mother, remarking that it was "about Devon." When Hughes began collecting Plath's fiction for publication in the volume *Johnny Panic and the Bible of Dreams,* the book's editor, Fran McCullough, implored Hughes to "please, please remember to look up the fragment of the novel (and the notes)"—in the United States, readers were suspicious of the motives of the Plath estate, McCullough said. Hughes knew there were rumors about a missing novel, so he explained, in his introduction to *Johnny Panic,* "after *The Bell Jar,* she wrote some 130 pages . . . provisionally titled *Double Exposure,*" but "that novel disappeared somewhere around 1970." In 1995, Hughes gave yet another account: "What I was aware of was sixty, seventy pages which disappeared. And to tell you the truth, I always assumed her mother took them all, on one of her visits." No manuscript pages or notes for this novel appear among Plath papers in any archives.

Hughes's most shocking revelation about disappearances and losses from the Plath legacy was that he had destroyed the last of Plath's journals himself. "I did not want her children to have to read it (in those days I regarded forgetfulness as an essential part of survival)," he explained in the foreword he wrote for the abridged version of the journals published in 1982. When a critic reprimanded Hughes, comparing him to the literary executors of Lord Byron's estate who shredded his papers, Hughes defended his action not as a literary executor, but as a father—as if burning the pages was the only way to keep them out of the hands of the children.

He claimed that another notebook simply "disappeared." This was the journal Plath kept between 1959 and late 1962—that is, while she was writing her breakthrough poems. Olwyn Hughes said in 1989 that she thought "it went missing nearly twenty years ago." But Hughes apparently thought he had it in his possession as late as 1981; according to a letter he wrote to Alvarez, Hughes said he had kept track of this notebook until it "walked, not too long ago." Then, during the last months of his life Hughes passed along a mysterious rumor to Keith Sagar, that the missing journals had been "seen" in the 1960s—apparently contradicting what he said to

Alvarez in 1981 about its disappearance "not long ago"—but that "the scent had gone cold."

Not surprisingly, the ambiguities in Hughes's accounts of what happened to these lost writings have led fans to fantasize and fiction-eers to fictionalize wildly about them. In November 2000, an opera titled *Giuseppe e Sylvia* envisioned the meeting of Verdi and Plath in the afterlife, in a bar, to sort things out. In 2001, a novel based on Plath's journals by Emma Tennant—one of Hughes's paramours in the 1970s—devised sensational substitutes for those missing volumes of the journals, including a scene in which Ted Hughes deflowers the teenage baby-sitter. In 2002, a hoax news story posted on the Internet claimed that the lost journals of Sylvia Plath had been deposited at the British Library by a scholar to whom Hughes had entrusted them for safekeeping.

Is it possible that Ted Hughes did not destroy or lose the journals? Reasonable people have always doubted Hughes's claims that they were missing, and tantalizing evidence that at least one of them still exists has now turned up in his archives. In the draft of a long letter addressed to the literary scholar Jacqueline Rose in 1990, Hughes initiated a confession: "I have never told this to anyone—I hid the last journal—about 2 months of entries," a decision he now regarded as an expression of his "utter foolishness" at the time he did it. He says that only the last page might have proved damaging to their children; he was actually protecting "somebody else," whom he doesn't name. But even while drafting this disclosure, Hughes had second thoughts, and crossed out those self-incriminating words. He sent Jacqueline Rose a much less interesting—though still very interesting—letter. But he saved the evidence of his impulse to tell all. The whole slew of draft pages of this unsent letter went into his archive, fragments of the 2½-ton jigsaw puzzle he left to posterity.

The commercial success of Plath's work was producing another set of burdens in Hughes's life. In 1966, following the U.K. release of the correctly attributed *Bell Jar*, Hughes began hearing rumors that a pirated American edition was in the works. Owing to an obscure clause in U.S law, the estate was about to lose its copyright in the novel. Hughes had not offered the book to Plath's American publisher, out of respect for Aurelia's feelings. Aurelia had been mortified by the publicity surrounding the release of *Ariel*—"'Daddy' sold *Ariel*," she noted bitterly. *The Bell Jar* would be a vastly greater embarrassment; her friends and neighbors would easily recognize the characters as caricatures of themselves. But since the book was likely to be published anyway, Olwyn Hughes persuaded Aurelia to see the financial advantage that would accrue to the children if Aurelia abandoned her squeamishness. It was the kind of argument Aurelia was not disposed to refute, and so she reluctantly gave her consent.

The Bell Jar came out in the United States in April 1971, was optioned for a movie, and went immediately onto best-seller lists, where it stayed for twenty-four weeks. It was understood that *The Bell Jar* was autobiographical. The movie eventually precipitated a libel suit in which Hughes was a defendant in 1987: a vaguely lesbian relationship invented for the film loosely implicated a classmate of Plath's at Smith who was by then a psychiatrist in the Boston area, and she resolved to claim damages. Closer to home, public discussion of the book confirmed Aurelia's dread that readers would identify the heroine Esther with Sylvia, and Esther's mother with Aurelia. Aurelia responded by having a heart attack. When she recovered her health, she came up with a plan to recover her reputation: she proposed to Hughes that she edit a book of Plath's letters, which Aurelia hoped would counteract these negative images Plath had made so vivid in her fiction. Hughes very reluctantly consented. By July 1974, Aurelia had produced a manuscript of letters and commentary numbering 1000 pages. She now thought the book should be published in two volumes.

As holder of the copyright, Hughes felt obliged to read every word. Since Hughes wanted to correct what he considered to be exaggerations and misrepresentations in Plath's letters, he also consulted Plath's journals and his own diaries. And so it happened that during the mid-1970s, Ted Hughes relived through Sylvia Plath's letters the thirteen years between the day she entered Smith College in 1950 and the week before her death. By the time he finished, he was steeped in the details of Plath's life, the range of her expressiveness, and the evolution of her vocation. It was a refresher course that would prove directly useful to him for the rest of his own career.

Hughes worked through the manuscript carefully with Fran McCullough, then wrote his advice into a thoughtful and tactful letter to Aurelia. The task of transcribing and annotating the letters had been therapeutic for Aurelia; now she needed to shape the material into an effective literary work of which Plath was the author. In the absence of a full biography, this book would be seized on as a definitive source of background, he cautioned. Aurelia, attempting to neutralize the effect of *The Bell Jar,* had given too much emphasis to Plath's abundant "enthusiasm," as he put it—an important trait, admittedly, but one without shading. He encouraged Aurelia to consider that the sort of book she was preparing needed to be "fashioned as judiciously as a novel," and assured her she could trust the editorial judgment of Fran McCullough, Hughes's own editor at Harper and Row, who would bring more objectivity to the project than either he or Aurelia.

Hughes's several letters about this project provide an invaluable source of insight into the way he saw his own editorial activity on Plath's behalf. Like Aurelia, he would always be positioned defensively when presenting Plath to her growing audiences; the ideals he set forth in his letters to her were equally words of advice to himself. His letters to Aurelia also show that in the course of reviewing the manuscript of *Letters Home,* Hughes had taken a close look at his marriage to Plath, which he could now see from the vantage of middle age. In the long letter he wrote to Aurelia defending his intentions to cut the manuscript she had prepared, Hughes at last revisited the site of the ethical scar on his life, his desertion of Plath—not a word he uses, but an experience he acknowledges to Aurelia. The rage and humiliation Plath expressed in her letters home were "inevitable and natural," under the circumstances, he allows. But he feels that Aurelia's annotations disfigure the actualities. First, he insists, Aurelia must respect the boundaries he wishes to set around his own privacy and that of the children. Then he gets down to the grievances he still harbors. Plath could really be hard to take, he reminds Aurelia, who knew as well as he did about the "steely determination" with which Plath pursued every serious aim—the divorce she was insisting on, for example; it still baffled him. In her extremity she had mishandled the situation nearly as disastrously as he had, in his view. More to the point, her most serious aim throughout their marriage had been to ensure that she got in a morning of writing. Unless she was teaching, or they were traveling, her writing took priority in their married life; his would have to take care of itself, and that was that.

Hughes is filling page after page as he composes this letter, and finally, he arrives at a judgment that he seems to be discovering as he writes it. Seizing a phrase Aurelia quoted from one of Plath's letters—that Plath had "sacrificed everything" for Hughes—he snatches it from melodrama and revives it with ice water. Plath didn't "sacrifice" any more or less than he did, he asserts. Together, they had *both* found a way to "sacrifice everything to writing." Yes: for six years they had managed to remain faithful to one summons, no matter what else was going on in their lives, and everything else had secondary importance. Whatever it took to be writers, they would do. "No blame": he too had given priority to whatever it was that made his writing possible. And if they hadn't had each other, he asserts—more surprisingly—neither of them would have been capable of this "sacrifice." He would have wandered off to Australia and piddled around; she would have become a professor, and written books on the side. Maybe. But instead she had become one of the most important women poets who ever lived.

CHAPTER NINE

CURING HIMSELF
(1967–1998)

One night during the months following Assia's suicide, Ted Hughes sat alone at his desk and wrote a set of notes in verse. The emotions in the roughed-out poem that resulted are very raw. He tells himself that he has destroyed his own life in the course of destroying his loved ones; he feels that he is being burned at the stake, and "whoever comes to help me dies." Pressing on his consciousness is the ancient burial mound that lay not far from his study window at Court Green: he feels entirely surrounded by the accusing dead. He drives his pen across the page in torment, hoping for evidence that he has a soul.

This was the kind of poem Hughes would never publish, and it captures the dilemma of his career during the decade that followed Assia's death and produced Plath's fame. Scandal had created for his work an audience fixated on his private life, or so he imagined; and this self-consciousness clamped him into another double bind, damned by readers if he produced new work and damned by himself if he didn't. The accusing dead were the subject that history had singled him out to confront as an artist. Trying to position their power in works of art was the greatest pressure on his creative life.

But Hughes was heavily defended against these dead. During the long decade of the 1970s, attempting to subvert his own powers of sabotage, he produced works that were tediously abstract and eso-teric—even repellent: *Cave Birds, Prometheus on His Crag, Gaudete.* But all were efforts consistent with Hughes's belief in the power of art to bring about "mental cure." Without exception, they were baffling adaptations of what Hughes considered the master plot of important literature: the shaman's journey through the underworld. In the breakthrough book he published at the end of the decade, *Remains of Elmet,* Hughes finally developed a medium in which the dead were given "posthumous life" in symbolisms that fused the actual with the eternal—evidence that the "mental cure" he was seeking to articulate for a whole culture had somehow occurred in himself.

An artist's way is full of switchbacks, though, and before Hughes advanced he retreated into a deep depression. He told the poet Peter Redgrove that he had passed the year following Assia's death "in very strange darkness." To Lucas Myers he was telegraphic: "Planets bad. Reaping the whirlwind." Even the attention of literary critics disturbed Hughes during the early 1970s. He spelled out the dilemma in the clearest terms to the scholar Keith Sagar, who was working on *The Art of Ted Hughes,* the first full-length study of Hughes's work. "This much exposure intensifies my sense of being 'watched,'" Hughes said; so he requested that there be no biographical in-

Ted Hughes, February 3, 1969

formation in the book. It encouraged *"the wrong audience,"* Hughes explained, emphasizing the words. Only grudgingly, Hughes permitted Sagar to print a photograph of him as a frontispiece. He was superstitious—a photograph provided access for "telepathic interference" by the reader, he believed. But as he told Peter Redgrove, to *stop* producing new work would just kill him. He would simply have to find the right "shape" for what he had to say.

"Knot of Obsessions"

The theme of being inhibited by his prospective audience, of being watched by the wrong people, recurs in Hughes's letters throughout the 1970s. Its deadening influence can be felt in his work, and can be witnessed in the management of his emotional life as he struggled to recover his soul. After his marriage to Carol Orchard in 1970, Hughes wrote to friends about the satisfaction he felt in having secluded himself in Devon, where he could protect his privacy. He also took up a new occupation. In 1972 he and his wife bought a ninety-five-acre farm named Moortown, located five miles from Court Green, on the edge of Dartmoor. Her father, Jack Orchard, came out of retirement to manage the farm, and they began raising cattle and sheep. And Hughes became an ardent fisherman again, after a long lapse. He told Lucas Myers that he thought fishing "absorbed all my other follies."

But as a writer, Hughes was frequently stalled or idling through the mid-1970s. He thought the poems he was producing were "light weight," though he was probably at work on the very heavy poems published at the end of the decade in *Cave Birds* and *Prometheus on His Crag,* with titles such as "The Scream," "The Executioner," and "A Flayed Crow in the Hall of Judgment." He complained to his old friend Daniel Weissbort of being "weirdly prostrated"—the cause might be physical, he thought, but was more likely his involvement in the publication of Plath's letters: the unavoidable exposure of his private life made him look like "the freak in that story."

Mainly, Hughes worked at things that didn't call attention to himself: limited editions, commissioned anthologies, book reviews, plays for children, translations of other poets' work. But sometime in 1970 Hughes composed a work of criticism that clarified the way his own work would go forward after his depression lifted. This was his introduction to *A Choice of Shakespeare's Verse,* in which Hughes provided a rationale for the unorthodox anthology he had made.

Hughes had culled passages from Shakespeare's plays and then sequenced them to illustrate an idea he had about Shakespeare. He argued that beneath all the complexities of character and incident in Shakespeare's work could be found a single, repeating pattern. Hughes described it as a "knot of obsessions" that "has its taproot in a sexual dilemma of a peculiarly black and ugly sort." This, Hughes argues, is the psychological source of Shakespeare's power as an artist. Shakespeare's imagination was formed in the historical moment of the Protestant revolution in England, when "the newly throned god" of the Reformation and "the deposed goddess" of Catholic theology "tore each other to pieces." Shakespeare's plays show us how the religious conflict "became, at bottom, a sexual dilemma" that still prevails in the misogyny of contemporary culture, Hughes claims. His *Choice of Shakespeare's Verse* was organized to clarify the "symbolic fable" that could be discovered in Shakespeare's storytelling.

Eventually Hughes generalized this view of Shakespeare into a field theory of literary personhood. The idea is simple and clear. Hughes proposes that no single work of a writer's output stands alone, that a strong writer's work proceeds by accretion over time, unconsciously building a consistent, recognizable persona. The literary persona who enacts the poet's struggle can be glimpsed, always, in one early work that Hughes calls the "first," which contains, in a single image, "a package of precisely folded, multiple meanings." The origin of this image is a trauma, usually hidden from the writer's consciousness, that partakes in a wholly personal way of some destructive aspect of cultural life.

The greatest poets, Hughes argues, are those in whom the deepest spiritual issues of their time find pathways into complex psychological representations, or images. In an essay on T. S. Eliot, Hughes carries this point very far. He says that whatever in the poet is making the image is resisted by the poet's ego, yet emerges in successive creations that can be very different from each other. However, each work will contain a consistent self-representation, if you know how to look for it. Hughes calls this creative entity the Poetic Self, using capital letters; and he notes, "the first successful representation is likely to be a compact index of everything to follow." Eliot's "first" poem is "Death of Saint Narcissus"; in Shakespeare, the "first" image of the persona emerges in the "way of loving" expressed in the Sonnets, but the first poem containing him as a character is "Venus and Adonis."

And with each subsequent successful creation, the Poetic Self grows closer to being able to produce a full image of its "predicament." Characteristics of the image will be that it is "visionary . . . irreducibly symbolic . . . and dramatically complete."

Hughes's analyses of these themes in Shakespeare and Eliot cover many pages over many years. During those same years, Hughes began constructing an ideal personhood for himself. It begins in the poems of *Remains of Elmet,* written, he said, in his mother's voice; and reaches its "drama of completion" in "The Offers," where Sylvia Plath comes back from the dead and speaks to him. His own "knot of obsessions" was expressed in a pattern of advance and retreat, its stimulus the irresistible immediacy of a woman's voice.

But in the meantime, during the early 1970s Hughes found only one way to release his creativity. Hughes began writing verse that didn't "count" because he didn't intend to publish it. He adopted the habit, after a day's work among the livestock at Moortown Farm, of jotting notes, "to make a fleeting snapshot, for myself, of a precious bit of my life." One day he decided to set down his notes roughly in lines, and discovered that the effects of the rhythm deepened the impact of the details. These jottings weren't really poems, in his view; they were transfers of sense impressions, one after another. If he delayed making his notes for several days, he lost interest, even if he remembered what details he wanted to set down. "Their charge of importance had gone." Conversely, when he was shaping his notes into lines while dashing them off, he seemed to "move deeper and more steadily into reliving the experience," and to find he had been making patterns even though his aim was making records. Even so, he said he "regarded them as casual journal notes and made no effort to do anything with them" for several years. When he had regained his artistic confidence, he published them as *Moortown Diary.*

Hughes was more or less an extra pair of hands at the Moortown Farm. His father-in-law and his wife ran the operation day to day, leaving him free to keep up with his other obligations. This agreeable arrangement lasted until the summer of 1975, when Jack Orchard was diagnosed with cancer. He died in February 1976, in his sixtieth year. Hughes was deeply attached to Jack Orchard, and took his death very hard. In the days following Orchard's funeral, he began a draft of a poem covering many pages. Eventually he shaped this anguished, rambling lament into a touching and shapely elegy for Jack Orchard. But his initial version of the poem was very personal; it dwelt, with almost clinical precision, on Orchard's physical deterioration. Jack Orchard's body had rapidly been overtaken, grotesquely distorted, and rendered helpless by disease. Then suffering divested him of all his violent, thrusting energy. Now death had falsified all that was distinctive in him, bestowing on his corpse the appearance of calm acceptance. Hughes's private mourning goes beyond mere grief for the person; it conveys a strong sense of identification with the fate of that huge, strong, able man: "all your plans & schemes came to nothing."

This powerful emotional experience was still quite recent when Ted Hughes traveled to Australia a month later, in March 1976. Hughes had accepted an invitation to attend the Adelaide Festival of Arts in South Australia. He arranged to arrive beforehand to spend some time with his brother in Melbourne. He took his father along; Billie Hughes would stay on in Melbourne while Hughes performed at the festival in Adelaide. He was eighty-two years old, and had never visited Gerald's home, nor had Ted Hughes. His visit with Gerald delayed him; arriving in Adelaide later than expected, Hughes missed being met at the airport by Jill Barber, the press officer who had been assigned as his escort for the duration of the festival. It was a hot afternoon. He made his way to the writers' reception travel-weary and

Jill Barber, 1970s

burdened by a heavy leather coat; he was cross when he finally met Barber, and asked where she'd been. She was ready for him. Barber, an Australian who worked as a press agent in London, had accepted the assignment at the Adelaide Festival partly in order to visit her parents, who still lived there. Barber had seen Hughes's picture in the face-book of artists scheduled for the festival and had bet one of her colleagues that she would bed Hughes before the festival was over. Now she sat him down in the cool of the garden where the writers had assembled. Telling him she was "psychic," and therefore knew what he liked without being told, she served him an array of choice Australian wines.

She stood no chance of losing the bet. "Foxy" would be the adjective to describe Jill, even today, married to a successful lawyer, and the mother of a daughter in college. In March 1976 she was thirty-one, single, and ready to fall in love. She has told the story of their romance in a newspaper article published in 2001: how she drove Hughes in a big white limousine to a press conference the day after his arrival, where he was hectored by a mob of people holding placards and chanting, "You murdered Sylvia." She rescued him from the crowd and, later that day, from the tedium of an official gathering, where she drank too much champagne. When they arrived back at his hotel, she became horribly sick. This time he rescued her, removing her expensive borrowed dress to keep it from harm's way. And now they made love, many times over, and they spent every possible hour together for the next two days. When Hughes left Adelaide for England, she thought she would never see him again. But the day after his departure, she received a phone call: "Jilly, it's Ted. I'm in love with you."

Barber had not read Hughes's work when they met, and knew little about his life—except what everybody knew about him: that he had been married to Sylvia Plath, who committed suicide. "I assumed he was a single widower," she wrote in her article. She learned differently only when they reunited in London. Hughes began coming up from Devon to spend weeks at a time with Jill, and he began talking about marriage to her. He said that his body was full of "black electricity," that she could release him. "We had met in a Paradise, and we both felt that our love was destined to be," Barber said. At midsummer he brought her to Devon, "to be married in his style." They drove to Dartmoor, then parked the car and scrambled through barbed wire, and crossed the moor to the Marriage Rocks, Barber navigating around the cowpats in stiletto heels. She was wearing a white summer dress for this ceremony: he had told her that if they made love on the rocks they would be together forever. "I knew my role in his life: to love him, love him, love him," she said.

Hughes had been avoiding the literary scene in London for years; now, with Jill Barber, he gladly took up new artistic projects and friendships. He became co-editor of *Mars*, a literary magazine founded by Barber's friend Kristina Dusseldorp—"Ted found the poets," Barber said. "Nobody would turn him down." Hughes's publisher was delighted to have him back in circulation. When his book *Gaudete* came out in 1977, Hughes accepted his publisher's request that he undertake a publicity tour, and he took Barber with him to the United States.

They were openly a couple. Their love affair took place in the best restaurants over the best wine—good food and drink were interests they shared. Barber smoked Gauloise cigarettes, a habit she had picked up in France; Hughes took up smoking Gauloises so he could stand to kiss her. Barber's newly purchased flat was under renovation, so they had to "bed-hop all over London," as she tells it, and they were welcome everywhere. Hughes gave her the nickname Gypsy-girl. When her flat was finally ready for habitation, they worked on the moving in together: he was a "real nester," she recalled, and put up wallpaper for her, with more enthusiasm than competence. They also traveled together all over Britain and went fishing together. His poem "Sunstruck Foxglove," addressed to a "gypsy girl," commemorates a trip they made one Midsummer Eve to Northumberland, she thinks.

> Her loose dress falls open . . .
> You glimpse the reptile under-speckle
> Of her sunburned breasts

Hughes also took her to visit the grave of Sylvia Plath, in Yorkshire. Barber says that she considered this her introduction into his family.

Ted with a champagne bottle, 1976

With Jill Barber, Hughes had found a way to lead, at last, a double life, split between a home base and a hunting ground. When Hughes told Barber that his body was full of "black electricity," was he thinking of Will Brangwen, in D. H. Lawrence's *The Rainbow*? That novel deals with a man's emotional recoil from the cheerful housewife who replaces his ardent bride. Newly married, Brangwen cannot bear the way his wife rises from their ravishing sexual entanglement to busy herself in domestic tasks—"he became a mad creature, black and electric with fury . . . fiendish in his thwarted soul."

Hughes's own phrase "black electricity" gestures toward the themes of his most esoteric work of the 1970s, in which men grow murderous toward their women (in *Gaudete*) or, suffering some deep wound in their relationships to themselves, are destroyed, dismembered, cannibalized in order to reconstruct themselves spiritually (in *Cave Birds* and *Prometheus on His Crag*). Hughes explained that these works enacted symbolically the struggle to rescue the "atrophied" souls of men who had lost the "capacity to be part of the sacred mystery, or to act other than mechanically." Vitality could be restored only by a spiritual conjunction of masculine with feminine, bride with groom—in the alchemical sense, and in the symbolic sense to be found in *The White Goddess*.

Jill Barber was just such a force of renewal in his life; and under the spell of his passion for her he began writ-ing again: poems about his childhood home in the Calder Valley. When he introduced Jill Barber to Robert Graves in London, he told Graves, "This is my Muse. And when he talked about marriage to her and to other women with whom he was intimate, that was what he meant: a symbolic conjunction, the farthest thing from dailiness, child rearing, or homemaking; the wildness he craved and without which he could not find his way back into his creativity. He had once put the matter to Gerald in a kind of motto: "Energy is created by every activity that resembles the pursuit of quarry."

Ted Hughes, June 28, 1976

Barber was the first but not the only woman who reinvigorated Ted Hughes's psyche during the years he was seeking his soul in that dark decade of the 1970s. In September 1976, after he and Jill Barber had become a couple, Hughes met the writer Emma Tennant, who wanted to enlist him as a contributor to *Bananas,* a hip literary jour-nal she was editing. In a memoir, Tennant describes the affair that developed under cover of their literary negotiations. Hughes was drawn to her freewheeling style and to her obvious fascination with him. She was attracted by his bad press. Tennant says she had long been obsessed with the Sylvia Plath of *Ariel* and of rumor. "Like so many women who read Plath's famous last poems in the late '60's, I feel I've lived through a climate of feminism in which . . . Sylvia stands for the martyred female and Hughes for the murderous male." In Tennant's case, the danger emanating from Hughes was seductive; she calls this affliction "the Bluebeard syndrome": a need "to become involved with a man known for his terrifying and unacceptable treatment" of women. After they became lovers, Tennant hoped that sexual intimacy would make Hughes receptive to her questions about what happened between himself and Sylvia. "Like Bluebeard's bride, it appears, I have to know." One day while they were taking a drive, she initiated a conversation about Plath. Hughes abruptly ended the outing and told her, "Don't talk about Sylvia." And yet he teased her by offering gifts that he had given, or thought of giving, to Plath: an elm-plank writing table, a fox cub. "I think he was a very overexcitable person" Tennant said, suggesting that he probably would have offered the table "to anyone he found quite attractive." She added, "It was part of his carry-on. He fancied himself."

But to Tennant too, Hughes proposed: he wanted them to run away together to the wilds of Scotland, Tennant says. He returned to this fantasy, sporadically, over the couple of years that they were lovers. When their affair withered, Tennant came to the insight that all of the women he seduced, herself included, were merely "objects of his fancy, and don't belong to the 'real' world." Jill Barber arrived at the same judgment. When it became clear to her that Hughes had no intention of making a real home with her, and was dead set against raising a family with her, Barber decided to bolt. By then she had a thriving literary agency, with connections at a number of locations in Europe and America. "I was the only woman who ever walked away from him," she said. "You can have no idea of what it was like to be the focus of his love. But Hughes was an ambitious man, and he knew that his reputation couldn't survive the scandal of a divorce. He just wanted things to go on as they were between us. But I was broody. So in 1980 I moved my business to New York."

Tennant was right: no paramour was prized for being "real." On the contrary, what Hughes sought from each of them was immersion in a fantasy that could release the suppressed life that was expressing itself in massive depression. He needed to connect with his own underworld. As he put the matter in an essay published the same year he took up with both women, "this inner world we have rejected is not merely an inferno of depraved impulses and crazy explosions of embittered energy. Our real selves lie down there. Down there, mixed up among all the madness, is everything that once made life worth living."

The partnerships Hughes formed with women during the 1970s didn't have to be acted on sexually in order to have an important effect on his life, though. In the same year that Hughes met Barber and took up with Tennant, he also formed a creative alliance with Donya Feuer, an American who had come to Europe with Martha Graham's dance company and never left. By the time she met Hughes, she had become director and choreographer at the Royal Dramatic Theatre in Stockholm and had worked extensively with Ingmar Bergman on productions of Shakespeare. In 1976, Feuer came across Hughes's *Choice of Shakespeare's Verse* and was thrilled by its daring introduction. She wrote Hughes's ideas into a script for a one-woman soliloquy, in which an aging actress would recall her life in the theatre through a progression of speeches and reminiscences that would set forth and personalize the symbolic fable Hughes identified as the basis of Shakespeare's plays.

In 1977 Feuer came to London to present this script to Olwyn Hughes, in her role as Hughes's literary agent. As they were talking in Olwyn's flat, Ted Hughes came down the stairs to greet her—she never forgot her first glimpse of him, "a giant of a man." Hughes welcomed Feuer's plans with great excitement and, as she left, said, "Keep in contact with me." She did, for nearly twenty years. Though they never again met face-to-face, they spoke often on the phone, sometimes as often as weekly. When she was mounting a play, he gave her notes; when she was working out problems with the staging, she sorted them out with him. Over the years they became intimate confidants as well. While Hughes was editing Plath's work, he spoke to Donya Feuer very openly about his reawakened anguish over Sylvia Plath's death, she said; and she talked to him freely about the most personal aspects of her own complicated life.

But the principal focus of their long-distance friendship was a running seminar on every aspect of Shakespeare. In 1986 Feuer decided to base a more ambitious work on Hughes's thesis about the "symbolic fable" laid out and retold in the last fifteen of Shakespeare's plays. Coincidentally, Hughes was editing a new selection to be titled *The Essential Shakespeare,* for which he would develop a new introduction. Their telephone seminars became even more frequent and detailed. In 1990, Hughes asked if he could write letters to her that developed the ideas they had been discussing. And thus was set in motion the process by which Hughes composed the first draft of *Shakespeare and the Goddess of Complete Being.* Fifty-four very long letters arrived in Donya Feuer's mailbox between April 23—traditionally regarded as the date of Shakespeare's birth and death—and June 14. This was the way Hughes subverted the censor in himself. He could speak without constraint to somebody named "you," an empathic listener.

Sinking into Folk-Tale

Hughes undertook yet another partnership with a woman artist in the 1970s. His publisher commissioned from the photographer Fay Godwin a new publicity portrait to release with the publication of *Crow.* Hughes normally hated a photo shoot, but he and Godwin discovered they had interests in common, including the landscape of West Yorkshire. As they completed the session, Hughes mentioned the possibility of collaborating with her on a book. "He told me there was an area of the Calder Valley he wanted to write about, but felt the need for a 'visual trigger,'" Godwin explained. The project languished, on his side: these were the years of Moortown Farm and the trough of his depression. But in 1976, Godwin sent pictures that galvanized Hughes into action, as did the news she gave him, that she had been diagnosed with cancer. "Ted told me to 'turn the current positive' and get on with the book," and at once he began sending her what he referred to as "Elmet" poems.

Hughes took Godwin's photographs as his point of departure for poems that lay claim to his Yorkshire past. In notes about this project, he says he fought the temptation to center the poems on memories drawn from his childhood, feeling that it was "not right to requisition this whole region and landscape to my own autobiography." Instead, neatly circumventing his bristling defenses against the direct representation of personal experience in poetry, he based the book on the memory of his mother's voice, his mother's tales about the past. This is the book in which he "sank" his body "into folk-tale." Hughes confided to Ben Sonnenberg that writing these poems had been a trial to him because a tributary of grim, even hateful memories of family life ran alongside rapturous ones, and both were true. He was able to write the book only by situating himself in his mother's stories and then, more riskily, in his mother's feelings.

Hughes's poetry never addressed his mother directly while she was alive. But *Remains of Elmet*, which was published exactly a decade after her death, begins the process of investigating his mother's role in his vocation as a poet. This book is in many ways an appropriation of his Celtic lineage, and its dedication read, "In memory of Edith Farrar"—his mother's family name—not Edith Hughes. In the prefatory poem of *Remains of Elmet*, Hughes refers to the spoken transmission of this culture, his "inheritance" from the Farrars, as an "archaeology of the mouth." Hughes looked back to the Celts of Elmet because, he said, "it's false to say these gods and heroes are obsolete: they are the better part of our patrimony still locked up." Or in his case, his matrimony. Using his mother's memories as his starting point and interpreting her visionary powers as evidence of the continuing existence of forces worshiped by the pre-Christian Celts, in the Elmet poems Hughes endows the Yorkshire landscape with articulate spirituality.

In *Remains of Elmet*, the mother's body is literally the landscape itself, the mounds and fluid contours of the moors; the bony ridges and deep clefts of the valleys; the slow heave of the earth that is dismantling the ruined mills and cottages, tumbling the stone back to the site it was raised from; the speechless intelligence that Hughes believed lay patient within the land, awaiting release.

But a few of the poems are directly autobiographical, and one of them, "Leaf Mould," dramatizes the way Ted Hughes received his birthright as a poet from his mother. In "Leaf Mould," Hughes imagines himself enclosed within his mother's womb while she walks on Hardcastle Crags, in the Calder Valley, gathering material for her garden. While she walks she is communing with the dead soldiers she knew as suitors in her maidenhood. They come to her as voices in the forest around her. And she transmits this occult power to the infant riding in her womb.

> brainwashed by her nostalgias,
> You were her step-up transformer

At the time of his birth she bestows her second gift on him, the Calder Valley as his subject: she hangs it around his neck like the harp on which David made the Psalms.

> Now, whenever you touch it, God listens
> Only for her voice

God listens, that is, for the living voice of the dead. The poems about Elmet point actually not to ruination but to massive, slow-moving progress toward renewal. The tumbled Pennine stone building blocks of factories and cottages, erected during centuries of settlement, were now reburying themselves in the lap of the valleys and the breast of the moors, to be reborn as mere stone. That is his celebratory vision of Elmet—a landscape rapidly and purposefully proceeding into its prehistory, returning to its primal origins.

Writing the poems of Elmet sent a taproot into Hughes's deepest relation to Edith Farrar, the enigma of her sexuality, regarded from the vantage of "six years into her posthumous life." The whole book is a meditation on the posthumous life of the dead to whom he is attached in the Calder Valley, including Sylvia Plath. In the poem "Heptonstall Cemetery," Sylvia's gravestone and Edith's gravestone are seen as feathers on the wing of an angelic black swan, the "giant beating wing" of wind bearing the clouds toward the Atlantic. The inclusion of Plath is more than incidental, for the composition of these poems coincided with Ted Hughes's work on editing the stories and journals and poems of Sylvia Plath for publication. Gradually, he was drawing his mother and Sylvia Plath together as composite influences in the history of his vocation.

The decision to release Plath's manuscripts was more or less forced on Hughes by circumstance. By 1977, royalties from *The Bell Jar* had dropped what Hughes called a "money bomb" on his life. By 1977 an overwhelming tax bill loomed—Hughes lamented that he should long ago have moved to Ireland, where artists were immune from taxation. The scale of the annual earnings of the Plath estate "astonished" Ben Sonnenberg when he learned about it from Hughes in 1987, when it was probably about $150,000. Hughes claimed to Lucas Myers that he could, possibly, owe as much as 99 percent of the total earnings on all her books—"believe me, that is quite a sum." Hughes had invested the royalties in real estate and was cash-poor.

A sensible decision would be to liquidate his biggest asset, the Plath archive. Hughes knew a good deal about the money that could be made from manuscripts, because he had been keeping an eye on the literary marketplace that bustled on the fringe of trade book publishing and had been selling manuscripts of his own, now and then. The Emory archive holds amusing documentation of a transaction in August 1975, in a Devon pub, between Hughes and some antique dealers: in exchange for "a big coffer"—presumably an antique chest or trunk—Hughes swapped four folders, each containing one poem in manuscript along with its drafts, several with writing by Hughes on the reverse. Hughes's annotations on these manuscript folders include all the details a book dealer would look for in appraising them; and he added a list of possible buyers along with his own estimate of the current market value of one of his poems. For "manuscript pages of achieved poems," he should receive £35 per sheet; for the author's holograph of a published poem, £20 apiece. These prices represented a substantial rise in the market value of manuscripts—in 1963, Hughes had received £5 per poem, often many pages of drafting, and he had already become a well-known poet. In 1977, Hughes was reluctant to sell his own papers to raise cash because of the psychological impact he feared it would have on him. He was reluctant to sell Plath's papers because the prices were still rising.

But the tax bill forced his hand. By the end of 1980, he had sketched an inventory of Plath's papers—around 4000 pages of manuscripts and typescripts—and turned the negotiations over to Sotheby's. Plath's archive was purchased by the Neilson Library at Plath's alma mater, Smith College. The sale was consummated on August 22, 1981, "immensely to our advantage," Hughes informed Gerald. And soon the pages were crossing the Atlantic to be shelved in boxes that stood not far from the rooms at Smith in which Plath had written some of them, thirty years before.

From "Relic Husband" to "Her Husband"

Hughes was thinking about financial profit when he gloated to Gerald about selling Plath's papers. But another kind of benefit had accrued during his years of managing the estate. In the course of collating Plath's manuscripts, reading Plath's letters to assist Aurelia in the development of *Letters Home,* and sorting the materials for sale, Hughes had become interested in all of Plath's writing, not only her poetry. In the run-up to selling the papers, Hughes decided he was going to print absolutely everything printable, "to make one big final eructation of every last morsel, with some flashes of editorial discretion," he wrote to Lucas Myers. And he planned to be the editor of this work, to select and arrange everything that went out under her name, and to write all the introductions himself. Though relinquishing the manuscripts, he would take artistic control of the way *both* he and Plath were represented in print.

In this project, Hughes had the able assistance of Fran McCullough, whom he had met when she first joined Harper and Row in 1965. One of her earliest acquisitions had been Hughes's edition of *Ariel,* and in handling it she had become Hughes's most trusted American ally. Their letters suggest that they became good friends—McCullough shared Hughes's fascination with astrology, among other compatibilities. When the need arose to work in close proximity, McCullough would come to Court Green. Together in 1974 they had wrestled the billowing first draft of Aurelia's manuscript into a form suitable for publication. From 1973 through 1980 they dealt with the abundant textual and ethical problems presented by Plath's archive. The ethical problems arose from Plath's habit, in her journal, of satirizing even their closest friends. The textual problems arose from the disorderly state of the manuscripts, and questions about which were the latest versions of Plath's poems. In *Collected Poems,* the critic Judith Kroll is acknowledged as the person who "did much to establish many of the final texts in their detail."

Hughes appointed himself the task of presenting Plath to audiences who already thought they knew all about her. He believed he would be able to correct the misconceptions that had been created by the journalistic sensationalizing of *Ariel* and the misconceptions to be found in the recently published biography of Plath by Edward Butscher. Writing prefaces to her work presented him with a difficult rhetorical problem, however. Hughes had never wavered in his belief that Plath was a genius, and he was confident that he understood what she had accomplished as an artist. But he was widely thought to have been in some way responsible for her death. How could he exercise his authority as a shrewd judge of literary artistry in the context of assessing her tragically curtailed career? Hughes devised a successful solution, in the form of two personae. One was the *literary editor* who greeted readers at the door of the book, and introduced the author Sylvia Plath and the works she had produced. The other was a *literary character* inside the book: the man Hughes sometimes called TH, and sometime called "her husband."

The first publication Hughes selected and edited from these papers was *Johnny Panic and the Bible of Dreams,* a collection of Plath's prose, comprised of stories, journalism, and a few character sketches from the journals. The introduction to this book is the best essay Hughes ever wrote about Plath. Pleasure infuses his own prose as he recalls the circumstances under which she constructed these stories, and as he describes the peculiar difficulties that inhibited her. His comments assume but never acknowledge the privileged position he occupied as her husband in gathering this information— he refers to himself simply as "an editor of Sylvia Plath's unpublished writings," as if he were one among many. But he tells us, obliquely, something very interesting about Ted Hughes. Formerly, he had regarded all that wasn't poetry as dross. But he had now come to regard all of Plath's writings as equally illuminating of her distinctive gift. Her journals were as important as her poems. "The themes she found engaging enough to excite her concentration all turn out to be episodes from her own life; they are all autobiography. They have the vitality of her personal participation, her subjectivity." And as a result, the voice we hear in her prose—all of it—is continuous with her poetry. The selections in *Johnny Panic* were meant to illustrate that striking coherence: "I am more and more inclined to think that any bit of evidence which corrects and clarifies our idea of what she really was is important."

Yet when the time came to write an introduction to the journals, in 1980, Hughes fumbled. By then, *Letters Home* had come out, bearing big chunks of his biography in its teeth. Hughes recoiled from the prospect of further exposure to public curiosity; he told Lucas Myers that he never would have published the journals if it hadn't been for the tax bill: he had committed himself to the book before the whole archive was sold. When Fran McCullough presented him with the edited manuscript of the journals for approval, he dithered provokingly:

he pulled rank, he agonized endlessly, he required cuts and more cuts. He could demand omissions, as owner of the copyright. But at the opening of the book he would still have to explain why they break off in 1959: he would have to admit that he had lost one of the journals and destroyed another. His discomfort was evident in the brief, unenthusiastic foreword he contributed to *The Journals of Sylvia Plath,* where he speaks in the first person; the real impact on Hughes of reading Plath's journals would not be visible for another sixteen years, when he published *Birthday Letters.* Nor was he ever satisfied with the edited text; it was both incomplete and too full of details he didn't want to see in print. At the last moment he backed out of being described on the title page as the book's co-editor, and titled himself "consulting editor." In her editor's note to the published journals, McCullough showed only the faintest of the battle scars, remarking, mildly, that the cutting of "intimacies" from the journal has "the effect of diminishing Plath's eroticism, which was quite strong."

In Hughes's eyes, however, the most important item on the list of publications to be drawn from Plath's papers was her collected poems. Writing the introduction, Hughes transforms himself from that abject public figure, the "relic husband," into a knowing and engaging literary character, "her husband."

The editor in Hughes took charge of the literary department, and wrote a splendid introduction. He first produces an endearing image of Plath at work. Plath's attitude to writing poetry was "artisan-like," Hughes said; "if she couldn't get a table out of the material, she was quite happy to get a chair, or even a toy. The end product for her was not so much a successful poem, as something that had temporarily exhausted her ingenuity." He characterizes Plath's distinctive process of composing individual poems and organizing them for publication; he discusses the development of her art. Then he describes the look of the manuscripts of her last poems, "aswarm" with beautiful phrases "crowding all over the place" but cast off before she settled on a final version. His lovely phrasing conceals a metaphor, in which Plath's archive equals a hive, full of honeycombs yet to be gathered.

And he coolly delivers a bombshell—acknowledging for the first time that the *Ariel* he had published in 1965 was not the *Ariel* he had found in Plath's black spring binder after her death. "The more personally aggressive poems" were left out, he explains, being possibly "too hard for the reading public to take." Now he lists at the back of the book, in order, the forty-one poems of Plath's original *Ariel* manuscript. Within these last few paragraphs Hughes projects an evolution for the public understanding of Plath's work, a development of which he has taken charge, and is passing on to us. Now we have been given "her" *Ariel* to place alongside the one he devised back in 1965; and we have the hint or promise of some further, ampler representation of her processes of composition, a fuller collection that might include these handwritten drafts along with poems that have escaped the archive so far but will, presumably, be added as time goes by. Throughout the introduction Hughes speaks in the first person, rhetorically deft, only a smidgeon self-conscious, growing more and more present as a participant as the essay progresses.

Hughes also wrote the annotations at the back of the book. And it is there, under the protective cover of endnotes, that Hughes presents himself as a literary character: "TH," the husband of this artisan. The back matter of this book is so cluttered with apparatus that it is easy to miss the little gem embedded in fine print on pages 275–96, but Hughes has constructed a miniature autobiography containing a first-person narrator revisiting scenes from his marriage—apparently by consulting Plath's journals and his own. Each year has its own introductory note, followed by notes to individual poems. Hughes's narrative, despite the brevity required by the endnote format, has a leisurely, reminiscent tone, as if he is turning the pages of a photo album. "On 16 June, she married. . . . SP and her husband lived in Boston until June 1959. . . . She and TH drove around the United States. . . . TH had received a Guggenheim Foundation award, and adding this cash to what they had saved from their teaching and other work, they sailed for Europe in December. . . ."

Surprisingly, only a few poems for each year are singled out for annotation. Hughes is evidently not aiming for thoroughness. What is he aiming for?

His first note, regarding Plath's "Conversation Among the Ruins" (1956), establishes the model: he will supply what *only* he can supply, her husband, who was present at the creation. "Conversation Among the Ruins," he comments, is the title of a painting by Giorgio de Chirico, of which a postcard was "pinned to the door of the poet's room" in Whitstead. The shift within this sentence is from the level of information widely available (the title of de Chirico's painting) to information that only someone who had climbed the stairs to Plath's room could recall. Reading Hughes's note about the postcard, a reader familiar with the rest of Sylvia Plath's work will be led to remember the supercharged pages of writing Plath set down in her journal while she was hoping for Ted Hughes to climb those stairs in February 1956. She transferred her anxiety into the process of writing "Pursuit":

> The panther's tread is on the stairs,
> Coming up and up the stairs

But Hughes does not annotate "Pursuit"; Plath has already annotated it, in *Letters Home,* pages 222–26; and on pages 115 and 129 of the journals that will soon be in print.

The point, I think, is that, in this minor autobiographical tour de force at the end of Plath's most important book, Hughes has relinquished the role of editor—looking on and commenting on the poet at work, as he does in the introduction—to present himself in the character of Plath's working partner. His edition of the *Collected Poems* establishes 1956 as the year Plath became a poet we want to collect. It is the year they met. By placing himself inside the story from its beginnings, Hughes suggests that neither could be written about, as poets, without reference to the other. The prestige of his own standing as a poet, in combination with the privilege of his intimate association with Plath, gave him credentials as Plath's biographer that no one else would ever possess.

And in the spirit of the call-and-response practice that was the hallmark of their creative partnership, Hughes seems to have left an image of himself editing Plath's *Collected Poems* in *Birthday Letters.* In a thumbnail portrait tucked into the poem "Drawing," he is sitting at his desk, looking at one of Plath's ink drawings and remembering Plath on their honeymoon, sketching the marketplace in Benidorm:

> Here it is. . . .
> Our otherwise lost morning

The actual marketplace has been lost: razed to make way for the tourist trade; her drawing keeps it alive for him to revisit. And Plath's hand that held the pen too has been lost, under the earth of her grave in Heptonstall Cemetery,

> While my pen travels
> Only two hundred miles from your hand.
> Holding this memory

His pen, it might be said, makes the shaman's journey underground to retrieve this memory, for us, the living. Here it is. Otherwise, lost.

Conversation among the ruins. The editorial work Hughes performed in *Collected Poems* inaugurated the project of staking a claim in the territory of literary versions of Plath's life. In 1976 he had written to Gerald that he felt himself to be "on the threshold of some big new step for my work, but I just can't get through to it." The problems, he thought, could only be solved by "getting rid of Sylvia for good and all." Now, with her manuscripts safely archived in a library, Hughes was no longer the steward of her remains. He had crossed that threshold by reentering a creative alliance with Plath that would stimulate his work for the rest of his career.

CHAPTER TEN

THE MAGICAL DEAD
(1984–1998)

In December 1984 Ted Hughes became the Poet Laureate of England, a venerable honor that originated in 1616 with the pension granted to Shakespeare's younger contemporary, Ben Jonson. A Poet Laureate is appointed for life by the sovereign and becomes an officer of the royal household, with the expectation that he will compose commemorative or celebratory works for occasions of national importance.

Ted Hughes was not the only candidate who had been considered for this appointment. Following the death of John Betjeman, who had held the position since 1972, it was offered to Philip Larkin, who declined. Hughes accepted gladly. His attitude toward royalty was unusual among contemporary artists; Hughes envisioned the sovereign as a vital principle of connection among all of the nation's living people and all its past generations, an idea he expressed in the metaphor of a wheel stabilized by its hub:

> The Nation's a Soul
> With a crown at the hub
> To keep it whole

Hughes said he had acquired this attitude toward the nation from his mother, who had, he thought, a "tribal allegiance" to the land and to its "magical dead."

Poet of England

Hughes undertook the duties of his office with relish; the public occasions he chose to commemorate called upon myth-making skills he had been honing for many years. One of his first and most successful Laureate poems "Rain-Charm for the Duchy," celebrated the christening of Prince Harry, the second son of the Prince of Wales. Dated on the winter solstice 1984, it opened with the description of a thunderstorm that ended a five-month drought:

> You scrambled into the car
> Scattering oxygen like a drenched bush

As the rain falls and the rivers rise in the poem, the lines swell and overflow the line endings in a flood of verbal inventiveness. And though the poem shows no sign of needing footnotes, a wonderful layering of meanings can be glimpsed in the simile "drenched bush." Slyly suggestive, it points to an ancient belief in the relationship between the king's

Ted Hughes as Poet Laureate, September 26, 1986

fertility and the nation's health—the theme of *The Waste Land* of T. S. Eliot, without the agony but with the same metaphorically wet hair.

Many people considered the office of Poet Laureate as quaint and unnecessary, but Hughes's writing had something to offer political life, broadly conceived. At the time of his appointment, his most recent publications—*Season Songs* (1974), *Moortown* (1978), *Remains of Elmet* (1979), *Under the North Star* (1981), and *River* (1983)—had increasingly to do with British locales, and held a view of nature that resonated with contemporary policy debates about farming, ecology, the health of the rivers. Moreover, he had an attractive interest in educating the young. Throughout his career he had been writing books for children, producing works that became contemporary children's classics that are frequently reprinted: *Meet My Folks!* (1961), *How the Whale Became* (1963), *The Earth-Owl and Other Moon People* (1963), *Nessie the Mannerless Monster* (1964), *The Iron Man* (1968), and *What Is the Truth?* (1984). In 1967, *Poetry in the Making* was compiled from his radio broadcasts for the schools, and widely adopted as a textbook.

Hughes had a taste for the high life that was a perquisite of this office too, and greatly enjoyed his association with the royal household, as references in his letters to his brother show. In 1974, after receiving the Queen's Gold Medal for Poetry from the hand of the Queen herself, Hughes had reported that she surprised him by being "very lively and nimble, small, immediately likable," and that they had a "nice talk." Following his appointment as Poet Laureate, he was welcomed as a friend by other members of the royal family. On fishing expeditions to Scotland, Hughes was invited to stay at Balmoral, sometime residence of the Queen Mother, where he was pampered and entertained by his hostess. He enjoyed her company; he said that as a child he always thought that the Queen Mother pictured in the newspapers resembled his own mother: both had leonine faces. Poetry he wrote for her birthday celebrations reflects this feeling of intimacy. The Queen Mother was born August 4, 1900, under the sign of Leo, like Hughes. For her eighty-fifth birthday Hughes boldly constructed an ornate tribute, "The Dream of the Lion," on a fanciful connection between her birth sign and the totem lion on the royal family's coat of arms.

These occult themes in Hughes's work attracted the attention of the Prince of Wales; Hughes became a familiar visitor at his home in Highgrove, and a sort of "spiritual adviser"—it was said that the Prince shared with Hughes an "unconventional spiritual curiosity." After Hughes's death, Prince Charles commissioned in his memory a pair of stained glass windows for his private sanctuary, depicting scenes from nature and commemorating their friendship.

Hughes's term as Poet Laureate fundamentally redefined the ideal of service in this office and, as it turned out, he had exactly the right disposition for the role, which he performed like a charismatic schoolmaster. Quite a lot of the creative work Hughes produced during those years was not poetry at all. He made numerous recordings of poetry, his own and that of others, in conjunction with his belief that the voice, not print, was the true medium of the poet's art. And he wrote a number of ambitious essays focused on some of the great works of the English tradition—astute, beautifully written, urgently communicative essays about the poetry of Eliot, Yeats, and Shakespeare. One of the best is a stunningly learned disquisition on the innovative poetic meters in the work of Samuel Taylor Coleridge, in which Hughes rose to new levels of ingenious rhetorical charm, even for him. Much of the other work he produced as Poet Laureate was commissioned—often "versions" or translations of works by other writers, often for the theatre. At this point in his career, commissions suited him very well. Hughes had always thrived in collaborations, and well-paid commissions worked on him as releasing agents for the massive learning and technical expertise he had acquired through lifelong, unstinting practice of his craft.

The Drama of Completion

The recognition Hughes received as Poet Laureate sometimes felt intrusive and unwelcome to him in daily life—the correspondence alone was a perpetual and inescapable burden on his time. But it was unquestionably beneficial to the "secret" life of his imagination. Paradoxically, Hughes's public prominence seems to have diminished the pressure of his vexed relationship to audiences. It freed him psychologically to confront the question of how he might shape his legacy to literature, how he wished to be seen and known by posterity.

Hughes was aware that his esoteric works were difficult and offputting to many readers, but he also worried that *all* of his poems might become unfathomable, once he was no longer alive to present them in person. At public readings, he provided often quite lengthy remarks and explanations for his work: "poems need prose precincts" as he put it. He acknowledged that it was a mistake not to write up some version of these commentaries, to accompany his printed work— like animals, poems could become extinct if the poet didn't endow them with a "habitat."

It was surely with this problem in mind that Hughes began in the mid-1990s to consider selling his literary papers. He contacted Ann Skea, a young Australian scholar, asking whether she might be willing to perform the task of sorting and inventorying them. Skea had corresponded with Hughes for several years while researching a study of his poetry, *Ted Hughes: The Poetic Quest*, and she had proved herself to be a careful, thorough reader. In her letters to him she made canny guesses about obscure allusions in his work, and she asked the kind of questions he appreciated—impersonal questions. If Skea accepted his invitation to work on the papers, she would have to drop everything and travel halfway around the world to Devon, putting her personal and professional life on hold, possibly for a very long time.

Ann Skea agreed to drop everything, and had her plans for a temporary move to Devon well under way, when she received a letter from Hughes withdrawing the invitation. There was a note of panic in his terse message. He felt very awkward about having to write such a letter, but he had his reasons, five of them. The one that counted was his shock at what he had come across in a casual sampling of the collection. He told her frankly that he wanted no one but himself to look at some of the things he had rediscovered; he would have to handle and consider every single page; and if so, why not make the inventory while he was at it?

It took him several years to finish the work, and eventually the papers were sold in one lot to the Robert W. Woodruff Library at Emory University in Atlanta, Georgia, where the resources for acquisitions had been enriched by a legacy of stock in Coca-Cola. In March 1997 the archive of Ted Hughes left Court Green for permanent residence in America—108,000 items in eighty-six boxes weighing 2½ tons, plus materials sealed in a trunk that is not to be opened until the year 2023. In late autumn 1996, Hughes's wife, Carol, snapped a color photograph of him absorbed in this project: Hughes sitting forward on a wooden chair, elbows on his knees, turning the pages of a letter. His mouth is closed in a firm relaxed line; a couple of days' growth of beard blurs the outline of his jaw. On his nose are large spectacles with amber frames from which a cord runs under the collar of an olive shirt that has been left unbuttoned at the neck far enough to disclose the gray hair on his chest. He is wearing khaki pants. One dark brown shoe is in evidence, the other is lost behind the ranks of cardboard cartons that fill the whole foreground of the picture. On the table to Hughes's right, a chinoiserie lamp illuminates the pages in his hand, and a red Magic Marker lies within reach. On the wall behind him hang several prints, including an image by Leonard Baskin: a bird with feathers resembling the plates on a suit of Japanese armor. At Hughes's back we notice a wooden door.

If the picture conveys a sense of pathos, though, it is entirely in the eye of the beholder who knows the date of Ted Hughes's exit. The actual man will go on to publish six more books during the next two years. And at this particular moment he is completely unself-conscious, ignoring the camera, intent on the business at hand—selecting what to include, what to leave out.

An important consequence of Hughes's decision to organize his own archive was that only he would ever know what had been excluded from the record he was arranging for posterity. Hughes's calm posture in the photograph radiates confidence that he has done a good job. He is not only completing a business transaction, he is putting the finishing touches on the image that will survive him.

One item Hughes has set aside from these papers is the journal that he kept quite regularly during some periods of his life. Hughes well knew the value of a writer's journal—it supplied exactly the kind of "habitat" Hughes lamented that he had not provided for his own poetry. Its absence from the archive suggests that he didn't wish to supply posterity immediately with a master file of mere information, one that would diffuse the force of the persona that spoke in his work. There was a foxy aspect to this decision, a desire to elude the baying pack of biographers he knew would be off and away soon after his death. There was also an ethic in it. Hughes held the view that commentators on literature had an obligation to serve as stewards of the achieved human voice to be found in poetry. He thought that the aim of biographers was exactly the opposite: they were levelers and spoilers. This was one of the reasons he had always refused to assist would-be biographers of Sylvia Plath. He told Plath's mother that he thought a biography of Plath would diminish the stature of her work in the eyes of readers. All biographers wanted to do, he said, was "show how like the rest of us" a genius such as Plath "really" was.

Nothing can keep a biographer from piecing together a fairly accurate account of the ways in which Hughes was like the rest of us, if that's what we want to know. But Hughes's actions in assembling this archive apparently have another aim: to make available the immense pool of manuscripts in which the image of his persona had evolved. By the time Hughes undertook the sale of his papers to Emory, he appears to have assessed himself by the standards he applied to the great poets in his personal pantheon and concluded that he measured up. As far back as Hughes could look into his career, he found a consistent desire, a consistent shape to his vocation. To put it most simply, Hughes had lived for poetry, with single-mindedness of the sort he had long ago discerned in W.B. Yeats, the first poet who ever seized his imagination. Yeats had "formulated his life mission on the grandest scale," and had centered his work in a first-person point of view constructed to serve as a revivifying conduit of the great mythologies. And Yeats was a modern man, like Hughes, confronting the very real possibility that civilization might within his own lifetime disappear entirely. Hughes thought that he, by a similar path to that of Yeats, had reached an understanding of the very foundation of the human instinct for survival, the capacity for mythmaking that he believed was a biological endowment in human beings. This archive of his papers would provide posterity with background, the confluence of the personal and the historical dimensions of his struggle for creative self-transcendence.

Arguably, the position he filled as Poet Laureate provided Hughes with the confidence to complete a coherent self-mythology that accounted for the vocation he had conducted as a poet-shaman. He knew that a character flaw—"diabolical fear of subjectivity"—had always stood in the way of his writing "the kind of book that I wanted, and that others could relate to"—even when writing the poems of Elmet. He condemned himself for producing "impersonal mood pieces," when the book needed simply to be about his family. But after his appointment as Poet Laureate Hughes experienced a new surge of creativity that produced the "drama of completion," in his own work, of the story of his life. During the last decade of his life, Hughes produced the poems that bestow on himself a childhood, a marriage, a separation, and a reunion, each an episode that accounts for the poet he became.

Among the most important additions to the consolidation of Hughes's myth were those in which he found a place for his father. William Henry Hughes died in February 1981 in Devon, where he had been living near Court Green. His body was transported back to Yorkshire, for burial in Heptonstall Cemetery, directly above the body of his wife, Edith, and not far from the grave of Sylvia Plath. His death permitted Hughes to memorialize his father's role in the history of the Calder Valley. For Hughes the son and for Hughes the poet, that role was as a survivor of the First World War.

"Dust as We Are" is the most interesting of these poems. It dramatizes the moment in which Ted Hughes receives his inheritance, and knows it. A worried boy sits alongside an anguished, unspeaking father who is replaying, in his head, battle scenes that the boy is watching with him—"like TV," carnage seen not from the perspective of the history books, but through the terrorized sensorium of the soldier. Hughes's father had attended the debut of modern warfare, on the beaches at Gallipoli. And in "Dust as We Are," Hughes produces a fabulous image for the expression of who, or what, this was, "killed but alive," that returned from the Great War:

> I divined,
> With a comb,
> Under his wavy, golden hair . . . ,
> The fragility of skull. And I filled
> With his knowledge

For an Englishman to abandon his irony in public takes courage indeed, so it is important to appreciate that Hughes has deserted the stance of world-weary irony—good-bye to all that—with which he ends the earlier poem to his father, "Out." Hughes is being rewarded for his filial piety, one might say, by the gods—being permitted to "divine" through touch what lies beyond expression in words; the strands of hair are direct conductors of his father's knowledge, bypassing speech. This is an utterly deft moment in Hughes's poetry—a consummation of his struggle to affiliate his father with his masculine poetic vocation. His father has literally come back from the land of the dead, like a shaman; and he imparts the equivalent of a shaman's spiritual knowledge through his skull, to his son.

Discovering his father's body as a site of knowledge is a radical moment in Hughes's work. "Dust as We Are" establishes in Hughes's myth that his poems about his father *are* his poems about the twentieth-century's wars, and about his birthright as a poet: he, Ted Hughes, has been ordained to devise speech that might undo the damage. Since his father was dead, he could not be hurt by Hughes's appropriation of his wounds and nightmares.

The way Hughes formulated his mythic relationship to Plath, during the same era of his Laureateship, is more complex, because it required the affirmation of her undiminished energy as the defining influence in his life. That story was not about generational succession; it was about complementarity, and its plot can be discerned in that interesting interview Hughes and Plath conducted in 1961 for broadcast by the BBC, *Two of a Kind*.

The account Hughes and Plath each made of their creative partnership in 1961 said they were "very similar" and "very different"; they had one "shared" mind, but they conducted "secret lives" in their imaginations. At the time of the interview these contradictory forces were operating in dynamic balance; neither of them remarked on the kinds of trouble that might emerge in the course of lives so poised. By the time Hughes began writing *Birthday Letters,* he had read Plath's journals, and had felt the power of the "secret life" her imagination had been conducting. Not "secrets," in the sense of action undertaken furtively or deceitfully, but language that did not enter their everyday discourse. Plath had been an expert at transferring her subjectivity into words on a page. Her journal was a treasury of expression drawn from the "secreted," entirely personal reservoir of language that evolves from the beginning in each human being: "very different" yet paradoxically "quite similar" in each speaker of the common language.

But Hughes had learned something else from her journals, and from thinking about Plath's development into womanhood. He and Plath had each been conducting secret lives in their imaginations because they occupied *essentially* different human bodies: biologically different. The male of the species makes a fundamental error in assuming that the mind he shares with his consort is the same mind. At best, his mind is attuned to the fabulous complexity of the imagery that rises from her creative expression. But always thrumming beneath his powers of rational understanding and symbol-making is the zest of the sperm. Possibly, this is the idea signified in the unsettling title, *Capriccio,* that Hughes gave to the book he addressed to Assia Wevill, during this same period. In Hughes's myth, Assia's role is purely that of demonic attractant: "Her saliva pure amnesia," her gaze fueled by "trophies digested," as we recall. Being male, he was biologically predisposed to be her natural prey, as she was his. The myth underlying Hughes's account of his relationship to Sylvia Plath required a separation followed by a reunion, after the definitive biological differences have asserted themselves.

Birthday Letters is the story of that reunion. Hughes produced the

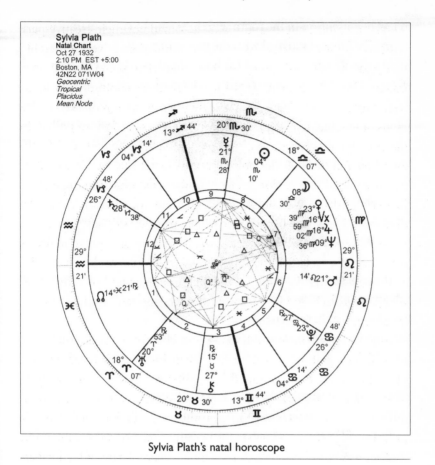

Sylvia Plath's natal horoscope

individual poems over a period of twenty-five years, but apparently the possibility of organizing them into a narrative only occurred to him in 1992: "My own drama with the dead," as he described the story he wanted to tell. He kept the plan secret from all but a few friends whose literary judgment he wished to consult; he thought the pieces might be artistically too "raw and unguarded." They had emerged from the repeated, intimate, troublesome contact with the voluminous pages of her manuscripts, in every genre, that had occupied him for years. Reflecting on that time, later, Hughes said that he began writing the verse letters to Plath as a way to thrust aside every other consideration, to feel her attention in the room with him, and to speak plainly to her, in privacy. He was satisfied with the pieces in which he found that "intimate wavelength," and in which he avoided merely poetic rhetorical effects. "I tried to . . . strip myself child-naked and wade in."

Birthday Letters opens, in "Fulbright Scholars," with Hughes's first sight of Plath in a newspaper article, as we have seen; but the plot—his "drama with the dead"—is generated by his first encounter with her journal, ten years after her death, in "Visit":

> Your actual words, as they floated
> Out through your throat and tongue and onto your page . . .
> Your story. My story

It is not the contents of her diary but the shock of her voice that galvanizes him; this is not the "I" of her poetry, but what Plath called the "diary I" of her journal, where she was consciously constructing a persona of her own, drafting notes that would evolve into *The Bell Jar*. More: he is learning that before their acquaintance was twenty-four hours old, its bewitchment by myth had begun. He has discovered a writer designing a Poetic Self, and turning him into a literary character—"the male lead in your drama"—at the same time.

In *Birthday Letters* he enters into partnership with this project: the imagination of himself as Plath's consort, in a story. In these poems, all details are metaphorical even when they are factual. Take, for example, Hughes's description in the poem "St. Botolph's," which presents Plath as if captured by a flashbulb, in a photograph that he is surveying from bottom to top, from her feet to her face:

> Swaying so slender
> It seemed your long, perfect American legs
> Simply went on up

A moment's thought will reveal the unlikelihood that Ted Hughes got a good look at Sylvia Plath's legs at the party on February 25, 1956. Plath's journal says she was wearing a tight skirt that night; and she always wore her skirts hemmed several inches below the knee, at the unflattering lower-mid-calf length dictated by 1950s fashion. Hughes appears to be referring not to her legs but to the photograph of her legs published on the front page of the campus newspaper, *Varsity*, in May 1956. It was reprinted in 1975 as one of the illustrations in *Letters Home*.

Throughout *Birthday Letters*, jolts of this kind cue us to recognize that the poet's access to the past has been thoroughly interfered with: actuality is always being absorbed into storytelling, and your story isn't my story. Sometimes the departures are so obvious that they call attention to themselves, as in "St. Botolph's," above, when Hughes recalls that on the night he first kissed Plath he stripped a blue headband from her hair; Plath's journal says it was red. In his poem about Plath's misadventure with a stallion, Sam, Hughes has Plath slipping off her horse and clinging to his belly, in life-threatening proximity to the pavement beneath her; Plath's letters and poem about the wild ride tell us she lost the reins and stirrups, and clung to Sam's neck. In the poem "Visit," Hughes recalls that the date on which they first made love was Friday, April 13, though the actual date was March 23; Friday the thirteenth was the day Plath returned from Europe and rejoined Hughes in London. But Hughes's myth needed a first sexual encounter on Friday the thirteenth, needed life-threatening danger from a ride on a horse, needed the color blue.

These specific details return as features of the poetic closure of *Birthday Letters* and *Howls and Whispers*. A good example is the way Hughes repossesses the color red from Plath's writing, and substitutes blue. Red was one of the colors Plath liked to have around her, and Plath's published poems and letters and journal are the unnamed but easily recognizable sources of Hughes's imagery in the last poem of *Birthday Letters*, "Red." But *Birthday Letters* shows that Hughes associated the color red with blood, and rage, and Plath's vivid defiance, and other disturbing influences in their life together. Blue is the color Hughes introduces like ritual magic at the end of the book, to restore balance,

> Blue was your kindly spirit—not a ghoul
> But electrified, a guardian

The image ties the ending of *Birthday Letters* back into their first night of love, in the poem "18 Rugby Street," where Plath wears "plumage of excitement,"

> A bluish voltage
> Fluorescent cobalt, a flare of aura
> That I later learned was yours uniquely

The last word in *Birthday Letters* is "blue," and in *Howls and Whispers,* a blue jewel is the metaphor for Plath's soul.

The apparent departures from fact in *Birthday Letters* and the subtle call-and-response effect of the imagery can be obvious only to readers saturated in Plath's works, however. That is the point, precisely. The clever subtext of Hughes's account of their marriage, in *Birthday Letters,* puts the Hughes persona, her husband, in dialogue not with an actual woman but with the vivid persona of Plath's well-known texts.

During most of the years that Hughes was in charge of Plath's posthumous reputation, he had considered it his duty to suppress everything that wouldn't show Plath at her best, and that definitely included those sprawling journals, with all their embarrassing personal details. Then, something happened that changed Hughes's mind about the status of Plath's personal prose. It seems he discovered that his introductions and forewords and essays about her achievements, and his pitying explanations about her disabilities had been . . . not wrong, exactly, but too emphatically *his.* In contrast, the subjectivity he discovered in the journals was rooted in female experience that stood quite outside his interpretations of it.

Now, writing *Birthday Letters,* Hughes turns to Plath's voluminous records of daily life as to invaluable depositions of their life together. As Plath's survivor, Hughes winced when he encountered the Lawrentian prose in which she described him to her mother. As her editor, Hughes required the omission of passages that he thought would not add to her luster in the world's eyes. But as the voice of *Birthday Letters*, he takes on the whole range of the subjectivity that can be discovered in Plath's writings. His apparent misquotations of her words are deliberate, ostentatious substitutions, for he is not remembering her words; he has been prompted by her words to enter into dialogue with that self she made in language. In order to do so, Hughes fetches that figure called "her husband," in the footnotes he wrote for Plath's *Collected Poems*, front and center, to speak in the first person. The intimate wavelength created between them in the first hours of love revives in the mythic space of these letters.

In short, he discovered the operation of a process in the works of Sylvia Plath that he had discovered in the works of Shakespeare and T. S. Eliot. At all times, she was composing a Poetic Self. This seems to have become clearest to him when he stumbled on those pages that contain the origins of Plath's poem "Pursuit," February 26 through March 11, 1956. Hughes observed, most disconcertingly, that the "lover" behind this love poem was a composite of himself and Richard Sassoon, with maybe a soupçon of Lucas Myers added for good measure. Moreover, Plath's love poem had little to do with him, much to do with her own appetites, and everything to do with the glorious pursuit of a metaphor: lust as a panther. In the pages of her journal, Plath tells how she went on red alert from the moment she heard the gossip that Hughes had been in Cambridge looking for her, and since she could not pursue him in person, stayed in her room and conjured him with obsessive word-magic, for pages and pages. ("Oh he is here; my black marauder; oh hungry hungry. I am so hungry. . . .") Forty years after the occasion, it shocks him again to remember the sudden pounce of her eyes, he says in "Trophies":

> The whiff of that beast, off the dry pages,
> Lifts the hair on the back of my hands

Hughes isn't talking only about Plath's abject lust, he is talking about the litany of her metaphors—he is watching her erotic fixation express itself in language supercharged with its prior use on him: "black marauder" and "hungry hungry" cycle back into her journal from their appearance in "Pursuit" and in her journal entries about their first meeting. His own metaphors in "Trophies" perform a similar conjuring act: he succumbs to her transformation of him—his sense of smell grows keen, his hair turns to fur—as if he were a character in one of Ovid's tales, and she one of the goddesses able to elicit from a man his expressive beast-form—such as Diana, in the myth of Actaeon.

Hughes's "Trophies" specifies that forty years have passed since he felt the impact of that fateful look in 1956. If so, "Trophies" was written in 1996, the year Ted Hughes was working on *Tales from Ovid,* his translation of selections from *Metamorphoses.* In his introduction he summarizes Ovid's achievement in a way that applies to "Trophies": "Ovid locates and captures the peculiar frisson of that event, where the all-too-human victim stumbles out into the mythic arena and is transformed." *Birthday Letters* is building exactly that case: that Ted and Sylvia each stumbled into the other's power to transform mere human beings into characters in a myth. He arranged to publish *Birthday Letters,* under the sign of Aquarius, on a day he selected by casting a horoscope and finding an alignment of the planet Neptune auspicious for the book's appearance. The editor at the London *Times* who bought some of *Birthday Letters* for serialization in the newspaper said Hughes required that this symbolic publication date, January 29, be printed alongside other publication details when the poems were serialized on January 17 and 22, 1998.

The poems of *Birthday Letters* stood in relation to the other book of poems drawn from the same pool of manuscripts, *Howls and Whispers,* as noon to midnight. The eleven *Howls and Whispers* are filled with nightmares. "The Offers," its most ambitious poem, also occupies an important position in Hughes's myth of the evolution of his poetic persona, her husband. It completes the story of his separation from his family into the role of consort to his female opposite, that alchemical Bride of his imagination, in a tale of magical reunion.

In "The Offers" Hughes describes a dream in which Sylvia Plath returns from the underworld three times, offering herself to his understanding. He first encounters her on the Northern Line of the London Underground, two months after her death. He boards a train at Leicester Square, heading home to the flat at Fitzroy Road, Sylvia's flat. The date is mid-April 1963. He takes a seat, and suddenly sees her sitting across from him, deliberately avoiding his eyes. He stares at her, appealing to be noticed. He observes that she is pale and sallow— it is the face he beheld in the morgue, only somewhat older and deeply melancholy. He gathers that she is being presented to him, that possibly she is being returned to him, but he does not speak, and when he rises to get off the train at Chalk Farm Station, she remains on the train and disappears into the tunnel of the Underground.

At the second of Plath's offers, she is younger and has assumed a different identity. He visits her at home in London. Now she is eager and gracious—he recognizes that she is flirting with him. She tells him that she has been living in Paris with her lover, and he realizes that, in this identity, she never returned from her trip to Paris in 1956, never came back to Cambridge and to his arms, never became a poet. (Hughes had probably been reading those pages in Plath's journal that worry the question of whether to marry Richard Sassoon.) He can't believe his eyes: it's really Plath! But he *knows* it isn't really Plath, it is some kind of spirit-demon who has taken her shape. She detains him until he recognizes that he has been breathing the gas of the underworld and is succumbing to its vapors. He kicks free, and she lets him go. But later she reveals that she has tricked him: sends him a postcard to tell him that she has ransomed herself by leaving him in the land of the dead, where, he now realizes, he has been stranded.

On her third visit, he is at home in a house he describes as "ruined." He is naked, running a bath, when she appears behind him. Now she is younger than he has ever known her, and more beautiful. She accosts him, and her voice reaches him across the tumult of falling water,

peremptory, as a familiar voice
Will startle . . . urgent,

Close: 'This is the last . . . This time
Don't fail me'

The sound of rushing water gives this beautiful scene the inflection of Hughes's passion for fishing: wading into rivers and holding still, relaxing his attention, releasing himself from dominance by the rational mind. Immersed in the river's force, he is carried deep into his animal nature.

This, for Hughes, is the ultimate experience of connection to everything that is not himself, the encounter with the sublime being of the White Goddess. "The Offers" dramatizes a "last" visitation of this goddess to this poet, as she tells him through the medium of Sylvia Plath. Robert Graves had said that the White Goddess must be approached with awe. But Hughes had learned to approach her also for the privilege of intimacy with her difference from him. Because Plath too was a writer and a mythmaker, it was she who could most productively enter the field of his continual reassessments of that fundamental dyad in nature, the reproductive sexual pair who had separated from the other animals by making language that outlasts death.

Their "last" encounter occurs not under the moon but under their roof, and reunites them. The scene is surely meant to show Hughes at the beginning of a new relationship to his authentic material, the relationship that made possible the poems comprising his autobiography. The three episodes of his dream in "The Offers" correspond to phases of a shaman's journey: a summoning by spirits; an ordeal in the underworld; and a return in a new body. This has, apparently, been the arc of Plath's travel in the underground as well, after she disappeared into that dark tunnel at the poem's opening. Her return to Hughes in a perfected form—he calls her "a flawless thing . . . a cobalt jewel"—completes the action initiated in the poem "Visit" in *Birthday Letters*, where her voice reached him like a thunderclap from the pages of her journals. In "Visit," she is imagined as buried under frozen earth, beyond the reach of his questions. In "The Offers," she has become the startling, embodied voice of the magical dead—"familiar . . . urgent"—addressing him directly. Since Plath was, indeed, the form taken by the White Goddess in Hughes's life, it had been her destiny to inflict devastation on Hughes, as well as release his creative fluency. These were the two aspects of her gift, as Robert Graves defined it: exaltation *and* horror.

"The Offers" is not only "the last" of Hughes's marriage poems, it is a "last" poem in his total oeuvre—a self-consciously performed "drama of completion" in the evolution of a Poetic Self of the kind Hughes described in his essay on T. S. Eliot. Only readers well acquainted with Hughes will glimpse the full inventory of references condensed into the last lines of "The Offers," but they coil a bright lasso around the themes of his life's work. And they answer the question posed in that "first" poem of the Poetic Self, the premonitory lament of "Song":

> When will the stone open its tomb? . . .
> You will not die, nor come home

That "you" who has always been and is not Sylvia Plath has come home, in the closing words of "The Offers." And he, on the occasion, is naked: vulnerable, undefended, receptive to her summons.

Ted Hughes died of heart failure, on 28 October 1998, one day after what would have been the sixty-sixth birthday of Sylvia Plath. His reputation had reached its zenith, and his books were climbing onto commercial best-seller lists, a rare occurrence in the career of a poet. First, *Tales from Ovid*, which received Britain's most prestigious literary prize, the Whitbread Book of the Year for 1997; then *Birthday Letters*, published in January 1998—his death in October would contribute to the book's astounding end-of-year sales figures: 110,000 copies in the United States, 75,000 copies in the U.K., making it the third highest-selling hardcover book of 1998. The fame and fortune that arrived together as 1998 opened continued to cascade upon Ted Hughes right up to the very month of his death, when the Queen bestowed on him the Order of Merit in a ceremony at Buckingham Palace.

Plaque on Ted Hughes's
birthplace, Mytholmroyd

Behind the scenes of these successes, Hughes the man was undergoing aggressive chemotherapy to arrest the development of colon cancer. He had been in treatment for eighteen months, but his illness was not discussed publicly, and the photographs that accompanied news of his awards perpetuated the image of a robust though moody Poet Laureate.

And despite his illness, Hughes had a couple of projects underway that he was particularly concerned to complete. During the summer preceding his death, he was finishing an adaptation of the play *Alcestis,* by the ancient Greek playwright Euripides. *Alcestis* is about the death of a wife, and her return from the underworld. Admetos, the much loved King of Thessaly, is doomed to die young unless he can persuade one of his kin to take his place. The elders of the family refuse but his wife Alcestis volunteers, and dies with great dignity. An unexpected visit from the god Heracles disrupts the funeral ceremonies; Heracles, remorseful about his apparent disrespect, volunteers to rescue Alcestis from Death. The god Apollo, who delivers the play's prologue, proclaims that what matters in this story is how Alcestis makes the gift, and how Admetos accepts it; like the late plays of Shakespeare in which wives come back from the dead, *Alcestis* is about the moral education of a husband. It was, coincidentally, one of the works of literature Sylvia Plath had been studying during the first year of their marriage: she had inscribed her copy of *Alcestis* with her new name—"Sylvia Hughes, Cambridge, 1957."

At the time Hughes was completing his version of *Alcestis,* he knew that his illness was terminal. Hughes was in touch with Barrie Rutter, a theatre director based in West Yorkshire who produced plays in an abandoned woolen mill in Halifax—only a few miles from the town where Hughes was born, and from the graveyard where his parents and Sylvia Plath were buried. Hughes told Rutter that he wanted

Alcestis to be performed first in West Yorkshire, because, wherever he traveled or lived, "his tuning fork was stuck firmly in the Calder Valley." Its characters would be posthumous vocal chords through which posterity would receive his last words as a poet-shaman about the loss and reclamation of the magical dead, enacted on the very ground of Elmet.

NAKED
(1998–   )

I n April 2000, the Department of Special Collections on the top floor of the Robert W. Woodruff Library at Emory University hosted a two-day celebration of the official opening of the Ted Hughes Papers, which had now been processed for use by readers. An exhibition of seventy items from this lode of treasures glowed in the vitrines at Emory. Of special interest were the notebooks filled with Ted Hughes's distinctive handwriting, pages on which he made the first drafts of poems and essays, sometimes pausing to rough out a horoscope or sketch an animal face.

The display cases also held photographs of Hughes at all stages of his life, alone or in the company of friends. Many of those friends, literary VIPs in their own right, could be seen leaning over the exhibitions, temporarily creating a double exposure: their young faces in miniature lying below the reflection of their living faces on the surface of the glass. Frieda Hughes, the family's representative, inspected the exhibition, elegant and poised as if unconscious of being covertly inspected herself. Lucas Myers and Daniel Weissbort chatted near the upright display of a rare copy of *St. Botolph's Review,* the little Cambridge literary magazine in which their writing had appeared along with that of Ted Hughes in February 1956, and which caught the eye of Sylvia Plath.

The artist Leonard Baskin was ill, and unable to attend. But he had been Hughes's friend and collaborator for over forty years, and their most beautiful joint production, *Howls and Whispers,* stood open in a place of honor on its own pedestal in the Woodruff Library through-out the days of celebration. *Howls and Whispers* had been published in an edition of 110 copies signed by Hughes and Baskin. Numbers 1–10 comprise a *very* special edition, each boxed volume containing an engraved copper plate for one of Baskin's etchings, and a handwritten page on which Hughes had drafted one of the poems. The Woodruff Library owns copy 7 of *Howls and Whispers,* which holds a draft page of "The Minotaur 2" that is enticingly crowded with canceled lines and inserted revisions.

In this poem, Hughes is developing a metaphor of Plath as one of the young women condemned to sacrifice herself to the Minotaur, in the myth about the Cretan monster imprisoned at the center of a labyrinth. At one point, Hughes's rapid pen has inscribed on this page, then scratched out, the words, "our secret quarrel suddenly a public show—." As we know, what interested Plath about that myth was the fate of Ariadne, who colluded with Theseus in destroying the Minotaur and was later deserted by him. Did Hughes suddenly think of this also? In any case, Hughes apparently didn't want to direct the reader's thoughts toward the misery of the last months of his mar-riage to Plath. He deleted the line about the secret quarrel. Yet he included the manuscript page in copy 7 of the published book. The personal allusion is there, and not there; it can be seen in only this one copy of *Howls and Whispers.*

"Suddenly a public show"—Hughes hated scrutiny by strangers. In death as in life, Hughes continues to baffle as well as to enable inquiries into his imagination's core. Deeper inside this building, not in sight, is the sealed trunk that waits to be opened and unpacked in the year 2023, the last bit of the Hughes legacy transferred to Emory by Hughes himself. He intentionally placed the contents of the trunk out of range of our inspection, though certainly not out of range of our curiosity. It's what's hidden—lying at "solar midnight"—in Hughes that draws us, the pressure of his still-undisclosed presence within these remains.

Hughes lures us into this labyrinth by hiding his secrets in plain sight, seeming to promise the possibility of reaching a locale of full disclosure, when—as he wrote to Aurelia Plath—"everything will be quite clear, whatever has been hidden will lie in the open." Every researcher becomes a Theseus with a thesis about that locale. Yet there is no "everything," not even here. Once you open what has been hidden, you have only advanced into another branch of the maze. Still, if something like a destination can be reached in this room, it is surely approached across the threshold of *Howls and Whispers,* in that beautiful poem "The Offers," where Plath accosts Hughes with a command that Hughes himself has written, "*This time, Don't fail me.*" Whose words are these, his or hers? Impossible to decide. The phrase forms in his ears only because the memory of Sylvia Plath has summoned them from his inner life, where she is still the guardian of his imagination's vitality, listening with her lively mind. *I am here.*

This is how she returns to consciousness, in her last apparition: as the life of words that quicken in the life of the hearer. Or the reader. Under Hughes's signature, Plath's words to Hughes become his words to us. Appropriately, this book is speaking with Plathian impatience. Yet you recognize what Hughes wants from you, the only thing the living can give the magical dead: empathic but pitiless attention.

Sources and Notes

Abbreviations

Frequently mentioned names, titles, and archival collections are abbreviated in the notes, as follows:

AP: Aurelia Plath
GH: Gerald Hughes
DM: Diane Middlebrook
SP: Sylvia Plath
TH: Ted Hughes

BL: Ted Hughes, *Birthday Letters.* London: Faber and Faber, 1998
CP: Sylvia Plath, *Collected Poems,* ed. with an introduction by Ted Hughes. London: Faber and Faber, 1981
JSP: The Journals of Sylvia Plath, 1950–1962, ed. Karen V. Kukil. London: Faber and Faber, 2000
LH: Sylvia Plath, *Letters Home: Correspondence 1950–1963,* ed. with commentary by Aurelia Schober Plath. London: Faber and Faber, 1975

British Library: The Department of Manuscripts, The British Library, London
Emory: Ted Hughes Papers, Special Collections and Archives, Robert W. Woodruff Library, Emory University, Atlanta, Georgia
Lilly: Sylvia Plath Collection, The Lilly Library, Indiana University, Bloomington, Indiana
Smith: Sylvia Plath Collection, Mortimer Rare Book Room, Smith College, Northampton, Massachusetts
Stanford: Department of Special Collections, Stanford University Libraries, Stanford, California

Other works by Ted Hughes and Sylvia Plath referred to in this book:

Unless otherwise indicated in this list, the publisher is London: Faber and Faber. Complete bibliographical information regarding works by and about Ted Hughes through 1995 can be found in Keith Sagar and Stephen Tabor, *Ted Hughes: A Bibliography, Second Edition, 1946–1995*, London and New York: Mansell Publishing Ltd, A Cassell Imprint, 1998. Complete bibliographical information regarding works by and about Sylvia Plath, through 1986, can be found in Stephen Tabor, *Sylvia Plath: An Analytical Bibliography*, London: Mansell Publishing Ltd., 1987.

By Ted Hughes:

The Hawk in the Rain, 1957
"England's Toughest Community" (review of Clancy Segal, *Weekend in Dinlock*). *The Nation*, July 2, 1960
"Arnold Wesker: 'A Sort of Socialism.'" *The Nation*, November 19, 1960
Lupercal, 1960
Meet My Folks!, 1961
How the Whale Became, 1963
Wodwo, 1967
Crow, From the Life and Songs of the Crow, 1970
Prometheus on His Crag, 1973
Gaudete, 1977
Cave Birds, 1978
Moortown Diary, 1989
Wolfwatching, 1989
Capriccio, engravings by Leonard Baskin. Hadley, Mass.: The Gehenna Press, 1990
Shakespeare and the Goddess of Complete Being, 1992
Remains of Elmet, photographs by Fay Godwin, 1979; revised and expanded as *Elmet*, 1994
Difficulties of a Bridegroom: Collected Short Stories, 1995
New Selected Poems 1957–1994, 1995
Tales from Ovid, 1997
Winter Pollen, 1997
Howls and Whispers, engravings by Leonard Baskin. Hadley, Mass.: The Gehenna Press, 1998
Racine's Phèdre, 1998
The Alcestis of Euripides, 1999

By Sylvia Plath:

The Colossus and Other Poems. London: Heinemann, 1960

The Bell Jar (under pseudonym "Victoria Lucas"). London: Heinemann, 1963; author identified as Sylvia Plath, Faber and Faber, 1966

Ariel, 1965

Johnny Panic and the Bible of Dreams and Other Prose Writings, ed. with an introduction by Ted Hughes, 1977; revised edition, 1979

Collected Poems, ed. with an introduction by Ted Hughes. London: Faber and Faber, 1981

The Journals of Sylvia Plath, ed. Fran McCullough; consulting ed. Ted Hughes. New York: Dial Press, 1982

The Journals of Sylvia Plath, 1950–1962, ed. Karen K. Kukil, 2000.

NOTES

Introduction: Becoming Her Husband

xv *literary marriage:* Counted from June 16, 1956, their wedding day, to October 11, 1962, the day they separated.

xv *"a marriage of opposites":* Two of a Kind: Poets in Partnership, TH and SP interviewed by Owen Leeming, recorded January 18, 1961. The BBC transcript is somewhat different from the recording; my account makes use of both. Transcript, p. 1/5. British Library.

xvi *"a single shared mind":* Ibid., p. 2/5.

xvi *"secret life":* Ibid., p. 2/1.

xvi *"Actually, I think . . .":* Ibid., p. 2/5.

xvi *"demons":* TH–AP, n.d. [December 1960]. Lilly.

xvii *"This is just like her . . .":* TH, "Sylvia Plath: *Ariel,*" Poetry Book Society Bulletin 44 (February 1965), reprinted in *Winter Pollen,* pp. 161–62.

xvii *"The Offers":* It is possible to retrieve a full copy of this poem, published October 18, 1998, by using the "back issues" search facility on the "archive" page of the Website of the London *Times:* www.thetimes.co.uk.

xviii *"knot of obsessions":* "The Great Theme: Notes on Shakespeare" (1971), *Winter Pollen,* p. 106.

xix *"An impartial scholar . . .":* TH–AP, January 12, 1975, "Notes on Letters Home, revised—January 1975." Emory.

Chapter One: Meeting (1956)

1 *"The solar system married us":* "St. Botolph's," *BL,* p. 14.

1 *St. Botolph's Review:* Details about the contributors in Lucas Myers,

Crow Steered, Bergs Appeared, p. 12, and about St. Botolph's Rectory, pp. 3–4.

2 *American magazines:* Plath's "Doomsday" had appeared in *Harper's,* May 1954; "Go Get the Goodly Squab" and "To Eva Descending the Stair" in *Harper's,* November 1954; "Circus in Three Rings" in *Atlantic Monthly,* August 1955; and "Temper of Time" in *The Nation,* August 6, 1955. See Stephen Tabor, *Sylvia Plath: An Analytical Bibliography,* pp. 106–10.

2 *"Quaint and eclectic artfulness":* Daniel Huws, review *of Chequer,* in *Broadsheet* (issues not designated), quoted in Keith Sagar, *The Laughter of Foxes: A Study of Ted Hughes,* p. 48.

2 *Plath was mortified: JSP,* February 26, 1956, p. 211.

2 *she had memorized:* SP had apparently looked at back issues of *Chequer* as well: her journal indicates that she also quoted a line from TH's poem "Casualty" that night ("Most dear unscratchable diamond"); it had been published in *Chequer* in November 1954. I am grateful to Keith Sagar for identifying the line and its publication date; e-mail to DM, author of this book, February 19, 2002.

2 *"frightfully pale and freckled": JSP,* February 26, 1956, p. 211.

3 *She cut in:* Lucas Myers, "Ah Youth," in Anne Stevenson, *Bitter Fame,* p. 312; Myers, *Crow Steered,* p. 32.

3 *"You like?": JSP,* February 26, 1956, p. 211.

3 *she bit him:* Ibid.

4 *Hughes deferred:* SP–AP, May 4, 1956, *LH,* p. 283.

4 *"without delay":* TH–GH, March 22, 1955. Emory.

4 *Hughes reactivated:* TH–Lucas Myers, March 18, 1956. Emory.

4 *"their blood before . . .":* The poem, "When Two Men Meet for the First Time in All," was published in *The Hawk in the Rain* under the title "Law in the Country of the Cats," p. 47.

4 *" 'I did it, I' ":* Other writers have assumed that SP was quoting from "Fallgrief's Girlfriends," but SP's unabridged journals indicate she was also quoting "I did it, I" from "When Two Men Meet for the First Time in All."

4 *Hughes had read:* TH acknowledged in an interview that Lawrence's writings "coloured a whole period of my life." Ekbert Faas, *Ted Hughes: The Unaccommodated Universe,* p. 202.

5 *"That big, dark . . .": JSP,* February 26, 1956, p. 211.

5 *195 pounds:* Donna Laframboise, "Ted Hughes' Private Letters Reveal Another Story," *National Post* (Toronto), July 29, 2000, p. B5.

5 *army-issue topcoat:* Stevenson, *Bitter Fame,* p. 73.

5 *class anxieties:* TH–SP, October 2, 1956. Lilly.

5 *"dressed in a weird . . .":* Karl Miller, *Rebecca's Vest: A Memoir,* p. 125.

5 *He bought his corduroy:* TH–Keith Sagar, October 10, 1998. British Library.

5 *"as though he'd . . .":* Glen Fallows, "Reminiscences," in "Ted Hughes Feature," *Martlet* (newsletter of Pembroke College Cambridge), issue 4 (Spring 2000), p. 8.

5 *"Ted was appalling . . .":* Philip Hobsbaum, "Ted Hughes at Cambridge," *The Dark Horse: The Scottish-American Poetry Magazine,* no. 8 (Autumn 1999), p. 6.

5 *self-conscious and shy:* TH–Sagar, October 10, 1998.

6 *"I felt like Hazlitt . . .":* Ben Sonnenberg, *Lost Property: Memoirs and Confessions of a Bad Boy,* p. 93.

6 *Hughes sitting immobile:* Emma Tennant, *Burnt Diaries,* pp. 71–75.

6 *"the biggest seducer . . .":* JSP, February 26, 1956, p. 213.

6 *somewhat fanatical undergraduates:* St. *Botolph's Review* published poems by Ted Hughes, Daniel Huws, E. Lucas Myers, David Ross, and Daniel Weissbort, as well as a prose sketch by Than Minton and a "Letter from a Painter" (George Weissbort). Emory.

7 *"I went up to Cambridge . . .":* Daniel Weissbort, quoted in Nicholas Wroe, "Speaking of Foreign Tongues," *Guardian,* June 30, 2001, p. 11.

7 *"A strange yowling . . .":* Peter Redgrove, " 'Gnat-Psalm,' " in *The Epic Poise,* ed. Nick Gammage, pp. 49–50.

7 *"almost a deadly institution . . .":* Quoted in John Horder, "Desk Poet," *Guardian,* March 23, 1965.

8 *"dark horse":* TH–Keith Sagar, June 18, 1998. British Library.

8 For Whitman and Rilke, see interview with Drue Heinz, *The Paris Review* 134 (Spring 1995), p. 61.

8 *Leavis's intellectual style:* "I might say, that I had as much talent for Leavis-style dismantling of texts as anybody else, I even had a special bent for it—nearly a sadistic streak there—but it seemed to me not only a foolish game, but deeply destructive of myself." Quoted in Sagar, *The Laughter of Foxes,* p. 46.

8 *Hughes had little taste:* "He rarely attended lectures, though he occasionally went to hear F. R. Leavis whom he found fascinating to watch and listen to and highly entertaining. . . . As for the wider life of Cambridge, Hughes belonged to no societies. 'Luckily' (he says) the Amateur Drama Club rejected him as an actor." Keith Sagar, *The Art of Ted Hughes,* pp. 8–9.

8 *team sports:* Ibid., p. 9.

8 *"There were Pembroke . . .":* Brian Cox, "Ted Hughes (1930–1998): A Personal Retrospect," *The Hudson Review* 52, Spring 1999, p. 32.

8 *"The Scope of Horror":* Fallows, "Reminiscences," p. 8.

8 *"He loved the opulent . . .":* Myers, *Crow Steered,* pp. 8–9.

9 *Hughes told versions:* "The Burnt Fox," *Winter Pollen,* 1993.

9 *dropping English literature:* TH–Neil Roberts and Terry Gifford, n.d. (c. 1977), regarding their critical work on his poetry (private collection).

9 *rank of II.1:* Information provided to DM by Professor Colin Wilcoxson, August 1999.

9 *"respectable but not dazzling":* Stevenson, *Bitter Fame,* p. 107.

10 *the visit impressed Hughes:* Colin Charles Fraser "Reshaping the Past: The Personal Poetry of Ted Hughes." (Ph. D. thesis, University of New England [Australia], 1998); pp. 40–44; and Eileen Aird, *Sylvia Plath: Her Life and Work,* p. 8 (Aird cites "files of the *Halifax Courier & Guardian*").

10 *the taste of claret:* Paris, 1954," *Howls and Whispers,* unpaginated.

10 *the big cats:* "Five Poems by Ted Hughes," ITV Schools *English Programme,* broadcast February 15, 1988.

10 *security guard:* TH–GH, October, 10, 1955. Emory.

10 *North Sea trawler:* Ibid.

10 *"The Jaguar":* TH–Ben Sonnenberg, n.d. Emory. Hughes misremembers the date of the poem's composition in this letter: "The Jaguar" was published in *Chequer,* November 1954; Hughes recalls writing the poem in a girlfriend's flat in January 1955.

10 *the Edgware Road:* Hobsbaum, "Ted Hughes at Cambridge," p. 10.

10 *Hughes greatly coveted:* TH–GH, October 10, 1955.

11 *"Ted in his hairy overcoat . . .":* Hobsbaum, "Ted Hughes at Cambridge," p. 10.

11 *too "forward":* Myers, *Crow Steered,* p. 45.

11 *" . . . the fingers themselves interweaving . . .":* Jane Baltzell Kopp, " 'Gone, Very Gone Youth': Sylvia Plath at Cambridge, 1955–1957," in *Sylvia Plath: The Woman and the Work,* ed. Edward Butscher, p. 66.

11 *"would pedal vehemently . . .":* Ibid.

12 *no photographs of Plath:* Nancy Hunter Steiner (who lived with SP before she went to Cambridge), *A Closer Look at Ariel: A Memory of Sylvia Plath,* p. 57. Janet Malcolm comments, "All the photographs of her disappoint me." *The Silent Woman,* pp. 122–23.

12 *"fat":* JSP, May 5, 1953, p. 181.

12 *thick mucus:* JSP, February 3, 1958, p. 321.

12 *testing the air:* Ed Cohen–SP, December 15, 1953. Lilly.

12 *gnawing her lips:* JSP, p. 328.

13 *her good posture:* Smith College Professor George Gibian mentioned this in an interview with Edward Butscher, *Sylvia Plath: Method and Madness,* p. 165.

13 *One of her boyfriends:* Peter Davison, quoted in ibid., pp. 178–80.

13 *"athletic"*: SP–AP, March 9, 1956, *LH*, p. 223. "You know I have loved Richard above and beyond all thought . . . all my conventional doubts about his health, his frail body, his lack of that 'athletic' physique which I possess and admire"; see also *JSP*, February 12, 1953, p. 173, and March 6, 1956, p. 217.

13 *not a good dancer*: The Bell Jar, p. 74.

14 *" . . . Betty Grable"*: Clipping of photograph from *Varsity* published in *LH*, p. 237.

14 *"German blond"*: Steiner, *A Closer Look at Ariel*, p. 57.

14 *"giddy gilded creature"*: Gordon Lameyer, "Who Was Sylvia?" (unpublished memoir) quoted in Stevenson, *Bitter Fame*, p. 59.

14 *redyed her hair*: SP–AP, September 27, 1954, *LH*, p. 141.

14 *wax . . . cellophane*: For wax, see Wendy Campbell, "Remembering Sylvia," in *The Art of Sylvia Plath*, ed. Charles Newman, p. 182; For cellophane, see Myers, "Ah Youth," p. 313.

14 *"the concentrated intensity . . ."*: Dorothea Krook, "Recollections of Sylvia Plath," in *Sylvia Plath: The Woman and the Work*, ed. Butscher, p. 49.

15 *"invariably lit . . ."*: Kopp, " 'Gone, Very Gone Youth,' " p. 65.

15 *"in her way . . ."*: *JSP*, July 17, 1957, p. 285.

15 *"that blond girl . . ."*: *JSP*, July 20, 1957, p. 289.

16 *"It's hopeless . . ."*: *JSP*, March 4, 1957, p. 273.

16 *creative writing course*: Linda Wagner-Martin gives no source for this information in *Sylvia Plath: A Biography*, p. 115, but recalled that it "came from Constance Taylor, who was then working in England . . . she had been at Smith and double-dated with Sylvia and him"; e-mail to DM, February 1, 2001.

16 *"part of me sleeps . . ."*: Richard Sassoon–SP, May 11, 1954. Lilly.

17 *"nervous boy . . ."*: *JSP*, January 7, 1958, p. 308.

17 *staying in a hotel*: Kopp, " 'Gone, Very Gone Youth,' " pp. 70–71.

17 *"being raped . . ."*: *JSP*, May 5, 1953, p. 181. Nancy Hunter Steiner associated Richard Sassoon with this strange insect metaphor, but unless Plath used it more than once, the reference was actually to Ray Wunderlich.

17 *she resolved to stop*: *JSP*, p. 202.

17 *writing* as if *to Sassoon*: *JSP*, p. 190.

18 *"the dialogue between . . ."*: *JSP*, February 25, 1956, p. 208.

18 *" . . . blast over Richard"*: *JSP*, pp. 208–9.

18 *"dark sideburns . . ."*: *JSP*, p. 211.

18 *"Fools Encountered"*: Myers, *Crow Steered*, p. 32.

18 *"sestinas which bam . . ."*: *JSP*, p. 211.

19 *"I started yelling . . ."*: *JSP*, pp. 211–12.

19 *"bang of blood . . ."*: "The Jaguar," *Chequer*, November 1954.

19 *"I can see how . . ."*: *JSP*, p. 212.

19 *"strong and blasting . . ."*: *JSP*, p. 212.

19 *" . . . blasting wind"*: *JSP*, p. 213.

19 *"banging and crashing . . ."*: *JSP*, p. 214.

19 *" . . . in bed"*: *JSP*, p. 225.

20 *"my black marauder"*: *JSP*, p. 233.

20 *"I have powerful . . ."*: *JSP*, p. 233.

20 *"tight, blasting . . ."*: *JSP*, p. 212.

21 *"I would like . . ."*: *JSP*, p. 212.

21 *"I could never sleep . . ."*: *JSP*, p. 214.

22 *"hungry, hungry those taut thighs . . ."*: "Pursuit," *CP*, p. 23.

22 *too focused on the theme:* "Passion as destiny is only *one* aspect and not the fatal holocaust I made it," she admits. *JSP*, March 1, 1956, p. 225.

22 *"Pursuit"* was published in *Atlantic Monthly*, January 1957, p. 65.

22 *on her honeymoon:* SP–AP, September 2, 1956, *LH*, pp. 269–70.

22 *Racine's theme:* TH translates the lines, "Everywhere in the woods your image hunts me." *Phèdre*, act 2, p. 26.

22 *"eats up . . ."*: *JSP*, February 27, 1956, p. 213.

23 *"You speak to me . . ."*: See Plath's probably unsent letter to Richard Sassoon, *JSP*, March 1, 1956, p. 216.

23 *Plath was deep asleep:* Myers's memoir, *Crow Steered*, recalls only one night of clod-throwing, as does Hughes's poem, but Plath's journal describes two.

Chapter Two: Romance (1956)

24 *Myers and Boddy returned:* Lucas Myers, *Crow Steered, Bergs Appeared*, p. 43.

24 *They found Hughes:* Michael Boddy, quoted in Elaine Feinstein, *Ted Hughes: The Life of a Poet*, p. 57.

25 *Plath was flustered:* Myers, *Crow Steered*, p. 43.

25 *"went in a barrel . . ."*: "18 Rugby Street," *BL*, p. 20.

25 *All night:* SP's journal records that their night of lovemaking left her raw and bruised. *JSP*, March 26, 1956, p. 552.

25 *sausages for breakfast:* Boddy, quoted in Feinstein, *Ted Hughes*, p. 57.

25 *"sleepless holocaust night . . ."*: *JSP*, March 26, 1956, p. 552.

25 *" . . . blood spilt"*: *JSP*, April 5, 1956, p. 564.

25 *no bathroom:* Ibid.

25 *mailed a postcard:* Anne Stevenson, *Bitter Fame*, p. 84; *JSP*, April 5, 1956, p. 565.

26 *planning Hughes's future:* SP–AP, April 29, 1956, *LH,* p. 243.

26 *nothing she'd rather do:* SP–AP, May 4, 1956, *LH,* p. 250.

26 *teaching job in Spain:* SP–AP, May 9, 1956. Lilly.

26 *bringing Hughes to America:* SP–AP, May 9, 1956, *LH,* p. 251.

26 *"I shall be one . . .":* SP–AP, May 26, 1956, *LH,* p. 256.

26 *seven children:* SP–AP, May 18, 1956, *LH,* pp. 254–55.

26 *provincialism of Australia:* SP–AP, May 9, 1956. Lilly.

26 *dead against negotiation:* Quoted in Ekbert Faas, *Ted Hughes: The Unaccommodated Universe,* p. 201.

26 *"new world":* "18 Rugby Street," *BL,* p. 24.

27 *vagabond life:* TH–GH, September 1956. Emory.

27 *Austria:* Warren Plath was enrolled in an Experiment in International Living project. Stevenson, *Bitter Fame,* p. 90.

27 *"the parish church . . .":* SP–Warren Plath, June 18, 1956, *LH,* p. 258.

27 *keep the marriage secret:* Ibid. pp. 257–59.

27 *"To find such a man . . .":* SP–AP, May 9, 1957, *LH,* p. 232.

28 *echolocation signals:* "Echolocation is a passive process for one party (the target in radar-speak) yet the nature of the echo is determined in many subtle ways by characteristics of the (passive) target, whether an obstacle or potential prey. In the case of bats, the echo is often complex and can reveal much more than simply the position of the target. In that sense echolocation is an interrogation in which the 'target' reveals something of its nature whether willingly or not." David Pye, e-mail to DM, October 15, 2001.

28 *"like brandy":* TH–SP, n.d. (postmark March 31, 1956) Lilly.

28 *"Ridiculous to call . . .":* TH–SP, n.d. (postmark April 9, 1956) Lilly.

29 *her face was bruised:* JSP, March 26, 1956, p. 552; "Fidelity," *BL,* p. 29.

29 *"somewhat sacred":* TH–AP, April 23, 1975. Lilly.

30 *"I had expected Ted . . .":* Lucas Myers, "Ah Youth," in Stevenson, *Bitter Fame,* p. 315.

30 *this flashy American:* Myers, *Crow Steered,* p. 34.

30 *"I'd rather have my Ted . . .":* Ibid., p. 45.

30 *Plath's attitude toward poetry:* Ibid., p. 7.

30 *"false" poets:* Miranda Seymour, *Robert Graves: Life on the Edge,* pp. 349, 352–54. Graves's lectures were later published as *The Crowning Privilege: The Clark Lectures,* 1954–5.

30 *Graves's militant stance:* See Myers, *Crow Steered,* pp. 6–13.

31 *Shaped his poetic conscience:* TH–Robert Graves, July 20, 1967, quoted in Seymour, *Robert Graves,* p. 328.

31 *"as such things . . .":* Interview with Drue Heinz, *The Paris Review* 134 (spring 1995), p. 85.

32 *"You stood . . ."*: "Song," *The Hawk in the Rain*, p. 19.

32 *reconstruct the poem:* Olwyn Hughes, conversation with DM, March 11, 2003.

32 *moon-worship:* Robert Graves, *The White Goddess*, p. 166.

32 *The earliest cultures:* Graves probably adopted this view from the scholarship of the Cambridge anthropologist Jane Harrison, according to Seymour, *Robert Graves*, p. 307.

33 *"mixed exaltation . . ."*: Graves, *The White Goddess*, p. 14.

33 *work of the mad:* Ibid., p. 12.

33 *woman behind "Song"*: Olwyn Hughes said that her name was Jean Findley (conversation with DM, March 11, 2003). A poem titled "Summer She Goes," dedicated to Jean Findley, is among TH's papers at Emory University.

33 *"demanded that man . . ."*: Graves, *The White Goddess*, p. 11.

33 *"no Muse-poet . . ."*: Ibid., p. 490.

34 *"She is either . . ."*: Ibid., p. 446.

34 *turn away from his Muse:* Ibid., pp. 490–91.

34 *"in her feathers of flame . . ."*: "Anniversary," *New Selected Poems*, p. 292.

34 *"A great bird, you . . ."*: "18 Rugby Street," *BL*, p. 22.

35 *high achievers academically:* Stevenson, *Bitter Fame*, p. 90.

36 *"I think I am . . ."*: SP–AP, March 3, 1956, *LH*, pp. 220–21.

36 *"larger, hulking, healthy Adam"*: SP–AP, April 13, 1956, *LH*, p. 233.

36 *cherry tree:* SP–AP, April 29, 1956, *LH*, p. 243.

36 *Adam is Ted:* SP–AP, April 21 and 18 May 1956, *LH*, pp. 239, 255.

36 *" . . . cows and coots"*: SP–AP, April 19, 1956, *LH*, p. 234.

36 *"world-wanderer, a vagabond"*: SP–AP, April 17, 1956, *LH*, p. 233.

36 *a big, unruly:* SP–AP, May 4, 1956, *LH*, p. 250.

36 *"No precocious hushed . . ."*: SP–AP, April 19, 1956, *LH*, p. 234.

36 *"cruel"*: For example, SP–AP, May 4, 1956: "Ted says himself that I have saved him from being ruthless, cynical, cruel and a warped hermit because he never thought there could be a girl like me. . . ." Lilly.

36 *What counts:* SP–AP, April 19, 1956. Lilly.

36 *she intends to reform him:* Ibid.

37 *"adam's woman"*: "Ode to Ted," *CP*, p. 30.

37 *"under yellow willows' . . ."*: SP enclosed "Metamorphosis" (retitled "Faun," *CP*, p. 35) and "Song" in her letter of April 21, 1956, *LH*, p. 239. The sexual reference quoted from "Song" was expurgated from the version titled "Song for a Summer's Day" published in *CP*, pp. 30–31.

37 *big loose pockets:* SP–AP, April 17, 1956. Lilly.

37 *meals in her hearth:* SP–AP, May 26, 1956, *LH*, p. 256.

37 *shrimp Newburg:* SP–AP, April 29, 1956, *LH*, p. 244.

37 *Ted was the first man:* Ibid.

37 *They were a matched pair:* Sam Middlebrook, conversation with DM, New York, December 1970.

37 *She bloomed with health:* SP–AP, April 29, 1956, *LH,* p. 243.

37 *Each was the other's best critic:* Ibid.

37 *resolved to make portraits:* SP–AP, May 18, 1956. *LH,* Lilly.

37 *Finish the Quotation:* SP–AP, April 21, 1956, *LH,* p. 235.

38 *"drunker than Dylan . . .":* SP–AP, April 29, 1956, *LH,* p. 243.

38 *the evidence now being in print:* My ear picks up the prenuptial influences on SP of TH's enthusiasm in *CP,* pp. 28–44. Most evidently: Dylan Thomas in "Ode for Ted" (p. 29), "Faun" (p. 35), and "Wreath for a Bridal" (p. 44); Hopkins in "Firesong" (p. 30); Yeats in "Strumpet Song" (p. 33), "Tinker Jack and the Tidy Wives" (p. 34), "Street Song," (p. 35), and "Recantation" (p. 41).

38 *pet names:* Words in quotation marks in this paragraph are used repeatedly in TH's daily letters to SP, October 2–22, 1956. Lilly.

38 *"ponky pooh chocolate for breakfast":* JSP, August 17, 1956, p. 258.

39 *the language of erotic ideology:* In 1951–1952, SP studied nineteenth- and twentieth-century literature with Helen Randall and Elizabeth Drew. The Plath archive at Smith has SP's notes from the course, including a few notes on *Women in Love.* Karen Kukil, e-mail, to DM, October 1, 2001.

39 *"mainly a learned process":* Ed Cohen–SP, December 17, 1951(?). Lilly.

40 *"justifying my life . . .":* JSP, n.d. (c. September 1950), p. 22.

40 *"soggy desire, always unfulfilled":* JSP, n.d. (Summer 1950), p. 20.

40 *edit them for publication:* Ed Cohen–SP, December 15, 1953. Lilly.

40 *"practical satisfactions":* JSP, September 20, 1952, p. 147.

40 *"physical rituals":* JSP, February 12, 1953, p. 174.

40 *" . . . tender pointed slopes":* JSP, p. 177.

40 *her psychiatrist:* SP's biographer Paul Alexander cites interviews with the late Ruth Barnhouse Beuscher as the source of his claim that Dr. Beuscher encouraged SP to engage in premarital sexual intercourse (*Rough Magic,* p. 135, and note, p. 374). *The Bell Jar* appears to be the source that SP's earlier biographer, Edward Butscher, called upon in making the same claim (*Sylvia Plath: Method and Madness,* p. 136).

40 *her virginity:* The date of SP's loss of virginity is contested. Both Alexander and Butscher cite interviews with Philip McCurdy as source of the information that he was Plath's first partner in sexual intercourse. Neither Linda Wagner-Martin (*Sylvia Plath: A Biography*) nor Anne Stevenson (*Bitter Fame*) follow Alexander and Butscher on this point. Stevenson claims that SP "was still anxiously a virgin" when she met Richard Sassoon in April 1954, and doubts that SP became sexually

involved with him until after the disastrous experience with the man SP fictionalized as "Irwin" in *The Bell Jar,* the episode that sent SP herself to a hospital emergency room in the summer of 1954 while she was attending classes at Harvard; but Stevenson does not acknowledge Butscher's different claim or give sources for her judgment (see *Bitter Fame,* pp. 52–57.) A note in SP's journal lists "Petting, parking, mismanaged loss of virginity and the accident ward" as a good topic for a story that could be "dredge[d] up from my mind" (*JSP,* p. 316), which suggests she may have contemplated eliding the parked car with the accident ward in fiction. Wagner-Martin is vague on the question of when SP and Sassoon became sexually involved but asserts that SP had intercourse with her longstanding boyfriend Gordon Lameyer following the episode with "Irwin," and cites interviews, letters, and an unpublished memoir of Lameyer as source (*Sylvia Plath,* pp. 114–17, and note, p. 252). Erica Wagner speculates in *Ariel's Gift* that Plath was still a "technical virgin" after her first night with Hughes, but this is certainly incorrect. According to Peter Davison (in *Half-Remembered*) he and SP became lovers during the summer of 1955; and it was his impression that he was not her first sexual partner.

40 *She avoided telling:* Wagner-Martin, *Sylvia Plath,* p. 116; her note, p. 252 cites Gordon Lameyer's recollections and unpublished memoir as her source.

40 *"what all these English boys . . .":* Jane Baltzell Kopp, " 'Gone, Very Gone Youth': Sylvia Plath at Cambridge, 1955–1957," in *Sylvia Plath: The Woman and Her Work,* ed. Edward Butscher, p. 68.

40 *Esther Greenwood's visit: The Bell Jar,* pp. 207–9. SP's biographer Anne Stevenson interprets a letter from Richard Sassoon as implying that Sylvia was careless about contraception, however, see *Bitter Fame,* p. 60.

40 *Plath was not keeping a journal:* That SP underwent one of Esther Greenwood's sexual misadventures—hemorrhaging from a vaginal tear incurred during a night with an acquaintance she met at Harvard summer school in 1954—is confirmed in the memoir of her roommate Nancy Hunter Steiner (*A Closer Look at Ariel: A Memory of Sylvia Plath,* pp. 85–92).

41 *Was now her vagina: JSP,* May 15, 1952, p. 103.

41 *"the appalling and demanding fire . . .":* Ibid., p. 104.

41 *"lull and soothe": JSP,* September 1951, pp. 98–100.

41 *"a polarization . . .": JSP,* May 15 1952, p. 105.

41 *" . . . like a star balanced . . .":* D. H. Lawrence, *Women in Love,* chapter xiii, "Mino." p. 149.

41 *"is only the branches . . .":* Ibid.

41 *"I plan not to step . . .": JSP,* May 15, 1952, p. 105.

42 *if Esther chooses to marry: The Bell Jar*, p. 75.

42 *"she had established . . ."*: Lawrence, *Women in Love*, chapter xxiii, "Excursus."

42 *"the only man in the world . . ."*: SP–WP, April 23, 1956, *LH*, 240.

44 *She encouraged Plath to enjoy:* Olive Higgins Prouty–SP, May 3, 1956. Lilly.

44 *living frugally in southern France:* SP–AP, March 20, 1956, *LH*, p. 230.

44 *"'mother and father' tongue":* SP–AP, January 16, 1956, *LH*, pp. 206–7.

44 *join Sassoon for the Christmas holidays:* SP–AP, January 29, 1956, *LH*, p. 212.

44 *" . . . people and art in Europe":* Ibid., pp. 212–13.

44 *"gray-clad, basically-dressed . . .":* SP–AP, October 13, 1954, *LH*, p. 144.

45 *She viewed her own cultivation:* SP–AP, January 29, 1956, *LH*, p. 212.

45 *"husband, lover, father and son . . .":* JSP, February 25, 1956, p. 199.

45 *a letter from Sassoon:* SP–AP, April 17, 1956, indicates that Sassoon had written letters from Spain that she didn't get until she returned to Cambridge (*LH*, p. 233). It was in her letters to Sassoon, as well as in her journal, that she expressed feelings of his abandonment. SP apparently corresponded with him on and off throughout spring 1956, and wrote to him about her decision to marry TH; such is the gist of the letter in which Sassoon writes elegiacally about their past, and tells her she sounds like an unhappy woman. Richard Sassoon–SP, n.d. (after June 16, 1956). Lilly.

45 *Adam to her Eve:* JSP, November 22, 1955, p. 193.

45 *"shudderingly relevant":* JSP, March 8, 1956, p. 229.

45 *"Little thin sickly exotic wealthy Richard":* JSP, February 25, 1957, p. 268.

46 *"Long before I was your* bien-amiée . . .*":* Richard Sassoon–SP, n.d. (after June 16, 1956). Lilly.

46 *Strong evidence suggests:* A. Alvarez, *The Savage God*, especially pp. 21, 38–41; and Judith Kroll, *Chapters in a Mythology*, especially pp. 166ff.

46 *"I was trying to be . . .":* JSP, January 10, 1959, p. 461.

47 *"the small waves break . . .":* Manuscript at Lilly (typescript carbon), dated June 10, 1949. Published in AP, introduction to *LH*, p. 36.

48 *The trapped train:* JSP, March 29, 1958, p. 359.

49 *"the motherly pulse":* "Ocean 1212-W," *Johnny Panic and the Bible of Dreams*, p. 21.

49 *"Because she asked me":* Reported but not attributed in Myers, *Crow Steered*, p. 46.

Chapter Three: His Family (1956)

50 *get along:* SP–WP, June 18, 1956, *LH*, p. 257.

51 *deceitful behavior:* SP–AP, July 25, 1956, *LH*, p. 256. "Ted and I have

decided to go stay with his family for the week before I go back to Cambridge and tell them we are married. I have been feeling very badly about his writing them as if he were alone . . . . so he is writing them . . ."

51 *Mytholmroyd:* "Holm," *Oxford English Dictionary* definition 3: "piece of flat low-lying ground by a river or stream, submerged or surrounded in time of flood. In living use in the south of Scotland (*howm*) and north of England, and extending far south in place-names; 'a flat pasture in Romney Marsh (Kent) is yet called *the Holmes*' (way)."

51 *delivered by a midwife:* TH–GH, February 2, 1994. Emory.

51 *We know the exact hour:* TH–Leonard Clark, n.d. (postmark 1974). Berg Collection, New York Public Library, New York.

51 *"fated to live . . .":* Ibid.

52 *"noon" . . . "midnight"* The technical terms for the noon and midnight positions as mapped on a horoscope are *Medium Coeli,* abbreviated MC (Latin for middle of the sky), and *Imum Coeli,* abbreviated IC (lowest part of the sky).

52 *geography is destiny:* I am indebted to Janet Booth and Joanne Wickenburg, professional astrologers, for notes about the term "solar midnight" and the significance of the planets in Ted Hughes's chart: e-mail, Janet Booth to DM, November 16, 2000.

54 *"For what . . . Darkness . . .":* "Pike," *Lupercal,* pp. 56–57.

54 *"symbols of really deep, vital life":* Interview with Thomas Pero, "So Quickly It's Over," *Wild Steelhead and Salmon* 5, no. 2 (Winter 1999), p. 50.

55 *"the poet of the Zodiac":* Julia and Derek Parker, *Parkers' Astrology* (London: Dorling Kindersley, 1994), pp. 124–26.

55 *"Conjunct your Ascendant exactly . . .":* "St. Botolph's," *BL,* p. 14.

55 *horoscopes in his pockets:* SP–AP, April 29, 1956, *LH,* pp. 243–44.

56 *"Fixed stars govern a life":* SP, "Words," *CP,* p. 270; TH, "A Dream," *BL,* p. 115.

56 *she chastises herself:* JSP, pp. 327, 517, 523, 525.

56 *a site of postindustrial wreckage:* Keith Sagar, "Hughes and His Landscape," in *The Achievement of Ted Hughes,* ed. Keith Sagar, p. 4.

56 *surrounded by mental patients:* TH–Nick Gammage, March 15, 1991. Emory.

56 *the "Myth" particle:* The village of Mytholmroyd has a web site, with links to photos of Ted Hughes's haunts: www.mytholmroyd.net.

56 *etymologically:* According to a local historian, the name means "the clearing—royd, a corruption of 'rode'—near Mithum," an old Yorkshire name for river mouth: that is, a settlement developed on a piece of

clear ground at the confluence of the Turvin and Calder Rivers. Mike Darke, *Mytholmroyd Heritage Walk*, p. 8.

57 *"Everything in West Yorkshire . . ."*: "The Rock" was recorded on April 3, 1963, broadcast September 11, first published in *The Listener*, September 19, 1963, and was reprinted in the anthology *Worlds: Seven Modern Poets*, ed. Geoffrey Summerfield; pp. 122–27.

58 *Scout Rock*: The Mytholmroyd Web site contains a recent photograph that illustrates Hughes's point: www.mytholmroyd.net/photos/scoutrock.htm.

58 *parsimony and cautiousness*: TH–GH, December 21, 1979. Emory.

59 *his father played football*: Nick Gammage, "'Nothing Will Connect': The Quest for Intimacy in Ted Hughes's New Selected Poems," in *Lire Ted Hughes*, ed. Joanny Moulin (1999), p. 63.

59 *his father's passion*: TH–Nick Gammage, November 29, 1989. Emory.

59 *"The ball jumped "up . . ."*: "Football at Slack," *New Selected Poems*, p. 157.

59 *the Great War*: See Colin Charles Fraser, "Reshaping the Past: The Personal Poetry of Ted Hughes" (Ph.D. thesis, University of New England [Australia], 1998), pp. 32–40, for a detailed reconstruction of William Henry Hughes's war service.

59 *Distinguished Conduct Medal*: "For the Duration," *New Selected Poems*, p. 128; citation quoted in Fraser, "Reshaping the Past," p. 40.

59 *a piece of shrapnel*: SP mentions this in "All the Dead Dears," her story about a visit to the Hughes's home that TH described as autobiographical, in *Johnny Panic and the Bible of Dreams*. See TH, introduction, pp. 1–6, and SP's story, p. 206 ff. Hughes refers to this incident in the poem "Out," *New Selected Poems*, p. 72.

59 *returned to the Calder Valley*: Leonard Scigaj, *Ted Hughes*, p. 54, citing Alan Moorhead, *Gallipoli*, pp. 360–61

60 *tobacconist's shop*: SP–AP, September 2, 1956, LH, p. 269.

60 *bookie*: TH–GH, c. June 21 ["Midsummer evening"], 1957. Emory.

60 *" . . . He's got his leg off . . ."*: "All the Dead Dears," p. 206.

61 *Pa was a raconteur*: TH–GH, c. June 21 ("Midsummer evening"), 1957.

61 *"My father sat . . . my father's survival"*: "Remembrance Day," part 3 of "Out," *New Selected Poems*, p. 74.

61 *how his father*: Emma Tennant, *Burnt Diaries*, pp. 178–79.

62 *squandered his life*: TH–GH, June 11, 1966. Emory.

62 *"Once you've contracted . . ."*: Interview with Drue Heinz, *The Paris Review* 134 (Spring 1995), pp. 69–70.

62 *"For the Duration"*: published in *The Listener*, May 9, 1985, first collected in *Wolfwatching* (1989), and then included in the revised and expanded version of *Remains of Elmet* published in 1994 as *Elmet*, and also in *New Selected Poems*; pp. 273–74.

62 *Everybody had his appalling tale . . . what you underwent?:* "For the Duration," *Elmet,* p. 128.

63 *"Out of the trench . . .":* Ibid., p. 129.

63 *"the soul's food":* "Dust as We Are," *Wolfwatching,* p. 11.

64 *The Farrars:* In 1471 the Farrars (other variants were Ferrer and Ferrar) settled there, and over the next 400 years grew wealthy, mainly buying and selling property. At the height of their prosperity they built a great house, Ewood Hall (a name derived from "yew wood"), which they relinquished as a residence in 1774; it was finally demolished in 1971. Information about the Ferrers/Farrars of Ewood is taken from Darke, *Mytholmroyd Heritage Walk,* p. 42.

64 *Farrar Straus:* TH–Leonard Scigaj, July 28, 1989. Emory.

64 *pregnant with their first child:* TH–GH, March 22, 1960. Emory.

64 *historical kingdom of Elmet:* TH notes that "Elmet is still the name for a part of West Yorkshire that includes the deep valley of the upper Calder and its watershed the Pennine moorland" (*Remains of Elmet,* p. 9).

64 *"book of invasions"* is Norman Davies's term for the Leabhar Gabhala Eirann, in *The Isles: A History,* pp. 34–39.

65 *married beneath herself:* Elaine Feinstein appears to disagree with this view. See her *Ted Hughes: The Life of a Poet,* p. 7.

65 *"half Moorish":* Anne Stevenson, *Bitter Fame,* p. 77. But Colin Fraser disputes this view: "Mary Alice Major's birth certificate suggests that Hughes's musing about Spanish blood is the product of family legend" ("Reshaping the Past," p. 68).

65 *all outsiders:* TH–Leonard Scigaj, June 18, 1981. Emory.

65 *Hilda, bore her only child:* JSP gives Hilda's birthdate (1908) and the date of birth of her daughter (1938), indicating that they have the same surname; if SP made any reference to the illegitimacy of this birth, it has not appeared in print, though of course it was known to the family. *JSP,* p. 703, n. 641.

65 Information about the ages of TH's parents at their wedding is drawn from Fraser, "Reshaping the Past," which is also the source for their occupations (p. 207).

65 *he monitors her appearance:* TH–GH, c. June 21 ("Midsummer evening"), 1957, et al. Emory.

66 *"connected-up writing":* Janette Lee, "Poet Laureate's Mexborough Memories," *South Yorkshire Times,* September 13, 1985, p. 13.

66 *the pen's resistance:* Heinz interview, pp. 64–65.

66 *"Ours wasn't a house . . .":* Ibid., p. 69.

66 *"Whatever other speech . . .":* quoted in Ekbert Faas, *Ted Hughes: The Unaccommodated Universe,* p. 202.

67 *a shelf of the classics:* "When my teacher began to make remarks about my writing my mother went out and bought a whole library—second hand—of classic poets." Quoted in Keith Sagar, *The Laughter of Foxes,* p. 43.

67 *"Eventually Olwyn . . .":* Ibid.

67 *"perpetual expectations":* Ibid.

68 *premonitory visions:* Various acquaintances, including SP, refer to Edith Farrar's visions; the most succinct source is TH's autobiographical story "The Deadfall" in *Difficulties of a Bridegroom.* For Hughes's comment on its authenticity, see his introduction, p. ix.

68 *gave him the elements: Difficulties of a Bridegroom,* p. viii. The direct reference is to "The Wound," but the plotting occurs elsewhere as well: most evidently in "The Rabbit Catcher" and "The Head."

68 *writings had turned out to predict:* TH–Ben Sonnenberg, n.d. Emory.

68 *an angel:* Faas, *The Unaccommodated Universe,* p. 139.

68 *The dream contained:* An inference drawn by the critic Ann Skea, which TH confirmed in a letter of November 3, 1984. Skea, *The Poetic Quest,* p. 243 and n. 3, p. 254.

68 *"dissolve yourself . . .":* "Source," *Wolfwatching,* p. 18.

69 *"Huge senseless weeping":* "The Last of the 1st/5th Lancashire Fusiliers," *New Selected Poems,* p. 291.

70 *painted lead animals:* "Capturing Animals," *Winter Pollen,* p. 10.

70 *Gerald was twelve:* Heinz interview, p. 59.

70 *Shooting was not a pastime:* "Capturing Animals," p. 11.

70 *became "obsessed": Two of a Kind: Poets in Partnership,* TH and SP interviewed by Owen Leeming, recorded January 18, 1961, BBC transcript, p. 4. British Library.

70 *the boy in the story:* Keith Sagar quotes Hughes as saying he was "about six" (*The Laughter of Foxes: A Study of Ted Hughes,* p. 38); Thomas Pero quotes Hughes as saying "Two or three" ("So Quickly It's Over," p. 1); Hughes writes "four" in *Winter Pollen.*

70 *"I had to scramble":* "Capturing Animals," p. 11.

70 *hidden in the corn:* Pero interview, p. 1. "So Quickly It's Over," p. 1.

71 *"a subsidiary brain":* Sagar, "Hughes and His Landscape," quoting 1961 radio interview *Two of a Kind.* p. 4.

71 *"he mythologized . . .":* Heinz interview, p. 59. The poem is available online at www.geocities.com/~spanoudi/poems/hiawatha.html.

71 *"I lived in his dream":* Heinz interview, p. 59.

72 *industrial waste:* Terry Gifford, "'Go Fishing': An Ecocentric or Egocentric Imperative?" in *Lire Ted Hughes,* ed. Moulin, p. 145.

72 *"long-handled wire-rimmed . . .":* "Capturing Animals" p. 11.

72 *"You're not only going . . ."*: Pero interview, p. 56.

72 *1938:* The date of the move has been variously reported. I am following information provided by TH to Janette Lee for a story in his hometown newspaper following his appointment as Poet Laureate: "Mr. Hughes vividly remembers arriving in Mexborough on September 13, 1938, just after his eighth birthday." Lee, "Poet Laureate's Mexborough Memories," p. 13.

72 *he joined the RAF:* Sagar, *Laughter of Foxes*, p. 41.

72 *a blonde party girl:* SP–AP, September 2, 1956; Lilly. Ted's parents "seem to find me more congenial than Gerald's wife, who visited them once, a blond flighty glamour girl from Australia, evidently very giddy and always wanting to go to parties and dances."

72 *aircraft engineer:* TH–Ben Sonnenberg, Emory.

73 *"blue-black" hair:* TH commented on this in a note to Keith Sagar, November 3, 1993. British Library, London.

73 *a widow's peak:* See figure 9, "Gerald, Olwyn and Ted Hughes, no date," in *The Page Is Printed: Ted Hughes, 1930–1998* (catalogue of an exhibition commemorating the life and work of Ted Hughes on the occasion of the opening of the Ted Hughes Papers, Robert W. Woodruff Library, Emory University, April 8–May 31, 2000), p. 4. A photograph of Edith Hughes with Ted was exhibited as item 7.

73 *"You are her best . . ."*: TH–GH, n.d. (c. autumn 1958) Emory.

73 *"Listening to the larks . . . for my brother":* "Anniversary," *New Selected Poems*, p. 292.

74 *"Two stepped down . . ."*: "Two," *Remains of Elmet*, p. 80.

74 *"'Two' is simply . . ."*: Skea, *Poetic Quest*, p. 200, quoting a letter from TH of November 10, 1982.

75 *buy some big houses:* TH–GH, October 10, 1955. Emory.

75 *mink farm:* TH–GH, October 16, 1954. Emory.

75 *Hughes took the rejection:* TH–GH, November 25, 1974. Emory.

77 *"We lived for it":* Pero interview, p. 54.

77 *fishing for pike:* Ibid., p. 50.

77 *By "divine" he means:* TH–Moelwyn Merchant, June 29, 1990. Emory.

77 *Through such moments:* Ibid.

78 *"Do you know Jung's . . ."*: TH–Terry Gifford, quoted in " 'Go Fishing,' " p. 154.

78 *"mutual predation system":* Ibid., p. 152.

78 *"went berserk: . . ."*: Pero interview, p. 55.

79 *"numb as a tree":* JSP, n.d. (September 1956), p. 580.

80 *"undeniable flashes . . ."*: "All the Dead Dears," *Johnny Panic and the Bible of Dreams*, p. 207.

81 *"Outside, the wind . . .":* Ibid.

81 *typing stories that Hughes dictated:* SP–AP, September 1, 1956; Lilly.

Chapter Four: Struggling (1956–1963)

82 *its grease and dust:* January 8, 1958, *JSP*, p. 308.

83 *Benidorm:* Plath's journal contains a detailed description of the site of Benidorm on August 18, 1956, *JSP*, pp. 577–78.

83 *"primitive":* Ted Hughes, "Notes on Published Works"(Emory, series 2, box 3, folders 6–12), folder 6.

83 *he planned to translate:* SP–AP, July 7, 1956. Lilly.

83 *he would read Shakespeare:* SP–AP, August 10, 1956. Lilly.

83 *bundle of scrap paper:* JSP, August 17, 1956, p. 259.

84 *Hughes normally exercised:* For an informative discussion of this practice, see SusanVan Dyne, *Revising Life: Sylvia Plath's Ariel Poems.*

84 *Walt Disney:* SP–AP, August 10, 1956.

84 *five times as rich:* TH–GH, February 24, 1957. Emory.

85 *short-sleeved jerseys:* "Drawing," *BL,* pp. 44–45.

85 *the same baggy sweater:* SP–AP, July 7, 1956.

85 *"linen . . . tie"* SP–AP, July 14, 1956. Lilly.

85 *far over budget:* SP–AP, August 2, 1956. Lilly.

85 *Samsonite luggage:* See Jane Baltzell Kopp, " 'Gone, Very Gone Youth': Sylvia Plath at Cambridge, 1955–1957" in *Sylvia Plath: The Woman and the Work,* ed. Edward Butscher, p. 63.

85 *rucksack:* Anne Stevenson, *Bitter Fame,* p. 92.

85 *Plath added:* JSP, August 14, 1956, pp. 253–54.

85 *The Joy of Cooking:* SP–AP, April 26 and May 8, 1956, *LH,* pp. 242, 253.

85 *cut it up with the scissors: The Bell Jar,* p. 7.

86 *romancing another woman:* Stevenson, *Bitter Fame,* p. 206; Dido Merwin is named as the source.

86 *"fatal bullet":* "The Inscription," *BL,* p. 173.

86 *"I could hardly . . . feeling unlikely":* "Fulbright Scholars," *BL,* p. 3.

87 *a poem by John Donne:* "Song: Go and catch a falling star . . ."

88 *"blessed Rombauer":* JSP, July 22, 1956, p. 249.

88 *"Good wine is only . . .":* SP–AP, July 14, 1956. Lilly.

88 *"to keep Ted from roaring protest":* JSP, July 22, 1956, p. 249.

88 *" . . . home-made water container . . .":* Ibid., p. 243.

88 *" . . . zucchini":* Ibid. p. 248.

88 *"myriad garnishes" . . . "like a Surgeon . . .":* JSP, August 17, 1956, p. 258. See also Irma S. Rombauer and Marion Rombauer Becker, *The Joy of Cooking,* p. 412.

88 *skinning a rabbit:* Rombauer and Becker, *The Joy of Cooking,* p. 425.

89 *"the French use wine":* Ibid., p. 413.

89 *"delectable":* JSP, August 17, 1956, p. 258.

89 *how he hunted:* TH–SP, October 6, 1956. Lilly.

89 *"Never did a new bride . . .":* JSP, July 22, 1956, p. 249.

90 *"most influential books:* Molly Finn, "First Things: Irma Rombauer, Joy of Cooking (1931)," *First Things 101* (March 2000), archived on www.leaderu.com/ftissues/ft0003/articles/rombauer.html.

90 *" . . . my own morality":* JSP, February 25, 1957, p. 269.

90 *"when she's faced by . . .":* Quoted in Donna Laframboise, "Ted Hughes' Private Letters Reveal Another Story," *National Post* (Toronto), July 29, 2000. p. B4.

91 *"When he won't eat . . .":* JSP, May 13, 1958, p. 385.

91 *"West-Yorkshire belly parsimony":* TH–GH, Spring 1957. Emory.

91 *"During her exams . . .":* Quoted in Laframboise, "Ted Hughes' Private Letters," p. B5.

91 *"atrocious" food:* SP–AP, September 21, 1956. Lilly.

91 *"burnt tough meat":* SP–AP, September 21, 1956. Lilly.

91 *"starchy little pottages . . .":* SP–AP, September 2, 1956, *LH,* p. 269.

91 *"It is all I can do . . .":* SP–AP, September 21, 1956.

91 *"Not just kippers . . .":* "Mother," *Meet My Folks!,* pp. 51–52.

92 *they planned to write:* SP–AP, July 14 and 25, 1956, *LH,* pp. 264, 265.

92 *"I recoiled . . .":* "Fever," *BL,* p. 47.

92 *"two silent strangers":* JSP, July 23, 1956, pp. 250–51.

92 *Hughes's memoir:* "Moonwalk," *BL,* p. 41.

92 *A year or so:* On dating "The Other Two," Karen Kukil writes, "We have an original typescript of 'The Other Two' with Plath's 9 Willow Street, Boston, address in the upper right hand corner. I agree that the poem is probably about Plath's honeymoon, but she may have written it as late as 1958–1959 when she lived in Boston. There is a lot of evidence in the Unabridged Journals that Plath used her journals as inspiration for poems. . . . Sometimes Hughes arranges Plath's poems chronologically by subject and sometimes chronologically by composition in Collected Poems. He is not consistent. In the case of 'The Other Two,' he probably should have included it with 1956 or 1959, but not 1957." Karen Kukil, e-mail to DM October 22, 2001.

93 *"He lifts an arm . . .":* "The Other Two," *CP,* p. 68.

94 *a delicious breakfast:* JSP, July 22, 1956, p. 247.

94 *"After a supper . . .":* JSP, May 3, 1958, p. 377.

94 *"I rose and made breakfast . . .":* JSP, May 11, 1958, p. 381.

94 *" . . . We woke in darkness . . .":* JSP, May 10, 1958, p. 380.

94 *the same association:* SP, October–November 1957 calendars. Lilly.
94 *"our good old sensible . . .":* Kopp, " 'Gone, Very Gone Youth,' " p. 68.
94 *"husband, lover, father and son":* JSP, February 25, 1956, p. 199.
94 *"We agreed on a Friday . . .":* JSP, December 27, 1958, p. 451.
94 *"sexual alliance through aggression":* Richard Larschan, e-mail to DM, October 2001.
95 *the first showers:* SP–AP, July 7, 1956. Lilly.
95 *"to use only five inches . . .":* Elaine Feinstein, *Ted Hughes: The Life of a Poet,* p. 22.
95 *gleaming-toothed physicality:* Suzette Macedo, conversation with DM, September 29, 2001.
95 *she mentions bathing:* For example, see *JSP,* April 13, 1958, p. 369.
95 *lacquers her nails:* JSP, April 15, 1958, p. 370.
95 *"How cleanliness rests my soul . . .":* JSP, May 13, 1956, p. 383.
95 *"A strong smell . . .":* JSP, Summer 1950, p. 14.
95 *"warm in bed . . .":* JSP, October 22, 1959, p. 520.
96 *"smelling lovely . . .":* JSP, July 20, 1957, p. 289.
96 *"after sweat and fury . . .":* JSP, February 5, 1958, p. 325.
96 *"I have run . . .":* JSP, February 22, 1958, p. 337.
96 *"his warmth . . .":* JSP, February 9, 1958, p. 328.
96 *"smelt of the heat . . .":* JSP, May 10, 1958, p. 380.
96 *"The Thought-Fox," New Selected Poems,* p. 3.
96 *"founded on the immortal enterprise . . .":* "Crow on the Beach," *Winter Pollen,* pp. 239–41.
97 *a "technology" developed:* TH–Moelwyn Merchant, June 29, 1990. Emory.
97 *"the shamans seem . . .":* "Regenerations," *Winter Pollen,* p. 58.
97 *The last four plays:* TH–Moelwyn Merchant, July 2, 1990. Emory. The plays in question are *Pericles, Cymbeline, The Winter's Tale,* and *The Tempest.*
97 *How the Donkey Became:* SP wrote a progress report in her journal on July 22, 1956, by which time TH had drafted fables about tortoise, hyena, fox, elephant, and cricket (*JSP,* p. 249). The book underwent significant revision before being published after Plath's death, on November 8, 1963. It was titled *How the Whale Became* and dedicated to Nicholas and Frieda. Hughes's "Notes on Published Works" at Emory describe having lost and rewritten the manuscript a couple of times before they were finally published.
97 *"At the end of a year . . .":* TH–GH, February 21, 1957. Emory.
98 *the "millions" of folktales:* TH–GH, n.d. (probably winter 1958). Emory.
98 *Alice in Wonderland:* TH–SP, October 19, 1956. Lilly.
98 *" . . . too much viciousness . . .":* Houghton Mifflin (Emilie W. McLeod)– TH, November 14, 1956. Lilly.

98 *"psychic symbols"*: TH–GH, n.d. (probably winter or spring 1958). Emory.

98 *"an American-trained dentist . . ."*: SP–Warren Plath, July 30, 1956. Lilly.

99 *"I took Ted . . ."*: SP–AP, May 18, 1956, *LH*, p. 254.

99 *"[M]uch cheaper in England . . ."*: SP–Warren Plath, 30 July 1956.

99 *"Sometimes strikes my finicky nerves . . ."*: *JSP*, April 1, 1958, p. 360.

99 *"Shut eyes . . ."*: *JSP*, September 14, 1958, pp. 419–20.

99 *". . . my own inner life . . ."*: *JSP*, July 7, 1958, p. 401.

99 *"superstitious fanciful . . ."*: TH–GH, February 24, 1957. Emory.

100 *". . . missing a train"*: TH–AP, May 13, 1963. Lilly.

100 *"I have never found . . ."*: *JSP*, January 3, 1959, p. 455.

100 *"oddly combined vehemence . . ."*: TH, draft introduction to CP, n.d. Emory.

100 *"I smell it . . ."*: *JSP*, May 19–22, 1958, p. 392.

100 *"I had a sprained thumb . . ."*: *JSP*, June 11, 1958, p. 392.

101 *"We have rousing battles . . ."*: SP–Warren Plath, June 11, 1958, *LH*, p. 344.

102 *"What would you make . . ."*: "Epiphany," *BL*, p. 114.

103 *the novel she was trying*: *JSP*, July 20, 1957, p. 290.

103 *"If I had grasped . . ."*: "Epiphany," p. 115.

103 *"Just one instance . . ."*: Quoted in Janet Malcolm, *The Silent Woman*, p. 143.

104 *"grand . . . bottom of a well"*: *JSP*, July 22, 1956, p. 248.

105 *"magic seven weeks"*: *JSP*, July 15, 1957, p. 283.

105 *"Slick stories . . ."*: Ibid., p. 284.

105 *"I underlined . . ."*: *JSP*, July 18, 1957, p. 286.

105 *". . . her children or mine?"*: *JSP*, July 18, 1957, p. 287.

105 *"Trouble-making Mother"*: *JSP*, July 18–20, 1957, pp. 288–90.

105 *"mother" for "month"*: *JSP*, July 25, 1957, p. 290.

106 *"a growing casualness about contraception"*: *JSP*, July 29, 1957, p. 294.

106 *"I have never . . ."*: *JSP*, August 9, 1957, pp. 293–94.

106 *"I couldn't write a word . . ."*: Ibid.

106 *"Ted should be . . ."*: *JSP*, June 20, 1959, p. 500.

108 *flat in Cambridge*: SP–AP, November 1, 1956, *LH*, p. 283.

108 *sitting on the bed*: TH–Keith Sagar, March 25, 1983. British Library.

108 *the narrow doorway*: *JSP*, September 6, 1957, p. 301.

108–110 *During the first three years*: Information about apartments in Northampton and Boston from AP editorial notes to *LH*, part 5, passim.

108 *"crammed up against . . ."*: *JSP*, June 20, 1958, p. 396.

108 *"a crow's nest"*: Peter Davison, *The Fading Smile: Poets in Boston, 1955–1960, from Robert Frost to Robert Lowell to Sylvia Plath*, p. 51.

108 *Plath borrowed:* Corinne Robins, "Four Young Poets," *Mademoiselle,* January 1959, p. 85.

108 *"cross and desperate":* JSP, October 19, 1959, p. 519.

109 *the luxury of solitude:* "I am so happy we can work apart, for that is what we've really needed." SP–AP, September 10, 1959, *LH,* p. 353.

109 *Tibetan Buddhist text:* Lucas Myers comments knowledgably on this text and its influence on TH in *Crow Steered, Bergs Appeared,* pp. 68–77.

109 *The House of Taurus:* SP did not give the title but described it as "a symbolic drama based on the Euripides play The Bacchae, only set in a modern industrial community under a paternalistic ruler." SP–AP, October 7, 1959, *LH,* p. 355. Apparently it was scheduled to be given a reading at the Poet's Theatre in Boston; but SP later wrote that Poet's Theatre "were willing to do a reading . . . & probably a performance if he rewrote it, but now we're withdrawing that, as he doesn't want it done." (SP–AP, June 11, 1960. Lilly.)

109 *At Yaddo they continued:* See Ekbert Faas's summaries in "Poetics," in *Critical Essays on Ted Hughes,* ed. Leonard M. Scigaj, especially pp. 86–89; SP refers casually to the practical uses of hypnotism in a letter home, October 13, 1959, *LH,* p. 355.

109 *"the underworld of her worst nightmares":* Ted Hughes, "Notes on the Chronological Order of Sylvia Plath's Poems," in *The Art of Sylvia Plath,* ed. Charles Newman, p. 192.

109 *"I have experienced . . .":* JSP, November 15, 1959, p. 530.

110 *"be true to my own weirdnesses":* JSP, October 22, 1959, pp. 520–21.

110 *"the experience that made* Ariel *possible":* "Publishing Sylvia Plath," *Winter Pollen,* p. 167.

110 *"an old shattered self . . .":* "Sylvia Plath and Her Journals," *Winter Pollen,* p. 183.

110 *"a statement of the generation":* JSP, July 20, 1957, p. 289.

110 *"peculiar, private and taboo subjects":* Peter Orr, "Sylvia Plath," in *The Poet Speaks,* ed. Peter Orr, p. 168.

111 *"she found herself . . .":* Hughes, "Notes on the Chronological Order," p. 192.

111 *"diagnostic labels:"* Frederick K. Goodwin and Kay Redfield Jamison, "Manic-Depressive Illness and Creativity," in *Manic-Depressive Illness,* pp. 342–56.

111 *"schizoaffective . . .":* Gordon Claridge, "Creativity and Madness: Clues from Modern Psychiatric Diagnosis," in *Genius and the Mind: Studies of Creativity and Temperament,* ed. Andrew Steptoe, pp. 237–38.

111 *Plath's mood swings:* See Kate Moses, "The Real Sylvia Plath" (review of

the unabridged journals, focusing on current scientific literature on PMS/PMDD), Salon.com May 30, and June 1, 2000.

111 *"I accepted her temperament . . .":* TH–Keith Sagar, June 18, 1998. British Library.

111 *"I feel, am mad . . .":* JSP, January 8, 1959, p. 459.

111 *"as if my life . . .":* JSP, June 20, 1958, p. 395.

112 *writing in bed:* SP–AP, February 25, 1960, *LH,* 367.

112 *Plath joked:* SP–Olwyn Hughes, quoted in Anne Stevenson, *Bitter Fame,* p. 224.

112 *"She had called out . . .":* Myers, *Crow Steered,* p. 77.

113 *"His wish, of course, . . .":* Hans Beacham–DM, e-mail, May 10, 2003.

113 *being "an ogre":* Hans Beacham, telephone conversation with DM, May 13, 2003.

113 *"tiny cubicle":* Interview with Drue Heniz, *The Paris Review* 134 (Spring 1995), pp. 63–64.

114 *she planned to wear slippers:* SP–AP, November 20, 1961. Lilly.

114 *"You bent over it . . .":* "The Table," *BL,* p. 138.

Chapter Five: Prospering (1957–1963)

115 *"she was a genius of some kind":* Interview with Drue Heinz, *The Paris Review* 134 (Spring 1995), p. 77.

115 *Hughes would eventually become:* JSP, March 29, 1958, p. 358.

116 *a wedding gift:* Donna Laframboise, "Ted Hughes' Private Letters Reveal Another Story," *National Post* (Toronto), July 29, 2000, p. B4.

116 *"Only did . . .":* "Flounders," *BL,* p. 65.

117 *"Sylvia is my luck completely":* TH–GH, February 24, 1957. Emory.

117 *Hill of Leopards:* SP–AP, May 7, 1957, *LH,* p. 311; for *Falcon Yard,* SP–AP, June 17, 1957, *LH,* p. 318; for *Menagerie with a Red Fox* and *The Girl in the Mirror,* JSP, July 20, 1957, p. 290.

117 *"because both of us . . .":* SP–AP, June 17, 1957, *LH,* p. 318.

117 *College teaching:* As an instructor of freshman English at her alma mater, Smith College, SP was paid $4200 for the full academic year, according to Elaine Feinstein, *Ted Hughes: The Life of a Poet,* p. 74. Feinstein notes that Plath's salary "was considerably more than a Cambridge lecturer's salary at the time" (no. 34, p. 250). Linda Wagner-Martin gives $4000 as SP's annual salary (*Sylvia Plath: A Biography,* p. 142). Neither cites the source of information. TH told his brother that as instructor of literature and creative writing at the University of Massachusetts in Amherst he was paid $2200 for half a year," TH–GH, n.d. (winter 1958). Emory.

117 *renewals of teaching contracts:* JSP, February 3, 1958, p. 322.

118 *"I wanted to keep . . ."*: Heinz interview, p. 62.

118 *grants and prize money:* SP noted the amounts. (*JSP*, September 5, 1958, p. 418 and in SP–AP, March 26, 1956, *LH*, p. 371, respectively.) The Hawthornden prize that TH received in 1960 for *Lupercal* included an award of £100, along with a "gold" medal; Anne Stevenson, *Bitter Fame*, p. 213.

118 *Saxton Fellowship:* SP–AP, November 9, 1961, *LH*, p. 436.

118 *"first reading" contract:* SP–AP, February 26, 1961, *LH*, p. 411.

118 *$7000 that year:* SP–AP, September 26, 1962. Lilly.

118 *the stubs went:* The scrapbooks are in the Hughes archive at Emory University.

118 *methodically saving:* SP mentions that they had accumulated $5000 by June 1960 (SP–AP, June 30, 1960, *LH*, p. 388). They withdrew all of it for a down payment on their home, but immediately began saving a portion of their income to repay their mothers for the loans that helped them buy the house.

119 *the sale of manuscripts:* TH sold the SP papers in his possession to Smith College in 1981, and sold his own papers to Emory University in 1997. The price that the libraries paid for their manuscripts is not public information; however, according to the *Times Literary Supplement*, the Hughes manuscripts fetched £600,000 in 1997. Aurelia Plath noted on her copy of the agreement that her right to sell the papers had been challenged by the estate ("Olwyn challenged!"—date indecipherable) (photocopy of "Agreement of Purchase," private collection). She donated later correspondence with the Plath estate to Smith in 1983 and received a $15,000 tax credit (Richard Larschan, e-mail to DM, November 18, 2001). TH also sent AP copies of the valuable fine press editions of SP's work produced by the Rainbow Press (Richard Larschan, e-mail to DM, November 18, 2001).

119 *"one of the richest British poets"*: John Ezard, "Ted Hughes Leaves £1.4m to Wife," the *Times* (London), April 20, 1999.

119 *calls his mother-in-law Prospero: BL*, pp. 132–33.

119 *"postwar utility son-in-law"*: "A Pink Wool Knitted Dress," *BL*, p. 34. Information on AP's salary and sending SP to Smith is from Richard Larschan, e-mail to DM, November 12, 2001.

120 *She projected finishing: JSP*, July 15, 1957, pp. 282–83.

120 *"bridging the gap . . ."*: *JSP*, August 9, 1957, p. 293.

121 *Cambridge "eccentrics"*: TH–SP, n.d. (probably October 4, 1956). Lilly.

121 *J. D. Salinger's: JSP*, March 4 and 11, 1957, pp. 272–76. *Lucky Jim* had been published in 1954; *The Catcher in the Rye* in 1951; *The Horse's Mouth* in 1944.

121 *"fresh, brazen colloquial voice"*: JSP, March 4, 1957, p. 275.

121 *"love, a falcon . . ."*: JSP, July 15, 1957, p. 284.

121 *"a vivid diary of reminiscence"*: JSP, February 24, 1957, p. 268.

121 *"the voyage of a girl . . ."*: JSP, March 4, 1957, p. 275.

121 *second Cambridge winter:* JSP, March 11, 1957, pp. 276–79.

122 *"I have experienced love . . ."*: JSP, November 15, 1959, p. 530.

122 *"pale with a mouth . . ."*: JSP, February 18, 1958, p. 333.

122 *"garish Leger cityscapes . . ."*: JSP, May 13, 1958, p. 384.

122 *"ravaged by years of sandblasting"*: JSP, March 18, 1958, p. 353.

122 *" . . . bartering and fingering"*: JSP, March 20, 1958, p. 354.

122 *"Secret sin . . ."*: JSP, February 5, 1958, p. 325.

122 *"Grit into art:"* JSP, January 12, 1958, p. 309.

122 *"My voice must change . . ."*: JSP, January 26, 1958, p. 320.

123 *"This be my secret . . ."*: JSP, January 22 and February 4, 1958, pp. 318, 324.

123 *factory-stamped pages:* Karen Kukil, editorial note 381, JSP, p. 694.

123 *the "new" journal:* JSP, May 13 and July 4, 1958, pp. 382–83, 401.

123 *"Sentimental"*: For example, "Let me not be sentimental," February 20, 1958, JSP, p. 334.

123 *"feminine" aspect:* SP–Warren Plath, June 11, 1958, LH, p. 343.

123 *a city full of poets:* See Peter Davison's lively book about literary Boston, *The Fading Smile: Poets in Boston, 1955–1960, from Robert Frost to Robert Lowell to Sylvia Plath.*

124 *"who also wrote"*: Diane Middlebrook, *Anne Sexton*, p. 103.

125 *the tiny table:* Davison, *The Fading Smile*, p. 172.

125 *an entire meal:* JSP, January 27, 1959, p. 465.

125 *"felt like regression"*: Ibid.

125 *"We would pile . . ."*: Anne Sexton, "The Bar Fly Ought to Sing," in *The Art of Sylvia Plath*, ed. Charles Newman, p. 174.

125 *"mental hospital graduate"*: Quoted in Davison, *The Fading Smile*, p. 175.

126 *"the marvelous enviable casualness"*: Ibid.

126 *"without ever having . . ."*: JSP, March 20, 1959, p. 475.

126 *"Who rivals? . . ."*: JSP, March 29, 1958, p. 360.

127 *Plath longed to "eclipse"*: Ibid.

127 *"What is my voice? . . ."*: JSP, January 21, 1958, p. 315.

127 *"Her novels make mine possible"*: JSP, July 20, 1957, p. 289.

127 *"One fig was a husband . . ."*: *The Bell Jar*, p. 75.

129 *Plath's overwhelming desire:* TH–AP, January 12, 1975. Emory.

129 *he called it "nagging"*: JSP, September 14, 1958, p. 421.

129 *Early in 1959:* SP's entry for December 31, 1958, indicates that she thought she was already pregnant by that date; her entry for March 20,

1959, notes the onset of menstruation "after a long 40 day period of hope." *JSP*, March 20, 1959, p. 474.

130 *"Sylvia was wearing her hair . . .":* AP, editorial note, *LH*, p. 356.

130 *Ted's family at a distance:* SP–AP, August 27, 1960. Lilly.

130 *"despite being of an enormous . . .":* SP–AP, February 11, 1960, *LH*, p. 366.

130 *three-volume edition:* Ibid.

131 *"the Greek islands . . .":* SP–AP, March 24 and 26, 1960, *LH*, pp. 370–71.

131 *fancy Greek restaurant:* SP–AP, March 3, 1960, *LH*, p. 368.

131 *" . . . nuclear wars":* A. Alvarez, *Where Did It All Go Right?*, p. 189.

131 *"so small that everything . . .":* A. Alvarez, *The Savage God*, p. 5.

131 *"a man who seemed . . .":* Alvarez, *Where Did It All Go Right?*, p. 198.

131 *"briskly American" that day:* Alvarez, *The Savage God*, p. 6.

131 *"He didn't recognize"* The publication of "Night Shift" in the *Observer* is not listed in Stephen Tabor, *Sylvia Plath: An Analytical Bibliography*, but Alvarez quotes from it in *The Savage God*, pp. 8–9.

131 *"In those days, Sylvia . . .":* Alvarez, *The Savage God*, p. 6.

132 *"tall, trim American wife . . .":* SP–AP, March 28, 1960, p. 372.

132 London *had previously published:* "The Sleepers" and "Full Fathom Five," *London Magazine*, June 7, 1960, pp. 11–13.

132 *"I must get them . . .":* SP–AP, March 3, 1960, *LH*, p. 369.

133 *"Oddly enough . . .":* SP–AP, May 5, 1960, *LH*, p. 380.

133 *"I felt to be sitting . . .":* Ibid. p. 381.

133 *"were instrumental in Ted's . . .":* Ibid.

133 *Hughes kept aloof:* Alvarez, *The Savage God*, p. 4.

133 *"self-assured and self-possessed . . .":* Alvarez, *Where Did It All Go Right?*, p. 198.

134 *Look Back in Anger* opened at the Royal Court Theatre May 8, 1956, directed by Tony Richardson; a film version was released in 1958, with Richard Burton as Jimmy.

134 *"translated from the French":* SP–AP, November 25, 1960. Lilly.

135 *"projected illuminated mandalas":* TH quoted in Ekbert Faas, *Ted Hughes: The Unaccommodated Universe*, p. 205.

135 *a dancer to mime:* Details from TH–AP, n.d. (c. December 21, 1960). Lilly.

135 *"a sort of Buddhist mass":* Ibid.

135 *the genre of the verse play:* TH–Olive Prouty, June 21, 1960. Lilly.

135 *"psychic entities":* TH–AP, (c. December 21, 1960).

135 *"early commercial acceptance . . .":* SP–AP, July 9, 1960, *LH*, p. 389.

135 *Eliot had expressed:* SP–AP, July 9, 1960. Lilly.

136 *"marvelously amusing and vivid":* SP–AP, June 11, 1960, Lilly.

136 *listening to the BBC radio production:* TH–AP, n.d. (c. December 21, 1960). Lilly.

136 *"theatricality"*: Ibid.

136 *"verse-piece for voices"*: Ibid.

136 *"and what they say . . ."*: TH–Lucas Myers, n.d. (winter or spring 1961). Emory.

136 *A soldier with a head wound:* In Keith Sagar's interpretation, the sergeant is dead and the play is taking place in the underworld; but Ripley is not dead, and returns (*The Art of Ted Hughes*, p. 81).

136 *the soldier, Ripley,:* TH may have named his protagonist after George Ripley (1415–1490), the most famous English alchemist and author of a widely known allegorical work on alchemy written in verse: *The Compound of Alchymy*. Ripley was from Yorkshire.

136 *". . . all the stock imagery . . ."*: TH, interview in Adelaide, Australia, March 1976.

137 *Hall also developed productions:* Peter Hall, *Making an Exhibition of Myself*, p. 166. *"I couldn't be happier . . ."*: SP–AP, April 5, 1961. *LH*, p. 416.

137 *"dark opposite to Shakespeare's* Tempest*"*: SP–AP, February 26, 1961. Lilly.

137 *"redeem" his reputation:* TH–AP, n.d. (c. December 21, 1960). Lilly.

137 *authentic level of intensity:* Fred Rue Jacobs, quoting a telephone interview with TH (no date), "Hughes and Drama," in *The Achievement of Ted Hughes*, ed. Keith Sagar, p. 158.

138 *"were fascinated . . ."*: Peter Davison–TH, December 4, 1961. Emory.

138 *". . . we'll be wealthy yet"*: SP–AP, April 5, 1961, *LH*, p. 416.

138 *Plath too recycled:* For discussion of poems drafted by Plath on versos of *The Calm* which are housed in the Smith archive, see Lynda K. Bundtzen, *The Other Ariel*, pp. 78–82.

138 *"a technology"*: TH–Moelwyn Merchant, June 29, 1990. Emory.

139 *"rhetorical and empty"*: Peter Hall–TH, September 27, 1965. Emory.

139 *"discursive intelligence"*: TH–AP, n.d. (c. December 21, 1960).

140 *keep Ted writing full-time:* SP–AP, July 9, 1960, *LH*, p. 389.

140 *"invested"*: SP–Lynne Lawner, February 18, 1960, quoted in Stevenson, *Bitter Fame*, p. 182.

140 *"besetting insecurity"*: Dido Merwin, "Vessel of Wrath: A Memoir of Sylvia Plath," published as Appendix II in Stevenson, *Bitter Fame*, p. 325.

140 *Plath's spotless, well-equipped kitchen:* Edith Hughes–AP, n.d. (postmark June 12, 1960). Lilly.

140 *get a salaried job:* SP–AP, June 30, 1960, *LH*, p. 386.

140 *in 1960 the purchase price:* Ibid., p. 387.

141 Average incomes and house costs are from dMarie Time Capsule, dmarie.com/timecap/.

141 *She noted wistfully:* SP–AP, August 31, 1960, *LH,* pp. 392–93; also see *LH,* p. 386.

141 *During their first ten months:* SP–AP, October 8, 1960, *LH,* p. 396. SP wrote, "Ted is going to buy a cheap radio this week," because so much of his work was scheduled for broadcast in the ensuing months.

141 *upstairs neighbor:* SP–AP, May 5, 1960. Lilly.

141 *writing retreat:* Dido Merwin says they meant the flat to be available only to TH (Stevenson, *Bitter Fame,* pp. 325–26).

141 *named for Aunt Frieda:* SP–AP, June 24, 1960, *LH,* p. 386.

141 *"We're all besotted . . .":* Al Alvarez, conversation with DM, September 3, 2002.

142 *"Wish I could":* SP–AP, April 21, 1960. Lilly.

142 *"like a kind . . .": Two of a Kind: Poets in Partnership,* TH and SP interviewed by Owen Leeming, recorded January 18, 1961, BBC transcript, p. 2/3. British Library.

142 *"At times she seems . . .":* TH–AP, May 30, 1960. Lilly.

142 *"she's found her talking voice . . .":* TH–Olive Prouty, June 21, 1960. Lilly.

142 *By Christmas:* TH–AP, n.d. (c. December 21, 1960). Lilly.

142 *"about the most interesting thing . . .":* TH–Merwins, n.d. (early August 1960). Emory.

142 *"The Devon dream . . .":* TH–Keith Sagar, June 18, 1998. British Library.

142 *"knock over the occasional deer":* TH–Keith Sagar, August 15, 1997. British Library.

142 *she had a few plans:* Stevenson, *Bitter Fame,* p. 248, refers to a letter by AP but does not indicate to whom it was written or where it was found.

143 *Court Green:* AP wrote to Warren that TH and SP would get Court Green for £4500 ($12,600); the asking price had been £4800 (July 30, 1961). Lilly. But SP wrote later that the owners had accepted £3600 ($10,800); SP–AP, August 7, 1961. Lilly.

143 *one edge of the:* Information about the house's location from SP–Marty Plumer, February 4, 1963. Smith. SP says the garden is 2.5 acres, not 3 (as in TH's letter to GH).

143 *buy Court Green:* Information about outright purchase of the house is from Stevenson, *Bitter Fame,* p. 219.

144 *Plath wanted fresh paint:* SP–AP, December 7, 1961. Lilly.

144 *forty-minute drive:* TH–Lucas Myers, n.d. (November 1961). Emory. TH mentions the distance to Exeter, not washing the clothes.

144 *"color tonic":* SP–AP, June 11, 1960, *LH,* p 385.

144 *fine red Wilton:* For the rugs in the house, see SP–AP, December 7, 1961.

145 *Hughes's collection:* See various TH–GH letters at Emory, for instance in folder 14 (1965), folder 21 (1972), and folder 24 (1975).

145 *"leading, at last . . .* : SP–AP, September 15, 1961, *LH,* p. 429.

145 *"I could cradle . . . With your hand":* "The Rag Rug," *BL,* pp. 135–37.

145 *raspberry bushes:* Suzette Macedo, conversation with DM, August 2002.

145 *They counted:* SP–AP, September 27, 1961, *LH,* p. 430.

146 *Devonshire:* I am indebted to Kate Moses for identifying the varieties of apples in the Court Green orchard.

146 *apple pie for breakfast:* SP–AP, April 25, 1962. Lilly.

146 *flowering trees:* WP–AP, September 10, 1961. Lilly.

146 *"digging and dragging and chopping":* TH–GH, July 2, 1962. Emory.

146 *Hughes was suffering:* "The Lodger," *BL,* pp. 124–25.

146 *his ashes:* The *Sunday Times* of London reported on February 4, 2001: "Ian Cook, a close friend of Hughes, . . . was entrusted by Hughes with the task of scattering his ashes on Dartmoor."

147 *" . . . hotline to his unconscious":* A. Alvarez, "Ted Hughes," in *The Epic Poise,* ed. Nick Gammage, pp. 209–10.

148 *a promising young poet:* TH's interview with Drue Heinz dates "The Thought Fox" to about 1955 (p. 77): "The earliest piece of mine that I kept was a lyric titled 'Song' that came to me as such things should in your nineteenth year. . . . Between that and the next piece that I saved, the poem I titled 'The Thought Fox,' lay six years of total confusion. Six years!" This is inaccurate, though, because TH published a number of poems as early as 1954 that he "kept"—i.e., published in a book and included in successive collections of his work. See the "Contributions to Periodicals" section in Keith Sagar and Stephen Tabor, eds. *Ted Hughes: A Bibliography,* pp. 278–79 et passim. SP wrote to her mother that *The New Yorker* had originally rejected "The Thought Fox," which indicates that it was one of the poems Plath had submitted for TH when she was attempting to find American outlets for his work. Hughes gave Plath credit for submitting the manuscript of *The Hawk in the Rain* for the prize it won, and *The New Yorker* acquired the poem from Harper Brothers before the book was published.

148 *immediately acquired for reprint:* In the United States, the anthologist Oscar Williams chose three poems from *The Hawk in the Rain* for the revised edition of his anthology of modern verse, in which the "The Thought Fox" would be the last poem (TH–Lucas Myers, n.d. [early summer 1958]. Emory); in the United Kingdom, A. Alvarez included it in his influential 1962 anthology *The New Poetry.*

148 *"apprehends the unwritten poem . . .":* A. Alvarez, "Tough Young Poet," the *Observer,* undated clipping at Emory, Series 6.

148 *"The window . . .":* "The Thought-Fox," *New Selected Poems,* p. 3.

149 *"Terrifying . . .":* Ibid. p. 39.

149 *"Carving . . . "*: Ibid., p. 40.

149 *"mining it to the limit"*: TH–Keith Sagar, June 16, 1998. British Library.

149 *a part of his brain*: TH–Keith Sagar, March 25, 1983. British Library.

149 *"special" to him*: TH–Keith Sagar, April 11, 1981. British Library.

150 *"Well, you write about . . ."*: "On Writing for Radio," TH interviewed by Anthony Thwaite, recorded January 16, 1963, transcript p. 8. British Library.

150 *"What am I? . . ."*: "Wodwo," *New Selected Poems*, pp. 88–89.

150 *"continually in a state . . ."*: Quoted in John Horder, "Desk Poet," the *Guardian*, March 23, 1965, p. 9.

151 *a state of "alertness"*: TH–Keith Sagar, April 22, 1980. British Library.

153 *"much superior"*: TH–Keith Sagar, n.d. (postmark March 13, 1981). British Library.

153 *"Here the hand . . ."*: "Lines to a Newborn Baby" was never collected into one of TH's books, but Keith Sagar reprinted the whole poem in *The Achievement of Ted Hughes*, pp. 316–17.

153 *"I'm no more . . ."*: "Morning Song," *CP*, p. 157.

153 *"My method was . . ."*: Heinz interview, p. 77.

156 *flavor of this partnership*: TH was commenting on the volume *Wodwo*. Ted Hughes, "Notes on Published Works." Emory, series 2, box 3, folder 6.

156 *"I'm a castaway . . ."*: Ibid.

158 *"the nervous strain . . ."*: TH–GH, July 2, 1962. Emory.

158 *Europe was too full*: TH–Lucas Myers, n.d. (September 1961). Emory.

159 *funerary*: I use the term "funerary" as descriptive of the tone of the book's ending, not indicative of chronology. Two of these poems had been published before SP's death: "Pibroch" (*Critical Quarterly*, Winter 1960) and "Mountains" (*Observer*, August 5, 1962). According to a letter TH wrote to Keith Sagar, two were lying on her desk at the time of her suicide: "Heptonstall," and "Pibroch"; and he wrote "Song of a Rat" and "The Howling of Wolves" a couple of weeks after her death (TH–Sagar, June 18, 1998. British Library).

Chapter Six: Separating (1962–   )

159 *young peach tree*: TH–AP, May 1, 1962. Lilly.

159 *"soaked with hot sun . . ."*: Ibid.

159 *radio play*: *Three Women*, directed by Douglas Cleverdon, recorded August 2, 1962, broadcast August 19 (repeated September 13, 1962, and June 9, 1968). All on BBC Third Programme. *CP*, pp. 176–186.

159 *she showed Hughes*: TH–AP, January 12, 1975 (reediting LH). Emory.

159 *"Sylvia is beginning . . ."*: TH–AP, May 14, 1962. Lilly.

160 *Poets should meet poets:* Suzette Macedo, conversation with DM, March 9, 2003, London.

160 *eager conversationalist:* Ibid.

160 *"old-fashioned . . . interested him":* Helder Macedo, conversation with DM, March 9, 2003, London.

161 *met the preceding spring:* Ruth Fainlight, conversation with DM, August 25, 1999.

161 *"nobodies":* Elaine Feinstein, *Ted Hughes: The Life of a Poet,* p. 118.

161 *"Elm":* "Elm" is dated April 19, 1962; the dedication was apparently added after Fainlight's visit. *CP,* pp. 192–93.

161 *"Love is a shadow . . .":* Ibid., p. 192.

162 *food for the table:* "Rabbit stew," appears on February 26, March 11, and June 25 in SP's 1962 diary. "Jugged hare" appears March 10. Smith.

162 *breakfasts of trout:* TH–GH, n.d. (May 1962). Emory.

162 *"the strangling quality of our closeness":* TH–AP May 13, 1963. Lilly.

162 *"was always looking . . .":* Helder Macedo, conversation with DM, March 9, 2003.

162 *"the loving slovenliness of motherhood":* JSP, "The Tryers: George, Marjorie (50), Nicola (16)," p. 632.

162 *"cowlike bliss":* SP–Marcia Brown Plumer, February 4, 1963. Smith. Also to AP, same day, she lamented being "catapulted from the cowlike happiness of maternity into loneliness" (*LH,* p. 498).

162 *a big baby:* In contrast, Frieda was seven pounds, four ounces. *JSP,* p. 647.

162 *Her writing conveys:* Ibid., p. 644.

163 *"nosing" and "sniffing" Nicholas:* Ibid., pp. 638, 641.

163 *"little sweet-smelling peach":* SP–AP, February 24, 1962, *LH,* p. 447.

163 *"well-behaved . . . Farrar-looking":* SP and TH–GH, n.d. (May 1962). Lilly.

163 *"I could do . . .":* TH–Lucas Myers, n.d. (September 1961). Emory.

163 *"He has a most complicated smile . . .":* TH–AP, May 1, 1962. Lilly.

163 *"perhaps the handsomest . . .":* Peter Porter, "Ted Hughes and Sylvia Plath: A Bystander's Recollections," *Australian Book Review,* August 2001, p. 23.

164 *"a Fitzgerald . . . Gary Cooper":* Tamsin Todd, quoting William Trevor, in "My Wife, the Other Woman," the *Observer* (London), February 15, 1998, p. 5.

164 *"Babylonian":* Richard Murphy, *The Kick,* p. 229.

164 *the family had immigrated:* Assia's history is summarized by Eilat Negev in "Haunted by the Ghosts of Love," the *Guardian,* April 10, 1999.

164 *artistic talents:* According to Eilat Negev, "Assia not only sketched, she also painted in watercolours, and was quite gifted. She didn't have any proper schooling, but judging from what we saw, she was definitely not

amateurish" (e-mail to DM, May 8, 2002). Lucas Myers observed Assia's watercolors hanging on the walls of her living room in her London flat in 1964 (*Crow Steered, Bergs Appeared*, p. 128).

164 *dabbled in poetry:* Eilat Negev quotes a poem by Assia in "Haunted by the Ghosts of Love"; unsigned manuscripts tentatively attributed to her can also be found in the Ted Hughes archive at Emory.

164 *beef stew and gingerbread:* Handwritten notes in block for May 18, 1962, SP's 1962 diary. Smith.

165 *"intelligent, witty, interested, good company":* Quoted in Anne Stevenson, *Bitter Fame*, p. 242.

165 *This dining table:* SP–AP, September 4, 1961, *LH*, p. 427.

165 *Before going to bed:* Stevenson, *Bitter Fame*, p. 242.

165 *"You are like the sunlight":* "Sunlight," dated October 1962, North Tawton. Emory. Unpublished manuscript drafts.

166 *Hughes describes a dream:* "Dreamers," *BL*, pp. 159–60.

166 *On Saturday afternoon:* SP's calendar diary for May 18–19, 1962, indicates that the Wevills were not expected to stay over Saturday night (Smith); this understanding was affirmed in a letter David Wevill wrote to Anne Stevenson after publication of *Bitter Fame*. Wevill contested the implication that Plath had "reacted badly" (*Bitter Fame*, p. 243) to their visit and had sent them home early. See Feinstein, *Ted Hughes*, p. 123.

166 *a tapestry kit:* Assia Wevill–SP, May 22, 1962. Courtesy of Elizabeth Compton.

166 *"gros point of gross roses":* SP–Marvin and Kathy Kane, June 9, 1962. Lilly.

166 *the next five weeks:* SP entered "tapestry" or "gros point" on her calendar diary for May 29, June 13 and 23, and July 1. Smith.

167 *"rapacious":* A. Alvarez, *Where Did It All Go Right?*, p. 209.

167 *big cats that hunters prize:* "Folktale," *New Selected Poems*, pp. 309–10.

167 *divorce seems to be brewing:* TH and SP–Gerald, Joan, Ashley, and Brendan Hughes, June 10–11, 1962. Lilly.

167 *study German:* TH–GH, July 2, 1962. Emory.

167 *"I have come . . .":* Feinstein quotes the note as recalled by Suzette Macedo, *Ted Hughes*, p. 124.

167 *folding a rose:* Ibid. Feinstein notes that in "Chlorophyl," published in a limited edition of poems about Assia (*Capriccio*), the message is carried not by a flower but by a grass blade.

167 *"a shipful of strangers . . .":* "The Rescue," *Wodwo*, pp. 36–37. TH identified "The Rescue" as a speech from *The Calm* in his "Notes on Published Works." Emory series 2, box 3, folder 6.

168 "*Love cannot come . . .*": "Event," *CP*, pp. 194–95.

168 "*hands round a tea mug . . .*": "The Rabbit Catcher," *CP*, p. 194.

168 *unmistakably a response:* Mentioned by Christina Britzolakis, in *Sylvia Plath and the Theatre of Mourning*, p. 105.

168 "*Rabbit Snared in the Night*": *Complete Poems* by D.H. Lawrence, vol. 1, p. 230.

168 "*Yes, bunch yourself . . .*": Ibid.

169 "*itched and kindled*": *JSP*, February 23, 1958, p. 337.

169 " *. . . Why do I feel . . .*": Ibid.

169 *celebrate the signing:* Linda Wagner-Martin, *Sylvia Plath: A Biography*, p. 170.

169 *surreal, violent fantasy:* "The Harvesting," *Wodwo*. Keith Sagar notes in his bibliography of TH that an initial draft of the story was among Hughes's very first publications, the essay "Harvesting," published in the Mexborough Grammar School magazine *Don and Dearne* (1:20–21, 26–27), Whitsuntide 1946. Sagar and Stephen Tabor, eds., *Ted Hughes: A Bibliography*, 2d ed., p. 277.

170 *Plath sent:* Stevenson reports that SP sent "Event," *Bitter Fame*, p. 244. Alvarez accepted "Event," and it was published in *Observer* on December 16, 1962. "The Rabbit Catcher" was not published until 1971, in *Lyonesse*, a limited edition book assembled by Olwyn Hughes and brought out by the Rainbow Press, the publishing venture she undertook with TH. However, SP read "The Rabbit Catcher" in her interview with Peter Orr on October 30, 1962, recorded by the British Council for the BBC.

170 "*In those snares . . .*": "The Rabbit Catcher," *BL*, p. 146.

171 "*Think of the many . . .*": Terry Gifford, " 'Go Fishing': An Ecocentric or Egocentric Imperative?" in *Lire Ted Hughes*, ed. Joanny Moulin, p. 145.

171 "*Up to the age of seventeen . . .*": Interview with Drue Heinz, *The Paris Review* 134 (Spring 1995), p. 59.

172 "*The blood jet is poetry . . .*": "Kindness" (manuscript dated February 1, 1963), *CP*, p. 270.

173 "*at its loveliest*": Edith Hughes–AP, June 5, 1962. Lilly.

173 *Plath festooned:* I am indebted to Kate Moses for teasing out the list of locations of hearts and flowers.

173 *a warm and breezy romance:* SP's work on the novel can probably be dated to around March 4, 1962, when she wrote to AP, "I am beginning work on something amusing which I hope turns into a book (novel) but may be just happy piddling" (*LH*, p. 448). In *Bitter Fame*, the existence of this novel is strenuously contested in a note that was probably contributed by Olwyn Hughes. However, the Hughes archive at Emory contains fifteen pages of notes and narrative that identifiably belong to the novel project titled *Falcon Yard* in SP's journal. Twelve pages are apparently from the same typescript—draft, with many strikethroughs—now titled *Venus in the Seventh*, which carries the novel as far as typescript p. 79. Smith has one sheet (p. 25) from what is apparently this same typescript of *Venus in the Seventh*. TH used these typescript pages to draft poems published in *Wodwo*, which indicates that Plath typed these pages of the novel after 1960.

173 *One evening when Aurelia*: AP, unpublished manuscript of *LH*. Lilly.

174 *entering slogan contests*: *JSP*, April 13, 1958, p. 365.

174 *"oppressive silences"*: Notes from AP's travel diary, in unpublished manuscript of *LH*.

174 *"I have everything..."*: AP editorial note, *LH*, p. 458.

174 *Plath silently passed*: Details from AP's travel diary, unpublished manuscript of *LH*. AP does not mention that SP ripped the phone wires out of the wall. That detail appears for the first time, without a source note, in Edward Butscher's *Sylvia Plath: Method and Madness*, p. 352; the context suggests that Butscher's source was an interview with one of the female friends in whom SP confided after her separation from TH.

174 *"... embarrassing position"*: AP, November 1986, outtakes of interview with Richard Larschan for *Voices & Visions/Sylvia Plath*, PBS documentary. Courtesy of Richard Larschan.

174 *Hughes was making*: TH–AP, January 12, 1975. Emory.

175 *"with a strange little laugh"*: Notes from AP's travel diary, in unpublished manuscript of *LH*.

175 *She wanted him out*: AP's notes do not describe the conversation, but it can be inferred from her (unsent) letter to Warren Plath, written from the home of Winifred Davies, July 17, 1962. Lilly.

175 *"every scrap of paper..."*: TH–AP January 12, 1975.

175 *"Sylvia had built..."*: AP–Leonard Sanazaro, May 4, 1982. Courtesy of the estate of Aurelia Plath.

175 *Another source*: Clarissa Roche, "Sylvia Plath: Vignettes from England," in *Sylvia Plath: The Woman and the Work*, ed. Edward Butscher, pp. 85–86.

175 *empty marriage bed*: AP–Elizabeth Compton, May 18, 1976. Courtesy of Elizabeth Compton.

176 *"She told me..."*: Elizabeth Sigmund (now Compton), "Sylvia in Devon: 1962," in *Sylvia Plath: The Woman and the Work*, p. 104.

176 *Hughes would later claim:* TH–Elizabeth Compton, n.d. (annotated by her, "July '63"). Courtesy of Elizabeth Compton.

176 *gushy sentimentality:* In his memoir, Lucas Myers ascribed this trait to Aurelia's immigrant family background, which he thought made her particularly eager to please; she was, he wrote, "the cupbearer of a mixture of treacle of very familiar components, American, New Englandish and German" (*Crow Steered,* pp. 59–60).

177 *"Violent and animal":* Nathaniel Tarn, diary notes dated July 19, 1962. Stanford. Tarn's first notes summarize the history of the affair, according to Assia, in notes made July 16, 18, and 19, 1962. Ibid.

177 *as thrilled as she was alarmed:* Suzette Macedo, conversation with DM, August 2002.

177 *a poem that he published twice:* The poem that begins "Friday created Adam . . . ," titled "Capriccios," was the first in a sequence of twenty poems in the volume *Capriccio,* published by Leonard Baskin's Gehenna Press in 1990, with engravings by Baskin, in a limited edition of fifty copies; for a description, see Keith Sagar and Stephen Tabor's *Ted Hughes: A Bibliography, 1946–1995,* pp. 145–46. All of the poems in *Capriccio* appear to be reflections on Hughes's relationship with Assia Wevill. The same poem, retitled "Superstition," is the last poem in *Howls and Whispers,* the volume addressed to Sylvia Plath published by Gehenna Press in 1998 in a limited edition of one hundred ten copies.

177 *Hughes misremembered:* Date confirmed in Keith Sagar, "Ted Hughes," *New Dictionary of National Biography.*

177 *"child-husband":* Nathaniel Tarn, diary notes dated July 19, 1962.

177 *working order:* SP–Olive Prouty, November 2, 1962; SP tells Prouty she's now got a new phone and new number. Lilly.

177 *He promised to work:* Nathaniel Tarn, diary notes dated July 19, 1962.

177 *"having hysterics":* Ibid.

178 *run it off the road:* Al Alvarez disclosed this information in *The Savage God,* pp. 14, 18. Nathaniel Tarn's diary notes put an earlier, and probably more reliable, date on this event than is given in Stevenson's *Bitter Fame,* p. 252, note.

178 *Hughes continued to show up:* SP–AP, August 27, 1962. Lilly.

178 *moving in a "civilized" fashion:* Stevenson, *Bitter Fame,* p. 252.

178 *"this woman . . . can't have children":* SP–AP, September 23, 1962. Lilly.

178 *"fish on a slab":* Suzette Macedo, conversation with DM, September 3, 2002.

178 *"a clean break" and was "going . . .":* SP–AP, August 27, 1962, *LH,* p. 460.

178 *"desertion" and about "his utter . . .":* SP–AP, August 27, 1962. Lilly.

178 *a recuperative holiday:* Elaine Feinstein quotes the recollection of
Elizabeth Compton that SP thought the trip to Ireland "might be 'a
possible renewal of their marriage'"; Feinstein also quotes a letter SP
wrote to Ruth Fainlight in September inquiring about facilities in
Spain, which suggests SP thought she and the children might accompany TH (*Ted Hughes,* pp. 127–28). A letter from SP to her mother is
ambiguous about whether she meant to be living with TH in Spain.
(SP–AP, August 27, 1962. Lilly). A letter from Winifred Davies to AP
indicates that SP had expressed optimism about a reconciliation in
Ireland: "I hoped great things from the Irish holiday but apparently
things have gone from bad to worse" (Davies–AP, September 22, 1962.
Lilly).

179 *"mutual":* TH–AP, January 12, 1975.

179 *". . . thought the best thing . . .":* Richard Murphy, *The Kick,* p. 225.

179 *fishing or grouse shooting:* Richard Murphy, "A Memoir of Sylvia Plath
and Ted Hughes on a Visit to the West of Ireland in 1962," Appendix III
in Stevenson, *Bitter Fame,* p. 352. Murphy says that SP told him TH had
gone fishing with Barrie Cooke; to her mother, SP wrote, "Ted deserted
me again in Ireland, saying he was going grouse-shooting for the day
with a friend. I believed him, as he had said he would tell me the truth,
however difficult. He left me to come home alone with all the heavy
baggage." SP–AP, September 23, 1962).

179 *A telegram from Ted:* SP–AP, September 23, 1962.

179 *Hughes was in Spain:* Nathaniel Tarn, diary notes dated October 1,
1962. Stanford, and Eilat Negev, Assia Wevill's biographer, public lecture at the University of Indiana, Bloomington, October 2002.

179 *"Ted has deserted us":* SP–AP, September 23, 1962.

180 *temporary insanity:* TH–AP, May 13, 1963. Lilly.

180 *"We can't invest . . .":* TH–GH, July 2, 1962. Quoted in Donna Laframboise, "Ted Hughes' Private Letters Reveal Another Story," *National Post*
(Toronto), July 29, 2000, p. B4.

180 *"flew down . . . little wiser":* JSP, April 19, 1962, p. 641.

180 *"The one factor . . . married to":* Quoted in Laframboise, "Ted Hughes'
Private Letters" pp. B4–5.

180 *"He says all the kindness . . .":* SP–Olive Prouty, September 29, 1962.
Lilly.

180 *"he now thinks all feeling . . .":* SP–AP, September 26, 1962. Lilly.

180 *thrown herself into nesting:* TH pointed this out, though compassionately,
in a letter to AP as early as December 1960: "Tending Frieda and recovering from having her . . . really absorbed Sylvia utterly until a month ago."
TH–AP, n.d. (December 1960). Lilly.

181 more *babies:* SP wrote to her mother, "I think having babies is really the happiest experience of my life. I would just like it to go on and on" (March 12, 1962, *LH,* pp. 449–50).

181 *"Now the storm-centre . . .":* TH–GH, n.d. (December 1962). Emory.

181 *"she was quite . . .":* TH–Keith Sagar, May 23, 1981. British Library.

181 *"natural supply . . . I exist":* TH–GH, July 2, 1962. Emory.

181 *there wasn't much sex:* Feinstein, *Ted Hughes,* p. 122, quoting Suzette Macedo.

182 *"His attunement to her . . .":* During the autumn of 1961, Hughes read over the BBC his children's book *Meet My Folks* and presented, over the BBC's Home Service for Schools, three essays about writing that were later collected in *Poetry in the Making,* "Capturing Animals," "Writing a Novel—Beginning," and "Writing a Novel—Going On"; these were broadcast in the regularly scheduled program *Listening and Writing.* His radio broadcasts for use in the schools continued sporadically through the 1970s. See Sagar and Tabor, *Bibliography,* pp. 357–64.

182 *"The main grief . . .":* Quoted in Laframboise, "Ted Hughes' Private Letters," pp. B4–5.

Chapter Seven: Parting (1962–1963)

183 *a borrowed flat:* Hughes probably stayed in this flat in Bloomsbury from the time he left Court Green until around Christmas, which he spent with his family in Yorkshire. By the new year he had rented a flat in Soho. Kate Moses, e-mail to DM, December 2000.

183 *a borrowed car:* TH–GH, n.d. (December 1962). Emory.

183 *"fed me the truth . . .":* SP–AP, October 9, 1962. Lilly.

183 *back in April 1956:* SP–Warren Plath, April 23, 1956. Lilly.

183 *"reverting to type":* SP–Warren Plath, October 12, 1962. Lilly.

184 *"no man . . . the male":* Winifred Davies–AP, September 22, 1962. Lilly.

184 *"Her saliva . . .":* "The Mythographers," *Capriccio* (unpaginated).

184 *Hughes was humming:* SP–AP, October 9, 1962. Lilly.

184 *taking pills:* Plath's doctor in Devon had prescribed drinamyl, according to a partial typescript describing Plath's last days, which was apparently based on interviews, identified only as Hinchcliffe, among the papers of A. Alvarez at the British Library, London.

185 *Plath followed this advice:* SP–AP, September 24, 1962, *LH,* p. 461.

185 *"If I am divorced . . .":* SP–AP, October 9, 1962.

185 *engaged a detective:* Nathaniel Tarn, diary notes dated October 10, 1962. Stanford.

185 *"I have never been . . .":* SP–Olive Prouty, October 25, 1962. Lilly.

187 *"to live with the rich . . .":* JSP, March 8, 1956, p. 230.

187 *"I made a model . . .":* "Daddy," CP, p. 224.

188 *". . . well be a Jew":* Ibid. p. 223.

188 *hooting with laughter:* Anne Stevenson, Bitter Fame, p. 277.

188 *Plath got rid of* all: AP, interview with Richard Larschan, "Sylvia Plath and the Myth of the Monstrous Mother," episode 108, Poets of New England (video, produced by The University of Massachusetts, 2001). In his biography of SP, Paul Alexander claims that Aurelia saw Plath burn them, but Aurelia does not mention this in the interview with Larschan. See Rough Magic, p. 286.

188 *ugly, muddled poem:* "Medusa," CP, pp. 224–26.

189 *"I was absolutely stunned . . .":* SP–Anne Sexton, August 21, 1962. Quoted in Diane Middlebrook, Anne Sexton, p. 174.

189 *"Wonderfully craftsman like . . . breakdown . . .":* Peter Orr, "Sylvia Plath," in The Poet Speaks, ed. Peter Orr, p. 168.

190 *"Under the gold bowl . . .":* These lines were dropped in the version published in Plath's collected poems, but are printed in Stephen Tabor, Sylvia Plath: An Analytical Bibliography, p. 143.

190 *"You are the one . . .":* CP, p. 242.

190 *"A spider's web . . .":* "Full Moon and Little Freida," Wodwo, p. 182.

191 *aching abandonment:* Excerpts from CP—"Event," p. 194; "Death & Co.," p. 255; "Child," p. 265; "Words," p. 270; "Confusion," p. 271.

192 *lying on Plath's desk:* TH–Keith Sagar, June 18, 1998. British Library.

192 *"having to take on . . .":* SP–Dot, December 14, 1962. Lilly.

192 *condescending amusement:* Ronald Hayman, The Death and Life of Sylvia Plath, p. 177.

192 *confidence in riding:* According to Kate Moses, who interviewed the riding mistress, "starting in November 62, SP took her horseback riding lessons 2x a week . . . she was, according to her Dec. letters, off the leading rein by the end (meaning she was riding free, presumably with instructor nearby, but not with the two horses attached by a leading rein). But that doesn't change the fact that by her birthday, she couldn't have been proficient enough to gallop and probably wasn't even at the canter (unless on the leading rein, in a ring)." Kate Moses, e-mail to DM, May 14, 2001.

192 *"at one with the drive . . .":* "Ariel," CP, p. 240.

193 *"Terrific stuff . . .":* SP–AP, October 12, 1962, LH, p. 466.

193 *"I shall go better . . .":* JSP, July 17, 1957, p. 286.

194 *"so they won't picture me . . .":* SP–AP, October 25, 1962. Lilly. Editing LH, AP omitted "deceived": see p. 477.

194 *party sponsored by PEN:* SP described the party to Olive Prouty in a letter of November 2, 1962. Lilly. Nathaniel Tarn noted a conversation

with Peter Porter about SP's behavior, diary notes dated December 7, 1962. Stanford. Plath is also remembered at another PEN party shortly before Christmas, in Chelsea; see Stevenson, *Bitter Fame*, p. 283, and Peter Porter, "Ted Hughes and Sylvia Plath: A Bystander's Recollections," *Australian Book Review*, August 2001, p. 25.

194 *"It was like coming . . .":* SP–AP, December 14, 1962, *LH*, p. 488.

194 *Highbury Fields:* Nathaniel Tarn, diary notes dated December 7, 1962. Stanford.

194 *Suzette felt sure:* Suzette Macedo, conversations with DM, August 2002.

197 *"I am out of Ted's shadow":* SP–Olive Prouty, December 21, 1962. Lilly.

197 *Hughes didn't like blue:* SP–AP, December 21, 1962, *LH*, p. 492.

197 *"bee colors":* Ibid.

197 *This bright room:* Ibid., p. 490.

197 *literary salon:* SP–AP, October 21 and October 23, 1962, *LH*, pp. 473 and 475.

197 *Hughes had turned over:* TH made an account of this arrangement in the letter he wrote to AP at the time he was going over the manuscript of *LH;* TH–AP, January 12, 1975. Emory.

197 *The Snake Pit:* Mary Jane Ward's *The Snake Pit* was published in 1946; the movie was released in 1948.

198 *"Sylvan Hughes":* JSP.

198 *"semi-autobiographical . . .":* SP–Olive Prouty, November 20, 1962. Lilly. Plath specified the title *Doubletake* [sic] and also told Prouty that she had considered titling the novel *The Interminable Loaf.*

199 *"several contemporary English novels . . .":* TH–AP, January 12, 1975, regarding requests for final cuts for *LH.*

199 *Martha Quest:* By 1963 Lessing had published three of what eventually became a five-book series with the overall title *Children of Violence.* The titles SP had probably read were *Martha Quest, A Proper Marriage,* and *A Ripple from the Storm.*

199 *"incandescent desperation":* Stevenson, *Bitter Fame*, p. 286.

199 *Hahn's coolly mind-boggling account:* Emily Hahn, "The Big Smoke," *Times and Places;* first appeared in *The New Yorker.*

200 *"Beyond the Gentility Principle":* A. Alvarez, introduction to *The New Poetry.*

200 *"I am not very genteel . . .":* Orr, "Sylvia Plath," p. 168.

200 *"relevant to the larger things . . .":* Ibid., pp. 169–70.

200 *"I speak them to myself":* Ibid., p. 170.

200 *"Now that I have attained . . .":* Ibid., p. 171.

201 *"'heroine' . . .":* Judith Kroll, *Chapters in a Mythology*, p. 66. In an e-mail to DM of July 2, 2002, Kroll specified that she had seen "no

pages or chapters of a novel at Court Green, just a brief chapter-by-chapter outline on a large (ca 5x8?) index card, with little notes scribbled on it as well."

201 *"rival says to heroine..."*: Kroll, *Chapters in a Mythology*, n. 56, p. 130.

201 *two French films:* Ibid., n. 52, p. 229.

201 *"Much better than..."*: A. Alvarez, conversation with DM, September 3, 2002.

201 *"I enjoyed transactions..."*: Ben Sonnenberg, "Ted's Spell," *Ravitan*, Spring 2002, p. 240.

202 *"You're not as important..."*: Ben Sonnenberg, *Lost Property*, p. 148.

202 *"energetic, hypnotic, unstoppable"*: Sonnenberg, "Ted's Spell," *Ravitan*, p. 243.

202 *"The Jaguar"*: "Five Poems by Ted Hughes," ITV Schools *English Programme*, broadcast February 15, 1988.

202 *"I can't have liked Sylvia..."*: Sonnenberg, *Lost Property*, p. 148.

203 *"When I come home..."*: Just before the memoir went to press, Sonnenberg sent the manuscript to TH, worrying whether he'd got it right. The manuscript had already cost him Bill Merwin's friendship, he confessed. But apparently, TH did not dispute these memories. Ben Sonnenberg–TH, January 11, 1991. Emory.

203 *Sonnenberg himself went on:* Sonnenberg eloped with Alice Swan (called Wendy Adler in *Lost Property*) in March 1964; Sonnenberg, conversation with DM, November 18, 2002, New York. Quotations from *Lost Property*, pp. 160, 161.

203 *Plath made tentative excursions:* SP is remembered at another PEN party, in Chelsea shortly before Christmas; see Stevenson *Bitter Fame*, p. 283, and Porter, "Ted Hughes and Sylvia Plath," p. 25.

203 *"As the months..."*: A. Alvarez, *The Savage God*, p. 26.

204 *"We were both..."*: A. Alvarez, *Where Did It All Go Right?*, p. 209.

204 *"seemed to entitle her..."*: Alvarez, *The Savage God*, p. 20.

204 *"hard, factual"*: Ibid.

204 *He has written:* Al Alvarez, *Where Did It All Go Right?*, pp. 201–10.

204 *"Love, the world..."*: "Letter in November," *CP*, pp. 253–54.

205 *It appears that she:* According to Linda Wagner-Martin, during January 1963 "she worked on her new novel, now titled *Double Exposure*, about the gradual corruption of a naïve American girl who revered honesty by a powerful and inherently dishonest man"; *Sylvia Plath: A Biography*, p. 236. Wagner-Martin does not cite a source, but seems to be paraphrasing SP's November 20 letter to Olive Prouty, misquoting the novel's current title.

205 *Hughes was still deeply:* TH wrote to Bill and Dido Merwin from Dido's flat, sending greetings from Assia, on January 21, 1963. Emory.

205 *David Wevill knew:* Nathaniel Tarn, diary notes dated January 5, 1963. Stanford.

205 *"dangling":* SP–Olive Prouty, January 22, 1963. Lilly.

205 *"The brimming power . . .":* "The Pit and the Stones," *Capriccio* (unpaginated).

205 *Frieda's undisguised sorrow:* SP–Prouty, January 22, 1963.

205 *"sometimes is nice . . .":* SP–AP, January 16, 1963, Lilly.

205 *train a nanny:* SP–Prouty, January 22, 1963.

206 *the same issue: Observer,* January 27, 1963.

206 *keenly perturbed:* Trevor Thomas, "Sylvia Plath: Last Encounters," photocopy 104, 1989, pp. 9–13. Courtesy of Richard Larschan.

207 *"feeling a bit grim . . .":* SP–AP, February 4, 1963, *LH,* p. 498.

207 *"Everything has blown . . .":* SP–Marcia Brown Plumer, February 4, 1963. Smith.

207 *"I can feel . . .":* Quoted in Hinchcliffe typescript, p. 39; apparent source is Ruth Barnhouse Beuscher. According to the curator of the Plath papers at Smith College, "We have two responses from Beuscher, but not the letters that Plath originally wrote to Beuscher. I think they may have perished"; Karen Kukil, e-mail to DM, May 16, 2002. Beuscher's extant letters to Plath are dated September 21 and 26, 1962 (according to Karen Kukil, e-mail to DM, May 24, 2002), before Plath's mind began "disintegrating," which suggests that the correspondence was more extensive than can now be ascertained.

207 *prescribed the antidepressant:* Hinchcliffe typescript, British Library. Parnate is a monoamine oxidase inhibitor with the generic name tranylcypromine (in the United States), which "often produce[s] clinical improvement within about ten days" (Ellen L. Bassuk, Stephen C. Schoonover, and Alan J Greenberg, eds. *The Practitioner's Guide to Psychoactive Drugs,* 2nd ed., p. 63).

207 *within ten days:* Ibid. p. 57.

208 *"almost completely repaired . . .":* TH–Keith Sagar, May 23, 1981. British Library.

208 *"closer than we'd been . . .":* TH–AP, March 15, 1963. Lilly.

208 *"[W]e were beginning to get on . . .":* TH–AP, July 13, 1966. Lilly.

208 *"The whole crazy divorce . . .":* TH–AP, January 12, 1975.

208 *resume their life together:* Ibid.

208 *a letter he drafted some years later:* TH to [no name], n.d.; incomplete draft of letter about an unidentifiable typescript of a biography of SP.

Emory, box 63. These details also appear in TH's poem "The Inscrip-
ton" in *BL*.

209 *"We ran out of time . . .":* TH–Sagar, June 18, 1998.

209 *Plath could not be left:* Jillian Becker, *Giving Up: The Last Days of Sylvia
Plath,* p. 8.

209 *hostility to Hughes:* Ibid. pp. 4–7; also see interviews with Becker in
Stevenson, *Bitter Fame,* pp. 291–96.

209 *Dr. Horder probably:* Wagner-Martin, *Sylvia Plath: A Biography,* p. 242,
and Stevenson, *Bitter Fame,* p. 296.

209 *he heard her pacing:* Thomas, "Sylvia Path: Last Encounters," p. 15.

209 *Others inferred:* Lucas Myers reported, "Ted told me that he was sure
Sylvia had intended to be rescued" (*Crow Steered, Bergs Appeared,* p. 80).

209 The nurse attempted to fufil her obligations, but when no one
answered her knocking at the flat, she went in search of a public
phone box from which to ring the doctor's office to confirm the
address.

210 *Unfortunately, the medication:* Dr. John Horder, letter to Linda Wagner-
Martin, quoted in Stevenson, *Bitter Fame,* p. 298.

210 *"allergic":* TH–Sagar, June 18, 1998.

210 *The whole catastrophe:* TH–AP, July 13, 1966.

210 *"She should not . . .":* AP referred to the problematic medication as SP's
"sedative"; she thought that if the dose wore off during Plath's sleep,
"there would be a dip down and she was to have taken that next dose,
to keep her on a level." AP, November 1986, outtakes of interview with
Richard Larschan for *Voices & Visions/Sylvia Plath,* PBS documentary,
Courtesy of Richard Larschan.

211 *Details of SP's actions that morning from Hinchliffe,* typescript,
A. Alvarez papers, pp. 49–50. British Library.

Chapter Eight: Husbandry (1963–1998)

212 *autopsy:* Hinchliffe typescript, pp. 51–52. A. Alvarez Papers, British
Library. This manuscript indicates that the autopsy was performed
by the University College Hospital pathologist the same day and that
the saturation of Plath's blood by the fatal compound "was 76.5%, an
extraordinarily high amount."

212 *Hughes gave Alvarez:* A. Alvarez, *Where Did It All Go Right?,* p. 206.

212 *"as if we had started anew":* TH, interview with Eilat Negev, Israel,
March 1996; published October 31, 1998, The *Guardian.* The children
"'grew up without knowing she committed suicide,' he said. 'I don't

know what was the right thing to do, but after her death I wanted all of us to live as if we had started anew.' "

212 *"It was either her or me"*: Suzette Macedo, conversation with DM, August 2002; see also Jillian Becker, *Giving Up: The Last Days of Sylvia Plath*.

213 *"a man's deeper sufferings . . ."*: Ted Hughes, "Orghast: Talking Without Words," *Vogue*, 1971.

213 *"rippling . . . like a flounder"*: TH revised "Ballad from a Fairy Tale" (*Wodwo*, pp. 166–167) and retitled it "The Angel" for its later publication in *Remains of Elmet*, p. 124. The phrase "like a flounder" occurs in the later version.

213 *"funerary furnishing"*: I am indebted to Ann Skea's *Ted Hughes: The Poetic Quest* for pointing out the recurrence of the square of satin. In a note (p. 254, n. 3 to chapter 10) to her discussion of "The Angel," Skea says that in a letter dated November 3, 1984, Hughes confirmed her inference that the square of satin was "a piece of funerary furnishing."

214 *"What are they dragging . . ."*: "The Howling of Wolves," *Wodwo*, p. 178.

214 *"unmoving and dead"*: The poem is "Fishing Bridge"; *BL*, p. 88.

214 *"I had never examined . . ."*: "The Deadfall," *Difficulties of a Bridegroom*, pp. 17–18.

214 *"Where the wolves . . ."*: "Life After Death," *BL*, p. 183.

215 *"pitchers of milk, now empty"*: "Edge," *CP*, p. 272.

215 *A couple of fierce poems*: The poems are "The Laburnum" and "Howls and Whispers."

216 *"What I didn't . . ."*: TH–A. Alvarez, n.d. (mid-November 1971). British Library.

216 *"bitterly sad"*: TH–Michael Ratcliffe, n.d (following publication of Journals). Emory, box 63, folder 6.

216 *"all she wanted . . ."*: TH–AP, March 15, 1963. Lilly.

217 *"suicides have a special language . . ."*: Anne Sexton, "Wanting to Die," *The Complete Poems*, p. 142.

217 *"That death was mine"*: For an account of Sexton's response to SP's suicide, see Middlebrook, *Anne Sexton;* pp. 198–201, 215–17.

217 *manuscript of forty-one*: TH describes the black spring binder in his introduction to the *CP*, p. 14.

218 *in a note to herself*: TH quotes SP without identifying his source; it was probably one of the lost journals. See ibid., pp. 14–15.

218 *Plath had considered*: For possible book titles, see Lynda K. Bundtzen, *The Other Ariel*, p. 22.

218 *and both contained*: I am indebted to Kate Moses for pointing out that *Lupercal* is a book of forty-one poems. Moses speculates that a marginal note in the *Ariel* manuscript, contemplating the omission of "The

Swarm," indicated SP's desire to retain this symmetry. Kate Moses, e-mail to DM, June 30, 2002.

218 *most of which he had never seen:* TH said that SP had shown him "a selected few" of the *Ariel* poems during their separation. Ted Hughes, "Publishing Sylvia Plath," the *Observer*, November 21, 1971; reprinted in *Winter Pollen*, pp. 163–69.

218 *read them aloud:* Elaine Feinstein, *Ted Hughes: The Life of a Poet*, p. 146.

218 *"no other woman poet . . .":* TH–AP, March 15, 1963.

219 *". . . a violent temperament":* TH–Keith Sagar, May 23, 1981, commenting on a review essay by Hugh Kenner. British Library.

219 *"I think she got . . .":* TH–Keith Sagar, March 13,1981. British Library.

219 *"The poppy is a wound . . .":* "Out," *Wodwo*, p. 156.

219 *"The Road to Easington"* was reprinted in *English Poetry Now*, ed. C. B. Cox and A. E. Dyson as *Critical Quarterly Supplement*, No. 3 (November 1962), p. 6; and in *New Lines 2*, ed. Robert Conquest, p. 58.

219 *"mocking the rhythms . . .":* TH–Sagar, March 13, 1981.

219 *"Whose is that . . .":* "The Bee Meeting," *CP*, p. 212.

220 *dreadful message:* TH–Sagar, March 13, 1981.

220 *She had moved:* Nathaniel Tarn, diary notes dated February 16 and March 12, 1963. Stanford.

220 *"crushed":* Nathaniel Tarn, diary notes dated February 16, 1963.

220 *Hughes's aunt:* Trevor Thomas–AP, April 27, 1976. Lilly.

220 *informal gatherings:* SP's downstairs neighbor, Trevor Thomas, subsequently gossiped to AP that Assia hosted noisy parties in the flat, but this impropriety is denied by others. Ibid.

220 *"hypnotized":* Nathaniel Tarn, diary notes dated June 23, 1963. Stanford.

220 *"detestable and contemptible":* Nathaniel Tarn, diary notes dated March 12, 1963.

220 *secretly read Plath's journals:* Nathaniel Tarn, diary notes dated June 23, 1963.

220 *shocked and hurt:* Suzette Macedo, conversations with DM, August 2002.

220 *"Maybe I'll end up . . .":* Nathaniel Tarn, diary notes dated June 23, 1963.

220–221 *Hughes was superstitious:* Nathaniel Tarn, diary notes dated March 12, 1963.

221 *"born to conduct . . .":* Lucas Myers, *Crow Steered, Bergs Appeared*, p. 127.

221 *"She was a touch . . .":* Lucas Myers, " 'Ah, Youth . . . ' " in Anne Stevenson, appendix 1, *Bitter Fame*, pp. 319–20.

222 *"no longer have . . .":* TH–AP, May 13, 1963. Lilly.

222 *"a good try"*: Warren Plath–AP, February 20, 1963. Lilly.

222 *She did not intend:* AP–John Horder, September 23,1963. Lilly.

223 *it recalled visiting:* Olive Prouty–TH, June 20, 1966. Lilly.

223 *he poured out:* TH–AP, May 13, 1963.

223 *"An extraordinary woman . . ."*: TH–Anne Sexton, August 9, 1967. Harry Ransom Humanities Research Center, The University of Texas at Austin.

224 *"gallant and generous"*: Feinstein, *Ted Hughes,* p. 67.

224 *". . . motherhood herself"*: Ibid., p. 152.

224 *"steals in a mysterious way . . ."*: TH–Lucas Myers, July 2, 1967. Emory.

225 *"some strange drastic secret motive"*: TH–GH, September 9, 1965. Emory.

225 *"sea blue eyes . . ."*: Assia Guttman Wevill–Lucas Myers, March 13, 1965. Emory.

225 *"almost forgotten . . ."*: Edith Hughes–AP, January 30, 1965. Lilly.

225 *pressure he was feeling:* TH–GH, April 27, 1967. Emory.

226 *He had planned, initially:* TH–AP, May 13, 1963.

226 *"We were like two feet . . ."*: John Horder, "Desk Poet," the *Guardian,* March 23, 1965, p. 9.

226 *"She was most afraid . . ."*: Ted Hughes, "Sylvia Plath: *Ariel,"* *Poetry Book Society Bulletin,* no. 44, (February 1965); reprinted in *Winter Pollen,* pp. 161–62.

226 *"The woman is perfected . . ."*: "Edge," *CP,* p. 272.

227 *"concern for certain . . ."*: Ted Hughes, introduction to *CP,* p. 15.

227 *Hughes's* Ariel: Publishing history of *Ariel* is from Stephen Tabor, *Sylvia Plath: An Analytical Bibliography,* p. 20; for *The Bell Jar,* see ibid., p. 16.

227 *five-year fellowship:* TH–AP, n.d. (arrived. c. March 21, 1966; according to AP's annotation). Lilly.

228 *tour down the Rhine:* Ted Hughes, "Notes on Published Works." Emory series 2, box 3, folder 7.

228 *Hughes confided:* TH–Ben Sonnenberg, August 10, 1967. Emory.

228 *"mental cure"*: Ibid.

229 *"a hurtling momentum . . ."*: TH, "Notes on Published Works." Emory, series 2, box 3, folder 7.

229 *"changing the audience"*: TH–Lucas Myers, December 10, 1967. Emory.

229 *"songs with no music"*: Quoted in Ekbert Faas, *Ted Hughes: The Unaccommodated Universe,* p. 208.

229 *"Who owns these . . ."*: "Examination at the Womb Door," from *Crow, New Selected Poems,* pp. 90–91.

230 *"The Crow is another word . . ."*: TH, "Notes on Published Works." Emory, series 2, box 3, folder 7.

230 *". . . something to eat"*: "That Moment," from *Crow, New Selected Poems,* p. 93.

230 *"obliquely," "inadvertently"*: TH–Keith Sagar, June 18, 1998. British Library.

230 *a recording: Crow*: Faber-Penguin Audio books, 1997. Keith Sagar summarizes the plot of *Crow* in *The Laughter of Foxes: A Study of Ted Hughes*, pp. 170–80.

231 *"Auschwitz"*: Emory, series 2, subseries 1, box 2: notebook (n.d.) included in ms. of "Shakespeare and the Goddess" contains a poem titled "Auschwitz" ("Down there, far from the Vistula; at Auschwitz, / My love, far from the Norse moors . . .").

231 *Hughes designated it*: Emory. Unpublished manuscript drafts, folder labeled "MS Provisional poem list of bits & pieces TH's note," which indicates TH was planning to include "Auschwitz" in what was eventually published as *Wodwo*. The list is on the back of an envelope forwarded from North Tawton to Doonreaghan House, Cashel, Galway, Ireland, postmarked March 4, 1966.

231 *"brightening on the words"*: Emory, series 2, subseries 2, box 1, folder "Tutorial" (*Recklings*). The untitled, unfinished poem is drafted on the same page as the beginning of a draft of "Tutorial."

231 *Yehuda Amichai*: According to Eilat Negev, "It was TH who admired Amichai's poetry and thought it will be a good idea if AW, who knew Hebrew from the time she lived in then-Palestine, will do the translation. Amichai, who served in the British army during WW2, knew English enough to approve Assia's translation. Apparently he was very pleased with it." E-mail to DM, May 31, 2002.

231 *broadcast by the BBC*: "Yehuda Amichai," poems translated and introduced by Assia Gutman and read by Ted Hughes, recorded June 28, 1968, broadcast December 12, 1968, Radio 3.

231 *"made a glamorous couple"*: Feinstein, *Ted Hughes*, p. 159.

232 *Assia pilfered*: Eilat Negev, e-mail to DM, February 16, 2002: "I found out that already in the early 1960's, Hughes was aware of the price of manuscripts, and sold quite a few, and enjoyed the fact that he got quite a bit for a sheet of paper. Assia was aware of the commercial value of writers' manuscripts, and to secure her child's future, sent her sister, as a premium bond to be sold when needed. Eventually, in 1970, they were returned to Hughes."

232 *"quite a lot"*: Quoted in Eilat Negev, "Haunted by the Ghosts of Love," in *Guardian*, April 10,1999.

232 *"greatly taken to" baby Shura, "fortunately"*: TH–Lucas Myers, March 1966. Emory.

232 *"a beautiful precocious little girl"*: TH–Lucas Myers, n.d. (Emory says winter or spring 1967, but internal evidence suggests autumn 1966). Emory.

232 "... *I've withdrawn all investments* ...": TH–Lucas Myers, December 10, 1967. Emory.

232 "*serious*" *depression:* Eda Zoritte-Megged, unpublished memoir quoted in Feinstein, *Ted Hughes,* p. 170.

232 "*I have been literally suicidal* ...": Assia Wevill–Celia Chaikin, n.d. quoted in Negev, "Haunted by the Ghosts of Love."

233 *habitually "tested":* Negev, "Haunted by the Ghosts of Love."

233 "*it was nothing new*" ... : Ibid.

233 *She drew a mattress:* Ibid.

233 *he fled to Ireland:* Olwyn Hughes–Dido and Bill Merwin, April 24,1969. Emory.

233 "*petty fetters*": "Gulliver," *CP,* p. 251.

233 "*tied & married*" ... "*bitter misunderstanding*": Folder marked "Crow Notebook, ca 1968–1969 (Hughes #41)." Emory.

233 "*People who live with me* ...": TH–GH, April 14, 1969, quoted in Donna Laframboise, "Ted Hughes' Private Letters Reveal Another Story," *National Post* (Toronto), July 29, 2000, p. B5.

234 "*threw my whole nature negative*": TH–AP, April 14, 1969. Lilly.

234 "*which has gradually* ...": Ibid.

234 "*psychological inferno*": TH–AP, May 5, 1969. Lilly.

234 *Hughes believed:* TH–AP, July 14, 1969. Lilly.

234 *he thought that intimacy:* TH expressed his sense of responsibility in two undated poems, for which internal evidence indicates composition between May and October 1979. The first lines of these poems are "So here I sit, composing futile poetry ..." and "So now on a mid-October morning[,] mist ..." Both in "Unpublished or Unidentified Work found with *Gaudete* '77 material." Emory.

234 *an enormous house:* Hughes had just received the City of Florence Poetry Prize, using the money (£6000) to purchase Lumb Bank. TH–Ben Sonnenberg, May 19, 1994. Emory.

234 *like trying to bury:* "So now on a mid-October morning[,] mist ..." in "Unpublished or Unidentified Work found with *Gaudete* '77 material."

234 "*housekeeper*": Hilda Farrar–AP, November 6, 1969. Lilly. Elaine Feinstein gives a detailed account of this period in *Ted Hughes,* pp. 174–77.

234 "*retreat* ... *die*": "So now on a mid-October morning[,] mist ..." in "Unpublished or Unidentified Work found with *Gaudete* '77 material." Emory.

234 *They wed very:* TH and Carol Ann Orchard were married in the Registry Office, Hampstead; his address at the time is listed as 10 Arkwright Road, London NW3. Orchard was twenty-two. Marriage certificate no. MX765834. Colin Charles Fraser, "Reshaping the Past:

The Personal Poetry of Ted Hughes" (Ph.D. thesis, University of New England [Australia], 1998), p. 207.

234 *Hughes wrote to his friend:* TH–Peter Redgrove, n.d. (1970). Emory.

235 *"Carol has pulled . . .":* TH–AP, July 7, 1972. Lilly.

235 *Hughes once remarked:* TH–AP, April 3, 1975. Lilly.

235 *Olwyn Hughes adopted a stance:* See Linda Wagner-Martin, preface to *Sylvia Plath: A Biography,* pp. 13–14; Jacqueline Rose, *The Haunting of Sylvia Plath,* pp. xi–xiv; Patrick Parrinder, "Quote Unquote," *Textual Practice* 14 no. 1, (2000); Bundtzen, preface to *The Other Arie,* pp. ix–xiii; and Jacqueline Rose, "'This Is Not a Biography,'" *London Review of Books* 24, no. 16, August 22, 2002.

236 *mere "sentimentality":* TH–GH, n.d. (postmark unclear, probably December 1976). Emory.

236 *"Sylvia's unpublished literary legacy . . .":* Myers, "Ah, Youth . . ." pp. 320–21.

236 *"everything that had her . . .":* TH–Joan Hughes, n.d. Emory.

236 *Sylvia's fountain pen:* "Apprehensions," *BL,* p. 140.

236 *memorabilia hunters:* TH–AP, n.d. (December 1965; AP's annotation). Lilly.

236 *disguise the theft:* TH–GH, February 1, 1980. Emory.

236 *on "centipede legs":* TH–GH, April 27, 1967. Emory.

236 *"my easygoing general readiness . . .":* TH–Keith Sagar, March 9, 1984. British Library.

237 *"about Devon":* Olwyn Hughes–AP, July 2, 1968. Smith.

237 *" . . . look up the fragment . . .":* Harper & Row (Fran McCullough)–TH, March 1, 1973. Emory.

237 *"after The Bell Jar . . .":* Ted Hughes, introduction to *Johnny Panic and the Bible of Dreams,* p. 1.

237 *"What I was aware of . . .":* Interview with Drue Heinz, *The Paris Review* 134 (Spring 1995), p. 98.

237 *No manuscript pages or notes:* During her work on the Plath manuscripts in the mid-1970s, Judith Kroll saw a card of notes in SP's handwriting regarding the novel; *Chapters in a Mythology,* pp. 66, 229.

237 *"I did not want . . .":* Ted Hughes, foreword. *The Journals of Sylvia Plath* (1982 edition; not *JSP*), p. xiii.

237 *Hughes defended his action:* TH–Michael Ratliffe, n.d. Emory.

237 *"it went missing . . .":* Olwyn Hughes, "Sylvia Plath's Biographers," *The New York Review of Books,* December 7, 1989.

237 *"walked, not too long ago":* TH–A. Alvarez, October 16, 1981. British Library.

237 *a mysterious rumor:* TH's letter seems confused, however, as if his mind

were not clear on the matter. TH–Keith Sagar, March 5, 1998. British Library.

238 *an opera titled:* Adriana Hölszky's *Giuseppe e Sylvia,* was performed in Stuttgart, Germany, in November 2000.

238 *deflowers the teenage babysitter:* Emma Tennant, *Sylvia and Ted,* p. 99–101.

238 *hoax news story:* "BIG NEWS—Lost Sylvia Plath Journals Discovered," *www.bbc.co-inc.com,* posted on the Sylvia Plath Forum on March 31, 2002.

238 *"I have never told this...":* TH–Jacqueline Rose, draft letter, n.d. (c. September 1990). Emory, box 63, folder 6. Rose quotes the letter she received from Hughes, in *Haunting of Sylvia Plath,* p. 243, n. 1 to chapter 2.

238 *much less interesting:* See Rose, *Haunting of Sylvia Plath,* pp. 242–43, and chapter 3, "The Archive," pp. 65–113.

239 *lose its copyright:* Feinstein notes that "Fran McCullough, an editor at Harper & Row, discovered that U.S. copyright law only gave protection for seven years to a book published abroad by an American citizen" (*Ted Hughes,* p. 184).

239 *"'Daddy' sold Ariel":* AP, autograph note on reverse of letter from Olwyn Hughes dated July 2, 1968. Smith.

239 *vastly greater embarrassment:* AP–Olwyn Hughes, June 22, 1968. Smith.

239 *financial advantage:* Olwyn Hughes–AP, May 28 and July 2, 1968. Smith.

239 *resolved to claim:* Jacqueline Rose discusses the lawsuit in *The Haunting of Sylvia Plath,* pp. 104–11. TH reported to Keith Sagar that the suit had finally been settled after five years of litigation, and that legal costs of his defense amounted to $180,000. TH–Keith Sagar, March 15, 1987. British Library.

239 *Aurelia had produced:* AP–Winifred Davies, n.d. (December 1974). Lilly.

239 *Plath's journals and his own diaries:* An inference that can be drawn from TH's long letter of January 12, 1975, to AP disputing passages in Plath's letters. Emory.

240 *"enthusiasm" ... "fashioned...":* TH–AP, July 6, 1974. Lilly.

240 *"inevitable and natural":* TH–AP, January 12, 1975.

241 *"steely determination":* Ibid.

241 *her writing took priority:* Ibid.

241 *to "sacrifice everything to writing":* Ibid.

Chapter Nine: Curing Himself (1967–1998)

242 *"whoever comes to help me dies":* "So here I sit, composing futile poetry..."; verso *of "Peterson, Jimmy / Entry No:* 17982" (unidentified poetry contest) dated 1969. Emory.

243 *"in very strange darkness"*: TH–Peter Redgrove, n.d. (1970). Emory.

243 *"Planets bad. Reaping the whirlwind"*: TH–Lucas Myers, n.d. (February 1971?). Emory.

243 *"This much exposure . . . wrong audience"*: TH–Keith Sagar, n.d. (1974?). British Library.

243 *"telepathic interference"*: TH–Keith Sagar, May 27, 1974. British Library.

243 *right "shape"*: TH–Peter Redgrove, n.d. (1970).

244 *secluded himself in Devon:* TH–Lucas Myers, n.d. (July 1972?). Emory.

244 *Moortown:* Elaine Feinstein, *Ted Hughes: The Life of a Poet,* p. 186.

244 *Jack Orchard:* TH–Leonard Scigaj, n.d. (photocopy appended to letter of July 28, 1989). Emory.

244 *"absorbed all my other follies"*: TH–Lucas Myers, n.d. (Summer 1975?). Emory.

244 *"light weight"*: TH–Lucas Myers, n.d. (1974?). Emory.

244 *"weirdly prostrated"*: TH–Daniel Weissbort, n.d. (probably late 1975). Emory.

244 *A Choice of Shakespeare's Verse:* selected with an introduction by Ted Hughes. The introduction was later reprinted as "The Great Theme: Notes on Shakespeare," in *Winter Pollen,* pp. 103–121.

245 *"knot of obsessions"*: "The Great Theme," *Winter Pollen,* p. 106.

245 *Shakespeare's imagination was formed:* Ibid., p. 111.

245 *"became, at bottom, a sexual dilemma"*: Ibid. p. 119.

245 *"a package of precisely . . ."*: Ted Hughes, *Shakespeare and the Goddess of Complete Being,* p. 33.

245 *"the first successful representation . . ."*: "The Poetic Self: A Centenary Tribute to T.S. Eliot," *Winter Pollen,* p. 277.

246 *"visionary . . ."*: Ibid.

246 *"to make a fleeting snapshot . . ."*: Preface, *Moortown Diary,* p. x.

246 *"Their charge of importance . . ."*: Quoted by Craig Robinson, "The Good Shepherd: Moortown Elegies," in *The Achievement of Ted Hughes,* ed. Keith Sagar, p. 258.

246 *"move deeper . . ."*: Ibid.

246 *regarded them as casual: Moortown Diary,* p. xi.

247 *This agreeable arrangement:* TH–Lucas Myers, September 1, 1975. Emory.

247 *his initial version of the poem:* Folder marked "Prose and poetry written at the time of Jack Orchard's death." Emory.

247 *"all your plans . . ."*: Ibid.

249 *"to be married in his style"*: Jill Barber, "Ted Hughes, My Secret Lover," *The Mail on Sunday,* May 13, 2001, p. 51.

249 *"I knew my role . . ."*: Jill Barber, conversation with DM, March 5, 2003, New York.

249 *"Ted found . . ."*: Ibid.

249 *"Her loose dress . . ."*: "Sunstruck Foxglove," *Flowers and Insects*, p. 44.

249 *visit the grave:* Barber, conversation with DM, March 5, 2003.

250 *"capacity to be part . . ."*: TH–Leonard Scigaj, June 18, 1981. Emory.

251 *"This is my Muse"*: Barber, conversation with DM, March 5, 2003.

251 *"Energy is created . . ."*: TH–GH, July 22, 1963. Emory.

252 *"Like so many women . . ."*: Emma Tennant, *Burnt Diaries*, p. 48.

252 *"to become involved . . ."*: Ibid. p. 49.

252 *"Like Bluebeard's bride . . ."*: Ibid. p. 159.

252 *"Don't talk about Sylvia"*: Ibid. pp. 153–54.

252 *"I think . . . fancied himself"*: Quoted in Suzi Feay, "The Ghost Writer," *Independent on Sunday*, May 20, 2001.

252 *"objects of his fancy . . ."*: Tennant, *Burnt Diaries*, p. 181.

252 *"I was the only woman . . ."*: Barber, conversation with DM, March 5, 2003.

253 *"this inner world . . ."*: Ted Hughes, "Myth and Education," in *Writers, Critics and Children*, ed. Geoff Fox et al.; reprinted in *Winter Pollen*, p. 149.

253 *"a giant of a man"*: Donya Feuer, conversation with DM, March 20, 2003.

254 *"He told me there . . ."*: Fay Godwin, "Ted Hughes and *Elmet*," in *The Epic Poise*, ed. Nick Gammage, p. 106.

255 *"not right to requisition . . ."*: Ted Hughes, "Notes on Published Works." Emory, series 2, box 3, folder 10.

255 *grim, even hateful memories:* TH–Ben Sonnenberg, n.d. (probably January 1991). Emory.

255 *"In memory of Edith Farrar"*: This dedication appears only in the limited edition of *Remains of Elmet*, published April 1979 by Olwyn Hughes's Rainbow Press. In the trade edition, published by Faber and Faber on October 31, 1979, the dedication read, "Poems in Memory of Edith Farrar." In the revised and expanded trade edition, retitled *Elmet* and published in 1994, the dedication read "In memory of Edith Farrar and William Hughes."

255 *"archaeology of the mouth"*: *Remains of Elmet*, p. 7.

255 *"it's false to say . . ."*: Ted Hughes, reviewing *Myth and Religion of the North*, by E. O. G. Turville-Petre, *Listener*, March 19, 1964, pp. 484–85. Quoted in Patricia Haberstron, "Historical Landscape in Ted Hughes's *Remains of Elmet*," *Critical Essays on Ted Hughes*, ed. Leonard Scigaj, p. 206.

256 *"brainwashed . . . her voice"*: "Leaf Mould," *Elmet*, p. 28.

257 *"six years into her posthumous life . . ."*: *Remains of Elmet*, p. 7; retitled "The Dark River" in *Elmet*.

257 *"giant beating wing,"*: "Heptonstall Cemetery," *Elmet*, p. 122.

257 *"money bomb"*: TH–GH, n.d. (probably December 1976). Emory.

257 *moved to Ireland*: TH–GH, n.d. (probably September 1971). Emory.

257 *"astonished"*: TH told Sonnenberg at the time of a lawsuit over the film of *The Bell Jar*, settled out of court in January 1987, that "costs to the estate had been considerable. 'One year's earnings,' he said." Beir Sonnenberg, conversation with DM, November 18, 2002. Estimate of Plath Estate earnings for 1987 based on Paul Alexander, *Rough Magic*, pp. 362–63; Alexander had information from AP, among others.

257 *"believe me, that is quite a sum"*: TH–Lucas Myers, January 16, 1977.

257 *"a big coffer"* ... *£20 a piece*: TH–Alan and Marcia Jones, August 23, 1975. Emory.

258 *Hughes was reluctant to sell*: TH–GH, April 12, 1977. Emory.

258 *4000 pages*: Karen Kukil, e-mail to DM, June 19, 2002.

258 *"immensely to our advantage"*: TH–GH, n.d. (September 1981). Emory.

258 *"to make one big final ..."*: TH–Lucas Myers, n.d. (c. December 1980 or January 1981). Emory.

259 *recently published biography*: Edward Butscher, *Sylvia Plath: Method and Madness*. Butscher's book was written without him having access to Plath's papers, but relied instead upon interviews with many sources, and their recollection of events was occasionally wrong. Butscher's book is still very useful because it contains these interviews.

260 *"The themes she found engaging ..."*: Ted Hughes, introduction to *Johnny Panic and the Bible of Dreams*, p. 5.

260 *"I am more and more inclined ..."*: Ibid., p. 9.

260 *tax bill*: TH–Lucas Myers, November 10, 1982. Emory.

261 *"... quite strong"*: Fran McCullough, editor's note to *The Journals of Sylvia Plath*, p. x.

261 *" if she couldn't get a table ..."*: Ted Hughes, introduction to *CP*, p. 13.

262 *"... too hard for the reading public ..."*: Ibid., p. 15.

262 *"On 16 June ..."*: Ted Hughes, "Notes on Poems 1956–1963," *CP*, pp. 275–96.

263 *"The panther's thread ..."*: "Pursuit," *CP*, p. 22.

264 *"Here it is ... this memory"*: "Drawing," *BL*, p. 44.

264 *"on the threshold ..."*: TH–GH, n.d. (postmark December 22, 1976?). Emory.

Chapter Ten: The Magical Dead (1984–1998)

265 *it was offered*: Philip Larkin died on December 2, 1985, but his throat cancer was not diagnosed until after TH's appointment as Poet Laureate:

apparently, he did not decline on grounds of poor health. See www.philiplarkin.com/.

265 *"The Nation's . . ."*: Epigraph to *Rain-Charm for the Duchy and Other Laureate Poems*.

265 *"magical dead"*: TH–Ben Sonnenberg, n.d. (probably late January 1991). Emory.

266 *"You scrambled . . ."*: "Rain-Charm for the Duchy," *New Selected Poems*, p. 286. Prince Harry was born September 15, 1984; Hughes's poem is dated December 21, 1984.

267 *most recent publications*: List and dates refer only to trade publications; Hughes was regularly bringing out work in limited editions during those years as well.

267 *"very lively and nimble . . ."*: TH–GH, November 25, 1974. Emory.

267 *leonine faces*: TH–Keith Sagar, January. 1986. British Library, 19.

268 *"unconventional spiritual curiosity"*: Nicholas Hellen and Richard Brooks, "Prince Makes Shrine to Ted Hughes," London *Times*, February 4, 2001.

268 *Coleridge*: "Myths, Metres, Rhythms," *Winter Pollen*, pp. 310–72.

269 *"poems need prose precincts"*: TH–Keith Sagar, February 18, 1982. British Library.

269 *"habitat"*: TH–Leonard Baskin, March 9, 1992. Emory.

269 *withdrawing the invitation*: TH–Ann Skea, October 1, 1995. British Library. TH notifies her he has changed his mind after asking her (on June 12) to inventory his archive. He apologizes and offers her some holiday time at the cottage on his property in Devon.

270 *Robert W. Woodruff Library*: Emory began acquiring Ted Hughes manuscripts in 1985, and made a series of small purchases in the late 1980s from a variety of different manuscripts dealers. In late 1995 or early 1996 Stephen Enniss, curator of literary collections at Emory, received a phone call from Roy Davids, Hughes's agent, inquiring whether the university would be interested in acquiring Hughes's literary archive. In November Ennis went to England to see the materials firsthand. Negotiations continued over the winter, and in February 1997 Enniss returned to pack and ship materials to Emory. The archive was officially opened for research in April 2000.

270 *108,000 items*: Lucas Myers, *Crow Steered, Bergs Appeared*, p. 38, probably drawing on newspaper reports.

270 *color photograph*: Steve Enniss dated the photograph in a conversation with DM, October 14, 1999.

271 *"show how like the rest of us"*: TH–AP, n.d. (March 1966). Lilly.

271 *"formulated his life mission . . ."*: TH, "The Poetic Self: A Centenary Tribute to T. S. Eliot," *Winter Pollen*, p. 271.

272 *biological endowment in human beings:* Evidence for this view is in Hughes's comments on the work of Vasco Popa, quoted in Ekbert Faas, *Ted Hughes: The Unaccommodated Universe,* p. 207, and his essay on Vasco Popa in *Winter Pollen,* pp. 220–28.

273 *"I divined . . .":* "Dust as We Are" was first published in *Listener,* January 2, 1986; reprinted in *Wolfwatching* (1989; quote from p. 11), and in *New Selected Poems.*

275 *"My own drama with the dead":* TH–Ben Sonnenberg, May 17, 1992. Emory.

275 *"raw and unguarded":* Unidentified letter of Ted Hughes read by Frieda Hughes at the Whitbread Prize award ceremony, January 26, 1999, broadcast over BBC1–TV.

276 *"I tried to . . .":* From a letter to Hughes's German translators, enclosed in TH–Keith Sagar, June 16, 1998. British Library.

276 *"Your actual words . . .":* "Visit," *BL,* pp. 8–9.

276 *"the male lead in your drama":* Ibid., p. 7.

276 *"Swaying so slender . . .":* "St. Botolph's," *BL,* p. 15.

276 *a tight skirt: JSP,* February 26, 1956, p. 213.

277 *she lost the reins:* "Whiteness I Remember," dated July 9, 1958, *CP,* pp. 102–3.

278 *"Blue was your . . .":* "Red," *BL,* p. 198.

278 *"plumage . . . uniquely":* "18 Rugby Street," *BL,* p. 22.

279 *"The whiff of that beast . . .":* "Trophies," *BL,* p. 18.

280 *"Ovid locates . . .":* Introduction, *Tales from Ovid,* pp. ix–x.

280 *Hughes required:* Erica Wagner, *Ariel's Gift,* p. 25.

281 *"peremptory, as a familiar . . .":* "The Offers," *Howls and Whispers* (unpaginated).

282 *end-of-year sales:* For the sales history of *Birthday Letters,* see Dan Glaister, "The Rise and Rise of Ted Hughes, Deceased," *Guardian,* January 12, 1999, p. 3.

284 *inscribed her copy:* Noted in the inventory TH prepared at the time of the sale of SP's papers and her library to Smith College in 1981. Smith.

285 *"his tuning fork . . .":* Barrie Rutter, quoting TH, in "Poet's Last Play Gets Homely Opening," *Guardian,* February 2, 2000.

Coda. Naked (1998–   )

288 *"everything will be quite clear":* TH–AP, January 12, 1975, "Notes on Letters Home, revised—January 1975." Emory.

Bibliography

Aird, Eileen. *Sylvia Plath: Her Life and Work.* New York: Harper & Row, 1973.

Alexander, Paul. *Rough Magic,* 2nd ed. New York: Da Capo, 1999.

———— ed. *Ariel Ascending: Writings About Sylvia Plath.* New York: Harper & Row, 1985.

Alvarez, Alfred. *The New Poetry.* London: Penguin, 1962.

————. *The Savage God: A Study in Suicide.* London: Weidenfield & Nicolson, 1971.

————. *Where Did It All Go Right?* London: Richard Cohen Books, 1999.

Barber, Jill. "Ted Hughes, My Secret Lover." *The Mail on Sunday,* May 13 and May 20, 2001.

Bassuk, Ellen L., Stephen C. Schoonover, and Alan J Greenberg, eds. *The Practitioner's Guide to Psychoactive Drugs.* 2nd ed. New York: Plenum Medical Book Co., 1984.

Becker, Jillian. *Giving Up: The Last Days of Sylvia Plath.* London: Ferrington, 2002.

Bentley, Paul. *The Poetry of Ted Hughes: Language, Illusion, and Beyond.* London: Longman, 1998.

Bere, Carol. *"Birthday Letters: Ted Hughes's Sibylline Leaves."* In *Lire Ted Hughes New Selected Poems, 1957–1994,* edited by Joanny Moulin. Paris: Éditions du Temps, 1999.

Bishop, Nick. "Ted Hughes and the Death of Poetry." In *The Challenge of Ted Hughes,* edited by Keith Sagar. London: Macmillan, 1994.

Brain, Tracy. *The Other Sylvia Plath.* New York: Longman, 2001.

Britzolakis, Christina. *Sylvia Plath and the Theatre of Mourning.* London: Oxford University Press, 1999.

Bundtzen, Lynda K. *The Other Ariel.* Amherst: The University of Massachusetts Press, 2001.

Butscher, Edward. *Sylvia Plath: Method and Madness.* New York: Simon & Schuster, 1976.

————, ed. *Sylvia Plath: The Woman and the Work*. New York: Dodd, Mead, 1977.

Byrne, Sandy. *The Poetry of Ted Hughes: A Reader's Guide to Essential Criticism*. Duxford, U.K.: Icon Books Ltd., 2000.

Churchwell, Sarah. "Ted Hughes and the Corpus of Sylvia Plath." *Criticism* 40, no. 1 (Winter 1998), pp. 99–132.

Claridge, Gordon. "Creativity and Madness: Clues from Modern Psychiatric Diagnosis." In *Genius and the Mind: Studies of Creativity and Temperament*, edited by Andrew Steptoe. New York: Oxford University Press, 1998.

Cornwall, John. "Bard of Prey." *Sunday Times Magazine*, October 3, 1999.

Cox, Brian. "Ted Hughes (1930-1998): A Personal Retrospect." *The Hudson Review* 52, (Spring 1999).

Darke, Mike. *Mytholmroyd Heritage Walk*. Todmorden, U.K.: Waddington & Sons, 1987.

Davies, Norman. *The Isles: A History*. New York: Oxford University Press, 1999.

Davison, Peter. *Half-Remembered*. New York: Harper & Row, 1973.

————. *The Fading Smile: Poets in Boston, 1955–1960, from Robert Frost to Robert Lowell to Sylvia Plath*. New York: Knopf, 1994.

Enniss, Stephen. *The Page is Printed: Ted Hughes, 1930–1998*. Catalogue of an exhibition commemorating the life and work of Ted Hughes on the occasion of the opening of the Ted Hughes Papers, Robert W. Woodruff Library, Emory University, April 8–May 31, 2000.

Faas, Ekbert. *Ted Hughes: The Unaccommodated Universe*. Santa Barbara: Black Sparrow, 1980.

Fallows, Glen. "Reminiscences," in "*Ted Hughes Feature*." *Martlet* (newsletter of Pembroke College, Cambridge), issue 4 (Spring 2000).

Feay, Suzi. "The Ghost Writer," (interview with Emma Tennant). *Independent on Sunday*, May 20, 2001.

Feinstein, Elaine. *Ted Hughes: The Life of a Poet*. London: Weidenfield & Nicolson, 2001.

Fraser, Colin Charles. "Reshaping the Past: The Personal Poetry of Ted Hughes." Thesis submitted for the degree of Doctor of Philosophy of the University of New England (Australia), May 1998.

Gammage, Nick, ed. *The Epic Poise: A Celebration of Ted Hughes*. London: Faber and Faber, 1999.

Gifford, Terry. " 'Go Fishing': An Ecocentric or Egocentric Imperative?" In *Lire Ted Hughes New Selected Poems, 1957–1994*, ed. Joanny Moulin. Paris: Éditions du Temps, 1999.

————. "Interview with Fay Godwin." *Thumbscrew*, no. 18, (2001).

————, and Neil Roberts. *Ted Hughes: A Critical Study*. London: Faber and Faber, 1981.

Gilbert, Sandra. "In Yeats's House: The Death and Resurrection of Sylvia Plath." In *Coming to Light: American Women Poets in the Twentieth Century,* edited by Diane Middlebrook and Marilyn Yalom. Ann Arbor: University of Michigan Press, 1985.

Goodwin, Frederick K., and Kay Redfield Jamison. *Manic-Depressive Illness.* Oxford University Press, 1999.

Graves, Robert. *The White Goddess.* London: Faber and Faber, 1961.

Hahn, Emily. "The Big Smoke." In *Times and Places.* New York: Crowell, 1970.

Hall, Peter. *Making an Exhibition of Myself.* New York: Vintage, 1993.

Hammer, Langdon. "Plath's Lives." *Representations* 75 (Summer 2001).

Hannon, Paul. *Walking Country: Calderdale.* Keighley, U.K.: Hillside Publications, 1996.

Hardwick, Elizabeth. "On Sylvia Plath." In *Ariel Ascending: Writings About Sylvia Plath,* edited by Paul Alexander. New York: Harper & Row, 1985.

Hayman, Ronald. *The Death and Life of Sylvia Plath.* New York: Birch Lane Press, 1991.

Heinz, Drue. "Ted Hughes: The Art of Poetry, LXXI" (interview with Ted Hughes). *The Paris Review* 134 (Spring 1995).

Helle, Anita. "'Family Matters': An Afterword on the Biography of Sylvia Plath." *Northwest Review* 26, no. 2 (1988).

Hirschberg, Stuart. *Myth in the Poetry of Ted Hughes: A Guide to the Poems.* Portmarnock, County Dublin: Wolfhound Press, 1981.

Hobsbaum, Philip. "Ted Hughes at Cambridge." *The Dark Horse: The Scottish-American Poetry Magazine* 8 (Autumn 1999).

Holbrook, David. "The Crow of Avon? Shakespeare, Sex and Ted Hughes." *Cambridge Quarterly* 15, no. 1 (1986).

Horder, John. "Desk Poet." *Guardian,* March 23, 1965.

Jacobs, Fred Rue. "Hughes and Drama." *In The Achievement of Ted Hughes,* edited by Keith Sagar. Manchester: Manchester University Press, 1983.

Kendall, Tim. *Sylvia Plath: A Critical Study.* London: Faber and Faber, 2001.

Kopp, Jane Baltzell. "'Gone, Very Gone Youth': Sylvia Plath at Cambridge, 1955–1957." In *Sylvia Plath: The Woman and the Work,* edited by Edward Butscher. New York: Dodd, Mead, 1977.

Kramer, Peter D. *Should You Leave?* London: Phoenix, 1997.

Kroll, Judith. *Chapters in a Mythology: The Poetry of Sylvia Plath.* New York: Harper Colophon, 1976.

Laframboise, Donna. "Ted Hughes' Private Letters Reveal Another Story." *National Post* (Toronto), July 29, 2000.

Larschan, Richard. Interviews with Aurelia Plath, November 1986. Program 8, "Sylvia Plath and the Myth of the Monstrous Mother"; and Program 9, "Sylvia Plath and the Myth of the Omnipresent/Absent Father." *Poets of New England* (video series). Amherst: University of Massachusetts Academic Instructional Media Services, 2001.

Lawrence, David Herbert. *Women in Love.* With an introduction by Richard Aldington. Phoenix Edition, London: Heinemann, 1954.

———. *The Rainbow,* Phoenix Edition, London: Heinemann, 1957.

———. *Complete Poems.* Phoenix Edition, 3 vols. London: Heinemann, 1957.

Lee, Janette. "Poet Laureate's Mexborough Memories." *South Yorkshire Times,* September 13, 1985.

Lenti, Paul. " 'Animals Tend to Come Up When I'm Not Careful.' " *Mexico City/The News,* August 22, 1982.

Lessing, Doris. *Martha Quest.* London: Michael Joseph, 1952.

———. *A Proper Marriage.* London: Michael Joseph, 1954.

———. *A Ripple from the Storm.* London: Michael Joseph, 1958.

———. *The Golden Notebook.* London: Michael Joseph, 1962.

Malcolm, Janet. *The Silent Woman.* With a new afterword. London: Picador, 1994.

Meyering, Shelley L. *Sylvia Plath: A Reference Guide, 1973–1988.* Boston: G. K. Hall, 1990.

Middlebrook, Diane Wood. *Anne Sexton: A Biography.* Boston: Houghton Mifflin/A Peter Davison Book, 1991.

———. "Channeling Plath." *Mirabella.* December 1993.

———. Introduction, to *The Bell Jar,* by Sylvia Plath. New York: Knopf/Everyman's Library, 1998.

Miller, Karl. *Rebecca's Vest: A Memoir.* London: Hamish Hamilton, 1993.

Moi, Toril. *What Is a Woman?* New York: Oxford University Press, 1999.

Moses, Kate. *Wintering, a novel of Sylvia Plath.* New York: St. Martin's, 2003.

Moulin, Joanny, editor. *Lire Ted Hughes New Selected Poems, 1957–1994.* Paris: Éditions du Temps, 1999.

Murphy, Richard. *The Kick, A Memoir.* London: Granta Books, 2002.

Myers, Lucas. "Ah, Youth . . . : Ted Hughes and Sylvia Plath at Cambridge and After." *Grand Street* (Summer 1989); reprinted as Appendix 1 in Anne Stevenson, *Bitter Fame: A Life of Sylvia Plath.* Boston: Houghton Mifflin, 1989.

———. *Crow Steered, Bergs Appeared.* Sewanee, Tenn.: Proctor's Hall Press, 2001.

Negev, Eilat. "My Life with Sylvia Plath, by Ted Hughes." *Daily Telegraph,* October 31, 1998; continued in "Poetry Is a Way of Talking to Loved Ones When It's Too Late." *Daily Telegraph,* November 2, 1998.

———. "Haunted by the Ghosts of Love." *Guardian,* April 10, 1999.

Newman, Charles, ed. *The Art of Sylvia Plath: A Symposium.* Bloomington: Indiana University Press, 1971.

Ostriker, Alicia. *Writing Like a Woman.* Ann Arbor: University of Michigan Press, 1983.

Orr, Peter, ed. *The Poet Speaks.* London: Routledge & Kegan Paul, 1969.

Paulin, Tom. "Laureate of the Free Market? Ted Hughes." In *Minotaur: Poetry and the Nation State.* London: Faber and Faber, 1992.

Peel, Robin. *Writing Back: Sylvia Plath and Cold War Politics.* Rutherford, N.J.: Fairleigh Dickinson University Press, 2002.

Perloff, Marjone. "The Two Ariels: The (Re)making of the Sylvia Plath Canon. "*American Poetry Review,* November-December 1984.

Pero, Thomas. "So Quickly It's Over" (interview with Ted Hughes). *Wild Steelhead and Salmon* 5, no. 2 (Winter 1999).

Phillips, Adam. *The Beast in the Nursery.* London: Faber and Faber, 1998.

Pierpont, Claudia Roth. "Memoirs of a Revolutionary: Doris Lessing." In *Passionate Minds: Women Rewriting the World.* New York: Knopf, 2000.

Pinker, Steven. *The Language Instinct: How the Mind Creates Language.* New York: William Morrow, 1994.

Porter, Peter. "Ted Hughes and Sylvia Plath: A Bystander's Recollections." *Australian Book Review,* August 2001.

Rhodes, Neil. "Bridegrooms to the Goddess: Hughes, Heaney and the Elizabethans." In *Shakespeare and Ireland,* edited by Mark Burnette and Ramona Wray. London: Macmillan, 1997.

Robins, Corinne. "Four Young Poets." *Mademoiselle,* January 1959.

Roche, Clarissa. "Sylvia Plath: Vignettes from England." In *Sylvia Plath: The Woman and the Work,* edited by Edward Butscher. New York: Dodd, Mead, 1977.

Rombauer, Irma S., and Marion Rombauer Becker. *The Joy of Cooking.* Illustrated by Ginnie Hofmann. New York: Bobbs-Merrill, 1953.

Rose, Jacqueline. *The Haunting of Sylvia Plath.* London: Virago Press, 1991.

———. " 'This Is Not a Biography.' " *London Review of Books* 24, no. 16, (August 22, 2002).

Rose, Phyllis. *Parallel Lives: Five Victorian Marriages.* London: The Hogarth Press, 1984.

Sagar, Keith. *The Art of Ted Hughes.* Cambridge: Cambridge University Press, 1975.

———. *The Laughter of Foxes.* Liverpool: Liverpool University Press, 2000.

———. "Ted Hughes." *New Dictionary of National Biography.* London: Oxford University Press, 2003.

———, ed. *The Achievement of Ted Hughes.* Athens: University of Georgia Press, 1983.

———, ed. *The Challenge of Ted Hughes.* London: Macmillan, 1994.

Scigaj, Leonard. *Ted Hughes.* Boston: G.K. Hall, 1991.

———, ed. *Critical Essays on Ted Hughes.* New York: G.K. Hall, 1992.

Sexton, Anne. "The Barfly Ought to Sing." In *The Art of Sylvia Plath: A Symposium,* edited by Charles Newman. Bloomington: Indiana University Press, 1971.

Seymour, Miranda. *Robert Graves: Life on the Edge.* London: Doubleday, 1995.

Sigmund, Elizabeth. "Sylvia in Devon: 1962." In *Sylvia Plath: The Woman and the Work,* edited by Edward Butscher. New York: Dodd, Mead, 1977.

Skea, Ann. *Ted Hughes: The Poetic Quest.* Armidale, New South Wales: University of New England Press, 1994.

———. *Poetry and Magic:* An analysis of *Birthday Letters* and of Ted Hughes's use of Tarot and Cabbala. Online commentary, www.zeta.org. au/~annskea/BLCabala.html.

Sonnenberg, Ben. *Lost Property: Memoirs and Confessions of a Bad Boy.* New York: Summit Books, 1991.

———. "Ted's Spell." *Raritan* 21, no. 4, (Spring 2002).

Steiner, Nancy Hunter. *A Closer Look at Ariel: A Memory of Sylvia Plath.* New York: Popular Library, 1973.

Stevenson, Anne. *Bitter Fame: A Life of Sylvia Plath.* With additional material by Lucas Myers, Dido Merwin, and Richard Murphy. Boston: Houghton Mifflin/A Peter Davison Book, 1989; reprinted with a new preface by Anne Stevenson, 1998.

Swift, Graham. "An Appreciation of Ted Hughes." *Granta* 65 (Spring 1999).

Taylor, Michael R. *Giorgio de Chirico and the Myth of Ariadne* (catalogue), Philadelphia: The Philadelphia Museum of Art, 2002.

Tennant, Emma. *Burnt Diaries.* Edinburgh: Canongate Books, 1999.

———. *Sylvia and Ted, a novel.* New York: Henry Holt, 2001.

Thomas, Trevor. "Sylvia Plath: Last Encounters" (unpublished memoir). Photocopy numbered 104, dated 1989. Courtesy of Richard Larschan.

Uroff, Margaret Dickie. *Sylvia Plath and Ted Hughes.* Urbana: University of Illinois Press, 1979.

Van Dyne, Susan R. *Revising Life: Sylvia Plath's Ariel Poems.* Chapel Hill: University of North Carolina Press, 1993.

Wagner, Erica. *Ariel's Gift.* London: Faber and Faber, 2000.

Wagner-Martin, Linda. *Sylvia Plath: A Biography.* New York: Simon & Schuster, 1987.

Wright, Carolyne. "What Happens in the Heart." *Poetry Review* (London: publication of the Poetry Book Society) 89, no. 3 (Autumn 1999).

Wurst, Gayle. "The (Non) Americanization of Ted Hughes." In *Lire Ted Hughes New Selected Poems, 1957–1994,* edited by Joanny Moulin. Paris: Éditions du Temps, 1999.

Index

Page numbers in *italics* refer to illustrations.

PHOTO CREDITS